THE COMPLETE FUNDRAISING handbook

5th edition

Nina Botting Herbst
Michael Norton

Contributors: Supriya Horn,
Jay Kennedy, Rebecca Ryland
and John Smyth

DIRECTORY OF SOCIAL CHANGE

In association with
the Institute of Fundraising

Published by
Directory of Social Change
24 Stephenson Way
London NW1 2DP
Tel. 08450 77 77 07; Fax 020 7391 4804
E-mail publications@dsc.org.uk
www.dsc.org.uk
from whom further copies and a full books catalogue are available.

Directory of Social Change is a Registered Charity no. 800517

First published 1992
Second edition 1993
Third edition 1997
Reprinted 1999
Fourth edition 2001
Reprinted 2003
Reprinted 2005
Reprinted 2006
Fifth edition 2007
Copyright © Directory of Social Change 2007

ISBN 978 1 903991 84 8

British Library Cataloguing in Publication Data
A catalogue record for this book is available from the British Library

Cover design by Keith Shaw
Text designed by Sarah Nicholson
Typeset by GreenGate Publishing Services, Tonbridge
Printed and bound by Page Bros., Norwich

CONTENTS

FOREWORD

Fundraising is a little bit like map reading. As soon as you think you have totally mastered it and your confidence is right up there, you get lost. You then have to revert to reminding yourself of the fundamentals and key principles to guide you back again.

The new edition of this title – a trusted source of fundraising advice since 1992 – has been significantly updated, making it even more relevant to fundraisers. The book is divided into three parts, covering fundraising principles and strategies, sources of funding and fundraising techniques. New material in this edition on income generation and contracts, the National Lottery, government funding, company giving and the European Union ensures the title explores all of the latest developments in fundraising. A new selection of case studies brings to life the practical advice on all aspects of fundraising *The Complete Fundraising Handbook* provides.

This book is a good reference point for your journey as a fundraiser – the publication is ideal for those starting out in fundraising – and experienced fundraisers will also find the reference sections at the end of each chapter useful sources of both networking and training advice.

Fundraising in the UK has never been stronger or more successful than it is today. And however you go about it, fundraising is the public face of charity – representative of an organisation's work, its cause and the people caught up in that cause. I wish you every success in your future fundraising campaigns and urge you to channel your passion for your organisation by taking a planned, strategic and professional approach.

Lindsay Boswell
Chief Executive
The Institute of Fundraising

ABOUT THE AUTHORS

Michael Norton founded the Directory of Social Change in 1975. He is no longer directly involved with DSC, but he went on to found the Centre for Innovation in Voluntary Action and to chair Changemakers, a charity which works to promote voluntary action among young people. Changemakers is part of the consortium that set up unLTD, the foundation for social entrepreneurs, which bid successfully for the £100 million endowment previously controlled by the Millennium Commission. unLTD uses the funds to make awards to individuals to set up projects that will benefit their communities. Michael Norton also spends about a fifth of his time working on projects that relate to the development of the voluntary sector in India, where he has set up the charity Books for Change.

Nina Botting Herbst started her fundraising career in 1993 as an account manager at Pell and Bales, the telemarketing agency. From there she went on to work for Shelter, Amnesty International UK and Tate, mainly concentrating on supporter development – legacies and committed giving. During this time Nina became actively involved with the Institute of Fundraising as a member of its Standards Committee, and by sitting on the working party that produced the first Code of Practice for Legacy Fundraising as well as chairing the group that developed the first Code for the Personal Solicitation for Committed Gifts. She was a member of the board which organised the 2001 National Fundraisers' Convention and has been a frequent speaker at fundraising conferences.

In 2002 Nina moved to the US and is currently an Associate Director for Development and Alumni Relations at the University of Chicago.

Introduction

I have heard charities and voluntary organisations referred to as 'money monsters' by funders. I think this is an amusing and actually quite fair description (although perhaps not the monster part!) The reality is that most charitable organisations need funds in order to do their work. And the fact that the public and the media doesn't really understand this doesn't change it.

Not only do we need to raise funds, but nowadays our ability to fundraise is hedged with rules, regulations, reporting mechanisms, application forms, interviews, checklists, media hype ... the list goes on *ad infinitum*.

And we are fundraising in a changed voluntary sector. Changed in the sense that there is now more money available from the state; that in many cases what were previously grants have been converted into contracts; that a lot of government funding is being driven by short-term priorities; that increasingly the larger charities are taking a bigger share of the available funds; that larger amounts are being given to fewer charities and that we are all being urged to work in partnership on joint funding arrangements.

All this makes the job of a fundraiser even more challenging than it has been in the past, and this is why this new edition of *The Complete Fundraising Handbook* has never been more needed.

The book is divided into three parts covering:

- Fundraising principles and strategies
- Sources of funding – including individual donors, grantmaking trusts, central and local government, the National Lottery and the European Union
- Fundraising techniques – from house-to-house collections and challenge events to direct mail and capital appeals.

The book now includes much-needed information on other sources of revenue generation, company giving, money from the EU and relevant information on the new Charities Act.

The advice and information given is sensible, practical and do-able. Michael and Nina have, as always, been honest about the challenges as well as inspiring and positive about the possibilities available.

There are so many ways to raise money and so many sources to go to that it can be completely overwhelming, even for the most experienced fundraiser. This book helps you to navigate this increasingly complex and specialist field of work in a simple and easy to understand way.

The challenges are great but the opportunities exist. To paraphrase a well-known saying: 'Go forth and multiply ... your funding opportunities!'

Debra Allcock Tyler
Chief Executive
Directory of Social Change

Acknowledgements

The publisher and authors are grateful to the following individuals and organisations who have given so freely of their time and experience in order to provide text, examples, case studies and advice:

Harry Brown; Nicola Eastwood; Imelda McGuigan (Action Aid); Joanna Dunstan (Amnesty International UK); Stephanie Papaefthemiou (Arts Council England); Andrew Watt (Association of Fundraising Professionals, USA); Márcia Balisciano (Benjamin Franklin House); British Heart Foundation; Kirstin Gaymer (Business in the Community); Chris Bates (Cancer Research UK); Charities Aid Foundation; Daniel Charles, Alex Wood (Christian Aid); Sally Woods (Compton Hospice); Catherine Graham-Harrison (Consultants to the Not-for-Profit World); Gary Connell (Department for Education and Skills); Hugh O'Daly (European Social Fund); Samantha Wilson (Fundraising Standards Board); Howard Lake (Fundraising UK Ltd); Clare Butler-Henderson, Louise Lane (Heritage Lottery Fund); Neil Skinner (ICOM); Laurence Wattier (IDs); Joe Murphy (Institute of Fundraising); Clare Cooper (Jerwood); Meg Abdy (Legacy Foresight); Crispin Ellison (Legacy Link Consultancy Ltd.); Gill Jolly (Director of Merlin Fundraising & Management Consultants); Roxy Ryan (National Deaf Children's Society); Catherine Lewis (National Trust); Tim Hunter, Dominic Evers, Stephen George and Denise Derbyshire (NSPCC); Mick Aldridge (PFRA); Emma Bockhop (Remember A Charity); Nicola Hanna (Shelter); Richard Radcliffe (Smee & Ford); Alison Benjamin (deputy editor of Society Guardian); Jacki Reason (Solutions to Publishing Challenges); Jonathan Bruck (Sport England); Theresa Lloyd (Theresa Lloyd Associates; Consultants to Charities and Arts Organisations); Volunteering England.

We are also grateful to the following organisations for permission to reproduce their copyright material as illustrations:

Action Aid, Benjamin Franklin House, Christian Aid, NSPCC, National Trust, Practical Action, Shelter.

The chapter on government funding was originally contributed by Susan Forrester and re-written for this edition by Jay Kennedy. The appendix on data protection was written by Paul Ticher. The chapter on companies was updated by John Smyth, the national lottery chapter was updated by Supriya Horn and the chapter on the European Union was updated by Rebecca Ryland. We thank them for their time and expertise.

This edition also draws extensively on material in previous editions and we gratefully acknowledge the contribution of Sam Clarke, the original author.

Dedication

This book is dedicated to Luke Fitzherbert, who played a leading role in creating the Directory of Social Change. Luke's energy and tenacity opened up grantmaking to far greater public scrutiny and accountability. Luke's talents as a teacher inspired a generation of fundraisers, particularly from smaller organisations, to rise to the challenge of raising money for their cause. Luke tragically died in a road accident in January 2007. He is sadly missed.

PART ONE

GETTING STARTED

1 **BACKGROUND**

In this chapter we look at the importance of fundraising to your organisation, the main challenges facing fundraisers, the intended readership and the structure of the book.

1.1 Fundraising today

Few traditional or service charities can finance themselves exclusively from the interest on huge endowments or investment portfolios. Nor do many voluntary organisations have the kind of routine annual surplus to enable them simply to absorb new work without the need for additional external finance. And given the short-term nature of most current grants regimes, many organisations find themselves on a kind of financial treadmill – how do we pay for this activity or that piece of work once the three-year grant has run out?

Rightly or wrongly, fundraising is a fact of modern voluntary sector life. For some it is a necessary chore, for others a marvellous and stimulating opportunity; for most of us, it is something in between. However you feel about it, fundraising is critical to the success of your organisation's work. The main reasons are set out below.

Survival

Every organisation needs money to keep going from this year to the next – to meet project costs and develop programmes for the future; to pay the wages and office overheads; to keep buildings and vehicles in a good state of repair; and to pay for new equipment. And the stark truth is that if the money is not raised, the organisation will not be able to do its work, and if the work is not done, pressing needs in society that the organisation exists to tackle will not be met.

The tool you will use to manage your fundraising is your annual budget. This will show the amount of money you plan to spend. It will also indicate the amount of money that has already been raised or has been promised, and what extra support still needs to be raised during the year so that you can meet your outgoings.

You will monitor your progress in fundraising through keeping records of all money received or promised, and by preparing and discussing management accounts at regular management meetings. If your income isn't coming in as planned, then you will need to take some sort of action – step up your fundraising programme, find and develop new sources of funds, cut costs, defer planned projects, or agree to subsidise the deficit out of your reserves.

Expansion and development

If your organisation is to meet the challenges of the future, you may need to expand and develop your work: improve your services; extend your work into other regions and areas; evaluate your impact; undertake research and campaigning alongside your basic service delivery work; experiment and innovate. This all requires more money – money that will need to be raised.

You will really need to prepare a business plan, or at least an outline budget, for the next few years so as to identify the resources you will need for your ongoing programme of work and any proposed major developments. Remember, fundraising always takes longer than you think. The more you plan ahead, the more successful you will be in getting the resources when you need them.

Reducing dependency

Many organisations are funded by only one or a handful of major donors or funders. This can put the organisation into a state of dependency. If one of the grants is withdrawn, this can create a financial crisis. It may also be difficult to determine your own agenda if you are constantly having to adapt to the priorities of a key donor/funder.

Broadening your fundraising base can reduce this dependency. You need to decide whether your organisation is too dependent on any one source. You might then see if you can build some stability by negotiating some form of long-term commitment from your existing funders, or you could try to develop alternative sources of income.

Building a constituency

Fundraising is not just about money; it is also about numbers of supporters. Each supporter is important to you. Many can be persuaded to give again and to give even more generously. They may be able to volunteer or to find friends who are willing to support you. They provide an indication of the level of support that your organisation is attracting, and therefore can add strength to your lobbying and campaigning work.

You need to think about the sorts of constituencies that you would like to mobilise and who your work will appeal to. Is it a particular type of business or profession? Or students and activists? Or women? Or retired people with time on their hands? Or parents? Or some other category? You will need to think about how best to identify them, the sort of message they will respond to and in what format this should be.

Creating a viable and sustainable organisation

Fundraising is not simply about generating the resources you need to survive from this year through to next year, or finding the funds for any expansion and development. It is also about helping create a viable and strong organisation which is able to sustain itself into the future.

There are many ways of doing this. One is to build a substantial and active donor base – getting people to support you who sympathise with your aims, and who will continue to give their support over a long period. Other ways include: organising fundraising events (which can create a regular and continuing source of income); creating capital within your organisation, such as a capital fund or buildings and equipment (especially when this reduces your need for running costs or can help you generate an income); and developing income generating schemes for the organisation itself.

Many organisations are addressing long-term needs – for example through community development, which will not yield immediate results, or in looking after disabled or older people where there is a continuing commitment to provide care well into the future. You need to create an organisation that is financially strong in the long as well as the short term, rather than one that is plagued by annual deficits and is at or near bankruptcy. Financial concerns can affect the morale of the whole organisation. Crisis fundraising is time-consuming and increasingly difficult – and in the end you will find you run out of goodwill. You need to find ways of strengthening the financial position of your organisation and this means developing a sensible fundraising strategy for the future.

1.2 The challenge for fundraisers

Responding to growing need

The UK, along with many other countries, is facing growing needs and rising expectations of what should be provided. There is a shortage of resources to meet health, welfare, educational and other modern-day societal needs. Greater life expectancy, persistently high levels of unemployment and family poverty in some regions, changing family structures, rising costs of service delivery, the need to introduce high technology solutions, new issues such as refugees and asylum seekers and a growing Islamaphobia are all making it difficult to respond to every need.

All the evidence shows that, despite rising national wealth, the poor are growing relatively poorer year by year, and despite all the government's efforts, too many of our children are growing up in poverty. There is also an expectation that voluntary organisations will intervene as providers of last resort, since the state seems to have withdrawn from this role.

It is not just a matter of raising more money to provide more or better services. The challenge for voluntary organisations is to develop solutions to people's needs rather than simply provide services that, while improving the quality of people's lives, leave the fundamental problems unresolved. If they can create more imaginative and effective approaches to the problems that exist in society, they can respond to the growing levels of need without necessarily increasing the demand for funding that is just not there. This role as innovator is one of the strengths of the voluntary sector. It is also something that many funders welcome.

Recognising the competition for funds

The fundraising world is extremely competitive. More and more organisations are started, which then need to think about fundraising and how to develop independent sources of income for themselves. This means that all the more obvious sources, such as grantmaking trusts, the larger local companies and rich individuals, are receiving increasing numbers of requests for funding – and they can't respond positively to them all, however worthwhile the cause.

Your job is to try to show that your organisation is successful, effective, cost-effective and lively – in short that it is the best recipient for a donor's funds. Alternatively, you can think about developing new sources of money that nobody else is yet exploiting – the large trust that nobody seems to have heard of and which is not yet listed in any of the grant guides, a rich individual who has 'just made it', a new and exciting way of raising money before everyone else has tried to imitate it.

Keeping up to date

The fundraising world changes continually. In April 2000 the tax structure changed completely to encourage people to give more tax-effectively. New technology offers major opportunities both for fundraising and for communicating with donors. There are also new laws on Data Protection and Freedom of

Information. In 2006 the government appointed a Minister for the Third Sector and a new Charities Act became law in November 2006. New government programmes are being introduced, some of which dwarf more traditional sources – for example FutureBuilders, a £125 million investment fund to help voluntary organisations deliver better services or 'V', a new charity set up as a result of the Russell Commission to raise and distribute £150 million over three years with government matched funding support. A successful fundraiser needs to keep on top of all these changes and developments.

Scrambling for funds

'There is intense competition for funds. Groups feel they must apply for whatever funds are available, although they know that their chance of success is low. There are so many initiatives from central and local government that it is difficult for voluntary organisations to respond without a full-time fundraising department. There is that sense of scrambling for funds whether or not they are appropriate for the organisation's current needs. Small groups are told they should market themselves, when they are already fully occupied providing services in often impossible circumstances. Most voluntary groups cannot confidently see beyond the short term. It is very difficult for them to get funds for long-term development, and they continue to hang on in the hope that somebody – a regeneration budget, the Lottery, a future government – will rescue them.'

[Tim Cook, formerly Clerk to the City Parochial Foundation]

Developing long-term solutions for your fundraising

There is an increasing emphasis on financial sustainability. Many trusts and companies, for example, don't like the organisations they support to continue to be dependent on them for more than a few years. They want to be able to withdraw their support so as to be able to back new ideas and new projects. At the same time, you can find that you have accessed all the ready sources of money, and that fundraising is then becoming more and more difficult. At this stage, if you can develop mechanisms for bringing money into your organisation on a continuing basis, this will provide you with the financial strength and confidence for a more successful future.

Different organisations deal with this problem in different ways. A committed membership paying subscriptions or giving by monthly direct debit; a major fundraising event which can be run annually; a network of local supporters' groups; service agreements and other forms of funding partnerships with local authorities – these are some of the ways of developing continuing income and reducing the need to fundraise.

Generating your own income

Income generation is another way of bringing income into your organisation. Charging for services, selling training and publications, hiring out facilities, can all pay their way or even contribute towards overheads. But to develop this successfully requires new thinking, new approaches and new skills. There is growing prominence given to this, as the 'social enterprise agenda' develops, although much of the emphasis of fundraising is still on the actual raising of money. Many more organisations are becoming happier with the idea of a more 'commercial' approach.

1.3 Who should read this book?

The simple answer is that everyone who has any sort of fundraising responsibility needs to understand the fundraising process.

- Board members (the generic term used for trustees and management committee members) may, in small organisations, be responsible for fundraising themselves, and in any case will want to know what to expect of fundraisers, how to employ them, what qualities they should have and what support they will need to succeed. They will also want to know the options for income generation schemes.
- The director and other senior managers may also be involved in fundraising and developing a fundraising strategy for the organisation. They will want to know when it is time to employ a specialist fundraiser or a fundraising consultant and how to manage them to achieve the best results.
- Fundraisers will of course need to have a good understanding of the many techniques that are available, so as to be able to decide which are likely to be the most relevant to them.
- People in other departments should be encouraged to find out more about the fundraising process and its impact on their work.
- People who are looking to move into fundraising (from inside or outside the voluntary sector) will find that this book will show them how fundraising works and which of their current skills may transfer.
- Volunteers involved in raising money could generate good ideas for improving their own contribution.
- Independent consultants and advisers who are specialists in one area of fundraising will get a broader perspective so that they can then advise their clients better.
- Trainers may wish to use some of the material as handouts for their courses.

This book has been written from as many points of view as possible, taking into account the perspectives of both large and small organisations, those with some experience of fundraising and those considering the possibility for the first time.

1.4 How this book is structured

The book is divided into three main parts, and within these it is divided into chapters. Each chapter starts with a summary of what it covers and ends with a list of resources and further information, covering the organisations and publications most relevant to the chapter.

Part 1 Getting started

Chapter 1: Background, which is this section, sets out why fundraising is important and what the challenges are for fundraisers.

Chapter 2: First principles describes some of the key principles of fundraising (to give a better understanding of the process) and some of the personal skills required in a fundraiser (so you will know your strengths and weaknesses for the job). It also shows how to construct your case, which will underpin all your fundraising efforts.

Chapter 3: Developing a fundraising strategy describes some of the factors to take into account and suggests ways of developing a fundraising strategy for your organisation, so you can decide where to concentrate your fundraising efforts. Resourcing your fundraising is also dealt with here: alongside having a strategy, it is equally important to have the resources available to implement your fundraising plans successfully. Equipping a fundraising office, recruiting a fundraiser and using a consultant are all discussed. This chapter also covers testing, evaluation and control, to enable you to be more cost-effective in your fundraising.

Part 2 Sources of funds

Chapters 4–11 cover getting support from individuals, grants from trusts and foundations, company giving and business sponsorship, grants from government and other statutory sources and programmes, the National Lottery and the European Union, and a range of other possible sources for you to consider. This part will give you an understanding of how money is given away and the ways donors can give, and will help you identify opportunities for getting support for your own organisation.

Part 3 Techniques

Chapters 12–16 cover a range of fundraising techniques that you can use with different kinds of donor, covering everything from house-to-house collections and direct mail to organising a fundraising event, running a capital appeal or writing an application to a trust. There is also advice on using the media and working with volunteers. The full list of topics covered in this part is given on the contents pages.

The book ends with:

- appendices, covering data protection and a list of the codes of practice produced by the Institute of Fundraising;
- a list of the key sources of information and advice;
- an index.

2 FIRST PRINCIPLES

This chapter covers some of the key aspects of fundraising. It will help you identify the people, the attitudes and the approaches that you will need in order to get a successful fundraising programme under way.

Details of organisations and publications referred to in this chapter are on page 34.

2.1 The key principles of fundraising

You have to ask

A major charity once asked non-supporters what was their main reason for not giving. The answer was simple – they had never been asked. The whole purpose of fundraising is to raise money. It is often forgotten that the call to action – communicating the punch-line that actually asks people to give – is the essential piece of the message.

When asking for money you need to be clear exactly what you want, while also being aware of what that particular donor is able and willing to give. You must also make it as easy as possible for the donor to respond.

'All of the reading of fundraising literature, planning, strategising, writing case statements and attending fundraising training cannot and will not raise money. Only implementing your plan – taking action – will raise money. So make this your motto: "Today someone has to ask someone for money".'

[Kim Klein, Fundraising for Social Change]

The personal approach

The general rule is that the more personal you can make your approach, the more effective you will be. So:

- asking someone face to face is better than ...
- telephoning someone to ask for support, which is better than ...
- writing a personal letter to someone asking for support, which is better than ...
- giving a presentation to a group of people, which is better than ...

- putting out a request on your website (at least the people who visit it are likely to be interested in what you are doing), which you can consider alongside ...
- sending an appeal to lots of people.

Many fundraisers prefer to send letters asking for support and this is sometimes the only way to reach a large group. However, it is not the most effective way of asking, especially when compared with:

- a meeting at your project where the prospective donor can see your work and meet some of the beneficiaries;
- a request from someone who has given or from a high profile person (such as a business leader or expert in the field). This can be far more effective than a request from a fundraiser or from the project director. Part of the skill in fundraising is knowing who is the best person to make the ask.

Understanding the donor's viewpoint

When deciding to give, a donor may experience a whole range of feelings and thoughts. It is important for the fundraiser to understand this process.

The act of giving includes elements of faith, hope and charity: faith that the fundraiser truly represents the cause and will act as an efficient conduit for the donor's money; hope that the gift, however small, will make some difference; and charity, which is an act of altruism, a gift without the expectation of any material return.

The donor may have a personal reason for wanting to give. People may support a cancer charity, for example, through concern that they might get the disease, or because a family member or close friend has recently died of it. They may feel strongly about an issue – such as the environment – and want to do something about it. In supporting your cause they are also supporting *their* cause, doing something they feel needs doing and that they want to see done. You need to recognise this and try to discover what will trigger a response from the person you are asking.

Fundraising is a people business

People do not give to organisations or to abstract concepts. They give to help other people or because they want to create a better world. Your job as a fundraiser is to show how you help them to achieve this. One way of doing this is through case studies – illustrating your work with examples of who you have been able to help, how you have been able to change their lives and the difference that a donation can make.

Another way is to focus your fundraising on particular aspects of your work: the community care project you are planning to introduce on the housing estate, and how it will transform people's lives; the YouthBank UK programme that enables young people to act as grantmakers to other young people in their local community and where you are all full of enthusiasm and excitement about its potential. By focusing on specific projects rather than the overall work of the organisation, it makes it easier to excite and enthuse your donors.

Fundraising is selling

Fundraising is a two-stage process. It is about showing people why your work is important and only then persuading them to give.

You must show people that there is an important need and that you can do something useful about it. Then, if they agree with you that the need is important and that something should be done and that your organisation is capable of doing something to make a difference, and if you can show them how the support you are asking them for could be used – then asking for money becomes easy. Once people have been sold the idea, then they will want to give.

Credibility and communication

People prefer to give to organisations and causes they have heard about and think well of. So your organisation's credibility and reputation are important. Media coverage of your work, trumpeting your successes in the newsletters you send to supporters, getting endorsements about the quality of your work from experts and prominent figures can all help give people confidence that you are doing a worthwhile and successful job – which then makes it much easier when you come to ask for support.

How much to ask for

Donors often don't know how much to give. They may not want to give much. Equally, they may not want to give too little and so seem mean. There are various ways of asking for money, some of which give more guidance than others.

- Ask for a specific sum to cover a particular item of expenditure (for example, £500 to sponsor a park bench at a nature reserve).
- Give a shopping list of different items at different prices (for example, if you are equipping a hospice, you can list all the items you will need to purchase, put a price against each and ask a donor to contribute to one or more). The price does not have to be just the direct cost of buying the item, but can include a reasonable overhead allocation.

- Show the cost per client as a unit cost, and ask the donor to support one or more units (for example, at a homework club, show how much it costs for a child to attend for a week or a term, and ask a supporter to sponsor a child for a week, a term or a year).
- Give examples of gifts already received.
- Break down your appeal total into numbers of gifts of different sizes that you need if you are to reach your target. This technique is commonly used in major capital appeals.

Example of a shopping list

Practical Action, formerly ITDG (Intermediate Technology Development Group), is a development agency that provides practical answers to poverty in developing countries.

Here is how it presents the sort of projects a monthly gift to the charity might support:

'You could help us with a *regular gift* each month by banker's order, enabling us to plan ahead with confidence, securing the long-term future of poor communities worldwide.

- £4 per month could buy a series of smoke-reducing interventions to test in a Maasai home in Kenya.
- £6 per month could help train more people in the money earning technique of dyeing and embroidery in Bangladesh.
- £10 per month could help Practical Action run village workshops on affordable ways to protect houses from earthquakes in Peru.'

Saying thank you

Saying thank you is extremely important. It recognises and values the donor's generosity. It makes them feel better about your organisation. And it may also prompt them to give again.

A former director of a major aid charity made a point of telephoning donors who had given £500 or more at home in the evenings to thank them personally. 'We're thrilled with your support. We're going to put it to good use immediately by using it to help establish a new health clinic for the Turkana. And we'll keep you in touch with progress.' This makes the donor feel that the charity is doing a good job and that their money is having a real impact. This is a very personal approach to thanking and may not be something you are able to do. However, even if you can't show your appreciation for every gift made, you should make sure you thank your donors periodically – at least once or twice a year. See chapter 4, section 4.7, for more on looking after your supporters.

Long-term involvement and commitment

What you really want are people who will give to you regularly and substantially. All the effort to find a donor and persuade them to give will really only bear fruit if they continue to give over many years, maybe increasing their level of giving over time. To achieve this means getting them involved with the work of the organisation and committed to its success by:

- saying thank you immediately and telling them what you plan to do with their money;
- regular reporting back, showing them what you have achieved with their money;
- sharing your ideas and hopes for the future;
- encouraging them to visit you and meet some of the people they have been helping;
- inviting them to meet with the staff and volunteers who are actually doing the work, and with prominent personalities associated with the cause.

Accountability and reporting back

When you accept a donation from somebody, you are responsible for seeing that:

- the money is spent on the purposes for which it was raised – failure to do this is a breach of trust;
- the money is well spent and actually achieves something.

You should always report back to the donor to show them that you have used their money effectively, and what difference their support has made. You can do this by sending a personal letter, a project report or a newsletter, by post or by e-mail. This is not only polite, it is good fundraising practice – an enthusiastic donor who has seen the money make a difference may consider becoming a more committed supporter.

If it turns out that the project has not worked, you can still present this positively. Many voluntary organisations are in the business of innovation, and this inevitably involves risks and occasionally failure. But you will have tried, and you will have learned. The experience can lead to new ideas and new ways of working. Even if you have made a serious blunder (for example purchased an unroadworthy vehicle from a dealer that then went out of business), admit what has happened and put it down to experience. Truthfulness is one of the key skills needed in a fundraiser, as we discuss in the next section.

As you develop your fundraising programme you should also be aware that with the growing variety of methods and media used by charities to fundraise from their existing supporters and the general public, e.g. face to face 'clipboard' fundraising, emails and SMS, the accountability of charities to the people who support them has become a very hot topic. In recent years the Institute of Fundraising has lobbied for the industry to be self-regulatory rather than there being a great deal of government regulation and control, and in 2006 the Fundraising Standards Board (FRSB) was launched to oversee this system of self-regulation. See Appendix 2 for more information on the FRSB.

2.2 The skills required in a fundraiser

Successful fundraisers need a number of key skills and qualities. It is helpful to reflect on what these are and whether you have them.

Enthusiasm and commitment

Commitment is one of the most important qualities in any fundraiser. You must really believe in the cause you are addressing and in the work that your organisation is doing. Your enthusiasm and commitment will encourage others to become equally committed through their giving.

The starving child syndrome

You are watching TV. There is a programme about a refugee camp in the Sudan. People have arrived there with nothing, absolutely nothing. They have walked days to get there and are near starvation. A picture flashes up of a starving child, who seems to be crying out to you 'Help me. Please help me. Please.' How can you resist giving your support to the aid charity running the feeding programme at the refugee centre? Then you think about the cause you are working for. 'If only I were having to raise money for starving children, it would be so much easier,' you think.

But your cause is important too. You have to make it seem as important to yourself and to others as feeding these children. Interestingly the fundraiser for the development charity probably believes that it would be much easier to be raising money to save endangered animals from being poached, and the animal fundraiser would much prefer to be raising money for a cancer charity.

You have to believe wholeheartedly in what you are doing, and make your cause compelling to others. If you can do this, fundraising will become very much easier.

The ability to ask

If you feel uncomfortable with the notion of asking for money, it will make your fundraising life difficult. Whether the task in hand is to write an appeal letter, telephone a business executive to ask for an in-kind donation, organise a committee to run a fundraising event, or pay a personal visit to seek the support of a major donor – it requires an ability to ask effectively for what you need.

Persuasiveness

People have lots of competing demands on their money. Your job is to persuade them that supporting your organisation is a really worthwhile investment of their hard-earned cash. You need to make a good case and use selling and communications skills to present it in a persuasive way. You need to be able to marshal compelling arguments, write letters which excite interest, talk fluently and interestingly about your cause in public or in private, create a sense of excitement through your enthusiasm, and share your hopes and visions for the future.

Confidence and dealing with rejection

When you are asking for money, you need to radiate confidence. If you are apologetic or hesitant, people are less likely to give to you.

'Some years ago I produced an environmental colouring book for children for a schools education programme. I thought that this might be sold to the public, so I decided to see whether bookshops might be interested in taking copies. I went first to my local bookshop. "Not our sort of book", they said. "No thank you." I had a similar experience at the next three bookshops I visited. I really was beginning to feel that nobody wanted the book. But I decided to go to one more bookshop before giving up. It was just as well that I did. "That's just the book we've been looking for. We'll take 70 copies for our Christmas table. What's the next title in the series, as we'd also be interested in that?" I felt elated. It is exactly the same with fundraising. Your next approach might be your big success! So keep trying.'

[Michael Norton on his book *Colour in Your Environment*]

One of the biggest problems is maintaining your confidence in the face of rejection. Since more people are likely to say 'No' than say 'Yes' – that's a fact of fundraising life – it is very easy to get downhearted. Many approaches will be unsuccessful, whether because of the enormous competition for funds, or just through bad luck. After a couple of rejections, you may begin to believe that nobody wants to support you. You might then start *acting* as if nobody wants to support you. You become apologetic and you talk as if you expect to be refused and maybe you even avoid asking – so as not to be rejected.

A good fundraiser has to be able to cope with rejection, starting each fresh approach as if it were the first, and learning from experience – so that the next approach is better than the last.

Persistence

Most fundraisers give up too soon. People often take 'no' to mean 'no' – rather than as a challenge to try to convert the 'no' into a 'yes'. If you give up immediately, then there's no chance at all. If you feel that someone really should be supporting you, you will try to find a way of getting them to change their mind, or find something else that they might like to support. You approached them in the first place because you need support and you felt they might give it. Don't just give up at the first setback; persistence really does pay.

Persistence pays

A group of fundraisers who were approaching charitable foundations were asked to telephone them when they had received a letter of rejection, to find out why their application had been turned down, whether there was any possibility of it being reconsidered, or what else they might apply for. What was interesting was how many eventually succeeded in getting a grant. If you are a donor receiving hundreds of applications, there is a tendency to say 'no' as an immediate response to any request. It is far harder to continue to say 'no' to someone who feels that they have a good project which you really should be interested in and who has the courage to come back and try to enter into a discussion with you – especially if their project falls within your priorities.

Truthfulness

Fundraisers have to be truthful at all times. The need to persuade people creates a pressure to tell partial truths and to claim more for your work than you can deliver. There is also a tendency to present the beneficiary as a victim because this makes it easier to elicit sympathy and support. This is as true for people with physical disabilities or families needing support as it is for those suffering from hunger or disease in the less developed world.

Attempting to present a sensitive but truthful case, whilst making it powerful enough to persuade donors to give, can cause conflicts within your organisation. Potential beneficiaries may object to the way in which you have portrayed them. Project workers may feel you are putting them under too much pressure to deliver impossible results. Beneficiaries may feel that they are being patronised. To resolve this demands sensitivity and understanding from the fundraiser.

Understanding your donors

'A fundraiser should never give up. Much depends on their approach and personality. To ask for financial or other support for people who are in need does not mean that you should look unhappy or ugly. Your good appearance, open smile, courage and challenge should light a beam in the heart of your donor. Your belief in the people you are helping should convince the donor. It is useful to remember that the donor is also a human being who lives in the same world as you, and is anxious to do their bit to improve the community. My modest experience in fundraising says that it is very important to create feedback with your donor. Generous people do not necessarily need to be praised up to the sky, but they will be delighted to know that their support has helped improve something or made a better world for somebody. We have become close friends with many of our donors and we try to build long-term relationships with them.'

[Contributed by Ekaterina Kim, a fundraiser in Moscow]

Contacts and the ability to make contacts

A lot of fundraising boils down not just to who you know, but also who can you *get* to know. One key contact can open up a hundred fundraising doors either by making introductions or, better still, by doing the asking for you. Ask yourself who you need to know in your local area or in the business networks you are trying to break into. Then ask yourself how you can get access to them. Then do it!

Good organisational skills

Fundraising can involve keeping in touch with thousands of supporters, ideally in a way that makes all of them think they are special and that you have a personal relationship with them. Good organisation is essential. Fundraisers should keep records of correspondence and information on all donations made. These files and your database must be organised and kept up to date so that no past event or piece of generosity is forgotten.

Good social skills

A good fundraiser needs confidence, patience and tact. Confidence, because a confident appeal is harder to refuse. Patience, to deal with the particular concerns of donors (for example, when they ask to hear about the income ratios of the organisation for the third time). Tact and sincerity, when asking a supporter face to face for a legacy, or to suggest a variation in a will. A good fundraiser should really enjoy meeting and dealing with people. A good memory for names and faces also helps.

Imagination and creativity

Imagination is an invaluable fundraising asset. It will enable you to dream up new activities to inspire existing supporters and create events to enthuse the public. You should aim to present your work in an exciting and imaginative way. Since the work of your organisation is constantly evolving and new opportunities are emerging, you can use this to identify new approaches instead of simply relying on what has been done in the past.

Opportunism

You should be ready to grasp every opportunity that presents itself. For example, when a well-known supporter sells their business, should your letter asking for support not be in their in-tray next morning? Or if a leading company has just announced a major hike in profits or has been awarded a major construction contract in your area, then a cleverly constructed appeal for funds might just succeed.

The annual calendar provides opportunities at different times of the year. For example, in Christian communities, Christmas and the New Year provide extremely good fundraising opportunities. Other faiths have similar points in the year. There are also anniversaries, centenaries or events such as a Jubilee, which can be used as a basis for major appeals.

Example

How Zubin Mehta, the Indian-born international conductor and Music Director for Life, became involved with the Shalom India-Israel Centre in Mumbai, in 1991

'Having nurtured the dream of an India-Israel Centre, I visited Israel in 1991, tramping the offices of umpteen cultural institutions, following up on every tenuous connection, meeting with Israeli government officials. Finally, on my way back to the airport, I felt the kind of empty fatigue that comes with carrying a load of promises but nothing tangible. I knew we needed a respected and powerful patron, and many names came up, including Zubin's. But it needed both familiarity and courage to access high places. That first time, in 1991, I'm not sure I had both. Suddenly, there was Zubin before me in the bustling airport. On impulse I went up and congratulated him, and said that he had done every Indian proud. He thanked me politely, then it was over. "In that crowded place," I anguished with myself, "I could have done more." Two hours later, airborne, I noticed Zubin up front, reading glasses perched on his nose. I mustered the courage to send a polite note requesting to talk to him. From that and many subsequent meetings I realised that I was with a very special human being. Zubin's warmth and easy accessibility, his ability to get as excited as a child with an idea, astonished me. Here was something he had always wanted to do – to bring the people of the two countries he loved together culturally.'

[Salome Parekh, Hon. Director and Trustee, the Shalom India-Israel Centre, Mumbai]

The key skills: how do you rate?

	have	don't have	could do better
enthusiasm and commitment	❏	❏	❏
the ability to ask	❏	❏	❏
persuasiveness	❏	❏	❏
confidence/dealing with rejection	❏	❏	❏
persistence	❏	❏	❏
truthfulness	❏	❏	❏
contacts	❏	❏	❏
good organisational skills	❏	❏	❏
good social skills	❏	❏	❏
imagination and creativity	❏	❏	❏
opportunism	❏	❏	❏

You may not have all the skills that you will need. You will find the following helpful:

- assess your strengths, so you concentrate on doing the things you are good at;
- learn what skills you need to acquire, and set about obtaining the necessary training or experience;
- find ways of compensating for your weaknesses by getting others to help.

2.3 Making your case
Fundraising for projects

It is far easier to raise money for something specific than to appeal for administrative costs or general funds. As we saw with the 'shopping list' in section 2.1, donors prefer to feel that their money is going to fund something they are genuinely interested in, whether it is saving a local woodland or buying play equipment for disabled children to use. Thinking of your work in project terms and designing projects that will attract support is the basis of successful fundraising. This simply means focusing each time on a particular activity or piece of work rather than on your organisation as a whole. A fundable project should be:

- specific, an identifiable item of expenditure or aspect of your work;
- important, both to your organisation and to the need it is meeting – long-term impact is an added bonus;

- realistic and achievable, giving the funder confidence that you will be able to deliver the intended targets and outcomes;
- good value, so that it stands out in a competitive funding environment;
- topical, looking at current issues and concerns;
- relevant to the donor, meeting their known interests and priorities;
- a manageable size, so that it won't overload the organisation.

To cost a project properly, you need to include all the direct and indirect costs that can reasonably be attributed to the running of the project: an appropriate percentage of management salaries, the cost of occupying the building, using the phone, doing the photocopying and so on. Some funders say that they will not fund these core costs, but you will have to get them paid for somehow. (See chapter 6 for more on the issue of core costs.) If you are going to be responsible for raising funds, you need to have agreed with your management committee and relevant managers how you are going to present your work as fundable projects.

Six essential ingredients

Most donors, whether they are big trusts, major companies or individual members of the public, receive thousands of requests each year. How are you going to construct your case so that it stands out from the crowd? Before you start to fundraise, you need to ask yourself:

- Why would anyone want to support our work?
- What are the specific reasons why different types of donor (individuals, trusts, companies, government etc.) would want to support our work?
- What is so important about what we are planning to do?

Try out your answers to these key questions on a couple of friends who know nothing about your area of work. Are they convinced? Now you are ready to fill in the detail of your case with answers to the following questions.

- *Who are you?* In other words, are you reliable and respectable, with a strong track record of good work successfully completed?
- *What is the need that you intend to meet?* This should not simply be an emotive statement, but should include factual evidence about, for example, whether the situation is local or national; how many people it affects; why it is urgent.
- *What is the solution that you offer?* This is where you can describe what you intend to do, the results you expect to obtain and how these will be measured. You may want to use examples of how similar projects have worked.
- *Why should you do it?* This is where you establish your credibility. What other work have you done? Have you had good publicity for this? Do you

involve volunteers and/or beneficiaries in your work? Do you have a track record in attracting funding?

- *How much do you need?* You need to have a clear idea of the total, who you intend to approach for the money, and how the total could be broken down for donors who want to contribute but could not possibly fund the whole thing.
- *What future do you have?* If you can show that you have thought ahead and attempted to achieve long-term stability, funders will be more inclined to support you.

Once you have the answers to these key questions, you will be able to use them in your fundraising, when you write an application to a trust or company (see chapter 15 for more on this), or when you put together a mailing to the public.

2.4 Organising your fundraising

Equipping a fundraising office

Some items of equipment are essential for a fundraiser; others are extremely useful. The main items are as follows.

1 *Telephone* This is absolutely essential. Ideally you need a line of your own, because of the volume and length of your calls, and to have it in a quiet place, so calls can be made in privacy. Fundraisers are often out of the office, so you need to ensure either that someone is there to answer your calls or that you have an answer machine. A mobile phone will enable you to make calls when you want and to be more accessible.

2 *Computer* A computer together with a basic software package such as Microsoft Office (or OpenOffice.org, which is free) will help you produce high-quality letters and proposals as well as storing your database of supporters and perhaps your budget and financial records. You will also need a good printer, and as part of your start-up package you are likely to be offered a scanner, which can be useful when producing material such as publicity leaflets.

3 *Photocopier* This will help you prepare large volumes of printed material for circulation to supporters. If you don't have access to a photocopier, try to make arrangements with your local copy shop and ask them to give you a good price.

4 *Fax* From time to time you may need to fax a document. You can get a fax machine that will also do small volumes of photocopying. Or you can arrange things so as to send and receive your faxes by e-mail.

5 *E-mail and the internet* More and more information is sent by e-mail, and many funders now have websites. Computers now come with a built-in

modem, and broadband for fast data transfer is becoming cheaper and cheaper. You may want to have a second telephone line for fax and e-mail. All sorts of package deals are now available, from telecoms companies and internet service providers (ISPs).

6   A*nnual reports and brochures* If you are a registered charity you have to produce an annual report by law. However, it is also an important fundraising document, as many funders will want to see your report and accounts. They do not need to be expensively produced, but should be well prepared and presented. You may also need a small range of information leaflets for the public which include reply coupons to encourage a direct response. See chapter 15, section 15.3, for more on producing printed materials. Desktop publishing (DTP) software on your computer will help you produce simple leaflets and other printed materials rather than having to use a designer. However, beware of spending hours playing around with designs as an alternative to getting on with the hard fundraising graft!

7   *Books* Handbooks on fundraising, grants guides and technical informa- tion on tax are all very valuable. Directories of trusts and companies which list the major givers and provide information on their grants poli- cies are essential. A CD ROM will be more expensive but will enable you to search more easily. See chapters 6 and 8 (Resources and further information) for suggestions. You may be able to consult directories and CD ROMs through your local council for voluntary service, rural commu- nity council or public library.

8   *Cash collection facilities* You must have a bank account so you can pay in donations. If you expect to have large sums on deposit for any length of time you should have a high interest account. If you plan to do house- to-house or street collections you will need to have the appropriate envelopes or collecting boxes. See chapter 12 for more on this.

9   *Letterheads* Most organisations will need stationery such as letterheads, compliments slips, business cards and reply envelopes. Letterheads need to include certain information (name and address, website, logo, legal sta- tus and charity registration number, etc.). The design of your letterhead is important; it is the first point of contact for many people. You can also spread your message through a strap-line explaining your mission or through an outright appeal.

10   *Display equipment* Fairs, exhibitions and shop windows can be good ways of gaining more interest in your work. You will need attractive equipment and good display material.

Setting up an office can be expensive. Some of the equipment you need you may be able to borrow from friendly organisations or supporters; other equip- ment you might get cheap or secondhand. You can also try to get equipment donated (local companies often have surplus equipment or furniture), or ask local suppliers for a heavy discount. You could also use a recycling scheme such as Morph or Green-Works. If you are a member of NCVO, you can take advantage of discounts it has negotiated on a range of products and services for its members.

You might want to prepare a shopping list of your needs and present it to a major funder as an investment package. It is in the funder's interest to get you set up as a fundraiser so as to reduce your dependency upon them.

Who should do the fundraising?

There are several options to consider.

1 The management committee

These people are legally responsible for ensuring that the organisation has sufficient funds to carry out its work and that it doesn't become insolvent. They should ensure that the fundraising is done effectively and on time, although they don't have to do it themselves. In smaller organisations, it is often the committee members who do most of the fundraising.

2 The chair

The chair occupies a special position of leadership. Part of the responsibility may be to deal with major donors, along with the director, and to attend meetings with foundations and businesses. In very small organisations, the chair may have to do all or most of the fundraising work.

3 A fundraising committee

Not all management committee members are good at fundraising, or even like doing it. So some organisations try to recruit only committee members who have good fundraising skills and personal contacts. But this is not always a good strategy. Any committee must include people with a range of skills, expertise and standpoints, as it is responsible for the proper management and strategic direction of the organisation as well as ensuring that it has sufficient funds.

It might be better to form a separate fundraising or development committee. This group can be charged with overseeing the fundraising, and even undertaking much of the work, and will include some members of the management committee plus others who are interested in or valuable to the fundraising process.

4 The director

The director of the organisation is the senior staff member and is in a good position to do the fundraising – with an expert knowledge of the work being done and sufficient seniority to be an effective persuader. Fundraising can be a creative process. When dealing with donors, you will be testing out ideas and getting feedback, negotiating different forms of support and having to think creatively about turning people's goodwill into cash. The director should know how far he or she can go.

One problem is lack of time, which means that the director may not always give fundraising sufficient priority. A possible solution is to give the director administrative assistance so that the fundraising part of the job can be done well.

5 A member of staff

Larger organisations, or those where fundraising is given a high priority, may create a specific post of fundraiser. This should ensure that someone with the time and skill to do the job properly is responsible for fundraising.

However, all too often organisations appoint a fundraiser and tell them to get on with the job, and then a couple of years later find that nothing has been achieved. If you decide to delegate the job of fundraising, both the director and the management committee need to keep control of the process – setting goals, monitoring progress, providing active support where needed and giving encouragement. It is also crucial to appoint someone who is capable of doing the job.

6 A volunteer

Another option is to find a part-time (or even a full-time) volunteer to do the fundraising or set up a fundraising group. Someone recently retired might find this an exciting challenge.

Volunteers are more often given responsibility for just one aspect of the fundraising, such as organising a fundraising reception or a gala film evening. This means that some of the fundraising work and responsibility can be handed over to someone else, but again you need to set targets and hold the volunteer accountable for their performance.

7 A fundraising consultant

Fundraising consultants or consultancy organisations are in business to help voluntary organisations with their fundraising – for a fee. Some specialise in major appeals, some in event organising, some in direct mail campaigns, some in corporate sponsorship, and some in working with smaller organisations to help them clarify their approach to fundraising and get started. Using a consultant can be expensive but, particularly where you are developing a major initiative, their experience and knowledge can add greatly to your fundraising efforts and help get things started. It is very rare that you will hand over all your fundraising work to an external consultant.

When you need a fundraiser

Not every voluntary organisation needs a paid fundraiser. Grant-funded bodies may leave the fundraising to the senior worker or to committee members. Smaller organisations might use volunteers. However, organisational growth or particular funding needs may make a paid fundraiser the best option.

A key issue is whether you can afford to employ a fundraiser, and what effect it will have on your administrative costs. Not many organisations are lucky enough to obtain sponsorship for their fundraiser, so you will have to meet their costs from the extra income you are able to generate. On the other hand, can you afford not to? Without a fundraiser, you may not have the capacity to raise the resources you need – as nobody else is prepared to do the work or give fundraising sufficient priority. As a rough guide, to employ a junior fundraiser full-time will cost at least £30,000 including overheads. To justify this, you will need to generate around £125,000 a year in extra revenue – although it may take some time to achieve results on this scale.

Initially it may seem that all the fundraiser is doing is raising the costs of their own salary. However, you need to take a long-term view. It takes several years to develop the full potential of the fundraising effort put in. Any fundraising appointment should be seen as part of the organisation's longer-term strategy.

Recruitment of a fundraiser

Once you have decided to recruit a fundraiser, you should consider the following:

1 Objectives

What are the objectives for the fundraising post? Is it to:

- develop alternative sources of funds to replace grants which are coming to an end?
- launch an expansion programme?
- run a major capital appeal?
- develop independent and local funding?
- create a large and active membership?
- develop corporate support?
- organise high profile events which will raise awareness as well as money?

You need to be clear about your objectives. This will help you write a job description and a person specification, so that you recruit someone with the experience and ability to do a good job. The objectives must be realistic: they should recognise your need for money, the opportunities that exist to raise it and a reasonable timetable for doing this which is not impossible to achieve.

There is always a learning process at the start when nothing much happens other than the fundraiser getting familiar with the work of the organisation, doing background research and developing contacts. But it is also important that results begin to flow reasonably quickly.

2 Budget

There is no point appointing a fundraiser unless you also provide a budget for equipment, operational costs and promotional activity. Without such a budget the fundraiser will be unable to do a proper job. The box below gives a list of headings that you will probably need to include.

Budget headings (employing a fundraiser)

Recruitment and training

Salary, National Insurance and pension contribution

Computer and printer

Mobile phone

Stationery, printing and photocopying

Share of office overheads

Travel

Subscriptions to professional organisations, magazines etc.

Purchase of directories / CD ROMs etc.

Design and print of leaflets and a presentable annual report

Mailing costs

---

3 Recruitment

Once you have decided your objectives and written a job description you will need to identify someone with the right:

- experience and expertise
- personal skills and qualities to do a good job
- ethical values and commitment to your cause.

The last two are really important. You can gain experience and expertise, but the personal skills and ethical stance come with the candidate. (The personal skills required in a fundraiser are discussed in some detail in section 2.2.)

There is always a chance that the appointment will not work out, that you have chosen the wrong person. It is advisable to include a six-month probationary period in the contract for a newly recruited fundraiser, as for most other key staff.

Where to recruit a fundraiser

- Circulate information about the job opportunity to your staff. This job might be something that a current member of your staff team might like to do.
- Circulate information about the job opportunity to your existing supporters and volunteers. They already have some commitment to the organisation. Someone might be just the right person for the job.
- Advertise in the local newspaper, the charity press, the Guardian's Society section, marketing journals, internet recruitment services, or via the Institute of Fundraising. These will reach the sorts of people you are looking for.

4 Induction

As for any other appointment, there should be a satisfactory induction process, which might include:

- meeting the management committee;
- meeting senior staff;
- site visits to projects to see the organisation at work, and discussions with project workers and beneficiaries;
- discussing and agreeing what the organisation stands for and how it should be presented to the public;
- discussing which donors the organisation is not prepared to accept support from and reviewing any formal donations policy;
- reviewing existing donor support, including meeting some of the more committed supporters, identifying problem areas and opportunities;
- agreeing the fundraising strategy and the targets for the first year, and sketching out what might be achieved over the first three years;
- being introduced to any key contacts, especially some of the larger funders.

Management and motivation of fundraisers

Fundraising is a demanding and often a lonely job. With all the difficulties inherent in raising money and a steady flow of rejections, it is easy to get downhearted. Proper management of the fundraiser's job means:

1 Keeping in touch with the work of the organisation

The fundraiser should be in regular touch with those doing the frontline work, visiting projects, talking to project workers and beneficiaries, getting a feel for the needs and the quality of the work, the issues, approach and ethos of the organisation. This will also help increase awareness of the fundraising process and the concerns and interests of your donors.

2 Setting targets and monitoring progress

Targets should be agreed with the fundraiser rather than imposed, and progress should be regularly monitored. It may not be the fundraiser's fault if targets are not being met. They may have been over-optimistic, or one large donation may have failed to materialise.

Try to learn from mistakes. You may want to create a small fundraising advisory group who will take a particular interest in the fundraising and with whom the fundraiser can discuss issues or refer problems.

Keep track of the time and effort put into each fundraising initiative. You can spend a lot of time chasing after marginal or unlikely sources, and too little developing those central to your future. Fundraising events can take up a lot of time for little financial return. Time is usually your most expensive item of cost, so use it effectively.

3 Giving fundraising due importance

Fundraising must be seen to be important, and the fundraiser needs support to do a good job. Fundraising which is just delegated and forgotten about, or starved of resources, will rarely work well. The director and the management committee must have confidence in the fundraising process and the fundraiser's abilities, and provide appropriate support and encouragement.

Your organisation should also do its best to recognise and celebrate any fundraising success.

4 Access to information

The fundraiser will represent the organisation and answer on its behalf in a range of situations. You need to be able to speak authoritatively to any interested parties. You must be kept informed of what is going on, how the organisation is doing financially and what new initiatives are in the pipeline.

5 Training and meeting other fundraisers

There are lots of fundraising courses and conferences taking place all over the country. These are good places to brush up on skills, share ideas and experiences, and meet and network with others doing a similar job. Fundraisers should be encouraged to find out what and how other organisations are doing, and to get hold of annual reports and other promotional material from rival organisations.

6 Free time to think

Some of the most creative fundraising comes from thinking about what you are doing, chatting to people about your ideas, meeting people and talking about your work (with no immediate intention of asking for money). The pressure to raise money means this creative time is often lost. This needs to be built into your work schedule.

Getting outside help with your fundraising

Periodically you may need help with your fundraising, whether to tackle a campaign, discuss new fundraising schemes or devise a new fundraising plan. You may just want a few words of advice or some administrative support or you might want some technical assistance. Different tasks require different skills with different costs associated with them. You must be absolutely clear about what you want, especially when you are briefing potential consultants.

Networking

When dealing with smaller problems or ones that only you can resolve, informal networks can help. The main body that can help facilitate this is the Institute of Fundraising which, at the time of writing, has over 4,000 individuals and 250 organisations as members. There is a strong culture of one fundraiser helping another despite the highly competitive nature of much fundraising today. The best way of accessing the network is to join the Institute of Fundraising. Membership gives you access to other members' contact information and your nearest regional group.

You can also attend training courses or conferences run by the Institute of Fundraising or by the Directory of Social Change, where you will meet people in similar situations to yourself.

Fundraising consultants

Many people now work as self-employed fundraising consultants. Consultants will say that their costs are small compared with the returns. However they would also admit that their costs are guaranteed while the returns are not. Costs tend to range from a low of around £250 a day to highs in excess of £1,000 a day plus VAT.

There are also fundraising consultancy firms. They would argue that they have a greater capacity to work for you and a wider range of skills. They are generally more expensive so it is more sensible to use them for things like advertising, capital giving, direct mail, payroll giving, (website) design and video or print production.

Since there are plenty of possible consultants and consultancy firms around, it is not difficult to find names. There are four main areas to look initially.

- The Institute of Fundraising members' handbook, *Who's Who in Fundraising*. This lists all current members and those that are independent consultants. It also has adverts for relevant services.

- The Association of Fundraising Consultants (AFC). This group contains both independent consultants and consultancy companies. It has its own code of practice.
- The National Council for Voluntary Organisations (NCVO) also keeps a list of consultants.
- The specialist press. Consultants often write articles to raise their profile or generate business. Others simply advertise. Have a look at *ThirdSector* and *Professional Fundraising* magazines.

Working with consultants

The use of consultants could be a major issue for your donors and supporters, who may positively dislike the idea that some of their donation will go to a paid consultant. You need to think very carefully before going down this particular road.

Once you have decided to go ahead, you must produce a clear brief against which you can compare quotes from different people (consultants expect to tender for business). Once you have identified your consultant, you must agree precise terms in a clearly-written contract. The Institute of Fundraising has a useful set of guidelines for charities wishing to appoint a consultant.

If you are paying someone not directly employed by you to sign appeal letters on your behalf, to visit donors or to make phone calls to donors, the Charities Act 1992 requires them to declare their status as a professional fundraiser and how they are being paid. The new Charities Act 2006 also contains requirements that professional or commercial fundraisers raising money for charitable purposes or institutions make statements about their role and how much of the money raised will benefit the charity or cause they are working for. There must also be a written agreement in a prescribed form between the charity and the professional fundraiser. A standard agreement can be obtained from the Institute of Fundraising, or see *The Fundraiser's Guide to the Law* for a model.

Payment by results

You may be tempted to pay commission rather than a flat fee to link cost with performance. This is problematic.

- Under the Charities Act 1992 (and still true under the Charities Act 2006), if the consultant asks for money they have to make a declaration that they will receive a part of the donation as commission, which can affect the chances of getting support (although if they simply advise on strategy or write out the letter for you to sign, no declaration needs to be made).

- The Charity Commission is not keen on commission fundraising. It feels that the charity should employ someone based on their competence to do the job and the expectation that they will succeed, and pay the consultant on this basis. But this payment could include a success fee if certain targets are achieved.
- If you have not made a financial commitment, you have less incentive to manage the consultant effectively.
- The consultant might cherry-pick – get those donations you were expecting anyway, and do little more.

If you can't afford a professional fundraiser, which is a common situation for small organisations, you could:

- look for sponsorship to cover the costs of the consultancy – show it as a cost-effective investment in the future of your organisation;
- seek a grant for an initial feasibility study – the Charities Aid Foundation makes grants for this purpose;
- find someone to do the work for nothing – this might be a long shot!
- do the work yourselves, but gather around you people with the required expertise to advise you.

How to select a consultant

Whoever you decide to choose, there are a number of steps to go through.

1. Be absolutely sure of the help you need. Is it just to devise the strategy, or do you need additional help with its implementation? Do you need someone to do a specific task, or just advise?
2. Write a good brief and clear job description covering what needs to be done, the timetable, and the specific objectives.
3. Have a selection of people or companies to choose from – ensuring that you choose the best.
4. Agree the basis of payment. Is this acceptable? What control over success and failure will you retain? How will expenses be charged? How much notice is required to terminate the arrangement if you are dissatisfied?
5. Obtain and follow up references. If you do not get good – or indeed any – references, proceed only with the greatest caution.

Resources and further information

See also general lists at the end of the book.

Organisations

AFC (Association of Fundraising
  Consultants)
Suite 316
Linen Hall
162–168 Regent Street
London W1B 4JN
www.afc.org.uk
Tel. 01582 762446

CAF (Charities Aid Foundation)
25 Kings Hill Avenue
Kings Hill
West Malling
Kent ME19 4TA
Tel. 01732 520 000
e-mail enquiries@cafonline.org

Institute of Fundraising
Park Place
12 Lawn Lane
London SW8 1UD
www.institute-of-fundraising.org.uk
Tel. 020 7840 1000

NCVO (National Council of Voluntary
  Organisations)
NCVO offers its members a growing
range of discounts on products and
services.
For information, contact:
Business Development Manager
Tel. 020 7520 2481
e-mail discounts@ncvo-vol.org.uk

Publications

The following publications are available from the Directory of Social Change.
Prices were correct at the time of writing, but may be subject to change.

Charitable Status, Andrew Phillips, 6th edn, DSC due early 2008, £12.95

The Fundraiser's Guide to the Law, Bates, Wells & Braithwaite and Centre for
Voluntary Sector Development, DSC 2000, £19.95

Other publications

Fundraising for Social Change, 5th edn, Kim Klein, Pfeiffer/Wiley 2006, £21.99
Pfeiffer/Wiley
Website: eu.wiley.com

Professional Fundraising, subscription £89 (charities), £120 (non-charities)
Plaza Publishing Limited
3 Rectory Grove
London SW4 0DX
Tel. 020 7819 1200
Fax 020 7819 1201
e-mail info@plazapublishing.co.uk

ThirdSector, published weekly, subscription £107 (non-charities),
£82 (charities)
Haymarket Professional Publications
174 Hammersmith Road
London W6 7JP
Tel. 020 8267 500

3 DEVELOPING A FUNDRAISING STRATEGY

This chapter will help you produce a strategic plan for your fundraising. It covers the preliminary stages of analysing your position and gathering information, as well as the follow-up work of monitoring and measuring your results.

Details of organisations and publications referred to in this chapter are on pages 55–56.

3.1 Planning your approach

Your strategy is the backbone of your fundraising. Getting it right requires a good deal of attention at an early stage, and should involve people both inside and outside your organisation, especially if you have major fundraising ambitions.

Headings for a fundraising strategy paper

Review of the current position
- Current strengths and weaknesses
- Past fundraising experience
- Existing fundraising strengths and resources

Projection of fundraising needs

Overall funding strategy

Proposed new sources of income

Suggested methods to meet fundraising targets

Resources needed to do this

Timeline for implementation

Strategy is about organising your ideas to produce a viable plan to take you forward beyond this year. If you just need £250 for equipment, all you may need to do is approach an individual or business sympathetic to your cause or organisation. This doesn't really require a strategic plan. However, if you have wider hopes or major existing commitments to fund, you will need to spend more time and be more creative in developing your fundraising strategy.

Your strategy will indicate where you want to be (in a period of, say, five years) and how you aim to get there. It is an integral part of your organisation's business plan. Obviously, not everything will go according to plan and you will need to incorporate new ideas as you go along. You should therefore aim to update your plan every year, and produce a revised strategy every two or three years.

Outlining your needs

The starting point for any fundraising strategy is to define the needs of the organisation. This can be done at three levels.

1 Just to keep going

How much money do you need to continue at your current scale of operation? How much is already assured, and how much do you need to raise to meet spending requirements? These calculations usually take the form of annual and rolling budgets for the short and medium term (up to three, or even five, years ahead).

2 To expand to meet growing need

Most organisations believe they are only scratching at the surface of the problem. If they had more resources, they could do much more to meet the need. Furthermore, the need may be growing or the problem getting worse. Ask yourselves the following questions:

- What is the current level of unmet need?
- What will happen if nothing is done?
- How are the needs growing and what changes do you foresee over the next few years?
- What should you be doing to respond to the challenges of the future?
- Who else is doing something to meet the needs?
- How does your plan fit in with what others are doing?
- Is your idea an effective way of addressing the needs, given the limited resources that are likely to be available?
- Could or should you be providing solutions to the problem rather than simply addressing the needs?
- Are there ways of collaborating with others which could combine efforts and resources for greater impact?

Future plans should be discussed and developed. Is it just a question of expanding what you are doing? Or will you be developing new mechanisms for addressing the problem? If the need is not significant and your role not clear, then developing a good fundraising case could be extremely difficult.

3 The future development of your organisation's work

Organisations do not stay still. There is often a momentum to develop, and even to expand. Success with one project gives an organisation confidence; it also throws up new ideas and brings greater credibility with potential funders and partners.

What developments do you have planned? What new services or projects will you want to run? Will you want to expand your work into other regions? Will you want to enter into major collaborations with funding partners to extend your work? Will you want to enter into partnerships with government authorities, working with them on a much wider scale to address the problem?

If you are a community development organisation, what about your relationship with the people you are helping? Are you empowering people to help themselves? If so, what happens to you when local people have the structures and skills to organise their own development? Will you extend and develop your work and maintain your development role? Or will you develop a withdrawal or exit strategy?

The future of your organisation starts with what you want to do. It is up to the chief executive to plan this, with input from other senior staff, from the fundraiser (if there is one in post), from the management committee and from the organisation at large. Then it is up to whoever is doing the fundraising to get the resources to put the plans into action.

However, it is vital that you do not do things simply because you can get the money. You must be led by the work that you want to do, the needs that you want to meet, rather than the money that you think you can raise. If you are not, you will soon find that the organisation will lose its sense of direction and will then become in serious danger of simply fizzling out.

Different approaches to fundraising strategy

Besides funding the work, you will also need to fund the organisation and its future. There are several factors to consider.

Capital developments

Capital developments, such as acquiring new buildings or IT systems, can have an impact on future fundraising needs in four ways. On the plus side:

- they can reduce operating costs;
- they can generate income from fees and charges (for example from letting out space);

- they can generate a greater capacity to fundraise (for example when organising a major appeal, you will be building a database of important contacts which you can utilise later on for further support).

On the minus side:

- they may increase your revenue costs if they require extra people to run them.

Endowment

Many organisations want to develop an endowment – that is, a capital reserve which can be invested to produce a regular income for the organisation. Some approach major donors for contributions to this fund; others set aside some of their income each year. They feel that this will give them greater financial security, remove some of the fundraising pressure or act as a reserve in times of unexpected difficulties. However, most trusts and companies prefer to fund your work directly rather than have their money tied up as an investment.

Examples of successful endowment fundraising

- The Campaign for Oxford endowed several professorial chairs by raising enough money to generate the annual income needed to support a professor.
- Community Links, a community-based project in London, organised a major appeal to take over a town hall in Canning Town and turn it into a community centre. The building was seen as an asset which could continue to be exploited for community benefit.

It takes a lot of hard work to raise an endowment. Might it not be better to spend that time on exciting and successful work? This would make the organisation more attractive to funders and make future fundraising easier.

Reducing dependency and developing independent sources of funding

There is a fundamental difference between an organisation that receives all its money from one source, and an organisation that receives money from several or many sources, each contributing towards the total requirement. Over-reliance on one source might give that donor too much power over what the organisation should be doing and where it should be going. It creates a risk of failure – that the organisation will not be able to survive if the grant is cut back or withdrawn.

You need to decide whether your organisation's funding base is too narrow and, if it is, how you can broaden it. You will need to think about all the possible sources of income, and decide which are the most sensible for your organisation to develop.

On the other hand, although it is good to have a broad base of support, there is a danger of taking this principle too far and having so many small-scale donors that all your fundraising energies go into servicing them without being able to develop your fundraising further.

Developing a membership and a supporter base

A strong membership or supporter base helps create financial independence by:

- creating a constituency of support (the number of people who support you add to your credibility as an organisation and give you lobbying power);
- building a local base for your organisation (your relationship with your local community will be much closer if the funding is drawn from it rather than obtained externally);
- creating opportunities for further fundraising. Each donor can be asked to give regularly and more generously, to recruit other donors, to volunteer their time and skills, to donate items of equipment, or even to leave a legacy. The more people who are supporting you, the more opportunities you will have for developing your fundraising.

Some key concepts

Before deciding who to approach there are some more general issues to think through.

- *Be cost conscious.* You need to monitor carefully the money you spend. You should ask supporters only for what is strictly necessary, and use as much as possible on the work of the organisation. Keeping your costs down is a factor in this.
- *Someone has to pay.* Many charities exist to provide a service to beneficiaries that is free or highly subsidised. This means that the amount raised determines the volume of work that can be undertaken. However, you may be able to charge for your services. You need to decide what is appropriate for you and your users. Alternatively, in the current contract culture, statutory bodies may be able to pay for the services you deliver. Either way, you must cost what you do carefully and accurately. Someone has to pay for it – your funders, your sponsors, your donors or your users.
- *Avoid risks.* The cash that you spend on your fundraising is intended to generate money to spend on your work. You shouldn't be squandering it on high-risk fundraising schemes where there is a real possibility that it might be lost. Fundraisers must minimise risk. You might need to pilot or test a new fundraising idea. You should identify the worst case scenario and take whatever action you can to avoid it, insure yourself against it or even scrap it if it looks set to fail.

- *The long-term approach.* You can simply concentrate on getting cash now, or you can devote some of your fundraising resources to ensuring the longer-term flow of funds into your organisation. For example, committed giving by individuals and appeals for legacies have high costs in the short term, but their long-term value usually far outweighs that of casual giving.
- *The multiplier approach.* A good way to maximise fundraising results is to cascade. A sponsored run can bring your organisation to the attention of large numbers of people. Every runner will sign up sponsors, and some of these may subsequently become interested in becoming a member or a regular donor (rather than in simply sponsoring a friend). This cascade effect will multiply the number of people supporting you and the amount you raise.
- *Sustainability.* In an ideal world, your organisation would be structured so as to minimise the need for permanent fundraising. Even if this is a mere pipe dream for you, there are a number of ways of making yourself more sustainable and therefore financially more secure:
  - develop a range of income-generating activities
  - develop partnerships with larger bodies capable of giving larger sums – government for example
  - raise an endowment fund
  - recruit volunteers and get support donated in kind
  - develop income sources that continue over many years, such as a membership
  - only organise events that are repeatable, so that if they work, they can be done again and again – and even better next time.
- *Time.* You need to be realistic about how long things will take. To go from £0 to £100,000 a year from grantmaking trusts may require years of patient fundraising effort. To land your first major company sponsorship requires professionalism and good relationships that you may not yet have. To get your first 5,000 supporters is far harder than getting the next 5,000. Everything can take longer than you expect. There is a danger of being over-optimistic. Try to be realistic about how long things will take.

3.2 Analysing your position

Analysing your current position is a good starting point for developing a strategy for moving forward. Not only will it help you answer some of the difficult questions you are often asked by funders, but it will also help you see your work in new ways and better understand your strengths and weaknesses.

The first step is to look at the work for which you are seeking funds.

- What is the need that you will be addressing?
- Who are the ultimate beneficiaries?

- What difference to the beneficiaries will your intervention make?
- Are there competing agencies, and does their work complement or duplicate yours?
- What is distinctive about your approach?
- Is the need you are addressing something that will continue – or is it occasional, seasonal or one off?
- Is the need expected to increase or change over the next few years and how will you respond to this?
- What are your medium-term plans?

Projection of financial need

The next step is to make a financial projection of the resources you will need to undertake your planned programme of work over the next three to five years. This must take in all planned expenditure and all probable income. It should show you two things: the funding gap that needs to be met, and possible fall-back options if funding is not received. This is best illustrated by the following example.

Example of a funding projection for a small organisation

Source of income	Current year	Next year	2 years' time	3 years' time
Current local authority grant	10,000	10,000	5,000	5,000
Grant from charitable trust	2,500	2,500	nil	nil
Membership subscriptions	250	250	250	250
Total committed income	**12,750**	**12,750**	**5,250**	**5,250**
Reserve at start of year	500	2,050	2,050	2,050
Current operational costs	10,000	12,500	15,000	15,000
New project costs	1,200	3,500	5,000	5,000
Projected fundraising target	**nil**	**3,250**	**14,750**	**14,250**

The example shows that your funding position for the current year is good, and that you have a small target to meet next year which is a realistic goal for your fundraising. However in two years' time, as your major grants run out, you will need to replace these, or develop new ways to fund your organisation.

Analysis of your environment

There are various ways in which you can explore your fundraising environment. These exercises are best done with a small group of people and a brainstorming approach.

1 SWOT analysis

The first, and most commonly used tool available is a SWOT analysis. This involves trying to identify your organisation's:

Strengths
Weaknesses
Opportunities
Threats

Strengths and weaknesses are internal to your organisation – those things that you know about your organisation which either give you an advantage or hold you back. Opportunities and threats relate to the external world – things which will impact on your work and your chances of raising money, both now and in future.

An example of a SWOT analysis for a small organisation

	Positive	Negative
Internal factors	*Strengths* Established team Experienced management Good relations with local authority Good reputation	*Weaknesses* Limited contact with funders Existing grants running out No evaluation undertaken
External factors	*Opportunities* Public interest in your issue New company in the area	*Threats* Change in benefit regulations Another local agency is expanding aggressively

2 PEST analysis

To explore the external factors in more detail, a PEST (sometimes also known as STEP) analysis can be useful. It is similar to a SWOT analysis, although you will be looking at the trends in society which are going to affect your fundraising and your work generally. This is done under the headings:

Political
Economic
Social
Technological

You are looking at the future and focusing on external changes which may affect you. For example:

- *Political:* what will be the impact on the voluntary sector if the ruling party changes at the next general election? What will the further contracting out of public services mean?
- *Economic:* what effect will the next budget have on the fundraising climate? How would increased public spending impact on the voluntary sector?
- *Social:* what will be the impact of people living longer, which is leading to a growing older population? What will be the results of the continuing fragmentation of the family?
- *Technological:* what does the internet mean for you and your users?

These and other factors will affect your organisation and your fundraising. There may be little you can do about some factors, but you should bear them all in mind as you develop your fundraising strategy.

PEST Analysis of a small employment charity for people with disabilities

Political: full implementation of the Disability Rights Act will bring advantages

Economic: improvements in economy will bring more work opportunities

Social: car-based society will continue to disadvantage those on low incomes with mobility problems

Technological: it will become possible for more people to work at home

These are the main factors that were identified. The next step is to consider what impact they will have.

---

3 Stakeholder analysis

Stakeholder analysis looks at all those groups that have an interest in your organisation and in its funding. For example, a refugee service concluded that it had a number of key stakeholders, which included:

- the local authority, which would otherwise have to provide support to refugee families;
- members of the organisation, who have joined because they feel strongly about the issues being tackled;
- refugee community organisations, which already provide direct services and advice to newly-arrived refugees;
- second generation refugees, who have stayed on in Britain and who wish to give something back to help other refugees.

This exercise should help you identify both who has a particular interest in supporting your work and why.

4 Auditing your existing fundraising

Even the smallest organisation will have some fundraising experience to build on. If your organisation is brand new, the people who are starting it may well have had experience and contacts from raising money for another organisation which will be useful – and you can always look at how similar groups have been able to raise the money they needed to get started.

You also need to find out where your organisation's funds are currently coming from, how easy it has been to raise the money, what other sources have been tried, what other fundraising techniques have been used with what results, and whether you are especially vulnerable to any particular source disappearing or being cut back.

Listing your fundraising sources

Source of funds	Funds received			% of total
	previous year	last year	this year	
Central government				
Europe				
Local government				
Trusts				
Companies				
Membership				
Individual donations				
Fundraising events				
Legacies				
Charges and fees				

You can also, if you wish, include the value of volunteer and in-kind support that you have received. This will give a better picture of the total resources you are mobilising.

5 Competitor analysis

You can glean a good deal of information from an intelligent look at your collaborators and competitors. The successful ones may have tried already to develop some of the fundraising ideas you are considering, but failed; or they may be succeeding with a source or a technique that you have not yet considered.

It is pretty easy to find out where other organisations get their money from – read their annual report and accounts. It may be harder to find out about their fundraising methods. Read the trade press, talk with colleagues in other organisations and ask them how they are doing. You will find many people who are happy to share their experience and ideas.

Assessing the opportunities

It is always worth comparing your current funding pattern with other possible sources you might consider. These include:

- a grant from a central or regional government department;
- a grant from a non-governmental agency (such as the Arts Council);
- a grant from a local authority or health authority;
- a contract or service-level agreement with one of the above to deliver a specified service;
- a contract with another body (perhaps a commercial organisation or another voluntary agency) to deliver a service;
- fees and charges from users;
- support from individuals through membership, donations or legacies;
- money raised from collections, fundraising events or entertainments, or other fundraising activities;
- grants from trusts, the National Lottery and other independent grant-making bodies;
- support from companies (including cash, in-kind donations, sponsorship, the provision of facilities or skills, or through a secondment);
- support from individuals who donate their time as volunteers;
- investment income and interest.

These are the main types of funding that are available. They are examined in more detail in Part 2 of this book. Not all will be appropriate to your organisation. You will need to select those that are right for your organisation's needs, and where you feel that you have the greatest chance of success. Here are some of the factors to take into account.

- *Past experience.* The results of your fundraising so far provide a good indication of both what to do and what not to do. Things that have gone well can be developed so that you do even better. Donors that have supported you can be encouraged to continue their support, perhaps at a higher level. New donors can be brought in to match the support you have been getting from existing donors. Invest effort and resources to develop those areas of fundraising that already appear to work well for you.
- *Scale of need.* If you need to raise substantial funds, these may be realised either in large grants from a few sources, or in smaller donations from a larger number of donors. You need to approach those fundraising sources that are capable of making a realistic contribution to your overall need.
- *The attractiveness of the cause.* Some causes are much easier to raise money for than others. People working with animals or children's cancer funds have causes that are extremely compelling. An overview of which cause areas the public gives to appears on pages 62 and 63. If your cause

is not a popular one, you will have to work that much harder to make it seem important, and to persuade donors to support you.

- *The style of your work.* Are you radical or conservative? Young or old? Innovative or steady? Every organisation will be able to identify institutions and individuals that share their vision and outlook. Equally there will be those that don't, and these will be much less likely to support you.
- *The resources and skills available to you.* Do you have the people to mount a collection, the contacts to develop a big gift campaign, or the organisational ability to run a major event? It is always best to concentrate on what you are good at.
- *Your natural constituency of support.* Is this the government? Trusts? Individuals? Who has a stake in the problem or need which you are addressing? Can you get them to share in its solution by becoming an investor in your work?
- *The type of organisation you want to be.* A membership organisation is very different from one funded by government; a fundraising organisation is different from one that relies on the sale of its services. Your fundraising provides the money to enable you to do what you want to do. Your fundraising strategy will help you become the sort of organisation you want to be.
- *Short term and long term.* Some sources are essentially short term, whilst others can develop into long-term relationships and partnerships. If you are there for the long term, you will need a sufficient proportion of long-term income. You will want to turn one-off donors into regular ones, to organise a successful fundraising event annually and make it generate more each year.

Assessing possible funding sources

Source	Past experience	Competitors' experience	Relevance to cause	Resources needed	Rating
Central government					
Local government					
Trusts					
Companies					
Big givers					
Members and supporters					
Events					

Clarifying the constraints

There will be limits on your fundraising, some stemming from the nature of your organisation, some which are created internally, and others which are externally imposed. Many of your constraints might even create some opportunities for you.

- *Geography.* An important constraint is the geographical remit of your organisation. Some funders only give to organisations with a national focus; others only give locally. Some companies may give nationally through head office, but make smaller local grants through local plants or branches. Local people are concerned about their own local communities. However, if what you are doing locally is particularly innovative or interesting, it may catch the interest of national funders, both because they like being associated with excellence and because your project may provide answers to similar problems in other areas.

- *Appropriateness.* Some sources are inappropriate because what the donor represents is the complete opposite of what the charity stands for. For example, cancer charities will not accept support from tobacco companies. If they did so, they would create bad publicity for themselves and problems with their other donors by endorsing a product which causes the problem. There may be other reasons for refusing a donation. For example, a campaigning organisation might not wish to be seen in the pocket of a vested interest or the government; and it might gain strength in its campaigning by being seen to be supported by a large membership. It is difficult to draw up a definitive set of rules on where you should and shouldn't fundraise. But it is important to discuss and try to agree a policy on what you are not prepared to accept before you set about asking, rather than creating problems for yourself afterwards.

- *Resources.* The resources available to you determine what you can and can't do. If you are planning a public collection, do you have or can you get sufficient people to do it? Money is another key resource. Much fundraising involves investing now to achieve a result later. Some fundraising, such as a direct mail, an advertising campaign or even a large building appeal, may require a substantial immediate expenditure. Anyone soliciting legacies is unlikely to see their efforts rewarded for some years. You need to know how much your fundraising is going to cost and when the results will come in, and then decide if you can afford to do it. Some fundraisers see these constraints as a challenge – they will find the people or the money they need somehow!

- *Contacts.* Your contacts can lead you to sources of money. If you have a good contact in the business world, they can ask other business people they know for donations. If you have celebrities wanting to get involved, you might use them as the anchor for a fundraising event. If you don't yet have sufficiently good contacts, think how you can develop these as a major challenge for your fundraising.

- *What other organisations are doing.* Not many organisations can expect to get away with being just imitators of others. You need to be – and need to be seen to be – distinctive.

3.3 Gathering information

Too many organisations assume that they know what their supporters and potential supporters think, what they are interested in and what they need to know about the work being done. This is dangerous. You need to check your assumptions and find out what your supporters really think about your organisation and its work. The more you can understand your donors and potential donors, the more you will be able to communicate effectively with them and motivate them to give.

There are various types of research that you can carry out, and for a wide variety of purposes. In this section we look at researching your own donor base, finding out what the public thinks of you, and using this research to identify potential new supporters.

Donor research

Whatever the size of your organisation you want to know who your supporters are and what they think of you. You depend on their time or money to carry out your work. If they are becoming disenchanted with what you are doing or can no longer meet your expectations, you have a problem which you will have to address.

Knowing who your supporters are will also help you identify other sorts of people you might try to recruit as new supporters – and it could indicate categories of people who you have not yet been able to reach out to and enlist.

You should try and chat informally to your supporters at events and open days, or whenever you come into contact with them. This shows them that you are interested in their opinions and will help you discover what they are thinking.

You may want to do more formal research, such as a survey. If you have a mailing list or can enclose the questionnaire with a newsletter, this will be relatively easy and cheap to do. You could also send your survey by e-mail or post it on your website, if you have one. You will probably want to find out your supporters' attitude to your organisation and its work. You may also want to get information which will help you communicate more effectively with them and develop some ideas for where to look for people with a similar profile. So, you might also want to ask about their:

- age
- sex
- marital status
- number of children
- income band
- working status
- job
- newspaper readership
- voting habits
- religious membership
- trade union and other membership
- giving methods to the organisation
- frequency of giving
- preferred areas of support
- support for other charities
- volunteering (whether and how much time they give)
- legacy intentions (whether they have made a will and if it contains a charitable bequest).

These simple questions and others that relate more particularly to your work can form the basis of a questionnaire you send out. But be careful when interpreting the results. Is the information from those who responded representative of the whole (which includes those who didn't respond)? Responders are likely to be more keenly interested than the average supporter. Also, poor survey technique can lead to misleading results. For example, if your questionnaire is too long, only those who have the time and interest will respond, so your results could be biased in favour of older people or those not in full-time employment.

Surveying your own supporters is not expensive. You can easily put some effort into doing it yourself, especially if you pay attention to the question composition and getting the replies back. You need to make the survey seem important and easy to respond to. Enclosing a reply-paid envelope for a mailed questionnaire and/or offering an incentive to those responding, such as free entry into a prize draw, can both lift response rates.

Public opinion research

Finding out what the public at large thinks is more difficult and expensive than a supporter survey. For some organisations it can be essential – for example, if you are trying to change the government's environmental policy, evidence of strong public feeling will add weight to your argument.

Postal surveys are not usually effective for this. A full public opinion survey using a specialist research company will be expensive – so you will need to assess whether the cost is worth it. Omnibus research may be appropriate: this is where a research company puts together questions from several organisations and carries out interviews asking all the questions in one survey. If you just want to know a few things, and the questions can be answered yes or no, this can be relatively cheap and quick. If you want to know how the public is likely to react to a proposed appeal or restyle of your organisation, then focus groups will be better (see below).

Interviews

Interviews take time, require professionals and are expensive. However, the findings can be invaluable. You can find out how you are perceived, how you compare with others in the same field, who are prospective supporters, and what their attitudes are to the cause and work being done. The questionnaire will be drawn up for you and you should get well-balanced responses and reliable results (including the differences between supporters and non-supporters). If you depend upon high levels of current public awareness of your cause for your success, this type of research will tell you how well you are doing.

Focus groups

Focus groups are useful when you want to explore key issues (for example, new fundraising materials, an advertising strategy, a new name, or attitudes to important issues). A focus group works by getting a number of people together for a period of discussion led by an experienced facilitator who helps steer the conversation and record the results. Group discussions can be held in different locations to give a geographic balance and help compare different types of supporter. Reports and transcripts will be made available to the client.

Sources of data

There are various good sources of information. The National Archives or the public library is always a good starting point, as is the internet. Reports from the census will contain a wide range of research at a national and local level. Market research companies produce interesting reports about people's behaviour and buying habits (these may be available in business libraries). Your local reference library or university social studies department should be able to tell you about any local research that has been carried out and help you find out about relevant academic research. This information can be particularly important in highlighting the importance of social problems and issues.

Statistics

Not all research data is reliable. Proper samples are needed to get meaningful results. Samples can suffer from several forms of bias. One is associated with the nature of the sampling process. For example, does it cover all areas of the country? Does it cover all age and income groups? Is the sample self-selecting? Have you only selected those who answered?

Equally important is sample size. There are statistical formulae to determine the sample size required to get a reliable conclusion 95% of the time. If you are doing your own survey, you might find a university lecturer or graduate student who has experience with statistics to volunteer to design your sampling procedures.

3.4 Developing a fundraising plan

Your choice of what sources of funds you will develop will have reduced your options for the fundraising techniques you can use. The next stage involves deciding what precisely you will do to raise the money you need.

The starting point for your plan will be to make a detailed list of the different sources and activities (direct mail to individuals, events, legacies, applications to trusts, company sponsorship etc.). Then for each, you need to work out the resources you will need – staff, volunteers, money, equipment, important contacts, specialist advice, etc.

Investment

Most fundraising techniques require investment – spending now to achieve some sort of return later on. For example, appeals to charitable trusts require a good deal of time to research the proposal, write it up, get others' views on it and get the presentation right; you will also have to spend equivalent time identifying suitable trusts to approach and tailoring the application to each. Other fundraising may require you to print leaflets, buy collecting boxes or spend money before you get anything back.

Before proceeding, you need to check whether you have the budget to do what you plan – money to pay for what you will have to purchase, and the time you will need to put in. The box overleaf gives some approximate start-up costs for different methods. All are dependent upon the scale at which you do them and whether you are lavish or frugal in your purchasing.

The costs of various fundraising techniques

Here are some rough estimates of the ratio of potential income to fundraising costs:

Twenty times

Donor mailings

Appeals to trusts

Ten times

House-to-house collections

Payroll giving

Lotteries and raffles

Two to five times

Temporary shops and stalls

Fundraising events

Radio appeals

Around break-even or less

Advertising

Cold mailing

Just as you need to invest in getting the fundraising going, so it will take time before you see the income. You need to organise volunteers, collecting boxes and leaflets well before you can carry out a collection. Some charitable trusts, especially the smaller ones, do not meet more than quarterly, so it could be up to six months from the time you post the application to the time you hear whether you have succeeded.

The planning times for fundraising

There will also be time between starting to develop any particular fundraising technique and seeing the results. Here are some rough estimates as to the amount of time to expect before your investment will begin to pay back:

One month:	Advertising for support, postal appeals, house-to-house collections, Gift Aid claims
Two to six months:	Lotteries, events, appeals to trusts and companies, radio/TV appeals, National Lottery applications, appeals to individuals
Six months to one year:	Government grants, payroll giving campaigns, Christmas cards
More than one year:	Legacies

3.5 Measurement and control of fundraising

Your fundraising strategy is not cast in stone – even though you may feel that after all the effort in creating it, you never want to see the document again! You should update your strategy from time to time to take account of changes both inside and outside your organisation. You should aim to review that strategy each year and rewrite it every three to five years.

The first step with a new or revised strategy must be to ensure that all your committee members, staff and key volunteers understand it and accept it. It will not be possible for everyone to be involved in producing the strategy document, so before you finalise it, make sure that all the issues have been widely discussed. This process of consultation will help everyone feel more committed to the outcome.

Monitoring progress

Without a strategy and a detailed plan, it is hard to monitor how you are getting on. Monitoring is important:

- to check your overall returns;
- to compare the effectiveness of different aspects of your fundraising;
- to justify the level of investment the charity is making;
- to help assess your fundraising's performance.

You will need to keep a particularly close eye on:

- costs incurred by each fundraising method;
- cash received;
- pledges of future support received;
- offers of help and support in kind received.

Monitoring is often easier for a small organisation. It can be surprisingly difficult for many larger organisations if their financial systems have not been designed to produce the information that fundraisers require.

To compare the effectiveness of each fundraising initiative, the fundraiser needs to know exactly how much time and money is being spent on it and what income it is producing. To do this, you can use the sample monitoring form below.

Monthly monitoring sheet

Appeal type	Income this month	Income this year	Budgeted income for the year	Direct costs	Indirect costs	Profit ratio
Collections						
Postal appeal						
Sponsored event						
General income						
Office costs						
Total						

Detailed measurement of fundraising

You can measure the effectiveness of your fundraising in a number of ways, although not all measures are appropriate to all situations. The most common measures are the cost ratio and the profit.

The cost ratio is calculated by taking the direct income generated and dividing it by the total costs that can be attributed to that activity (including an estimate of the indirect costs). This is then expressed as a ratio (for example, 5:1) or a percentage (for example, 20%). The main problem is that it does not tell you how much you have raised.

For example, you may discover that your public speaking to a wide range of local groups and appealing for support raised £2,380 and cost only £340 (a ratio of 7:1 or 14%). On the other hand, you raised £17,200 from trusts at an estimated cost of £6,500 (a ratio of 2.6:1 or 38%). This makes the latter look less successful and can be misleading.

1 You may have exhausted all the local speaking possibilities and so you cannot repeat your success, even if this has been your most cost-effective method of fundraising.

2 Although this was your most cost-effective method, it only generated £2,040, whereas you generated £10,700 in grants from trusts (both net).

The cost ratio is an important management tool for controlling costs, but on its own it is not a sufficient measure of fundraising success. There are other measures which you can use.

If you are using the telephone to recruit collectors for your street or house-to-house collections, you need to know how efficient your telephoning is. The first measure is the response rate to your request (divide the number of successes by the total number approached). This measure can similarly be used in postal appeals and payroll giving campaigns.

But knowing how many people will respond is not enough. You also need to know how they respond and how much they have given. It may be good to get 10 people in 100 saying yes; but if they only give £1 each, you will still be disappointed. The average donation is the measure of how much they give. You can then try to increase both the response rate and the average donation. For example, when you ask a supporter to renew their membership, why not suggest that they increase the level of their giving. When organising a sponsored event, you can ask people to sponsor by the minute rather than by the hour, and they are then likely to give more. If you ask a supporter to pay monthly contributions, you will receive more than if you ask for quarterly or annual contributions.

Another measure is the yield. This is the income received divided by the number of people approached. Thus, if you mail 1,000 people and receive £550 in donations, the yield would be 55p per donor mailed.

Finally you will need to have some way of measuring the impact of long-term or open-ended commitments. Your fundraising commitments have gained you a donor. You can measure the donation they have made. But many of them will go on to give further support, and the costs of getting this further support will be much lower than the costs of getting the first donation. A very few may even go on to make a major gift or leave you a legacy. This is valuable to you.

So another measure you can use is lifetime value. This is a useful measure because it helps you justify a higher level of initial expenditure on promotion and fundraising. For example, you mail 1,000 people and get 20 responses and a total of £550 in income. You predict that those 20 people on average will each make two further donations of the same amount. The total income you expect to receive from these donors is £1,650. The total cost is the cost of the initial mailing to 1,000 people plus the additional cost of further mailings to your 20 new supporters. From this you can calculate the lifetime value of these 20 donors and demonstrate that the costs of acquiring them were very reasonable.

Selecting appropriate measures to assess your fundraising is extremely important. It enables you to manage the process better – to control costs, to try to generate more income and more supporters, and to retain these supporters for longer periods. It enables you to see what works and what doesn't work, to develop new and better fundraising techniques, and to test out new ideas. It is important that you succeed in generating the money you have committed to raise and that you do this within your agreed budget. It is also important that you continue to improve your fundraising skills. The rest of this book is designed to help you do just this.

Resources and further information

See also general lists at the end of the book.

Organisations

Office of National Statistics
(for census data)
Segensworth Road
Titchfield
Hampshire PO15 5RR
www.statistics.gov.uk/census
Tel. 01329 813800

Publications

The following publications are available from the Directory of Social Change. Prices were correct at the time of writing, but may be subject to change.

The Complete Guide to Business and Strategic Planning, 3rd edn, Alan Lawrie, DSC 2007, £18.95

Other publications

Social trends
Regional trends

These and other Stationery Office publications can be ordered from:
TSO Orders
PO Box 29
Norwich NR3 1GN
www.tsoshop.co.uk
Tel. 0870 600 5522
Fax 0870 600 5533
e-mail customerservices@tso.org.uk

PART TWO

SOURCES OF FUNDS

4 INDIVIDUAL DONORS

Individuals are very significant givers to charity: according to figures in *UK Giving 2005/06*, compiled by NCVO and CAF, it is estimated that the sector received £8.9 billion in voluntary income from the UK population. The methods used to fundraise from individuals are far more varied and complex than those used to obtain funds from companies, trusts or government.

This section covers how and why individuals give. In Part 3 you will find some of the techniques that can be used to encourage them to support voluntary organisations.

Details of organisations and publications referred to in this chapter are on pages 94–95.

4.1 About individual donors

Every potential individual donor to an organisation has their own characteristics, motivations and preferred way of giving. You, as fundraiser, must be clear about which individuals you want to approach for a particular type of gift, and how you plan to attract the support of that group of people.

Potential donors to your organisation, excluding those who have already supported you, could include:

- those with personal experience of your cause or mission as well as those with none. For example, a parent of a disabled child will have a different perspective on disability than a member of the public but both may be just as inclined to give;
- young and older people. People may have different interests at different stages in their lives. Over recent years young people have shown a particular concern with the environment, AIDS, drug-related issues and homelessness; whereas the profile of donors to medical causes (such as cancer research and treatment or a hospice) or animal charities, is usually older. However, this does not mean that older donors would not be keen to give to 'young' causes or vice versa;

- people with large incomes as well as those who are less well off;
- individuals connected with institutions; these include philanthropic groups of local business people; churches and other faith groups; schools and colleges; trades unions and employers, and through them employees;
- people in specific cities or regions, as well as the UK population as a whole;
- the family and friends of existing supporters. People are more likely to give if asked by a relative or someone they know, who already has an interest in the organisation.

The clearer you can be about who your organisation's potential supporters are, the more successful you will be in reaching them. Start with your existing supporters; for example, a survey could help to find out what sort of people have supported your organisation in the past and why; or if you have a database of your supporters, you could start your analysis there.

Why people give

As mentioned in chapter 2, people support organisations for many different reasons. However, the more your fundraising message ties in with an individual's personal motivation the more successful that approach will be.

The following are some of the reasons why people give to charity.

- *Being asked.* A primary reason for people not giving is that they have not been asked.
- *Concern* is a strong motivator for many donors. They may be worried about the environment, or want to improve the plight of starving refugees or help stop the spread of AIDS. Making a donation provides them with an opportunity to do something positive for a cause they believe in.
- *Duty* is another strong motivator, particularly for older donors. Many faiths promote the concept of charity, with some recommending that their members allocate a certain share of their income each year for this.
- *Guilt* can motivate people to give. But unlike duty, if people give on impulse out of a sense of guilt, this is less likely to lead to a long-term relationship.
- *Personal experience.* People who have direct or family experience of cancer, heart disease or another illness might be especially motivated to give to this type of cause. Also, those with children at school may want to support their child's education or someone may want to 'give back' to an educational institution they attended.
- *Personal benefit.* Some people like the status or recognition that comes when their generosity is publicised. They may also like to be associated with prominent people involved with an organisation.

- *Peer pressure*. When people know that their friends and colleagues have given, or when these people are asking them to give, it can be hard to refuse.
- *Tax benefits* are unlikely to be a prime motivator for giving, but can be an important factor in encouraging people to make certain types of donation and to give more generously (see section 4.6 *Tax-effective giving*).

It is important to understand why supporters generally, and especially why the specific individual or group of individuals you intend to approach, might want to give to your particular organisation. You can then tailor the message to make it more relevant and interesting to them.

You also need to understand why people don't give. They may not be interested in your organisation and what it stands for. Or they may have given to something similar recently. Other demotivating factors might be that your cause has had some bad publicity, that it appears to have high administration costs, there is a concern the money is not getting to the intended beneficiaries, or that you have not looked after your donors particularly well in the past.

Making contact

Here is a suggested five point plan to follow when starting to approach individuals:

1 Identify your potential supporters, those people whose background and motivations make them likely to want to support your cause.
2 Create the right message to appeal to them, which:
    - builds on their motivation;
    - starts from their understanding of the cause;
    - takes account of their natural hesitations or reasons they might have for not giving.
3 Direct that message to those people in the right way. For example, if senior business people are your audience, they can be reached by a variety of means: through the business press; local Rotary Clubs, Chambers of Commerce and other associations of business people; personalised letters; or by asking business people who already support you to ask their colleagues and peers directly.
4 Make it easy for them to make their donation. Any materials that aim to get people to support you should include a clear means by which they can respond (whether by mail, phone, fax, e-mail or through a website) and clear contact details. To increase the likelihood of someone making a donation you could also consider the following:
    - A freepost facility. A donation should not be lost because the potential donor did not have a stamp! However, almost all organisations now suggest that if a stamp is used this will save the charity money.

- A dedicated telephone line for credit card donations and enquiries, with a named person on promotional literature and at the end of the line. This makes the facility more personal and shows a concern for customer care. You might also consider a freephone facility.
- A CharityCard donation facility for Charities Aid Foundation clients, which include approximately 100,000 individual donors and about 2,000 companies. Around 4,000 charities now welcome the use of the CharityCard and are listed with their telephone numbers in a CAF directory and on the CAF website (www.cafonline.org).
- A secure website, so that donations can be made online. See chapter 14, section 14.6, for more on using the internet for fundraising.

5 Support your fundraising with a good communications programme, as people are more likely to give to your organisation if they have heard about its work and the importance of the cause. Public relations is a key ingredient of successful fundraising, so if your organisation does not have a press officer, you will need to spend some time promoting the organisation and publicising its work yourself. See chapter 15, section 15.4, for more on external communications and dealing with the media.

Most popular causes

Figures in CAF's *Charities Trends 2007* show that the most popular causes in 2005/06, using voluntary income as the measure, were, in descending order of priority:

1	international agencies	6	children
2	arts/culture	7	religious – international
3	cancer	8	animal protection
4	religious – general services	9	heritage/environment
5	religious – missionary	10	general social welfare

The most popular cause remains international charities. International charities have seen huge growth over the last couple of years, mainly due to the number and scale of a string of disaster appeals: the 2004 Asian tsunami appeal, which provoked an unprecedented public response, was followed in 2005/06 by a series of further disaster appeals, including the famine in Darfur, Hurricane Katrina and the Pakistan earthquake.

It comes as no great surprise therefore that international charities continued to thrive in 2005/06 with extremely strong real-terms growth of 22% this year. International charities this year received 41% more revenue than their nearest rival cause, arts and culture.

Arts and culture organisations take second place due to the fact that, with the re-alignment of the data in response to SORP 2005, there are more arts and culture charities in this year's top 500.

The number of cancer charities in this year's top 500 has fallen from 22 to 19, which largely explains the apparent fall in voluntary income. But in reality this is only due to the re-shuffling of income with the introduction of SORP (2005).

CAF, *Charity Trends 2007*

Five things to remember when fundraising from individuals

1 If possible, state clearly and precisely how much money is needed.
2 Express the need in human terms, giving graphic images of the issue being tackled and how the organisation helps people. Avoid abstract statistics describing the global importance of the problem unless a particular point needs to be emphasised. The more people can understand and identify with a problem, the more they will feel they are helping real people, and the more successful the appeal will be.
3 Ask for exactly what you want. Prospective donors will not necessarily know the size or nature of the donation expected of them. It is also useful to suggest a range of values, so the donor can choose their own level of giving. If relevant, a 'shopping list' might be used showing what different amounts can achieve; this is sometimes called a list of tangible items.

Example of a shopping list from Amnesty International UK

£5 a month pays for four faxes to be sent as part of an Urgent Action campaign to save someone in imminent danger of torture or facing death

£10 a month enables us to continually place pressure on relevant politicians and policymakers to establish concrete measures to stop violence against women

£25 a month means that an Amnesty arms expert can attend international government meetings calling for tougher arms control

£30 ensures that our researchers can continue their country missions to investigate reports of torture

£200 pays to run a crisis response mission for one day, including setting up communication channels, collecting research and distributing information throughout the world.

[Amnesty International UK website]

4 Repeat the message that your organisation needs their help, and that with their support something can be achieved. Repetition reinforces the message, so try to:

- tell them what the appeal is about;
- then tell them again in more detail;
- finally remind them about what they have been told.

5 Target the appeal carefully, making the message as personal and relevant to the donor as possible. When approaching existing supporters, refer to their previous generous support and what has been achieved with it, or if approaching local people, focus on the local benefits of your organisation's work. The more targeted the message, the more successful it will be.

Building a supporter base

It is far easier to build on a base of existing supporters than to start from scratch. An existing donor is ten times more likely to support your organisation again than someone who has never given. However, if you have few or no current donors there are various methods you can use to acquire them.

1 Promotional or fundraising leaflets

Produce a leaflet giving details about your cause and illustrating your need for funds. This does not have to be expensive. Sometimes the simplest leaflet is most effective – for example, an A4 sheet, printed in two colours and folded to make a four-page leaflet with photographs of the organisation at work, and a reply coupon so potential supporters can express interest or make a gift. You might also give people options for how they would like to get involved, for example by giving money, becoming a member or volunteering their time. Remember to include your website address, if you have one. See chapter 15, section 15.3, for more on producing leaflets.

2 A membership or supporter scheme

Developing a scheme of this type can bring people closer to your organisation and keep them in touch with news and success stories. It can also provide a legitimate reason for communicating on a regular basis.

3 Supporter get supporter

Ask existing supporters to help by recruiting a friend, a colleague or a family member.

4 Mailing lists and reciprocal mailings

Look for another organisation, commercial or voluntary, whose customer or supporter profile is similar to yours and arrange to send an appeal to their list – for example, a health charity could send a leaflet and a short covering letter to doctors and other health workers. Once an organisation has built up its supporter base it is possible to carry out reciprocal mailings with others, where each organisation mails its supporters with the other organisation's literature. See chapter 14, section 14.2, for more on direct mail.

5 Local newspaper, radio and TV coverage

A paper, radio or TV station might be interested in running a feature about a local charity. To make this opportunity as effective as possible, you should make sure that your contact details are included so anyone who is interested is able to get in touch. See chapter 14, section 14.5, and chapter 15, section 15.4, for more on using the media.

6 House-to-house collecting or door-to-door canvassing

If your organisation is not well-known, one way of rectifying this is to approach people face to face. This can be particularly effective for a local cause. If you are considering this type of fundraising you should consult the relevant Institute of Fundraising Codes of Practice on House-to-House Collections and Face to Face Fundraising (see Appendix 1) and contact the PFRA, the organisation set up by charities themselves to advise on this area of fundraising. See chapter 12 for more on collections and chapter 14 for face to face fundraising (or personal solicitation).

7 Events

Potential supporters may be attracted to an event where they have the opportunity to visit an exclusive venue, hear a well-known speaker or participate in an entertaining evening. Once there they might well be receptive to hearing more about the cause that the event is to benefit. See chapter 12, section 12.1, for more on organising events.

Once a donor has been recruited the aim is to keep them involved so that they continue to give and, hopefully, develop their relationship with your organisation in other ways.

4.2 Major donors

Some of your donors may have the potential to do much more for you than others. They might identify themselves by making a significantly larger donation than the amount you asked for, or you might find out that they have greater potential through researching your supporter base. You might then decide to set up a fundraising programme specifically for these people.

Firstly you should make a decision about the point at which you will begin to treat people as major donors: this will be different for different organisations. For a small charity a major donation from an individual might be £250 or even less; for a larger organisation with a developed strategy for encouraging big gifts, their major donor programme may only kick in with those giving several thousand pounds.

To help you make this decision look at your current range of donations by value. You will probably find that there is a clear cut-off point above which donations become scarcer. Once you have identified these people, you need to decide whether they will get similar communications to your other donors but with higher levels of gift asked for, or a totally different type of letter concentrating on more ambitious ways in which they can help you. Either way, you should aim to make them feel more involved rather than simply sending a standard donor appeal.

You might organise special events and visits for them or get them involved in your fundraising itself – see chapter 13 *Capital and big gift campaigns*, and chapter 16 *Fundraising with volunteers*.

You may also find the book *Major Donor Fundraising* – details at the end of this chapter – a useful reference if you plan to concentrate on this group of your donor base.

Major donor programmes

If you feel that there are sufficient numbers of people who are or might become major donors, you could set up some sort of club to encourage them to increase their commitment to you. You could get your existing key donors to advise you on who else you might approach, or get them to approach their friends, colleagues and networks themselves to ask for support. You need to make sure that this is going to be cost effective for you, as these people are likely to take more of your time to look after, or steward, than your other supporters. Also, they may require particular types of benefits in return for their support, such as meetings with your chief executive or director, crediting in your literature (such as your annual report) and having some influence on the future of the organisation.

Example of a donor development scheme

The National Theatre has a four-tier programme, starting with the Supporting Cast level for a minimum gift of £400 every year, and going up to the Olivier Circle for people giving £10,000. Each level builds on the benefits of the one below, culminating with acknowledgements on the donor boards in the National Theatre foyer and access to the theatre's VIP room.

4.3 One-off donations and appeals

Individuals can support you in a wide variety of ways, for example with cash gifts of various types or gifts in kind, or by buying raffle tickets, attending events or volunteering their time. The following sections look at the main methods by which you can encourage people to donate money.

Asking existing or prospective supporters for a one-off donation to support a cause has been a key method of raising funds for many organisations for some time. This can be done on a large scale by approaching hundreds (or thousands) of individuals through direct mail or, more directly, face to face with individuals or small groups of people, particularly when asking for a high value gift.

One-off donation appeals are often used to encourage new donors to support you. Once that first donation is made you might go back and ask for another or offer other methods by which you can be supported, for example, by making a committed gift (see section 4.5 *Committed giving*/page 73). You will find that some people who have supported you with a single donation will be happy to become more committed, some will want to keep giving on an occasional basis and some will never give again.

4.4 Legacies

Legacies are an enormously important source of charitable funds: according to NCVO's *UK Voluntary Sector Almanac* they generated £1,643 million for the voluntary sector in 2004–05, accounting for 14% of total voluntary income (an increase of 2% on 2003–04). Legacy fundraising can often seem a mysterious activity which generates large sums with apparently little effort for the fundraiser. In fact, some of the largest legacy-earning charities have carefully planned strategies for developing this income. Like other forms of fundraising, what you get out depends on what you put in.

Types of legacy

There are several types of legacy. Each is of value in different circumstances.

- *Pecuniary legacy.* This is the most straightforward type of legacy, where a specified amount is given, for example, 'I leave £500 to the Cancer Research Campaign.' The main drawback is that over time the value of the legacy is eroded by inflation.
- *Residuary legacy.* Where either the whole or a proportion of the residue of an estate is given, after all pecuniary legacies and specific bequests have been made. These legacies are on average ten times larger than a pecuniary legacy. Residuary legacies will keep up with inflation better, as the main item of any worth is likely to be a property. Many people simply do not know their net worth, and would be surprised if they knew the potential value of their charitable bequest. With the decline in the birth-rate, the increase in life expectancy and property ownership, there will be an increase in the number of people with significant assets who may not have family to bequeath their estate to. This is a real opportunity for charities.

- *Specific bequest.* Where a donor leaves a specific item that can either be kept or sold by the beneficiary.
- *Long stop legacy.* This stipulates that if all the other provisions of the legacy fail, for example if all the named residuary beneficiaries have died, or if there are conditions attached which cannot be met, then the estate reverts to a charity. In these cases, it is unlikely that the charity will receive anything; but if it does, it is likely to be a substantial sum.
- *Reversionary or life interest.* Where an elderly relative needs to be cared for, a life interest clause is often used, such as, 'My house is given to the XYZ Charity with a life interest to my uncle Charles.' This gives the relative the right to live in the house during their lifetime, but on their death the right to the property reverts to the charity. This can be a useful way of carrying out a responsibility to the supporter's family while at the same time ensuring a valuable legacy to charity.

There are two other terms linked to legacies of which you should be aware.

- *Codicil.* A codicil is an addition to a will, containing supplementary instructions, and is drawn up and witnessed in exactly the same way as a will. It is a simple way in which people can add instructions to their will without having the whole thing redrafted. For example, they could draw up a codicil to add a £1,000 legacy to your charity.
- *Deed of Variation.* This is a way of changing a will after the person who made the will has died. This can only be done if all the beneficiaries of a will agree. Thus, if the deceased was a very keen supporter of the environment, then the family could instruct the executors (who are responsible for administering the will) to make a £500 bequest to an environmental charity. This has to be done through a legally drawn up Deed of Variation. Any amount given in this way to charity is exempt from Inheritance Tax.

Promotion and target audiences

The essence of legacy fundraising is that promotional effort is made now for a reward some years later. There will usually be a time-lag of between three to five years before you begin to see any financial benefit. Interestingly this is also the average period between a last will being made and when a person dies.

There are a number of ways to promote legacies.

- *Meeting donors face to face,* often in their own homes, to discuss the benefits of legacy giving and the work of your charity.
- *Direct marketing campaigns* (for example by mail and telephone) to supporters may seem less personal, but may be the most practical way of getting an initial legacy message across. However, if you plan to target the

general public this will require a very clear set of objectives, a sensitive package and good administrative back-up. One technique that has been used extensively by charities in the past is to offer a free booklet giving advice on drawing up a will.

- *Meeting solicitors face to face.* Solicitors draw up wills and may be asked for advice on charitable bequests. Some charities organise meetings or seminars targeted at professionals to which they invite a number of their own supporters. This provides an opportunity to discuss will-making.
- *Advertising in the press.* This needs to be well targeted, coded and analysed and should carry a challenging message. However, even taking all this into account, the response is often negligible.
- *Advertising in specialist legal journals and directories,* which are targeted at solicitors and other legal professionals. This will ensure that they are aware of you and have your correct details to hand.

Obviously, for anyone to receive a legacy, a person has to make a will (they are referred to as the 'testator' or 'legator') and they then have to die. The will that includes a bequest to your charity has to be their last will. They may make several wills during their lifetime, and vary their charitable bequests as their interests, family or financial situation change. Therefore charities that attract predominantly older supporters are more likely to receive legacy income in the immediate term. Given that women live longer than men and, if they marry, tend to marry older men, a female supporter is more likely than a male supporter to have no direct family to leave her money to.

Before developing a legacy campaign it is important to:

- decide whether you are the sort of charity that might expect to receive legacy income;
- find out who has left you legacies in the past and if they supported you during their lifetime.

There are several questions to answer in respect of targeting. Whether to go for existing supporters, which is where you are most likely to find support, whether to target the general public with a bias towards people aged 65 and over – the main target audience for legacies – or whether to target legal advisers, such as solicitors, who help in the drawing up of a will. Past experience, however, has shown that many solicitors are not keen to make specific suggestions to their clients regarding charitable legacies or mention the possible inclusion of these types of bequest.

One aim of having a supporter base is to build up a good understanding amongst your members of how they might help you. If some form of regular committed giving is a natural successor to occasional one-off gifts, then a legacy may be a step up from regular giving. In the process of communicating with donors, you will over time build relationships which will enable you to discuss legacies – which some people may consider a sensitive issue.

You might adopt an indirect approach, with regular mentions in a newsletter, or you might write directly to your supporters about making a will. One major charity mailed 100,000 of their existing supporters inviting them to request information on will making and indicate their interest in making a legacy. The resulting 3,500 enquiries may represent a huge success or little more than polite interest; only time will tell. However, the additional alternative option of sending a donation if supporters were unable to leave a legacy yielded £100,000 in immediate income.

One of the main stumbling blocks for charities is getting people to make their wills in the first place, but there are ethical issues linked to offering to write wills for your supporters, even when you have a legally qualified solicitor working for your organisation. If you want to suggest solicitors to your supporters, then it is best to give the details of at least three and allow the supporter to make their own final selection. A consortium of charities runs a biennial campaign with solicitors called Willaid (www.willaid.org.uk) which offers will making for a fixed donation to the consortium. The charities benefit from the donations, which are equally distributed, and may also receive legacies as a result, and the solicitors involved benefit by being associated with the promotion, and if they are appointed as executors they can charge normal professional fees. You could organise your own will making promotion, working with local firms of solicitors, or schedule your legacy promotion at the same time as Willaid, when public awareness of charitable legacies may well be higher.

The message

There are three main types of legacy message used by charities.

1 'Make a will (and leave a legacy to us).' This approach relates to the fact that a high proportion of people die without having made a will (intestate), and the State then distributes their estate according to pre-set rules. Thus if the testator wishes to have any control over how their money is to be distributed and to minimise inheritance tax liability they must make a will. According to data compiled by Charity Monitor only 41% of adults aged 65+ have made a will – so almost two thirds of your target market have not.

2 'Remember us by adding a legacy or codicil to your existing will.' This approach must necessarily be directed at those people who have made a will. Will making can be a complicated process, especially when there are significant assets and family interests to consider. The value of this approach is that it gets to people who know what you are talking about and who could do something quite quickly – namely, add a codicil to their existing will.

3 'Make a pledge to support us when you make or update your will.' This approach has several advantages. It allows you legitimately to keep the supporter on file and to keep in touch about the subject, whilst also allowing you to get a very direct measurement of the effectiveness of your promotion. Your aim is to get people thinking of leaving you a legacy to send you a pledge form, or some other indication of their future gift.

'In Memoriam' gifts

An 'In Memoriam' gift commemorates a person who has died. These donations are usually made by the friends and family in memory of the deceased, for example by placing small ads in the personal columns of the newspapers inviting friends and family to send donations to a favoured charity rather than to send flowers.

Legacy materials

When starting to promote legacy giving it is useful to produce some literature illustrating your organisation's need for legacies. Key points to make are:

- the importance of your charity's work and the need for continued support in the future;
- the importance of legacies as a source of income for your charity;
- the tax exemptions for charitable bequests;
- the legally correct forms of words, though you should always stress the importance of using a solicitor to draw up any will.

This information can either be mailed out to supporters or be used as an information pack for people enquiring about this method of giving.

Legacy administration

Getting people to leave a legacy is only the first step. You will want to keep in regular touch with those who have pledged to support you or told you that they have mentioned you in their will. If they make a new will, you want them to retain the legacy to your organisation or, possibly, increase the size of their legacy. Also there may be a good deal of administration to be handled once the testator has died. The process can at times be extremely protracted especially when you are sharing the residue with others, or when the will is contested. It is important to be prepared to carry out an effective chasing up function as well as being able to deal sympathetically with bereaved families.

The Smee and Ford Service

Smee and Ford, now part of Waterlows, provides two services on a commercial basis which can be useful to charities receiving legacy income. The 'Will

Notification Service' informs a subscribing charity when it has been mentioned in a will that has gone through probate, i.e. cleared by HM Revenue & Customs for distribution, so that the charity can notify the executors of its interest and press for an early distribution. The 'Discretionary Will Service' notifies subscribing charities of situations where money is left for charitable purposes to be distributed at the discretion of the executors, rather than to a specific charity or charities. In this instance a charity can contact the executors and present its case for some of these funds.

Investment in the promotion of legacies

One of the issues often confronted by fundraisers is deciding how much to invest in legacy fundraising since, as mentioned earlier, it can take time to see any return and it is often difficult to link actual legacy income to expenditure on promotion. However if you do nothing, you are unlikely to see any consistent development in your legacy income.

One idea is to use a percentage (say 10%) of your current legacy income for promotion. Another is to set a target for the number of pledges that you will receive each year. As time goes on you will find out both how many pledges turn into legacies and how much it costs to get a pledge. Coding your response form will give you an idea of the returns from each promotion.

Recent developments in legacy marketing and income generation

Charities are becoming increasingly sophisticated in the way they address the issue of legacy awareness and how the income from this area of fundraising can be grown. Two initiatives in recent years have illustrated these concerns.

A number of charities have made a concerted effort to raise public awareness of the value of legacies as charitable gifts. An organisation that was established with this object in mind is Remember A Charity. Launched in 2002, Remember A Charity is the largest charity consortium in the UK, made up of over 140 registered charities, and is hosted by the Institute of Fundraising. The consortium has its own website (www.rememberacharity.org.uk), providing information on will making, charitable legacies and its charity members to the general public and professional advisors. It also runs legacy awareness-raising media campaigns on television, radio and in the national press. Members of the consortium come from an increasingly diverse range of local and national UK charities, from NHS hospital trusts and educational establishments, to the RSPCA and Salvation Army.

Another campaign to broaden the opportunities for legacy fundraising is spearheaded by the Charity Tax Reform Group. The Lifetime Legacy initiative is focused on the introduction in the UK of tax-effective Charitable Remainder Trusts (CRTs), a giving vehicle common in the United States since the 1960s. They allow a donor to make an irrevocable gift to a charity during their lifetime of shares, property or cash, while retaining the benefit of the income or use of the gift for the term of the donor's life. The donor can make deductions against capital gains tax at the time of the gift and its value is not counted as part of their estate for the purposes of inheritance tax. CRTs resemble a charitable legacy or deferred gift but are advantageous to the charity receiving them, as the donor's commitment is irrevocable as opposed to the promise of a gift in their will, which may not actually materialise. The benefit to the donor is that they are able to support a favourite cause while still receiving income for themselves or another beneficiary.

4.5 Committed giving

Committed or regular giving is one of the most valuable and consistent ways your donors can support you and will provide one of the best financial returns for any direct marketing activity. Getting people to give their first donation can be expensive, and may not cover costs through the immediate income produced, but it is often the first step in building up a base of supporters. The follow-up mailings are what generate the real revenue – people who have already given, often known as 'warm donors', respond much better to any appeal than people who have never given ('cold donor prospects').

Getting your donors to commit to regular giving creates a continuing income stream, broadens your fundraising base and enhances your organisation's sustainability. Also you can apply income from regular givers to those parts of your work which are hardest to raise money for.

To encourage people to make committed gifts you need to:

- stimulate their concern for the cause and interest in your work;
- help them recognise the importance of long-term support – your work may take time to yield results and you depend on them continuing to give;
- make it easy for them to give regularly: one way is to set up some form of membership or friends scheme, with pre-set levels of giving;
- ensure that, where possible, donations are paid tax-effectively through the Gift Aid scheme;
- reasssure them regularly about the continuing value of their committed support.

This list will provide you with an agenda to develop your direct mail and donor acquisition programme, and then turn a new donor into a committed and enthusiastic long-term supporter.

Mechanisms for committed giving

There are three main ways in which committed giving can be developed:

- regular, usually monthly, payments which can be made tax efficient with Gift Aid (see section 4.6 *Tax-effective giving*);
- a membership scheme. This will not always be tax-effective as there are restrictions on the level of benefit that can be received by the member. Some schemes are concerned primarily with generating income, others aim for high membership numbers to enhance the credibility and campaigning ability of the organisation;
- payroll giving, which is also a tax-effective way of giving.

The specific mechanisms available for the actual transmission of money are:

- a banker's order, or standing order, where the payments are sent from the donor's bank to you;
- a direct debit, which reverses the control of the transaction: you, the charity, claim the payments from the bank when they fall due;
- regular payments via a donor's credit card;
- cash or cheque payments, though these are not so efficient to administer as you will usually need to remind donors when to send their payment.

Promotion

Not every donor will want to enter into a long-term commitment with you, but you should give all of them the opportunity to do so. Your strategy will depend on your answers to the following questions:

- What are the interests and motivations of your supporters?
- How much income do you need to raise, and how much are your donors prepared to give?
- How will you encourage your existing supporters to increase their commitment?
- Are there any other potential committed supporters that you can identify?
- What opportunities do you have for reporting back to your committed givers, so as to maintain their enthusiasm and support?
- What else can you do to get them to feel more involved in the work of the organisation and the cause it is addressing?
- Are you able to administer and steward such a programme?

Do not take your committed givers for granted. Keep in regular touch and tell them what you are doing. Always recognise their commitment so they understand that you are contacting them because of their regular donation, especially when there is an obviously good reason for an appeal, such as an emergency.

You can report back to your committed givers regularly through a newsletter, magazine or personalised letter from you or your chief executive. Committed givers tend to want to see their donations going to the cause rather being used on expensive communications so it is good to keep expenditure here to a minimum. Some charities hold events where donors can meet senior staff or see the organisation in action. This not only provides a good opportunity to thank them, but also enables the most committed to become even more involved, get more information and meet other supporters.

Promoting committed giving

The following are some of the promotional techniques you can use.

Approaching active givers

Analyse the response to your appeals. A number of your donors will have given more than once. These are your priority targets for committed giving. Contact them to point out the advantages of giving regularly and offer to send the appropriate forms. If there are only a few prospective targets, then contact them in person or by telephone.

Promoting committed giving more widely to your donor base

One strategy is to undertake an annual appeal to promote regular giving and encourage payment by standing order or direct debit. This may alienate those not able to give regularly. Another strategy is to mention the value of committed giving in each mailing, and allow people the opportunity to opt into giving in this way.

Regular upgrading of donation value

Once you have donors giving on a regular basis you might think about asking them to increase the value of their donation. It is easier to do this administratively if you have set up their donations via direct debit rather than a standing order, as the latter will require filling out a new form.

Using a sponsorship programme

Here the donor is linked to a specific project, community, family or person over a period. Such an approach can work well in fundraising terms, but has to be handled with care. Problems can arise where the donor really wants to help just one individual person (most projects provide support for the whole community), or where the donor builds up an expectation of a relationship with, for example, a sponsored child.

Recruiting large numbers of supporters with a low-value regular gift by direct debit

Some organisations such as Oxfam use this very successfully. Once donors are giving monthly donations, there is the opportunity to go back to them and ask them to increase the value of their donation.

'Welcome mailings'

These are sent following an initial gift to an organisation from newly recruited donors. There is a two-fold purpose to these mailings: to welcome new donors and tell them more about the cause they have given to, and to ask them for more and regular support, often suggesting a regular monthly gift through their bank.

'Member-get-member' or 'supporter-get-supporter'

This is simply an invitation to an existing member or supporter to nominate or recruit another. Various incentives (such as a free entry prize draw or some form of gift) can be used which are offered either to the original member or to the new one. This relies on the personal enthusiasm of existing members and their ability to persuade their friends and colleagues, but the technique generally works extremely well.

Membership schemes

Many voluntary organisations have membership schemes. Some are aimed primarily at people who are interested in getting more involved – helping the organisation campaign, attending cultural events, volunteering their time, but also giving money. Membership schemes of this type may have their annual subscription levels set deliberately low to encourage as many people as possible to join, therefore increasing the organisation's influence. Then there are those schemes that have a fundraising purpose – the primary aim being to generate income for the organisation.

Benefits of membership

1   Membership offers a convenient peg upon which to hang the request for committed and long-term support.
2   Membership can enhance your campaigning ability. Organisations like Amnesty International and Friends of the Earth invite people to become members to harness their support for the cause.
3   Membership can open up the organisation to democratic control through annual meetings, giving the members some feeling that they control the direction of the movement.
4   Your membership list is also a good place to look for donations. These people have demonstrated their commitment to the cause and so qualify as perfect prospects for obtaining further financial commitment.
5   Membership can easily be structured to invite different levels of contribution (to reflect people's commitment, ability to pay, etc.).

Why people become members

There are a number of reasons why people will sign up as members of your organisation.

- *Personal benefit:* the member joins principally because of the benefits they believe they will gain. Examples of this are the RSPB and the National Trust which give discounted entry into their reserves or properties to their members.
- *Support:* the member joins to express support for the work of the charity. In this case membership is organised to encourage members to subscribe at affordable rates as a way of making their contributions on a continuing basis.
- *Campaigning:* members are signing up to show their support for particular policies or causes.
- *Influence:* members join many local organisations simply to be able to influence their affairs. This will be done through regular meetings and AGMs.
- *'Clubs':* the member joins a club – such as the Friends of the Royal Academy – to signal their support for the work and also receive benefits from membership. Subscriptions may be higher in such cases and there may be expectations of involvement in activities and events.

Membership and regular giving

The value of membership subscription income depends on:

- the number of members – the more you have, the better. Once you have established a scheme, your aim should be to find ways of recruiting new members economically;
- the annual subscription level. This will depend on your objectives – to make money or to involve as many people as possible. Some organisations give members a choice of subscription levels;
- the cost of running the scheme. This includes the cost of member acquisition, collecting membership fees and communication costs (such as sending newsletters and annual reports). You need to analyse costs very carefully to establish the real net value of the scheme;
- the value of any additional income that is generated from further appeals to members.

It is most common to ask people to give on a monthly, quarterly or annual basis. You might even suggest a certain level of donation, and ask the donor to select the frequency. The value of encouraging regular giving is something that can be tested quite easily in a mailing. Usually requests for monthly or quarterly giving will be no less effective than an annual payment, and will produce much higher average annual donations.

Categories of membership

One of the key issues in this area is the way in which membership and committed giving are priced and styled. Membership fees have to take into account the possibility of attracting large numbers of people who are prepared to be identified with your organisation. They also need to allow concessions to people on low income and encourage higher levels of support from wealthy supporters, benefactors and corporate members. In fact you may want to set up a different scheme for people able to make larger donations.

Many organisations have several categories of membership with different levels of annual subscription. Other categories of membership can be created such as a sponsor or a patron. One organisation has three categories – 'Friends', 'Good Friends' and 'Best of Friends'; another has 'Gold', 'Platinum' and 'Silver' membership. The fundraiser's challenge is to lift members from one category to the next.

Life membership is an opportunity to get a single large payment in one go, as well as enabling a member to be seen as an important benefactor of the organisation. But life means life, unless you state otherwise, and you are committed to servicing the membership for the duration without any expectation of an annual income. Therefore the price needs to reflect this.

Administration

The administration of membership demands a high degree of organisation, especially if you wish to maximise the benefits of your fundraising efforts. There are several issues to consider.

1 How do you get members to renew their subscriptions?

The best system is where the member has to do nothing – the membership continues until cancelled, and the subscription is paid automatically through the donor's bank account by direct debit (or via their credit card).

If there is a fixed-term commitment and this comes to an end, you will want to ensure that as many people renew as possible. The usual way to do this is by sending reminder letters, either a few months before the expiry, giving them time to renew, or to coincide with the expiry, to remind them that renewal is due. A follow-up reminder after expiry, telling them that their membership will lapse if they do not renew, or a further follow-up some months later – a final reminder – might also be appropriate. You may want to test different sequences to see which works best for you.

The telephone is also a valuable tool for renewal. You will need to decide at what point in the renewal cycle you use the phone – before the renewal date, at renewal or afterwards. The phone is also a good medium for asking a donor to increase the value of their donation and reminding those who have just not got round to renewing to do so, and you can also gather useful information about why members may not be renewing.

Membership renewal can be done on one fixed date each year (for example with annual membership running from 1 January to 31 December). However you have the problem of what to do with members who join during the year – especially those who join later in the year and feel that they have already paid their subscription. An alternative is that each member's membership expires exactly 12 months after the annual subscription was paid. This requires more efficient organisation, as you will be dealing with renewals on a rolling basis throughout the year.

If you have a large membership you will need a reliable computer database to help you handle renewals. A key issue is the ability of the system to identify renewal points so that you can mail not only on the point of renewal but also before and after to stimulate the highest possible renewal rate.

2 Raising the subscription rate

Changing the annual subscription rate can be a very laborious process, because members have to be informed of the change and any standing orders you are administering will need to be cancelled and replaced with new ones for the appropriate amount. As a result, some organisations review their subscriptions quite infrequently (perhaps once every three or four years) and take a conservative view of the need to increase rates. This means that membership fees can often lag well behind inflation – although this is not so important during periods of low inflation.

One way around this problem is to ask for subscriptions to be paid by direct debit. You will still need to inform your members in advance of any rise in the subscription, giving them a chance to cancel if they do not want to pay the higher amount, and you have to agree to reimburse any sums debited from a bank account in the event of a dispute.

3 Making membership payments tax efficient

Under Gift Aid, any payment can be made tax effectively provided the donor is a UK taxpayer and has declared (by ticking a box or filling out a form) that they wish the charity to reclaim the tax paid on all their donations. The benefits received by the member are limited to 25% for a donation or subscription up to £100, £25 between £101 and £1,000, 2.5% above £1,000 with an overall benefit limit of £250. So if you want to make membership payments tax efficient you will need to check with the HM Revenue & Customs to make sure they accept that the membership benefits you offer are within these limits. If your primary aim is to generate funds, it makes sense for you to make your scheme tax-effective and encourage as many members to pay in this way as possible. In addition, if the member is a higher rate taxpayer, they will benefit from higher rate relief.

4 VAT liability on membership subscriptions

When more than an annual report and a right to vote at the AGM are offered to a member in return for their subscription, HM Revenue & Customs will treat the subscription payment as being partly a payment for a service, and some or all of it may be taxable (for those organisations registered for VAT, or where the taxable subscription income takes them over the VAT registration threshold). Many organisations are keen to offer benefits to encourage people to subscribe. If you are unsure about the tax implications, you should consult HM Revenue & Customs before finalising your membership scheme. More information can be found in *A Practical Guide to VAT.*

5 Maintaining donor records

Your committed givers and members will be giving money to you regularly and possibly supporting you in a number of other ways. You need to keep track of their support to identify people who might give you extra help when you need it, or to invite to special events such as receptions, or simply to personalise your appeals to them. All this information needs to be on one record not only in order to develop a full picture of each donor's support but also to avoid any duplication of mailings. If you are not yet ready to invest in one of the big tailor-made databases, the 'How to' guide *Building a Fundraising Database Using your PC* by Peter Flory will provide you with a step-by-step introduction to setting up a simple database using Microsoft Office. In collecting any data about your supporters you must of course ensure that you comply with the requirements of the Data Protection Act (see Appendix 4).

Payroll giving

Giving at work has been around for some time in Britain. Originally it involved large numbers of factory workers giving a few pence per week and signing an authorisation to have the amount deducted from their wages each pay day. In 1987, the government created a new scheme for tax-deductible payroll giving as part of its policy of encouraging charitable giving. It was seen as an opportunity for charities to mobilise support from the millions of people in employment and gave what had been a very marginal form of giving a completely new lease of life. In the past the scheme has not delivered anything like what was expected of it and still does not generate as much revenue for charity as it could. However, it is an established way of giving and provides charities with a mechanism for regular committed income.

Most recently the Institute of Fundraising has been working with the HM Revenue & Customs to promote this tax efficient opportunity for giving. As part of this scheme grants and matching funds have been offered to employers who wish to initiate payroll giving for their staff, as well as the award programme, the Payroll Giving Quality Mark. Currently more information on this area can be found at www.payrollgivingcentre.org.uk.

At the time of writing payroll giving is celebrating its 20th anniversary and the most recent figures, published by the Institute of Fundraising in February 2007, show that there are now 600,000 employees giving in this way, netting nearly £85 million for charities in 2005–06. It should be noted that on average, payroll donors give for around nine years, which is a substantial time for a regular gift. There are 9,000 employers registered to operate payroll giving schemes with five million employees having access to a scheme.

How payroll giving works

The donor wishing to make a payroll donation has to be an employee on the permanent payroll of an employer who subscribes to a payroll giving scheme. A company pensioner who is also on the company payroll can also give through the scheme. The donor signs a form authorising the employer to make deductions each pay day from their wages or pension to donate to a selected charity or charities. The donor can alter the beneficiaries or increase or reduce the monthly amount or even cancel the arrangement at any time. The donation is allowed against the employee's income when calculating his or her tax liability, but it does not affect the amount of National Insurance contribution that has to be paid, which is calculated on the employee's gross income.

An employer will contract with a payroll giving agency (PGA), who themselves are registered charities. Their role is to collect the money from the employer and distribute the payments to all the charities nominated by the employee. The employer then passes the money to a PGA charity together with the employee's instructions for distributing the money. The job of the PGA is to receive the money from the employer and distribute it to the charities selected by the donor. PGAs are licensed by HM Revenue & Customs to operate a payroll giving scheme. There are certain operating requirements for a PGA: the administration charges must be kept within 4%, the money must be passed to the beneficiary charities within 90 days, and a donor must be able to support any charity in the UK using the scheme. There are a number of approved PGAs, details of which can be found on www.hmrc.gov.uk/payrollgiving.

There is no upper limit on how much an individual can donate annually through payroll giving.

Example

At 20% Income Tax rate (2008–09 tax rates), a monthly donation works like this:

employee gives	£10	charity receives	£10
tax saving	£2.00	minus agency administrative charge 4%	£9.60
cost to the employee*	£8.00		

*For a higher rate taxpayer, with a tax saving of £4, the cost to the employee is reduced to £6.

Promoting payroll giving

There are several different ways of promoting payroll giving to benefit your charity:

- circulate details of the scheme to those of your supporters who are not already making regular donations. Remember that only some of them will be in employment and working for an employer who is running a payroll giving scheme, and if they are not, they will not be able to give in this way;
- ask your existing payroll supporters to canvas support from their work colleagues, and provide them with the necessary promotional materials to do this;
- contact companies operating payroll giving schemes, and ask them to allow you meet and talk to their employees;
- use a commercial promoter or professional fundraising organisation (PFO), to put your cause alongside others. This will usually involve a charge for each recruited gift;
- join a consortium which then employs a commercial promoter to reach employees;
- use leaflets inserted in company magazines to recruit employees direct.

How to get started

There are a number of important decisions to make when considering whether to develop payroll giving.

- Is it worth it? There are opportunities, but it is not a major source of charitable giving and it takes time and effort to get going. If you do decide to investigate further, then the first step would be to identify all the major employers in your area (public and private sector) and find out whether they have a payroll giving scheme.
- Do you do it yourself using your own staff, or by engaging a PFO?
- Do you promote your charity on its own, or are you part of a consortium?
- You will need to prepare promotional materials, including an explanatory leaflet for employees, which can include a deduction form for them to hand into their payroll department, and a poster to put up at the workplace.

- How will you fund the development costs, bearing in mind the long lead time involved before you actually begin to receive a flow of income?

How Compton Hospice encourages payroll giving

Terminally ill patients and their families who are looked after by Compton Hospice are benefiting from £100,000 raised each year through payroll giving. The money is raised by a part-time payroll giving officer who identifies and approaches local firms. A senior member of staff is always approached to arrange a meeting at which the Hospice requests an opportunity to promote payroll giving to the staff face to face. This can either be in small groups at team meetings, which proves the most successful, or by using an exhibition stand in the staff restaurant to promote interest and then being on hand to talk to employees when they are taking a break. As often as possible Compton advertises its visit in advance. It asks for a minimum donation of £6.40 per month on its payroll giving forms and the resulting average annual donation is £73 per donor. Compton's annual donor attrition rate for its payroll giving programme is approximately 14%.

Approaching employers directly

Some employers will be happy to recommend a charity or charities to their employees (for example, where a company adopts a 'charity of the year', or to supplement a donation or sponsorship that the company has undertaken). Other employers prefer to leave it to the employees to decide what to support, and may not want to give a particular charity the opportunity to canvass support in their organisation. A lot of UK employers, particularly smaller and medium-sized companies, still do not offer payroll giving facilities to their employees, nor are they likely to know much about the scheme, though their awareness may have improved with the recent promotion schemes by HM Revenue & Customs and the Institute of Fundraising. In such cases, you have to persuade the company to establish a payroll giving scheme first.

When approaching a company, you will want to do the following.

- Research what the company does, who makes the decisions, whether they undertake any charitable giving and, as mentioned earlier, whether they operate a payroll giving scheme.
- Approach the person who has the authority to allow you to set up a meeting to discuss your plans. For smaller companies, this will be the managing director.
- Discuss with that person how you might promote payroll giving to their staff.
- Arrange your payroll giving promotion in the company.

The best way to promote payroll giving is face to face. Indirect methods such as leaflets and posters on their own are less effective. You need to agree with the employer precisely what access you will be allowed to their staff. It is unlikely that you will be able to go round the offices or shopfloor and ask employees individually. It is more common that you will be talking to groups of people in their lunch break or at a pre-arranged meeting, or you may be able to set up a stand about payroll giving and your organisation in a common area of the building such as the entrance foyer.

Professional fundraising organisations (PFOs) for payroll giving

There are a number of PFOs which specialise in promoting payroll giving to employees. The most usual procedure is:

- you enter into a contract with the PFO;
- they put information about your charity alongside that of other charities they represent;
- they go into the workplace to promote payroll giving taking along information about the charities they represent;
- they then charge you for each donor who signs up to support your charity.

There is now an organisation of payroll giving promoters and consultants, the Association of Payroll Giving Professional Fundraising Organisations (APGPFO), to help ensure standards.

Consortia

For smaller charities, the use of commercial promoters is problematic, since the charity will have very little public profile. When a prospective donor is faced with a list of charities, those which are unknown are the least likely to be supported. This is where a consortium approach can be helpful. Consortia are set up by groups of charities specially to promote payroll giving. A consortium can include charities working for the same sort of cause (for example, there is a consortium of smaller children's charities called Childlife), or can be made up of a range of local charities. Donors are encouraged to support the consortium (which is usually constituted as a charity in its own right), and the proceeds are shared between consortium members, either equally or according to some formula agreed at the outset. Consortia have two important advantages:

- the costs are shared. This is a form of fundraising where many of the charities involved do not have any previous experience, so operating in this way can be less risky;
- the consortium is benefiting a range of charities. This can make it easier to gain access to a workplace, because the employer may not want to be seen as favouring one charity over another.

A charity wanting to get involved in payroll giving, but not wanting to go it alone, could attempt to join an existing consortium, or join with others to set up a new consortium. The consortium should have a catchy name, and comprise a compatible group of similar charities that are happy to collaborate.

4.6 Tax-effective giving
Gift Aid

The rules regarding tax-effective giving changed significantly on 6 April 2000, with the government's 'Getting Britain Giving' campaign. The main change for individual donors was that all tax-effective payments, whether made by regular donation or with a one-off gift, had to be covered by the Gift Aid scheme, and there would be no minimum level (previously it had been £250 for a one-off gift) for the size of donation. Therefore, in theory, any payment made to a charity by a taxpayer is eligible for tax relief as long as:

- the donor fills out a Gift Aid declaration (which replaced the existing Gift Aid certificate) which is then kept by the charity. This need only be a simple sentence included in the donation form that the donor signs and returns with the donation;
- the charity maintains an 'audit trail' linking the payment to the donor – the charity needs to record each donation separately and be able to prove to HM Revenue & Customs how much each donor has given.

At the time of writing research by the Institute of Fundraising shows that not all charities are taking advantage of Gift Aid, with only 6 out of 10 of the UK's smallest non-profits (those with a voluntary income of less than £100,000) making a Gift Aid claim in the last year. Therefore it appears that there is still work to be done in terms of promoting the benefits of Gift Aid to this group.

You can get further advice on implementing a Gift Aid programme from HM Revenue & Customs Charities or by visiting its website www.hmrc.gov.uk/charities/ (see also www.tax-effective-giving.org.uk which is a part of the Institute of Fundraising website). Here you will also be able to find exactly what information is required to be included in a Gift Aid declaration, and a model form. The Gift Aid declaration can state that it covers all donations from the date of the current gift onwards (and going back up to six years prior to the date of the declaration), so one declaration can cover all future claims, although the donor can cancel this at any time. The level of benefits the donor can receive are limited to 25% for a donation or subscription up to £100, £25 between £101 and £1,000, 2.5% above £1,000, with an overall maximum of £250.

So, in theory, you can add 25% (on 2008–09 tax rates) to the income from, for example, a sponsored run if:

- all your sponsors are taxpayers;
- they all complete or have completed a Gift Aid declaration;
- you can prove that they have made the payment.

Once you have proper record keeping in place, the system is now so simple that you can reclaim tax on almost any donation, whatever the size, as long as the donor is a taxpayer. However, you should be aware that there is now a time limit for making claims for tax on donations made by Gift Aid. Any charity which is a company for tax purposes must make any claim within six years from the end of the accounting period to which the claim relates; while a charity which is a trust for tax purposes must make any claim within five years of 31 January in the year following the end of the tax year to which the claim relates.

Tax-effective giving: who gets what?

For a basic rate taxpayer, paying tax at 20% (2008–09 rate)

A donor pays you £10.

This amount is net of income tax at the basic rate.

To earn this the donor will have to have earned a gross sum of £12.50.

To calculate this amount: $\dfrac{100}{100-20}$ or $\dfrac{100}{100-R}$ where R = rate of Income tax.

The donor pays 20% tax on £12.50, which is £2.50, in order to earn £10.

You are able to reclaim this £2.50 from HM Revenue & Customs. And this increases the value of the donation by 25% (at a 20% tax rate).

For a higher rate taxpayer paying tax at 40%

You reclaim £2.50, as above.

But the donor has paid 40% tax on the £12.50 of income.

This amounts to £5.00.

The donor is able to reclaim £2.50 from HM Revenue & Customs in higher rate relief (which can be done by a PAYE adjustment or when making an annual tax return).

Deeds of Covenant, which used to be an important mechanism for charities asking for regular gifts, no longer count for a separate tax relief and were made more or less obsolete when the Gift Aid scheme was rolled out in April

2000. Payroll giving (see pages 80–85) is another tax-effective form of gift, but here the donor receives all the tax benefit, and there is no additional tax that the charity can reclaim.

CAF accounts

Another method of giving tax effectively is where the donor uses the services of the Charities Aid Foundation (CAF). Here they pay a sum to CAF as a charitable donation and tax is reclaimed on this. The total amount, made up of the value of the donation and the tax reclaimed less an administrative charge to CAF and a compulsory donation to the National Council for Voluntary Organisations (which set up the scheme), is kept in an account for the donor. The donor can then make charitable donations from the account, either using vouchers which they give to the charity as they would a cheque, by quoting their CharityCard number, or by asking CAF to make regular direct payments to a charity from their account. In the first two instances the charity claims the sum given from CAF. Since the tax has already been reclaimed in respect of this donation, no further tax can be reclaimed by the charity.

Gifts of shares to charity

Since April 2000, individuals (and companies) have also been able to get tax relief on gifts of certain shares and securities to charity when calculating their income for tax purposes. The tax relief applies where the whole of the beneficial interest in any qualifying shares or securities is disposed of to charity either by way of a gift or by way of a sale at an undervalue. The following categories of shares and securities can be donated using this relief:

- shares and securities listed or dealt in on the UK Stock Exchange, including the Alternative Investment Market;
- shares and securities listed or dealt in on recognised foreign stock exchanges;
- units in an authorised unit trust (AUT);
- shares in a UK open-ended investment company (OEIC);
- holdings in certain foreign collective investment schemes – broadly, schemes established outside the UK equivalent to unit trusts and OEICs.

To check whether the shares or securities qualify for the scheme, contact HM Revenue & Customs Charities for advice.

Where an individual makes use of this relief, they are able to deduct the 'relevant amount' from their total income for tax purposes. The relevant amount is either the full market value of the shares (where the transfer is a gift), or the difference between the market value and the actual cash received (where the transfer is a sale at an undervalue). This figure is then adjusted by adding to it any incidental costs of disposing of the shares – for example brokers' fees.

Tax relief can be claimed at the donor's top rate of tax via their self-assessment tax return, and for Capital Gains Tax (CGT) transfer is deemed to have taken place at cost (so no CGT is payable) unless the shares are sold at an undervalue, where the sale price is taken as being the transfer price.

Since April 2002, the same tax relief has been available for donors who give land and buildings to charity.

Example

A donor paying tax at the higher rate of 40% gives shares valued at £25,000 to a charity. The shares originally cost £10,000. From the donor's point of view the disposal is deemed to have taken place at £10,000 and therefore the gift does not act as a gain or a loss for Capital Gains Tax (CGT) purposes. If the donor were to sell the shares for their current value (£25,000), there would be a capital gain of £15,000 which would be taxed at 40% (£6,000). The net amount received on the sale would only be £14,000. For tax purposes the donor's annual taxable income will be reduced by £25,000 (the value of the shares donated). At the 40% rate this reduces their liability by £10,000. The donor saves £10,000 in Income Tax and £6,000 in CGT as compared with selling the shares. The effective net cost of the gift to the donor is therefore only £9,000.

4.7 Looking after your supporters or stewardship

Your donors and supporters are a key part of your fundraising future. They have demonstrated their commitment to you through giving, and you should try to retain this commitment and strengthen their ties to your organisation. This is often referred to as donor or supporter care, stewardship or customer relationship marketing. This section concentrates on two aspects of developing your supporter relationships – thanking them, and increasing their involvement.

Thanking your donors

Being thanked makes donors feel good about their giving, and tells them that their donation has been received and is being put to good use. Thanking your donors gives you the opportunity to find out the depth of their interest, and perhaps some of the reasons why they support you. It can also enable you to tell them more about your work and your future plans. And all this will help you to get further support from them.

Your best prospects for a donation are those people who have already given to you, so when and how you thank them can be crucial. There are several ways of saying thank you.

By mail

Some charities reply to all donations, while others reply only to certain types or levels. It can be expensive to thank people for every donation whether large or small, especially if there are a lot of them, but there are important advantages in thanking donors at some point, even if you do not do it every time. If you are concerned about saving administrative costs, you might ask donors to tell you if they do not want an acknowledgement from you every time they give.

When you do say thank you, try to do it immediately, say within three days of receipt of the donation. Try and make the letter as personal as you can, recognising how long the person has been supporting you and their level of giving. It might be useful to develop a set of generic letters which you can then adapt as necessary. Some organisations get their chair or director to sign the letter. This is not necessary except for very large donations. Your smaller and regular donors may be more interested in getting to know you (the fundraiser) or a donation administrator, whom they will be able to contact if they have a query or want further information.

By telephone

If you want to respond quickly and personally, particularly for larger donations, the telephone is ideal. As soon as you receive an exceptional gift, ring the donor and thank them personally.

By e-mail

If you know a supporter's e-mail address, and this is something you should definitely be collecting along with their mailing address and telephone number, this can be an immediate way of thanking which also has the advantage of appearing very cost effective.

Face to face

Personally visiting important donors can be a time consuming business. However, it can also be extremely worthwhile. The visit should be made by an appropriate person. Depending on the level of donor, this might be the fundraiser, a member of the management or fundraising committee, or a trained volunteer. Donors may be wary about the object of such visits until they have actually received one. A simple chat to tell the donor more about your work and to thank them for their gift will often naturally lead on to discussing other ways they can help without your having to introduce the subject yourself or ask directly.

Through an event

If a face to face visit is not possible, another way of meeting and thanking supporters is by setting up an event, such as a reception or open day. A senior person from the organisation might attend and give a short talk; then staff, committee members or other volunteers can be on hand to talk to those who have been invited to the event. This requires careful planning and briefing of your staff, committees and volunteers to ensure that everyone is spoken to.

You might hold the event at your office. People are often interested in seeing how an organisation works, even when all there is to see are desks and filing cabinets. Or you could organise a site visit to see a project at work and enable the donors to meet some of the beneficiaries and the local community.

With a gift

Some fundraisers offer some sort of incentive or token in return for gifts of a certain size or type. This might be something heavily promoted by the charity to encourage a particular response, or a token of thanks used to build commitment and help spread the message to others. For example, a special Christmas card from your president; a certificate for a pledged legacy; or a wildlife print. Though giving is often a private matter, some supporters welcome opportunities to discuss their favourite cause with their friends. A thank-you token or certificate which they can display in their home can help them do this.

By public acknowledgement

You can also thank people through a public announcement – such as an advertisement in a newspaper or a mention in your newsletter, magazine or annual report.

Think carefully about your annual report. Not only can you credit your donors, but this also sends signals to others that you need donations and will publicly acknowledge any support you receive. Indicating the level of gifts creates a certain peer group pressure for others to give at similar levels. Perhaps more importantly it gives credibility – 'If those people have given, then it must be a good organisation.' As an organisation grows, the number of donors may get too large to list everyone; but the major donors should still appear. See chapter 15, section 15.3, for more on annual reports.

Taking paid advertising to thank donors might be expensive but can be worthwhile if there are other messages to communicate (for example that the cause has widespread or prestigious support). Remember to get the donor's permission before you do this and also check how they wish to be credited, as some will not want to see their names publicly in print.

Involving supporters in a campaign

In 1999 the NSPCC launched a national campaign to put a stop to child abuse, the Full Stop Campaign. This initiative had a fundraising target but also aimed to increase non-financial involvement among existing supporters and the general public. The campaign used both direct marketing and broader awareness raising methods such as television advertising – some involving celebrities – and billboard posters to encourage support.

Increasing donor involvement

The more your donors and supporters understand your cause, the issues and policies, your problems and failures as well as your successes, the more likely they may be to make a greater financial commitment to your organisation. There are a number of ways of giving donors a fuller picture of what you are doing that will help build their commitment and support.

Regular mailings

Mailings to supporters are crucial for keeping them in touch, whether these are purely to communicate information, or to ask for further donations. You can use them to report back on your progress and, by implication, how you have used their money. You might highlight successes and achievements, including any major grants received, and set out your future plans.

Obviously, you want your supporters to read what you have sent; you may also want them to respond. Both are difficult in a world where people are constantly receiving unsolicited information from all manner of sources. In order to make your letter stand out you might use a device such as a questionnaire or link your mailing with a particular campaign that your organisation is running. A questionnaire can tell you what your supporters think (and who they are), and you can use their views to make important campaigning points. For example, in the past Shelter used surveys to build connections between the organisation and its supporters, such as asking them to contribute their views on what the government's housing policy should encompass.

Sending a questionnaire to supporters in a regular appeal mailing can increase response rates. Some people will be motivated by the appeal and some will be motivated by the request to provide information. You can also use questionnaires to ask donors how they want to be involved or how they want you to communicate with them. You can include a postcard in your mailing asking supporters to return this to, for example, a government minister, either directly or through your office, and thereby engage them in your campaigning. This is something that Amnesty International UK has done for particular campaigns.

Other involvement techniques

Other ways of increasing involvement include the following.

- *Lectures and talks*. An event where your supporters can hear experts discuss a particular issue gives them the chance to understand more fully the cause you are addressing, and makes them feel that their contribution is important and useful. You can also highlight a new initiative that needs support. However, the essential purpose of such a meeting is not to raise money, but to build interest and involvement, thereby providing a solid platform for future fundraising.

- *Involving donors in your fundraising*. On the principle that the best person to ask is someone who has already given, you might try to find ways of inviting donors to accompany you to fundraising meetings, particularly where you know they are enthusiastic. If they can convey something of what motivated them to get involved, it can encourage others; equally importantly, it will cement their relationship with you. Another way of motivating existing donors to ask their friends and family to give to you as a favourite cause is through mechanisms such as Tribute Gifts. These can be promoted by charities as an opportunity for supporters to ask for donations to commemorate significant events like weddings or a special birthday or anniversary.

- *Friends groups*. By 'enrolling' donors as members of a friends group or a supporters club (either free or for a subscription) and sending them a regular newsletter which focuses as much on the donors and what they are doing for the organisation as on the work of the organisation, you can create a sense of belonging. You can then organise special events for these key supporters and also develop special appeals where you ask your existing supporters to raise a sum of money for a specific purpose. By giving them the responsibility for doing this and a target to achieve, this will encourage them to give generously.

- *Campaigning*. Many voluntary organisations campaign. The campaigning is usually spearheaded by the paid staff, but can often be reinforced by members and volunteers. Those who become involved in advocating a cause will develop a much deeper commitment to it and may become your best supporters in the long term.

Fundraisers should never allow fundraising to become divorced from the advocacy work. It is important to ensure that there are a number of ways for people to support an organisation: giving money, volunteering, fundraising and campaigning. Some people will only be able to do one of these. However many may want to do more – and by becoming more involved, this will strengthen their concern and commitment to you.

Challenges for the fundraiser

1   To get the donor to give again.
2   To get the donor to give regularly and frequently, ultimately on a committed basis.
3   To get the donor to increase their level of giving.
4   To get the donor to give in several different ways.
5   To encourage the donor to leave a legacy.

Recruiting volunteers from your donors

It is sometimes assumed that volunteers and donors are two separate categories of supporters which should not be mixed. Many charities feel that they should not ask their donors to volunteer, nor their volunteers to give money. This assumes that people compartmentalise their concern and their response, which is unlikely to be the case.

All those who are giving their time should also be given the opportunity to give money. You may feel that they should be protected from such requests, but some may be happy to give. Unless you ask them, you may miss out on their support. (See chapter 16 *Fundraising with volunteers*.) Donors can also be invited to become volunteers. Most will not have the time available or wish to, but some will – and they will continue as donors too. Even if they do not wish to volunteer, their support may be all the stronger when they are made aware that other people are volunteering their time.

Resources and further information

See also general lists at the end of the book.

Organisations

Association of Payroll Giving Professional Fundraising Organisations (APGPFO)
c/o Business in the Community
137 Shepherdess Walk
Islington
London N1 7RQ
www.apgpfo.org
Tel. 020 7566 8729
Fax 020 7253 1877
e-mail caroline.peat@bitc.org uk

Charities Aid Foundation
25 King's Hill Avenue
King's Hill
West Malling
Kent ME19 4TA
www.cafonline.org
Tel. 01732 520 000
Fax 01732 520 001
e-mail enquiries@cafonline.org

Charities Trust
Suite 22
Century Building
Bruswick Business Park
Tower Street
Liverpool L3 4BJ
www.charitiestrust.org
Tel. 0870 708 7878
Fax 0151 286 2360
e-mail info@charitiestrust.org

Charities Trust is a national payroll giving and corporate donation management agency approved by HM Revenue & Customs.

HM Revenue & Customs
(for Tax & VAT matters)
www.hmrc.gov.uk

Smee & Ford
Paulton House
Shepherdess Walk
London N1 7LB
www.smeeandford.co.uk
Tel. 020 7324 2312
e-mail info@smeeandford.co.uk

www.tax-effective-giving.org.uk
A part of the Institute of Fundraising website.

Publications

The following publications are available from the Directory of Social Change. Prices were correct at the time of writing, but may be subject to change.

Building a Fundraising Database Using your PC, 2nd edn, Peter Flory, DSC/CAF 2001, £12.95

Effective Customer Care, Amanda Knight, DSC 1999, £12.95

Legacy Fundraising, 2nd edn, ed. Sebastian Wilberforce, DSC/CAF/Institute of Fundraising 2001, £22.95

Looking after your Donors, Karen Gilchrist, DSC/CAF 2000, £14.95

Major Donor Fundraising, Margaret Holman & Lucy Sargent, DSC/CAF/Institute of Fundraising 2006, £22.95

A Practical Guide to VAT, 3rd edn, Kate Sayer, 2007, £14.95 new edition due in September 2007

Other publications

Institute of Fundraising Code of Practice on House to House Collections

Institute of Fundraising Code of Practice on Legacy Fundraising

Institute of Fundraising Code of Practice on Payroll Giving

Institute of Fundraising Code of Practice on Personal Solicitation for Committed Gifts

COMMUNITY FUNDRAISING

This chapter looks at three ways of fundraising at a local level:

- forming a local group specifically for fundraising;
- using local clubs and societies to mobilise support for your project;
- fundraising through schools, where you can get the support of young people.

Details of organisations and publications referred to in this chapter are on pages 110–111.

5.1 Fundraising through local groups

Whether you are an established national organisation or a small local group just starting out, raising money locally through events and collections and by other means can be an important source of income. However, this requires time and effort.

There are two main approaches: using paid staff to do the fundraising, or recruiting a group of volunteers. Wherever possible it is best to work through volunteers. The staff member's job is then to recruit and support those volunteers. The point of doing this is that the fundraising effort is taken on by the local group, leaving you free to concentrate on other tasks. It may not be cost-effective for a paid member of staff to spend time organising craft fairs, dinners or coffee mornings, although paid staff should be responsible for particularly important events – especially where there are large sums involved. The more you raise money yourself, the more you will have to do in the following years in order to maintain your level of income, and therefore the less time you will have to develop volunteers, so it is best to recruit your volunteers early on.

Local groups can raise money in a specified area or for a particular service. They may raise money through a specific activity (a special ball, for example). You can establish local fundraising groups in different towns and cities, or in different areas of the same city. They will work largely independently, but you will need to provide proper management and support. The more groups you establish, the more money you should raise, and groups work best when you have strong and committed volunteer leadership. It can take a long time (up to 18 months or sometimes even longer) to get a group established and raising money successfully, but the investment can be worth it. The volunteers you recruit, if properly supported, may stay involved with your organisation for many years.

Getting started

To establish a local fundraising group, you need to:

- be clear where you want a group and what you want the group to do;
- find people who are willing to put in the time to raise money for you, and in particular:
  - find leadership for the group;
  - establish the group with a constitution or set of guidelines, which defines how it will work and its relationship with the organisation it is raising money for;
  - work with the group to identify appropriate (and ideally repeatable) fundraising activities;
  - support the group in its fundraising work;
  - and THANK THEM!

The following example illustrates how you might set about forming a local fundraising group. The key is to follow up on every idea or contact, to ask persuasively – and to get the volunteers doing something.

Getting a local fundraising group going

I wanted to form a new fundraising group in the town. It was a fairly affluent dormitory town of about 10,000 people – a day-trip holiday resort. The Society used to have a fundraising group there a few years ago but it had grown old together and disbanded and no one could help anymore.

I contacted the local MP, who had expressed some interest in our work some years before but had done nothing. He suggested that I contact a number of his political colleagues in the area and was happy for me to say that he had suggested it. I contacted them all. Only one person showed any interest. He made it clear he did not want any long-term involvement, but would host a meeting for us if we wanted to invite people to an information-type evening.

I looked through the records of any donations or enquiries that had been made in recent years and came across a request for information from two mature students living in the town. I called them to see if they would be interested in coming to a meeting and they thought they would be. I took up the offer of the evening and discussed with the host who else we might invite. We sent out about 30 invitations and received eight acceptances, including the two mature students.

Only the two mature students turned up on the evening. They felt embarrassed by the non-attendance of the other people and said they would help. I suggested that they could organise a coffee morning/evening and invite their friends and neighbours. They did so, and about 40 people attended. I was there to talk to people and see if anyone else was interested – four were. I asked if the original two would think about organising another morning/evening and this time suggested involving the four other people. They were happy to – and we had the beginnings of a new fundraising group.

The next event came and went with another four or five people wanting to help. This exercise was repeated twice more – we had new people joining, and the original people began to withdraw. After 15 months we had a lively group of 22 young women eager to help and enjoying themselves in the process.

[Consultant Harry Brown, writing of his experience when at the NSPCC]

Recruiting the right people is another key to success. In particular you need to look for key people to chair/lead the committee or take overall responsibility for a particular area of fundraising. Identify the skills and resources that people will need for the job – time available, use of their home, contacts, ideas, initiative, enthusiasm, and so on. Allow plenty of time to find the people you need. Try to find out what motivates them. Do they want to meet new people? Do they need public acknowledgement? Do they want to make a name for themselves? Do they enjoy 'achieving' things? You can also ask the people you contact to suggest other people. Ask if they would be willing to make the approach or introduce you. If you are setting up a local branch of a national organisation, start with existing supporters who live in the area. They will already be interested in the cause, so may be keen (or may be persuaded) to help. As the group begins to organise fundraising events (and starts to be successful), you will find that there will be more interest in what you are doing and more people will be come forward to volunteer their time. At any stage in the process, good publicity in the local press or on local radio can bring further support.

Recruiting for a local committee

The steps you need to take are as follows:

- Research the area
- Identify key individuals
- Find ways to engage key individuals
- Meet them and seek contacts and leads
- Obtain the commitment from the 'leader' or leading people
- Build up a list of people they know

- Organise an inaugural meeting (try to get one of the interested people to host it).

Joining a committee is an opportunity to make a contribution to the welfare of the community in an interesting and enjoyable way, which leads to personal satisfaction.

It is an opportunity to acquire a personal profile and influence in an acceptable way, to meet other business contacts and be seen as the supporter of a national charity.

People of the calibre of those invited to join a committee have very limited free time, but are in a position to select and actively support fundraising events that fit into their lifestyles.

Funds raised through the efforts of the local committee ideally will be spent in the area on locally based projects.

There is satisfaction to be gained from becoming part of a (national) charity with the occasional opportunity to meet and talk with the decision-makers in the organisation.

Constituting the local group

You need people – and you need something for them to do. You also need a constitution, or a set of guidelines, which defines how the group will operate and clarifies their relationship with the charity they are raising money for. If you are setting up lots of local groups, you can draw up a model constitution. The local group can be simply a sub-committee or branch of the charity, with no separate legal identity of its own. Or it can be a separate organisation in its own right, constituted independently as a charity, with the object of supporting the charity it has been set up to raise money for.

A separate legal structure will be more expensive to operate, but it will give full responsibility and control to the local group – it will be completely accountable for what is raised and what the money is spent on. A structure with branches gives the parent charity direct control – and trustees responsibility for how the money is raised and spent. The most appropriate structure depends on a number of factors, including the time the committee has been in operation, the amount of money it is raising, the number of local groups around the country raising money for you, and the parent charity's own constitution and byelaws. *The Voluntary Sector Legal Handbook* covers this area in more detail (see publications list on page 111).

Make sure that the group operates in the interests of the parent charity and does nothing to bring it into disrepute. If the group is independently constituted, this can be done through a licence agreement, which authorises the use of the charity's name and logo provided that certain standards are met and values adhered to. The Charities Act 1992 provisions on unauthorised fundraising provide some safeguards against independent groups of people who decide to raise money for you without your permission.

Constitution of a local committee

The following are some of the headings for the constitution of a local fundraising committee. These responsibilities are not to be taken lightly.

- The committee and the charity
- Support to be provided by the charity
- Responsibilities of committee members
- Name
- Location
- Bank account / banking arrangements / transfer of funds raised
- Objects of the committee
- Structure including: patronage, election of officers, responsibility of officers, terms of office
- Meetings and operation: quorum for meetings, frequency of meetings, voting, resignations, termination of memberships, annual general meetings
- Remuneration of members, expenses policy
- Alteration of constitution.

Local fundraising activities

There is an enormous range of fundraising activities that a local fundraising group can undertake. Here are a few examples that have worked well in the past:

- coffee mornings and other types of social gatherings
- bridge tournaments and other games such as chess
- sponsored walks, jogs, cycle rides, fun runs – and anything else that can be sponsored
- heritage walks and cultural evenings
- craft fairs
- fashion shows
- film premieres
- concerts and other cultural events
- dinners and balls
- picnics and outings for families, if possible at interesting locations
- auctions of donated goods and 'promises auctions' (where a promise to do something useful or interesting is auctioned)
- sports events and tournaments

- getting supporters and businesses to advertise in calendars and diaries, brochures and annual reports
  (*Getting companies to advertise is covered in chapter 8*)
- local sales of your organisation's greetings cards
  (*Selling goods is covered in chapter 11*)
- public and house-to-house collections
  (*Public and house-to-house collections are covered in chapter 12*)
- raffles, lotteries and sweepstakes (which are regulated under the Lotteries Act)
  (*Lotteries and raffles are covered in chapter 12*)
- competitions with an entry fee to participants (which are not regulated).

Supporting and managing a local group

It is important to make sure any local group actually does the work, does it well, operates in accordance with the values and aims of the charity it is raising money for, and does not call unreasonably upon staff time. You will need to manage and support the group if you are to get the most out of it. Here are some ideas for how to do this.

- Provide the group with some form of induction, so that they understand the importance of the work being done by the charity, see the staff at work and meet and talk to staff and beneficiaries. They will then know what they are raising the money for and it will give them the enthusiasm they need to convince those they are asking. Make sure you provide them with appropriate literature about the work of the organisation.
- Help steer the group towards those fundraising methods that are most likely to work. Your experience will help, and you can also research what other local fundraising groups are doing. You may have a number of tried and tested ideas and be able to give them all the information they need to put them into practice.
- Give the group a budget (they will need to spend some money to raise money) and talk to them about fundraising targets. Don't expect too much too soon. It is best to start slowly, and to allow more time than they think will be necessary. If they are too optimistic at the outset, there will be a sense of failure when targets are not achieved.
- Continue to show your personal interest in what they are doing. Monitor their progress and be on hand with advice if they have difficulties. At every opportunity, acknowledge your appreciation of their hard work, find ways of celebrating their success, and thank them.

Your relationship with the leader, or chair, of the group is critical to its success. They will act as your key contact and their enthusiasm is vital to maintaining the overall energy and commitment of the group. A good leader will also help to ensure that a longstanding group does not slip into a rut where new ideas and people are blocked, and will get the group working as a team.

The characteristics of a good fundraising leader

1   The leader must be an efficient and capable **organiser**.
2   Leaders must be able to **plan** an event in every detail.
3   Leaders must be able to **communicate** with their helpers. They should enjoy working with people and should be able to lead without causing offence.
4   A leader must be able to **motivate** others and inspire them with enthusiasm and zeal.
5   Leaders must be good judges of people. They must get to know their committee and helpers well and be able to **recognise and use the talents and abilities of individual members of the group**. They must also be able to understand each person's strengths and weaknesses in order to be able to **direct** and **guide** them in a way that they can accept and enjoy.

[Sterrett, *Complete Guide to Fundraising*]

5.2 Local clubs and societies

There is a wide range of local groups and associations which can be extremely valuable for your fundraising. They can provide you with money, influence and human resources. There are many different organisations which can fulfil this role, but this section will concentrate on:

- local companies
- membership bodies
- local groups
- churches and other religious bodies.

These areas can be invaluable for their contacts and their ability to mobilise large numbers of people to volunteer, attend events, organise collections and give you access to their friends and colleagues. They can help raise your profile.

Local companies often want to support local groups. Many are looking for ways to get their staff engaged locally, to help build teams and to improve morale. Some will want to increase sales, others will simply want to get involved with the cause. Volunteers will often work in local companies and can be the best way into a company.

Membership bodies such as the Women's Institutes (mainly in rural areas) and Townswomen's Guilds (in urban areas), Young Farmers, Round Tables, Lions and Rotarians (and other similar bodies for men or women). Usually these organisations don't make large grants themselves, but they can encourage their membership to support a particular appeal and you might spot a potential key supporter amongst them.

Local groups such as Scouts, Cubs, Girl Guides, Brownies, sports clubs and dance schools can all help. You may be organising a sponsored walk or a fun run, or a fete or a fair, and require people to staff the event. Such organisations can be a useful source of helpers, perhaps in return for a small grant to their own funds.

A wide range of church and religious bodies give to charity. Many local congregations decide to allocate an annual collection to a particular cause – not all are religious in nature, and can be in addition to traditional collections such as Christian Aid Week. Groups within congregations often meet to explore particular themes and this will lead them, for example, to become interested in homelessness or poverty. At a diocesan and national level, the Churches have boards of social responsibility (or their equivalent) whose role is to mobilise support for social action. Other faiths and denominations too will operate in a similar way.

Each type of organisation is different; you will need to find out what they can do for you. Try to get invited to speak at a function. If you do, take plenty of literature with you that explains your organisation and the sort of help you are looking for. You could ask if you could appeal for support there and then. Or they might write about your appeal in their next newsletter. Or you might ask for permission to write to the membership afterwards. A few organisations have been able to develop significant support in this way. It is easier if there are one or two enthusiastic volunteers who you can use as speakers.

Support you can expect

Depending upon the organisation you are approaching, you could look for:

- a cash donation;
- a gift of equipment for a local project;
- mobilising the involvement of volunteers for your project or for a fundraising event;
- encouraging donations from their members or getting them to organise a collection for you;
- running a fundraising event;
- an invitation to speak at meetings or to appeal to their membership;
- an endorsement for your work;
- an introduction to key individuals who might be willing to support you and get involved in your work.

Groups to consider approaching

Local companies

Chamber of commerce

Professional associations

Institute of Directors

Membership organisations

- Rotary
- Lions
- Round Table
- Soroptimists
- Inner Wheel
- Women's Institutes
- Townswomen's Guilds
- Mothers' Union
- Ladies' Circle
- Rotoract

Other local bodies

- Student rag committees
- College student unions
- Scouts and Guides
- Young Farmers' clubs
- Police
- Fire brigade
- Hobby groups; e.g. amateur dramatic societies

Religious bodies

- Churches (Church of England, Catholic, Methodist, Baptist, Pentecostal and other denominations).
- Other faiths (Hindu temples, Moslem mosques, Sikh gurdwaras, Jewish synagogues).
- Boards of social responsibility for particular faiths and denominations.

Getting started

1   Consider what support you are looking for. Is it cash support from the organisation or its members? Is it people's time to help you as volunteers? Is it their ability to mobilise support for you from friends and contacts? Is it their access to individuals with influence? Is it their facilities you wish to

make use of? Or is it an endorsement of your work? Always create a strong case for support.

2 Review your records to see if they have supported you in the past, and what other similar organisations and networks have given you support.

3 Check with your own committees and supporters to see if they are members of any relevant organisations. This can provide a first point of contact.

4 Draw up a shortlist of possible organisations that you believe have the interest and the resources or membership to support you.

5 Make contact at the appropriate level and try to establish what might be of interest to them.

6 Follow this up with a specific proposal; make this something they could reasonably do for you.

5.3 Working with schools and young people
Some basic principles

There are four reasons for wanting to involve young people.

- You will be generating money for your work, although this will not always be a substantial amount. Young people are more likely to have time to give rather than money, but they do have the ability to raise money for you.

- You will be involving young people in your cause, giving them a better understanding of the issues involved and the work you are doing. They may need the help your organisation provides at some time. You may even find ways of encouraging them to volunteer.

- You will be laying an important base for future support. If people get involved in supporting charity when they are young, this can influence what they do and choose to support in later life.

- You will be reaching adults through young people. Raising money through young people inevitably includes their parents and parents' friends in a way that you otherwise might not be able to.

How you approach young people and what you ask them to do will depend on two factors: the institution you are approaching them through and their age. You can reach young people through the following.

- *Educational institutions*: these include not only primary and secondary schools (and middle schools where these still exist), but also FE and sixth form colleges, as well as universities, for the increasing number of young people who go on to higher education.

- *Youth clubs,* where there is more freedom to undertake creative activity.

- *Out-of-school projects*, which include out-of-school learning projects and after-school clubs as well as projects for young people with special needs.

- *Formal volunteering programmes*, including those funded under the Millennium Volunteers programme, which encourage young people to develop their own ideas and solutions in response to problems and needs.
- *New Deal employment projects* and projects funded through the Connexions Service, which aim to create further opportunities for learning and skills development for young people aged 13–19.

You also need to design your approach differently for different age groups.

- *Up to 5 years old*, children can be involved in fundraising via their parents' philanthropic interests or through pre-school groups and nurseries. Charity-organised national events such as Barnardo's Big Toddle, sponsored by Lloyds TSB, is one way that families with young children are being approached.
- *From 5 to 11 years old,* where children can be reached through primary schools, ideas need to be simple and have good educational content. At Key Stage 2 (age 8–11), young people are beginning to use their own initiative to do things.
- *From 11 to 16* (Key Stages 3 and 4), young people have Citizenship Education as part of their official curriculum, and they are encouraged to do active projects in the community. You should be aware that below the age of 16 there are legal issues involved for your charity if you organise projects for young people off school or youth club premises without a teacher or youth leader being present.
- *Post 16*, through to university and beyond, young people can be expected to organise activities independently, for example through a charity committee or by organising one-off events such as a disco or fun run in aid of a charity of their choice. The Youth Action Network encourages young people's involvement out of school. At university, volunteering is promoted by Student Volunteering.

There are three issues to take into account: the interests and concerns of the young people themselves; what they are capable of doing; and their educational needs. If you can design an approach that deals with all three, then you will find there is enormous potential.

Legal, ethical and safeguarding issues

If you are planning to raise money from young people, you should remember that you are dealing with a vulnerable and impressionable group. You need to approach them with care and be sensitive to their interests and their needs. You should not put undue pressure on them or their parents and families. Instead, try to get them to understand your work, the reasons for it and why it is important. There are several issues to consider.

- Legal constraints. Young people under the age of 18 are not able to enter into legal agreements, and should not be expected or invited to make contributions of any contractual nature. People working with young people under 18 and the trustees of charities undertaking this work may need to get a CRB (Criminal Records Bureau) check.

- Educational considerations. The role of a school is to educate young people and prepare them for their future life. Though charity and charity appeals certainly confront them with issues from the outside world, exploring these may best be done through classroom work rather than some fundraising event. The school must be the judge of what is appropriate, and many have tough stipulations on whether and how to work with charity appeals. This is well covered in the Institute of Fundraising Code of Practice on Fundraising in Schools.

- The pressure that children and young people apply, implicitly or explicitly, on their parents to give money or participate in an event ('pesterpower' as it is known in advertising). Most fundraising by younger children involves getting parents and close relatives or neighbours to contribute. Parents may react negatively to the number of times they are asked to give to through their children, and may even try to prevent them from taking part.

- Safeguarding. Children should not be encouraged to solicit support of any sort from people outside quite a narrow circle of family and neighbours, for personal safety reasons. There are also legal and safety issues relating to young people under 16 when they are taken outside school premises and parents will need to give permission. Further safeguarding advice is available from www.nspcc.org.uk/helpandadvice.

Making the approach

To obtain access to young people through a school, you will need the permission and support of the headteacher (or the support of a committed class teacher, who will then get the agreement of the headteacher). You can make the approach directly, or a committed supporter or volunteer who is a parent or a teacher could do this for you.

Most heads receive a large number of approaches from charities (some of the larger charities have departments that concentrate on this form of fundraising), and they will want to limit the number of activities taking place in the school. It is unlikely that you will be able to involve a school more than once a year, so you will need to contact as many schools as possible if you are to get a reasonable number involved in raising money for you. You need to be conscious of the time it takes to approach schools (ten visits to talk to groups of 30 students or one visit to talk to 300 students) and the effect that has on your own work – cost, income, hours available to work etc. Personal visits are the best way of making the approach. If this is not practical, a telephone call is better than a generic letter.

Some fundraising ideas for schools and young people

Some of these will work best with younger children, others will be fine right up to the sixth form:

- Cake and biscuit stall
- Carol singing
- Fancy dress or 'no uniform' day (teachers too!)
- Litter picking
- Picnic
- Promises auction (babysitting, ironing, gardening, bike servicing etc.)
- Raffle
- Recycling
- Sponsored event: walk, silence, swim etc.
- Summer fete with activities including:
  - face painting
  - puppet making
  - treasure map
  - book stall.

No school is going to invite you in if the only thing you plan to do is raise money. A useful guide is to make your activities:

- firstly fun
- secondly educational
- and only thirdly fundraising.

The usual starting point is to offer to give a talk about your organisation, the work it is doing, and the issues or problems it is dealing with. This will usually be to a school assembly or a relevant year group. Now that citizenship is a compulsory element of the curriculum at Key Stages 3 and 4, you may find secondary schools more willing. You will need to make your presentation as attractive and interesting as possible because this introduces the next step – the invitation to fundraise for you. This will either be taken up by the school or by a particular class if it fits into its educational programme.

Sponsored competitions are popular as they offer opportunities for learning, and sponsored events such as walks or swims offer an element of physical challenge which may be attractive. For secondary schools, the students themselves are in a better position to decide how funds should be raised and then organise the process.

The NSPCC developed a character called Will Stop to use in its schools materials for the Full Stop Campaign. In this illustration he appears in a colouring exercise which could also be used as a sponsorship vehicle – for every Will Stop the child found and coloured in they could raise money for the NSPCC.

Fundraising by and for schools

Competitive pressure on schools is increasing, with more and more charities competing to raise money from a fixed number of schools.

But there is also another sector of organisations seeking to raise money from young people and their parents – the schools themselves. Schools have realised that often the only way to expand or improve the quality of their education or to provide for extras is to raise money themselves. It is natural for the school to have first call on the generosity of both the students and their parents. Mostly this fundraising activity is carried out by Parent Teacher Associations, which comprise a group of active and already committed parents. Raising funds for the school itself can be carried out in a whole range of ways, many of them covered in this book: fetes, cake and book sales, quiz evenings, and designing and selling Christmas cards have all proved popular and effective.

Publications for schools

A number of the larger charities produce publications for children. These fall into two categories.

- School packs of teaching materials specially designed for use in the classroom (where they must be linked to the curriculum). Sometimes the pack is sponsored by a company whose interests overlap with the subject of the pack. The NSPCC, for example, received sponsorship from

Fern Training & Development for their schools pack, including the Where's Will illustration shown in this chapter.

- Simple information aimed at young people, which is sent in response to enquiries or as a thank-you for a donation. This could include a book or a pamphlet, a newsletter or an information sheet. You might even consider setting up a junior supporters 'club' to nurture the interests of young people. These undoubtedly build a strong loyalty to the organisations concerned and are an important ingredient of a successful fundraising programme.

National competitions

National and larger local charities might consider an award scheme for young people – such as an essay competition, an art competition, or an ideas competition. You will need to offer prizes, which can be to the young people or to the school – or perhaps to both. The prizes might be in cash, books, bursaries, or travel opportunities and they will usually represent around 10%–25% of the total cost of running the scheme. You also have to pay for publicity, printed material, judging, the awards ceremony, and all the administration involved. However, you may be able to get sponsorship from companies that are looking for ways to reach young people – they can get good publicity from having supported an exciting award scheme. For local and city-wide competitions, you might get a local newspaper to become a media sponsor, providing you with free publicity at all stages of the competition, rather than cash support.

Resources and further information

See also general lists at the end of the book.

Organisations

Youth Action Network
Crest House
7 Highfield Road
Edgbaston
Birmingham B15 3ED
www.youthactionnetwork.org.uk
Tel. 0121 455 9732
Fax. 0121 455 9697
email info@youthactionnetwork.org.uk

Student Volunteering
England www.studentvol.org.uk
Scotland www.studentvolscotland.org.uk

Publications

The following publications are available from the Directory of Social Change. Prices were correct at the time of writing, but may be subject to change.

Institute of Fundraising Code of Practice on Fundraising in Schools

Organising Local Events, John F Gray & Stephen Elsden, DSC 2000, £14.95

Schools Funding Guide, 2nd edn, Nicola Eastwood, Anne Mountfield & Louise Walker, DSC 2001, £19.95

Tried and Tested Ideas for Local Fundraising Events, 3rd edn, Sarah Passingham, DSC 2003, £16.95

Voluntary Sector Legal Handbook, 2nd edn, Sandy Adirondack & James Sinclair Taylor, DSC 2001, £50 (voluntary organisations) £80 (others)

6 TRUSTS AND FOUNDATIONS

Grantmaking trusts, sometimes known as foundations, are independent grant-making bodies. They get their income from investments or through their own fundraising. They are set up specifically to give money away for charitable purposes and for community benefit. The web resource www.trustfunding.org.uk (published by DSC) currently states that it has information on over 4,200 trusts which have a total of £3.1 billion a year to distribute. Trusts are a must for most fundraisers – for well-established national and local charities, but also for new and smaller community-based projects. This chapter gives the basic information you need to start fundraising from trusts.

Details of organisations and publications referred to in this chapter are on pages 126–128.

6.1 About trusts

Trusts come in all shapes and sizes, founded for a variety of reasons, with different social and political perspectives, and with different approaches to their grantmaking. Most trusts will not be interested in funding you, but there will be plenty that are. You will need to research carefully which trusts are worth approaching, what aspects of your work they will be interested in, the size of their current grants budget, and the range of their grants.

Most trusts say they receive far more applications than they can possibly support – but not enough good ones. Many generic letters are sent to a large number of trusts without being tailored to each one's particular interests and priorities: these are generally rejected on sight. The key to success is to make sure that each application you send is relevant to the particular trust and that you ask for an appropriate amount. See chapter 15, section 15.1, for advice on writing applications.

Many trusts see their key role as being to support innovation – new ideas, new ways of doing things, new needs, new organisations. They will be wary of anything that could be interpreted as simply compensating for cuts in statutory funding or continuing to fund the core costs of your organisation over a long period. Many organisations owe their existence to progressive trusts that were prepared to shoulder whatever risk there may have been during their early stages. The downside of this, of course, is that in order to obtain funding beyond the initial start-up period (usually a maximum of three years), organisations are compelled to repackage their work into 'new' projects, even if they are still addressing the same long-term need.

Successful fundraising from trusts involves identifying suitable trusts, finding out as much as you can about them, trying to get them interested in your work even before you approach them for money, finding an aspect of your work that they will want to support, and persuading them to say yes. What could be easier than that?

How a trust works

A trust has the following structure:

THE DONOR or FOUNDER
who provides the money
▼
A CONSTITUTION or TRUST DEED
which sets out how the funds are to be managed and distributed
▼
THE TRUSTEES
who ensure that the funds are properly invested and managed, and grants are made according to the terms of the trust deed
▼
ADMINISTRATIVE STAFF
Many of the larger trusts employ staff to manage the affairs of the trust, to deal with applicants and to assess applications (some use external assessors); the staff are accountable to the trustees, who retain the ultimate responsibility for the trust's decisions. However, the majority of trusts have no paid administrative staff at all.
▼
THE APPLICANT
who applies for a grant from the trust (that's you!)

The diversity of trusts

- The largest trust by far (after the Big Lottery Fund) is the Wellcome Trust. It gives mainly to medical and scientific research, and so is not relevant to the majority of fundraisers. Trusts like the the Garfield Weston Foundation have much broader remits – in 2004–05 it gave over £38 million in grants across a wide range of charitable purposes. At the other end of the scale are much smaller (usually local) bodies which may have just a few hundred pounds a year to distribute.
- Trusts may have an international remit, such as the Aga Khan Foundation, which funds in East Africa and Asia, and Comic Relief, which works predominantly in Africa (but also in the UK). Trusts may give nationally, such as the Joseph Rowntree Foundation or the Lloyds TSB Foundation. Or they may operate regionally or locally. Some local trusts are very large and if you are fortunate enough to work within their beneficial area, they may be your best source of funds. Not all areas of the UK are as well provided for as others in terms of local trusts, so the luck of geography can play a significant part in successful fundraising.
- Some trusts support a wide range of activities, while others specialise in providing funding for a particular type of work. Part of the knack of tailoring an application lies in identifying an area of work that a trust will support and highlighting that aspect in your proposal.
- Some trusts will give grants to individuals. Others only fund organisations. Many limit their support to registered charities.

6.2 Understanding how trusts work

There are various key factors that influence how each trust operates, and you need to develop an understanding of these in order to increase your chances of success.

Where trusts get their money from

Most trusts are established with a capital sum provided by a founder during his or her lifetime or in their will. This could be cash, shares in a company or even land. The founder could be a successful business person – such as Paul Hamlyn or David Sainsbury, who have both set up major foundations – but there are also many trusts set up by individuals with much more modest sums.

Some trusts are set up with donations from the public. The various royal Jubilee Trusts are examples, as are the Winston Churchill Memorial Trust and the Diana, Princess of Wales Memorial Fund, both of which were set up in memory of famous individuals.

Some trusts have no permanent funds, but rely on continuing fundraising to provide them with money for distribution. The largest of these are the BBC's Children in Need and Comic Relief, both of which raise money through major television appeals.

Some trusts are set up by companies as a vehicle for their charitable giving. Depending on the way this is done, some are truly independent, whilst others are obliged to follow company policy in their grantmaking (in which case you should probably approach them in the way that you would approach a company – see chapter 8).

How a trust is founded can have a significant impact on its grantmaking. Although the trust's declared area of interest may simply be recorded as 'General charitable purposes', the founder's wishes, sometimes set out in a letter attached to the founding trust deed, will guide the trustees in their grantmaking. The founder and his or her family may often play a leading role in the affairs of the trust as trustees, supporting concerns and projects which particularly interest them. This is perfectly legitimate; trusts are in one sense 'private bodies' set up for 'public benefit'. They are not, however, private in the sense of being permitted to keep information about their assets and grantgiving to themselves. Like other charities, all charitable trusts in England and Wales must be registered with the Charity Commission and file their annual accounts according to the requirements of the Statement of Recommended Practice (SORP). Over time, the founder's influence can diminish as outside trustees are appointed, which has happened with the Joseph Rowntree and Nuffield Foundations.

Examples of major trusts established by successful business people

- Esmée Fairbairn Foundation (Ian Fairbairn, M & G Group, unit trusts)
- The Gatsby Charitable Trust (David Sainsbury, J Sainsbury, supermarkets)
- The Paul Hamlyn Foundation (Paul Hamlyn, publishing)
- The Mackintosh Foundation (Cameron Mackintosh, musical theatre)
- The Wates Foundation (the Wates family, builders)
- The Garfield Weston Foundation (Garfield Weston, Associated British Foods)
- The Westminster Foundation (Duke of Westminster, landowner)
- The Wolfson Foundation (Sir Isaac Wolfson, retailing)

The trust's objects and policies

The trust deed, governing or founding document, sets out the objects or purposes of the trust, defining what can and cannot be supported. Objects can be very broad, defined only as general charitable or educational purposes, or quite specific: one of the objects of the Childwick Trust, for example, is to support charities for people who work or have worked in the mining industry in South Africa; and the Great Britain Sasakawa Foundation exists to support links between Great Britain and Japan.

The trustees can also decide on a policy and priorities for their grantmaking (so long as this falls within the objects of the trust). So a trust set up for the advancement of education might decide to give all its money for literacy and numeracy, or as bursaries to young people aged 16 to 18 in order to encourage them to stay on at school, or to primary schools to buy computers. You need to check to see whether your application falls within the trust's current grant policy and priorities. It is also worth looking at what grants it has given in the recent past, since this may help you to identify the trustees' preferences – although these can change from year to year; and just because a trust gave to a particular type of project one year, it may not intend supporting similar schemes the next year. It is also possible to misinterpret why a particular grant was given; funding for a church choir may have been given because the trust supports music, or it may simply support church-related activities, in which case there is little point in applying for money for a school music project. Not all areas of charitable work are equally supported; trusts determine their own priorities for giving, which may not relate to current needs or issues in society.

The beneficial area

Many trusts are restricted in where they can give support. Some can give throughout the UK, or even throughout the world. Many can only give locally. For example, the City Parochial Foundation and Trust for London, which work together, can only give grants for the benefit of the people of London, and the Cripplegate Foundation for those who live or work in South Islington and parts of the City of London. If you are lucky enough to operate within the beneficial area of a large trust then your chances of success are greater than if you are based in an area which is less well-provided for.

Community foundations

Community foundations work in a specific geographical area to provide grants for local charitable activity. They have been active in the UK since the 1980s, although the idea originated in America in 1914. Community foundations operate in two main ways:

- by building an endowment of capital given by companies, trusts and individuals in their area, and from legacies. The income from this is then used to make grants;
- they work with other donors to help them distribute their money more effectively. Donors can direct their funds to a favoured cause or within a

specified geographical area. Themed funds can address a particular issue, such as crime prevention, and projects can be supported with donations from several sources.

Community foundations are being promoted, supported and trained by Community Foundation Network. This is how they describe their role:

Community Foundation Network (CFN) aims to promote the concept of community foundations in the UK, stimulate and support their growth and best practice, and give support to individual community foundations and their networking with others.

CFN's objective is to ensure a network of thriving community foundations throughout the UK, each one able to strengthen their local community through strategic grantmaking and excellent service provision to donors.

To achieve its purpose, CFN upholds a number of external values, including:

- *proactively providing leadership, specialist knowledge and support to members and to the broader community foundation field;*
- *sharing and promoting knowledge and best practice within the worldwide community foundation movement.*

Community trusts are growing in importance, and at an impressive rate. In 1999–2000 there were 29 fully operational community foundations. Now at the time of writing in 2007, CFN claims a membership of approximately 60, which for the year 2005–06 gave out grants totalling £70 million. They can be key funders of local work, and may also give advice on raising money from other local trusts. You may even be able to use their support as a lever to obtain further funding; a national trust is likely to react more positively to your application if you can demonstrate that you have already successfully raised money locally.

Read the guidelines before applying

Most of the larger trusts publish guidelines to what they will and will not fund. It is important to read these before applying to see whether what you are proposing fits within their policies and does not fall within their exclusions. For example, the Bridge House Trust was established by the Corporation of London to distribute money surplus to what is required for maintaining Blackfriars, Southwark, London and Tower Bridges. The overall object of the trust is to apply these funds for the benefit of Greater London, but if you examine its guidelines more closely, you will see that its main grants policy is to concentrate giving in the following five areas, in Greater London:

1   access for disabled people
2   improving the quality of London's environment

3   children and young people

4   assistance to older people in the community

5   strengthening the voluntary and community sector.

It cannot fund:

- political parties
- political lobbying
- non-charitable activities
- work that does not benefit the inhabitants of Greater London.

It also does not fund:

- individuals
- grantmaking bodies to make grants on its behalf
- schools, universities and other educational establishments (except where they are undertaking ancillary charitable activities specifically directed towards one of the agreed priority areas)
- medical or academic research
- churches or other religious bodies where the monies will be used for religious purposes
- hospitals
- projects which have already taken place or building work which has already been completed
- statutory bodies.

Large and small trusts

Larger trusts are managed professionally and tend to have a clerk, secretary, administrator or director (the title varies), who is in executive charge of the grants programme, together with some administrative support. Some very large trusts have a team of specialist or regional grants officers. The director will report to a board of trustees. The trustees remain responsible for policy and grant decisions, but base their decisions on the recommendations of their staff. Most of the larger trusts have well-thought-through policies for what they are interested in supporting. Applications are assessed according to these and there is no point in applying if you cannot demonstrate that your project or organisation fits within the guidelines.

Smaller trusts are often run by the family or the individual who set them up. They may be administered by a firm of lawyers or accountants who will prepare the accounts, and sometimes provide an address for correspondence. They often do not employ professional staff to assess grant applications. Many simply support the interests of the founder or family that established the trust. Some will not even consider applications received from charities they have no contact or connection with – so good contacts with their trustees or some form of personal or local connections are often vital.

How grant decisions are made

Most trusts respond to the requests they receive for support, rather than seeking out projects they would like to support. So the first stage in the grant-making process is receiving a proposal from an applicant. What happens next depends on the size of the trust. Larger trusts will have a procedure for assessing applications, which could include:

- the trust director or a specialist grants officer assessing the application and making a recommendation;
- undertaking a site visit or meeting with the applicant;
- engaging a consultant to investigate and report (which would only be done for very large applications).

A report with recommendations is prepared for the trustees, with the final decision being made at the next trustees' meeting. Some of the very large trusts allow their staff discretion to decide smaller grants without reference to the trustees.

Smaller trusts tend to do everything through the trustees. Trustees read all the applications they receive, reject clearly inappropriate ones and discuss together which they will support, based on the information in your application.

Most capitally endowed trusts (the vast majority) distribute income as grants each year. On average – and as a very rough rule of thumb – this equates to around 5% of the value of the total endowment. However, income can vary considerably and is dependent on interest rates for cash, stock market performance for investments and chargeable rent levels for property.

Grant levels can be affected by other factors. For instance, some trusts will reinvest a portion of income to ensure the value of the capital endowment is not eroded by inflation. Other trusts may actually use some capital to increase the value of grants they can make (if the trust deed allows this).

A few trust deeds define how long the trust will exist. It is likely such time-limited trusts will distribute more capital in grants as the end date approaches, possibly leading to higher grant levels.

If a settlor (the person who established the trust) is particularly motivated by a cause they may make additional contributions to the trust in order to support at a substantially higher level than might appear possible from the trust's normal activity. This is rare and only likely if your organisation enjoys a very good relationship with the settlor.

6.3 Some important considerations

Charitable status of the applicant

Almost all trusts can only support charitable work. However, there are a few trusts which can support non-charitable work, the main ones being the Barrow Cadbury Trust and the Joseph Rowntree Reform Trust, both of which are associated with larger charitable trusts. This requirement to support charitable work does not mean that trusts can only give to registered charities, but they must support work for public benefit. Many trusts, however, have a policy of only giving to registered charities. Newly established organisations that have not yet obtained charitable status, or those which have decided not to register as charities, will not be able to obtain a grant directly from such trusts, although you can arrange for another charity to receive the grant on your behalf (some community foundations and local councils for voluntary service are prepared to do this).

There are also trusts which have been set up to support individuals in need or to give grants for educational purposes (see *A Guide to Grants for Individuals in Need* and *The Educational Grants Directory*). Some trusts also provide bursaries to individuals – for example the Prince's Trust supports young people, the Winston Churchill Memorial Trust provides bursaries for people to undertake study visits, and unLTD provides awards for people who wish to create change in their communities. Many trusts which make grants to organisations specifically exclude grants to individuals.

National or local projects

Many large trusts have a national or international remit. They support national projects, important local projects, or projects of national significance (such as pioneering local work that has implications for the way things are done in other parts of the country).

Some national trusts also make purely local grants. Many have a particular interest in supporting projects close to where they are based. Some also have defined areas of the country where they give their local support (on the basis that it is more effective to concentrate their resources on a particular area, and that it is difficult to assess applications from all parts of the country). For example, the Wates Foundation supports projects in South London. Such trusts usually also want to focus on need, so any local project should try to make a convincing case that local needs are particularly pressing – comparative local data, possibly from census figures, can be useful.

Some trusts have been established specifically to make grants in a local area, so if yours is a local project, you should start by finding out what trusts are active in your area. Trusts are, unfortunately, distributed unevenly around the country. The majority are based in the London and the South East. Some other areas are also quite well served. For example, although there are few trusts in Manchester or Wales, there are thriving trust networks in Scotland, Liverpool and Birmingham. If you come from an area with few local trusts, you will naturally find it harder to get trust support for a local project, although there are moves to encourage trusts that can give nationally to look further afield. You could try making a case to a national trust based not just on need, but on the lack of available local trust funding to meet that need.

One-off or continuing support

Most trusts either make one-off grants or give regular support for only a limited period (usually no more than three years, although a few trusts fund for longer than this), as they want to keep themselves free to respond to new requests. Many have a maximum grant limit. Trusts also want to feel that, unless you are proposing to eradicate a problem altogether, the work will continue once their support has ended. You therefore need to be clear about the long-term goals and funding strategy of the project and the organisation. Where the proposal is for a building or to buy some equipment, you need to show how the facility will be used and how the running costs will be met. Where the grant is towards running costs, you should show how you are going to fund your work once the grant ends, i.e. your 'exit strategy'.

Whatever kind of grant you get, if you are able to show that you have used the money effectively, the trust may well be willing to support another aspect of your work once the current funding runs out – although some trusts don't give a second grant to an organisation until at least a year has elapsed since the first grant terminated.

Grants or loans

Most trusts simply make cash grants. Some may make interest-free or low-interest loans, but you must be able to repay the loan and this can only happen if there is some return expected from the project. The Charities Aid Foundation (through its Venturesome Programme) and the Triodos Bank have set up social investment funds specifically to make loans to charities.

Trust preferences

Every trust has a different approach. Some prefer to give start-up or 'seed' money; others prefer the development of more established projects. Some favour capital projects; others revenue. Some prefer safer, more conservative work; whilst others are radical and pioneering. Some want to make a large number of small grants; whilst others concentrate on a few major projects.

Almost all trusts prefer to support specific projects and initiatives rather than to make a contribution to general costs. Terminology such as 'core costs' and 'overheads' has historically been used inconsistently by both fundraisers and funders, but a useful publication is produced by acevo (Association of Chief Executives of Voluntary Organisations) *Funding our Future: Core Costs Revisited*, which may help you to clarify what a trust is prepared to consider:

- **development funding**, through which the internal infrastructure costs of an organisation are met for a time in order for it to grow and develop;
- **strategic funding**, through which the funder recognises the need for an organisation to exist and is prepared to contribute over an agreed period;
- **full project funding**, in which all reasonable associated costs are met as part of a funding package.

An acceptance in particular of the term 'full project funding' by trusts will be enormously helpful in enabling organisations to apply for sufficient funding to cover the real costs of a project.

To summarise, in order to have the best chance of success, make sure that your application matches:

- *the trust's policies and priorities.* There is no point sending an application to a trust which has no interest in that sort of work;
- *their scale of grantmaking.* There is no point approaching a tiny trust for a large grant, or a major one for a small item of expenditure;
- *their ethos and approach.* You will have the greatest success with those trusts that share your outlook and values.

6.4 Getting started with trusts

The Directory of Social Change publishes a range of grant directories on trust giving for fundraisers, including its own *Guides to the Major Trusts* and *Guides to Local Trusts,* and the Charities Aid Foundation's *Directory of Grant Making Trusts.* The CAF directory covers more trusts, and reports what the trusts themselves say about their policies and grants, whereas the DSC guides include the results of independent research and analysis of what the trusts actually do in practice. They also go into greater detail, particularly for the larger trusts, where most of the money is.

All the information from both the CAF and DSC databases of trusts is also available on a single, comprehensive CD ROM which, although it is more expensive, makes the process of searching a lot easier and quicker. Or you can subscribe to the website version of the database, www.trustfunding.org.uk. Another useful database is maintained by an organisation called

FunderFinder. If you are short of funds, the directories and CD ROMs can be accessed at the DSC library and some local councils for voluntary service.

The internet will also give you access to a vast amount of information. Many trusts have their own website. Organisations such as the Association of Charitable Foundations (ACF) also have sites, which can provide useful information.

Finding the right trusts: a step-by-step approach

1 First of all, find out what contact you have had with any trusts previously, and whether they were successful. For applications that failed, try to find out why. Trusts that have supported you before are often likely to support you again – especially if you have done a really good job with their money.

2 Those that have turned you down are also likely prospects for future support. You have already identified them as being potentially interested in your work – but as yet, you have failed to convince them of the value of supporting you. Try to find something really interesting for them to support, and present a better case next time.

3 Go through the directories of grantmaking trusts to identify and match possible funders with aspects of your organisation's work. Divide the trusts in two ways:
    a) those that seem most likely to give to you
       those that might just be interested
       those that it is not worth contacting
    b) larger trusts which could make a reasonably sized grant
       smaller trusts where you could only expect to receive a small amount.

Your final contact list may only contain 20–30 trusts, but this is likely to be much more successful than a scattershot approach. Concentrate your efforts on approaching those that are most likely to support you. Find out whether the trusts on the list produce an annual report or guidelines for applicants; these can often be accessed on the web. Thoroughly research your application from the available information. Find out whether any of your trustees, volunteers or staff members have good links or personal contacts with any of the trusts you are planning to approach. Personal contact can be very useful and helpful when checking that your application is appropriately worded.

Trusts are unlikely to give a large grant to organisations they have never heard of. If you are looking for large sums, it may be better to apply for something small now, spend it well, then go back for something more substantial. Or maybe work in partnership with a larger, longer-established and better-known organisation. Their partnership with you will boost your credibility.

6.5 Making contact

Getting in touch with trusts is a process which has several stages:

1 General PR to make people aware of your organisation and its work, so that when you approach a trust, it has heard of you and understands the importance of your work. You can send copies of your annual report or relevant publications well before you intend to raise money; get coverage of your work and achievements in the media, and send copies of this to people who might be interested; or participate in radio or TV discussions, or in specialist conferences (as a speaker or asking questions from the floor).

2 A phone call to establish contact. Ask whether there is a best time in the trust's year to apply, whether the trust can support your type of work, and the procedure for applying for a grant. You may be able to get a clearer picture of the sort of work that the trust is likely to want to support. Find out the deadline for applications. Many trusts meet quarterly; but smaller trusts may only meet annually, or may not respond at all to applications from people and organisations not known to them. Sometimes the trust will suggest that you delay your application until the next meeting, as there are just too many requests this time for your proposal to stand any chance of success.

3 A written application setting out your request. Find out first whether there is an application form or whether a particular format is required. Make sure that you attach a copy of your latest accounts, together with your annual report (if you have one) or some other description of your organisation and its work (see chapter 15, section 15.1, for advice on writing a fundraising application).

4 Ask for an appropriate amount. Use your research to find out typical levels of grant that the trust makes and tailor your request accordingly. Some trusts make larger grants to larger national charities, and smaller grants to smaller or more local projects.

5 A trust will often back the ideas and energy of a key individual in your organisation. If you have such individuals, emphasise their strengths in your proposal, include a CV, and try to get that individual to meet the trust.

6 For a large proposal where you are unlikely to get all the money from one trust, think carefully about what to ask for. You could invite trusts to match the giving of another trust, or to money raised from elsewhere. For example, if you are seeking support for a community venture, getting the local council to pay for the staff and premises and asking the trust to cover the project costs can be an attractive way for both to give their support. Or you might try to get four trusts each to contribute a quarter of the project costs, where the total you require is beyond the reach of any one of them.

7 You might then telephone to check that your application has arrived, and to ask whether any further information is required. You might try to get the staff or trustees to visit you. It will considerably enhance your chances if someone has visited the project. Make sure that everything is working well, that the premises look well-kept and well-used, and that they meet some of your users who can speak enthusiastically about your work and the help you have given them.

8 If you have contact with a particular trustee, try to discuss your proposal with them and enlist their support before the matter comes up for discussion.

9 Remember to say thank you if your application has been successful. Note all the conditions attached to the grant and the reporting requirements – and make sure that you comply with these.

10 Keep in regular touch, and let the trust(s) know how the project is going, and tell them about anything that has been particularly successful. This helps build a relationship with them, which may lead to further support.

11 Keep a record of all the approaches you make, both letters and phone calls, and of the responses. This will be helpful when you approach them next time and avoid duplication and over-frequent responses.

12 If you find you have raised more money than you need as a result of approaching several trusts, be truthful and go back to them with alternative suggestions. Offer to extend the length of the project or improve it, rather than have to repay the money. They will almost always agree.

What trusts are looking for

1 Can you define the problem clearly?

2 How will you make a difference? And does it work?

3 Can you show what difference will be made?

4 How long will you need before you can demonstrate an impact?

5 How do you see the problem and your approach to it fitting in with the trust's priorities?

6 What skills will be needed for the project? Can you demonstrate that you have them? If not, how will you get them?

7 Have you supplied details of your training and past experience, if this is relevant?

8 What is innovative about the project? And how far can the innovative aspects be replicated in other situations?

9 If the project isn't innovative, why does the application merit a grant?

10 How do you propose to evaluate and disseminate any practical experience, outcomes and lessons learned from the project?

11   Do you have a clear management structure?

12   Does the application come from or clearly have the support of the senior people in the organisation – both the senior staff and the management board?

13   Have you supplied your latest annual accounts? And do they give a picture of a well-run, effective organisation?

14   What are the major sources of income for your work at the moment, and will these continue? If not, what are you planning to do to secure your organisation's future?

15   Is your budget realistic? Many applications undercost their projects.

16   What proportion of the total you require is being requested from the trust?

17   Where do you propose to obtain the balance? Have you already made other applications? Have any been successful? Are any pending, and when will the outcome be known?

18   What if you can't raise the whole of the budget you have proposed? Will you be able to work on less? Will you have to adjust your plans? Will you go ahead?

19   What will happen when the trust's grant runs out? Is there a strategy for obtaining continuing funding? Or will the project become self-sufficient or terminate at that point?

20   When do you need the funds? Most trusts have a decision process which takes several months to receive, evaluate and decide on the application. Many applicants apply far too late.

These 20 questions were adapted from a leaflet given to applicants by the Joseph Rowntree Charitable Trust. They are the sorts of questions you will need to address in your written application (see chapter 15) and in any subsequent discussions with a grants assessor.

Resources and further information

See also general lists at the end of the book.

Organisations

Association of Charitable Foundations (ACF)

Central House
14 Upper Woburn Place
London WC1H 0AE
www.acf.org.uk
Tel. 020 255 4499
e-mail acf@acf.org.uk

This is a network for trusts, which produces a newsletter, runs an annual conference for members, and organises special interest groups to keep members informed on particular areas of charitable work. Its website provides links to its members' sites and their funding information.

Community Foundation Network
Arena House
66–68 Pentonville Road
London N1 9HS
Tel. 020 7713 9326
e-mail network@communityfoundations.org.uk

FunderFinder
65 Raglan Road
Leeds LS2 9DZ
www.funderfinder.org.uk
Tel. 0113 243 3008
Maintains a database on disk to match your project proposals with funding opportunities. Your national association or your local council for voluntary service may have a copy you can use.

Publications

The following publications are available from the Directory of Social Change. Prices were correct at the time of writing, but may be subject to change.

The main grants directories are:

The Directory of Grant Making Trusts, CAF/DSC 2005, £95 (New edition to be published at the end of 2007.)

The Grant-making Trusts CD ROM (all the trusts from the CAF and DSC databases on one CD ROM), developed by FunderFinder for DSC 2006, £150 + VAT

A Guide to Local Trusts: four volumes covering local trusts in the North of England, the Midlands, the South of England, and Greater London, DSC 2006, £29.95 each

Guide to the Major Trusts, Vol 1: the top 400 trusts (making grants annually of at least £300,000), DSC 2005, £34.95 (New edition to be published at the end of 2007.)

Guide to the Major Trusts, Vol 2: the next 1,200 trusts (making grants annually of at least £30,000), DSC 2005, £34.95 (New edition to be published at the end of 2007.)

A Guide to Scottish Trusts: provides comprehensive coverage of trust-giving in Scotland, DSC 2006, £27.95

The Welsh Funding Guide: provides comprehensive coverage of trust and other giving in Wales, DSC 2005, £27.95

www.trustfunding.org.uk; www.grantsforindividuals.org.uk; www.companygiving.org.uk: these subscription websites allow you to access the same range of information as the Grant-making Trusts CD ROM, but are updated throughout the year. Annual subscription £160 + VAT (charities and voluntary organisations) £215 + VAT (statutory and commercial)

Directories of trusts that will fund individuals:

The Educational Grants Directory, DSC 2006, £34.95

A Guide to Grants for Individuals in Need, DSC 2006, £34.95

Specialist funding guides include:

Arts Funding Guide, 6th edn DSC 2002, £22.95

Environmental Funding Guide, DSC 1998, £8.95

International Development Directory, DSC 2001, £19.95

Sports Funding Guide, 2nd edn, DSC 1999, £16.95

Youth Funding Guide, 2nd edn, DSC 2002, £19.95

The following handbooks may also be useful:

Avoiding the Wastepaper Basket, 2nd edn, a practical guide for applying to grant-making trusts, Tim Cook, LVSC 1998, £5.50

Find the Funds, Christopher Carnie, DSC/CAF 2000, £16.95

Fundraising from Grant-making Trusts and Foundations, Karen Gilchrist & Margo Horsley, DSC/CAF 2000, £14.95

Writing Better Fundraising Applications, 3rd edn, Michael Norton & Mike Eastwood, DSC 2002, £18.95

Other publications

Funding our Future: Core Costs Revisited, 3rd edn, acevo 2004, £15.00

7 THE NATIONAL LOTTERY

The National Lottery is now the largest single source of funds for voluntary organisations, and for arts, sports and heritage projects. Between 1994 and 2005 some £19 billion was raised for 'good causes'. The Lottery is of such size and importance that many organisations gear a substantial part of their fundraising effort towards getting support from the various Lottery Distribution Bodies. This chapter gives an overview of how these operate.

Details of organisations and publications referred to in this chapter are on pages 142–143.

7.1 About the National Lottery

The National Lottery was launched in 1994, and rapidly established itself as a key funder of voluntary activity. There were early worries about the potential impact – competition with existing charity fundraising, and in particular longstanding charity lotteries; the encouragement of gambling; and the transfer of money from the poor to the rich.

Many voluntary organisations have applied for Lottery grants and many have succeeded. Over 50,000 UK charities and voluntary groups were helped by money from the lottery between 1994 and 2003. However, it takes time and effort to put together a good application, and the assessment process is a rigorous and demanding one.

7.2 How the National Lottery operates

The National Lottery is operated under licence until 2009 by Camelot plc.

Distribution of each £1 of Lottery income

Of every £1 spent on a lottery ticket, 50p goes on prizes, 28p on good causes, 12p to Camelot (0.5p profit), 5p to the Treasury and 5p to retailers. The 1993 Lottery Act set out five good cause areas that would benefit from money raised by the National Lottery: Arts, Sports, Heritage, Charities and voluntary organisations, and projects to celebrate the Millennium. At the time the money was shared equally by all good causes. In 1998, the government created the New Opportunities Fund (NOF) to fund health, education and the environment. NOF received a third of all good cause money.

In 2004, the Big Lottery Fund (BIG) was created, merging the Community Fund – originally known as the National Lottery Charities Board – and the New Opportunities Fund to create one body. The Big Lottery Fund receives 50% of all Lottery funds available for good causes.

The National Lottery Distribution Bodies are independent. They do however distribute public funds and their distribution policies are subject to a level of statutory control from the government. Their grantmaking is under close public and media scrutiny and is often the subject of wide-ranging debate. This has centred not only on certain recipients of grants but also on the short-term nature of revenue funding, and historically a perceived focus on capital projects in the areas of arts, sports and heritage, often seen as elitist.

In response to complaints about the short-term nature of their funding, a number of BIG's programmes now provide funding up to five years. Projects are also commonly asked to provide a realistic exit strategy that plans out how the project will continue after the funding from BIG has finished. One possible effect of this is that requests for larger amounts and for longer periods are made, which, over time, might lead to funding fewer, albeit better, projects.

The National Lottery operator (Camelot) does not have any influence on the distribution of the funds, although it has set up its own foundation (which operates in the same way as those of other prominent companies). In 2004 it gave £2.5 million in community contributions, concentrating on combating disadvantage (see *A Guide to UK Company Giving*).

7.3 The Big Lottery Fund (BIG)

In June 2004, the Community Fund and the New Opportunities Fund merged to become the Big Lottery Fund. It distributes 50% of all National Lottery good causes funding across the UK to the value of approximately £600 million per year. The responsibilities of the Millennium Commission have also transferred to this body, including its ability to fund major transformational projects. Lottery grantmaking is a 'devolved' activity and there are separate locally managed BIG programmes in England, Scotland, Wales and Northern Ireland. The first wave of funding within its new framework runs from 2005 to 2009.

Before the New Opportunities Fund and the Community Fund merged, the priorities of the New Opportunities Fund were set by the government. There was some concern that money from the Big Lottery Fund would be spent on government-led initiatives, betraying the longstanding policy of additionality (i.e. that Lottery funding should not substitute for Exchequer funding). However, this has not yet proved to be the case and the level of control over what BIG delivers is relatively loose. The Big Lottery Fund has undertaken that at least one third of the money will be delivered through 'demand-led' (see below for more details) and 'lightly prescribed' programmes and the remainder through a range of strategic programmes. Critics however say that many of the 'demand-led' programmes are in fact far from lightly prescribed, for example those restricted to advice, infrastructure or community buildings. This is covered in more detail under the 'Open application, demand-led programmes' section, page 132.

The Big Lottery Fund has now established two operational centres in Newcastle and Birmingham to administer funding applications and to provide core functions across the Fund. This is a clear change from the Community Fund's regional offices, which undertook application assessment and grant management. However, the Big Lottery Fund still has a strong regional presence (in each of the nine government regions), and its staff look to develop partnerships with local organisations, key regional stakeholders such as Government Offices, Regional Development Agencies and other Lottery distribution bodies.

BIG's mission is to 'bring real improvements to communities, and to the lives of people most in need'. It now calls itself an 'outcomes funder', which basically means that it is most interested in the difference that your project is trying to make to people's lives rather than its actual activities. BIG is clear about the wider changes that it wants its funding to make overall and each of its programmes has specific outcomes it wants to achieve through the projects it funds.

Underlying all BIG's programmes are three key themes:

1 Supporting community learning and creating opportunity
2 Promoting community safety and cohesion
3 Promoting well-being.

In England, these underlying themes are supported by four outcomes which BIG would like its funding to achieve:

Outcome 1: People having better chances in life, with better access to training and development to improve their life skills.

Outcome 2: Stronger communities, with more active citizens, working together to tackle their problems.

Outcome 3: Improved rural and urban environments, which communities are better able to access and enjoy.

Outcome 4: Healthier and more active people and communities.

To get funding from a programme you will need to show that your project will help BIG achieve one or more of the programme specific outcomes (in the case of some programmes, such as Community Buildings, you need to achieve at least five out of the eight programme outcomes). You will also be expected to set out your own outcomes for your project. During the assessment process the quality of your outcomes, in relation to the amount of money you are asking for, will be of high importance. If you are successful your project will be monitored by BIG, based on the outcomes you have set yourself. BIG has produced a document called 'The difference your project makes', which is a very useful guide to taking on an outcomes approach and can be downloaded from its website.

BIG is also committed to the principle of full cost recovery, which means that it will pay all overhead costs, and will provide funding for all relevant costs associated with delivering the projects. There is a particular interest in also paying for marketing and fundraising costs to ensure that the project becomes self-sustaining in the longer term. Grants can be for up to five years.

The programmes that most charities will be interested in are those that are referred to in BIG's jargon as 'demand-led'. This basically means that there is an open and competitive process by which organisations can apply, so long as they fit the programme criteria. Some of these 'demand-led' programmes are open to almost any group to apply, for almost any purpose (what they refer to as 'lightly prescribed'), such as Reaching Communities, whilst others are more specific about who is eligible and about what kind of work will be funded, such as Advice Plus, Basis and Well-being. Other programmes which are responding to a very specific, high level, strategic need, such as Children's Play Facilities and Community Libraries, are ring-fenced for grants for specific organisations to apply to – such as local authorities.

7.4 Open application, demand-led programmes

Many of the programmes, whether they are 'lightly-prescribed' or strategic are delivered in a 'demand-led' way. The key issue here is the spectrum within which the Big Lottery Fund's strategic programmes are being delivered. Awards for All should be seen at one end of the spectrum and direct contract grants with strategic organisations (like the grant it has awarded to the Children's Play Council, under the Children's Play initiative, to run 'Play England', which supports infrastructure development for Children's Play and will make a major long-term difference to how play is recognised, supported and delivered in future) at the other. Where a programme is on the spectrum is determined by how discrete an intervention it is (and will make) (i.e. to what degree it allows the Big Lottery Fund to achieve its goals).

Since announcing its funding portfolio, the Big Lottery Fund has developed a set of funding programmes which are responding to particular needs and looking to achieve certain outcomes, and are being delivered through a range of models. Details of the different programmes regularly change; it is therefore advisable to refer to the BIG website for the most up-to-date information.

Whilst Reaching Communities is seen as a real opportunity to access Big Lottery Fund money by the widest possible number of stakeholders, it is a highly over-subscribed programme, with a consequent low chance of success. BIG has therefore suggested that if a project fits within one of the more specific streams, it is better to apply there, or contact the lead agency delivering the funding first before applying.

Submission and assessment of applications

Each programme has a different application process, though they are all on the same 'outcome' based principles. The details for specific programmes can be found on the Big Lottery Fund website.

As mentioned above there are different delivery models that BIG uses for different programmes. Some of the main ones are listed below.

1 Outline proposal form and full application (e.g. Reaching Communities, Young People's Fund).
2 Two full application stages (e.g. BASIS, Community Buildings).
3 One full application stage (e.g. Advice Plus).
4 Portfolio partners – this is where organisations are asked to develop a portfolio of projects that will address an already specified need.
5 Award Partners – this is where organisations are asked to apply to administer grants to other organisations to address a pre-specified need.

Although all application procedures are slightly different, they have much in common. Once you have filled out an application form (in the case of programmes such as Reaching Communities, where there is an outline proposal form, you will only receive a full application after the outline proposal form has been approved) each application then goes through a rigorous process of assessment. This process differs significantly from that for the Community Fund where each question was ranked and scored. It is now the case that each application is looked at more holistically, rather than being based on whether particular questions were answered correctly.

As already explained, the process for different programmes varies widely. However, below are some general pointers, which are true for most of them.

- The applicant completes the form and meets all the requirements. Besides answering all the questions, you must submit a number of other documents, which are listed on the checklist at the back of each application. These will include up-to-date annual accounts, three months' worth of original bank statements, and signature pages.
- Stage 1 assessment by a grants officer (GO). Inadequately completed applications and applications from ineligible organisations are rejected at this stage.
- Full assessment by a GO, which includes an interview, normally over the telephone, but sometimes face to face or by e-mail.
- If there is a second application stage, those who pass the first assessment stage are invited to fill out the second application.
- Consideration by the Grants Committee for the specific programme.

Each of the application forms are slightly different and at the time of writing many of the questions on many of them were quite repetitive.

Applications will be allocated to a GO, and an effort is made to keep the same GO on the same application all the way through the assessment process. Full assessment by the GO is usually carried out over the telephone during an interview, which lasts approximately one to one and a half hours. A time is agreed when the interview will take place, and it is important that the right people are present to ensure that a correct presentation of the organisation and the proposal is given.

The criteria for each programme against which the application will be assessed are published in guidance notes. There are two sets of criteria for all demand-led programmes:

1 The project outcomes –
   a meet an identified need, and
   b help to achieve the programme outcomes.
2 The organisation can deliver the project well and achieve the proposed outcomes.

Types of grant

There are a number of restrictions relating to the size and types of grants you can get from the Big Lottery Fund. You can apply for:

- one, two, three, four or five-year funding
- some or all of the project's costs
- revenue costs (including core costs, as long as they are not being paid for by anyone else)
- capital costs.

You cannot normally apply for:

- endowments
- loans or loan payments
- retrospective funding
- making up deficits
- promoting particular religious beliefs
- sports, art or heritage projects (as these are the responsibility of other Lottery boards).

No grants will be awarded which replace (or may replace) lost statutory funding, nor where the money will subsidise statutory provision, nor where it will make up a deficit on a service otherwise funded by the state.

Dealing with an assessment – 10 tips to keep in mind when having your interview with the grants officer

1 Remember that not all GOs have experience of your kind of work. Do not assume too much knowledge of what you are trying to do and how you are proposing to do it.
2 Be prepared and have all your documentation to hand. When you arrange for a convenient time for the GO to call you, ask what information they will be looking for. It will save you time and stress, and make the assessor's job easier, if you are organised and prepared.
3 If they do make a visit remember that GOs are human. There's no need to go overboard but make sure they feel welcome. Cocktails and canapés are too much, but coffee and biscuits will be welcome.
5 Be open and honest. Don't be over the top or try to cover over the cracks. If your organisation is perfect, why do you need the money anyway?
6 See the assessment as a discussion not an interrogation.

7 Use friendly, jargon-free language. Be straightforward in your answers.

8 If your proposal is for a minibus or a building or a salary, you may need to supply copies of your supporting documentation to the GO if they don't have them.

9 Keep a record of what information you have been asked to provide. This will help you make sure after the assessment that you have fulfilled your side of things. At key points in the conversation, ask the assessor to reflect back their understanding of what has been said. This will avoid misunderstandings.

10 At the end of the assessment, do not be afraid to ask questions about anything you are unsure of. It should be a two-way process, and this is your chance to get some first-hand knowledge of when you can expect to hear, what happens next, or anything else that is needed.

Answering the GO's questions

GOs can, and sometimes do, seem to ask about anything and everything. In practice, they want to know the following.

- The basic question: What difference will your project make to people's lives? Are your outcomes SMART – specific, measurable, achievable, realistic and time bound?
- How does the project encourage the people who benefit to be involved in its planning and running? You need to show that you have actively consulted potential users or beneficiaries in the project planning and how they will be part of the management, monitoring and evaluation of what is happening (for example, by setting up a project steering committee which includes users).
- Is the organisation financially sound and well-managed? For example, does it produce annual accounts which show a reasonable surplus? Does it pay its bills on time? Does it have a reasonable amount of money in the bank? Does the management committee meet regularly and review what is going on? Does the organisation have a good track record in delivering the kinds of services it is applying for?
- Is the project properly planned and organised, and will it be staffed appropriately? Is there a project plan? Does it seem sensible? Does it have measurable targets? Are they realistic? Are the management structures clear?
- Is the budget accurate and does it offer value for money? Are all costs covered, including overheads? Do they seem appropriate for the work that is being done? Can you show that this is money being very well spent?
- Will the project be monitored and evaluated in a meaningful way? Are there clear targets for the project? Will there be regular progress reviews? What will happen if targets are not met?

- What will happen when the Lottery money runs out? Will the project simply stop? If you want it to continue, how is it going to be funded?
- Is the organisation committed to equal opportunities? A statement on a piece of paper is not enough. You have to show that you are genuinely representative of your community at management committee level, among the project leaders, volunteers and users. If you are not, what are you doing about it? (The argument that 'I don't think we have those kinds of people here' does not carry much weight.) How many people with disabilities are involved in your activities? What access do you offer to people with special needs?
- Does the organisation have the necessary financial and management experience to cope with the added workload and responsibility associated with a BIG grant?
- Have you researched the work of other voluntary groups in your locality, and are you certain that your project will not duplicate existing services?
- Are you doing what the government should be doing? Are you applying to BIG to make up for lost local authority funding? If so, you won't get a grant.

Getting started

Phone for an application pack for the particular programme you want to apply for or download it from BIG's website. You can apply to as many programmes as you like as long as it is for different projects. Application packs are available in printed and audio form. The guide to each particular round is also available in Braille and large print, in a variety of minority languages, and in a special edition for people with learning difficulties. Soon you will also be able to apply via the website.

Read through the guidelines, paying particular attention to the assessment criteria. Decide on the project you want to do and how it fits with the programme outcomes. On key questions, such as the level of need, the degree of benefit, the extent of user involvement, your equal opportunities approach, and the detailed breakdown of the budget, make detailed notes giving information in more detail than is required for the application form. This can then be referred to during the assessment process when particular questions are asked.

Send off the application form in the envelope provided, retaining a copy for yourself. Then wait to be contacted for the assessment process. You will hear whether your application has been submitted properly and can go forward for assessment. Once the assessment has taken place, you just have to sit and wait for the letter informing you as to whether the application has succeeded or failed.

7.5 Arts grants

Arts grants are handled by the four national Arts Councils – for England, Northern Ireland, Scotland and Wales.

Arts Council England funds activities that benefit people in England or that help artists and arts organisations from England to carry out their work. The grants are for individuals and organisations and are for time-limited activities.

Grants to individuals normally range from £200 to £30,000. The average grant given in 2004–05 was around £5,000. Grants to organisations normally range from £200 up to £100,000. The average grant given in 2004–05 was around £18,000. Grants for national activities normally range from £5,000 up to £200,000. The average grant given here in 2004–05 was around £41,000.

Between 2006 and 2008 Arts Council England will be investing £1.1 billion of public funds from the government and the National Lottery.

There are some exceptions to the geographical coverage mentioned above: for example, when artists are involved in professional development activities in other countries. Applications can be accepted from individuals or organisations based in the European Union.

The agenda for the arts 2006–08 sets six priorities:

- taking part in the arts
- children and young people
- the creative economy
- vibrant communities
- internationalism
- celebrating diversity.

There is a high demand for Arts Council grants. The following may give you an idea of the criteria.

They will look at whether your application:

- is from an individual or organisation that has not received funding from the Arts Council before;
- will benefit areas of the country with social deprivation (social and economic problems) or communities at risk of 'social exclusion' (not being able to take part fully in society because of, for example, poverty, prejudice or isolation);
- will benefit areas of the country or communities that have limited cultural opportunities;
- will contribute to arts development, regionally or nationally (or both).

Applications

There are no deadlines or programme closure dates for grants for the arts as it is a rolling programme. You can apply using the current application pack on the Arts Council website.

7.6 Sports grants

As part of its work to sustain and increase participation in sport and active recreation, Sport England invests in a range of projects across the country, as well as providing advice for partners involved in sport and promoting sport and its benefits.

There are two funding streams – national and community. At a national level, Sport England works with and invests in a range of national funded partners. These include national governing bodies of sport, plus partners with expertise in areas such as coaching, equity and volunteering. Investment is currently prioritised in 31 sports.

Sport England's community – or regional – funding stream is called the Community Investment Fund, or CIF. This is the National Lottery funding available through and managed by the regional offices of Sport England. Funding is awarded through an open application process.

Sport England Community Investment

The Community Investment Fund is the National Lottery funding available from the nine regions of Sport England. Sport England's nine Regional Sports Boards (RSB) make decisions about community funding (grants over £10,000) to projects in their region. These Boards comprise experts from sport and related fields and are responsible for the development of sport in the region. The regions have all developed a plan for sport and investment in their region, detailing their priorities.

When making investment decisions, the Boards look for evidence that projects will help meet these priorities and support Sport England's work to get more people involved in sport. Across the country there is a focus on hard-to-reach groups with the aim of helping them stay involved throughout their lives.

Sport England has produced a range of resources online to help an applicant with their funding application. These include information about a set of milestones that detail what is expected from an applicant – from an initial enquiry through to post-award support and reporting.

The award process

The award process has two stages. At Stage One the applicant completes a 'light touch' online application form. The relevant Sport England region then decides whether to encourage the application onto 'Stage Two', or discourage it. By encouraging an application, the applicant is given access to the Stage Two application form, and nominated a Sport England case officer to liaise with. Having completed the Stage Two application, this is taken to the Regional Sports Board for a funding decision.

Applications

Applications can be made at any time. For further information, ring your national Sports Council or visit the Sport England website (www.sport england.org/index/get_funding.htm) for an application pack.

7.7 Heritage grants

The Heritage Lottery Fund (HLF) enables communities to celebrate, look after and learn more about their diverse heritage. It funds the entire spread of heritage – including buildings, museums, natural heritage and the heritage of cultural traditions and language.

Since 1994 the HLF has awarded over £3.6 billion to more than 22,500 projects across England, Scotland, Wales and Northern Ireland.

The Fund's aims are to:

- conserve and enhance the UK's diverse heritage;
- encourage more people to be involved in and make decisions about their heritage;
- ensure that everyone can learn about, have access to, and enjoy their heritage.

It also aims to bring about a more equitable spread of grants across the UK and work towards this through teams with locally responsive development priorities based in Scotland, Northern Ireland, Wales and the English regions. Its development teams can offer advice and assistance to potential applicants. To date:

- 40% of HLF funding has gone to projects in the 25% most deprived local authority areas;
- 74% of grants have been for sums under £50,000.

And, since 2002 (the start of HLF's current Strategic Plan), nearly 50% of its funding has gone to community and voluntary sector organisations.

Funding programmes

HLF has a range of grant programmes which are designed for different types and sizes of heritage project. Its standard programmes include:

- *Your Heritage (grants of between £5,000 and £50,000)* Grants are available under this scheme for community-focused heritage projects which either conserve and enhance England's diverse heritage or encourage communities to identify, look after and celebrate their heritage. Projects must also increase opportunities for learning about community heritage and open up heritage resources and sites to the widest possible audiences.

- *Heritage Grants (grants of £50,000 or more)* Projects under this scheme must conserve and enhance England's diverse heritage, or encourage more people to be involved in their heritage, or both. They must also make sure that everyone can learn about, have access to and enjoy their heritage.

- *Awards for All scheme (grants of between £300 and £10,000)* HLF also contributes to the Awards for All scheme, which is administered by the Big Lottery Fund. For more information see section 7.8 *Awards for All* and visit www.awardsforall.org.uk.

In addition there are targeted schemes which include:

- *Young Roots (grants of between £5,000 and £25,000)* The scheme aims to involve 13–20 year-olds (up to 25 for those with special needs) in finding out about their heritage, developing skills, building confidence and promoting involvement in the community.

- *Repair Grants for Places of Worship (grants in England are awarded up to £200,000, in Scotland up to £250,000, and in Northern Ireland and Wales up to £100,000).* This programme is designed to help conserve and sustain heritage at risk, through urgent repairs to places of worship. The UK-wide scheme is delivered through programmes in England, Northern Ireland, Scotland and Wales.

- *Landscape Partnerships (grants of between £250,000 and £2 million)* This initiative supports schemes led by partnerships representing a range of heritage and community interests which aim to conserve landscape areas of distinct local character throughout the UK.

- *Parks for People (grants of between £250,000 and £5 million)* This programme helps with the restoration and regeneration of public parks and gardens, including squares, walks and promenades throughout the UK.

- *Townscape Heritage Initiative (grants of between £250,000 and £2 million)* Through this initiative, HLF make grants that help communities to regenerate the historic parts of their towns and cities.

Applications

To apply for a grant from the HLF, you should first obtain an application pack, which gives full details of the process.

HLF requires all applicants to have a constitution and a bank account. If you are a profit-making organisation or a private owner you may not be eligible for a grant.

7.8 Awards for All

This is a small grants programme for local groups administered on a separate regional basis in England, Northern Ireland, Scotland and Wales. The Arts Council England, the Big Lottery fund, The Heritage Lottery fund and Sports England (only BIG and Heritage in Wales) work together and make grants in the range of £300–£10,000; again this range varies regionally.

Applications

Ring 0845 600 20 40 for an application pack or download a copy from the website.

Resources and further information

See also general lists at the end of the book.

Organisations

Arts Council England
www.artscouncil.org.uk/funding
Tel. 0845 300 6200
e-mail enquiries@artscouncil.org.uk
Textphone 020 7973 6564

Awards for All
www.awardsforall.org.uk
Tel. 0845 600 2040

Big Lottery Fund
1 Plough Place
London EC4A 1DE
Tel. 0845 4 10 20 30
Fax 020 7211 1750
Textphone 0845 039 0204
e-mail general.enquiries@biglottery_fund.org.uk

Heritage Lottery Fund
7 Holbein Place
London SW1W 8NR
www.hlf.org.uk
Tel. 020 7591 6000
Fax 020 7591 6271
minicom 020 7591 6255
e-mail enquire@hlf.org.uk

The National Lottery now has a central website and enquiry line:
www.lotteryfunding.org.uk
Tel. 0845 275 0000
Textphone 0845 275 0022

Regional Arts Councils

East
Tel. 0845 300 6200
Textphone 020 7973 6564

East Midlands
Tel. 0845 300 6200
Fax 0115 950 2467

London
Tel. 0845 300 6200
Fax 020 7608 4100
Textphone 020 7973 6564

North East
Tel. 0845 300 6200
Fax 0191 230 1020
Textphone 0191 255 8585

North West
Tel. 0845 300 6200
Fax 0161 834 6969
Textphone 0161 834 9131

South East
Tel. 0845 300 6200
Fax 0870 242 1257
Textphone 01273 710659

South West
Tel. 0845 300 6200
Fax 01392 433503
Textphone 01392 433503

West Midlands
Tel. 0845 300 6200
Fax 0121 643 7239
Textphone 0121 643 2815

Yorkshire
Tel. 0845 300 6200
Fax 01942 466522
Text phone: 01942 438585

Sport England
Community Investment Fund
3rd Floor Victoria House
Bloomsbury Square
London WC1B 4SE
www.sportengland.org
Lottery line: 08458 508 508

Publications

The following publications are available from the Directory of Social Change. Prices were correct at the time of writing, but may be subject to change.

A Guide to UK Company Giving, John Smyth & Denise Lillya, DSC 2007, £39.95

8 COMPANIES

According to *The Guide to UK Company Giving* companies give more than £700 million a year to charity (this excludes funds raised by staff but not matched funding). About half of this is in the form of cash donations; the rest is gifts in kind, secondments, sponsorships, joint promotions and goodwill advertising. This chapter covers all aspects of company giving.

Details of organisations and publications referred to in this chapter are on pages 170–171.

8.1 About company giving

Most companies give out of enlightened self-interest rather than pure altruism or charity, and they see their giving as 'community involvement' or 'community investment'. Though giving by companies is not as significant as that of individuals, government or trusts and foundations, they are still a funding source that should be considered both on a local and national level.

The main reasons why companies give are as follows.

- To create goodwill: to be seen as good citizens in the communities where they operate and as a caring company by society at large.
- To be associated with causes that relate to or are potentially impacted by their business. For example, mining and extraction companies might support environmental projects; pharmaceutical companies, health projects; banks, economic development projects; retailers and insurance companies, projects working with young people and crime prevention; and so on. One motive for this might be to enhance their image, but it could also help build contacts and gain market intelligence and therefore increase sales and consequently profits.
- Because of pressure from the government to support particular initiatives which contribute to government policy.
- Because they are asked and it is expected of them. There can be peer pressure amongst companies in a particular sector of business – banks, oil companies, pharmaceuticals, insurance companies, etc. They are concerned to see that the quantity and quality of their giving is appropriate to their status as a company.

- Because the chair or other senior directors are interested in that cause (and perhaps support it personally).
- Tax: giving to a charity can be done tax effectively. This will be an added benefit for the company, but seldom a determining factor.

For privately owned or family controlled companies their giving is often little different from personal giving. For public companies, where it is the shareholders' funds that are being given away, the company will want to justify its charitable support. You can help them to do this by telling them not just why you want the money, but why supporting you should be of interest to them. You can also tell them about any benefits they will get in return for their money and about the impact that their donation will make on your work.

Remember too that companies like thanks, recognition and good publicity for their support, whether in newsletters, your annual report by having their branding on your materials, or through media coverage.

What companies like to support

There are fashions in what companies like to support. For example, in the 1980s, AIDS/HIV and homelessness were not generally supported, but today companies do support these causes. The following are some of the areas that companies find attractive.

- Important local projects in the areas where the company has a significant presence. Business in the Community organises 'Seeing is Believing' events for business leaders, when they take them to visit local projects to see problems at first hand and explain how they can make a significant contribution.
- Activities that relate to their product. For example, NatWest has a schools programme, Face2Face with Finance, promoting financial literacy, and banks in general target their giving at young people (who are potential customers); BT's Community Connections programme supports projects around the theme of communication.
- Economic development projects – because a flourishing economy benefits business. Shell, for example, supports LiveWIRE, an award scheme for new enterprise, and the STEP programme, which provides undergraduates with work experience during the summer vacation.
- Environmental projects – United Utilities, through its United Futures partnership with the Groundwork Trust, will provide funding for a number of environmental projects in local communities across the UK.
- Educational projects – as education and training are an investment in future employees.
- Sporting events and competitions, and other activities that attract keen public interest or mass participation, such as the London Marathon and Comic Relief's Red Nose Day.

- Initiatives that have the backing of very prominent people. Who knows who is always important in getting support from companies. The Prince's Trust is able to capitalise on this in its fundraising 'finding that doors open for them without having to be pushed'.

Freshfields Bruckhaus Deringer – employee volunteering and *pro bono* work

Freshfields Bruckhaus Deringer's community and *pro bono* programme has four themes – access to justice, human rights, young people and homelessness. Strategic direction is given to the programme by the community and *pro bono* committee. Each of the firm's offices is responsible for interpreting the strategy in order to maximise its impact and engagement locally.

Employees throughout the firm are encouraged to spend one working day each year on community activities or, for those with legal or other appropriate skills, to support various *pro bono* initiatives.

In 2005, 34% of London staff took part in community and *pro bono* work, contributing nearly 28,000 hours in total.

Within its chosen programme themes, Freshfields Bruckhaus Deringer's has:

- helped GCSE students at Haggerston Girls' School in Hackney to improve their language skills in French and Spanish;
- provided work experience through the 'Ready for Work' programme to some 110 homeless people, 13 of whom have taken up full- or part-time work at the firm;
- provided volunteers to build with Habitat for Humanity in Poland, Romania and London;
- provided free legal advice to individuals and community organisations in need, e.g. for homeless and vulnerably-housed people at the Dellow Centre.

There are certain areas that companies will not generally support:

- local appeals outside areas where they have a business presence – there is no business reason for them to do this;
- purely denominational appeals for religious purposes, although they may support social projects run by religious bodies;
- mailed appeals, which are printed and sent to hundreds of companies;
- controversial campaigns which might bring them bad publicity, although they may support 'unpopular' causes such as homelessness or mental illness;
- overseas development work, unless the company has a business presence in that country, when support will more likely come from a local subsidiary – although some companies do support emergency and aid appeals on the basis that this is the sort of thing that their staff are interested in.

Special initiatives by companies in a particular industry

CRASH is the construction industry charity for single homeless people. Through CRASH, contractors, property owners, construction companies, builders' merchants, interior designers, architects, surveyors and engineers combine to help charities working with homeless people to improve their premises and facilities, and the accommodation they provide for individuals.

CRASH is funded entirely by its supporters from the construction and property sectors, from whom materials and in-kind help is also gifted to assist with building projects. Further funds are raised through various events and conferences, including the following during 2007: Red Friday; *Building Magazine's* Dragon Boat Challenge; No Christmas Card campaign; and the Interbuild photography exhibition showing work by homeless and formerly homeless clients.

Projects currently being supported by CRASH include:

- building searches
- detox support
- night shelters
- social businesses.

CRASH had total incoming resources of £376,000 in 2005, of which just under half was donated by 'patron' companies, i.e. those that have pledged financial and material support for a minimum of three years.

WaterAid is a charity set up by the water industry to focus charitable giving and technical expertise for water projects in 17 countries in the developing world. It mobilises support from the water companies, employee volunteering and giving, and through appeal leaflets sent out by the UK water industry to its clients.

In 2005–06, fundraising support from the water industry totalled £3 million. This was raised through initiatives developed by the regional fundraising committees in water utilities, and major hospitality and challenge events run by contractors, consultants and suppliers.

What companies give

There is a variety of ways in which companies can support charities:

- a cash donation (usually a one-off grant);
- sponsorship of an event or activity such as a museum exhibition;
- sponsorship of promotional and educational materials;
- sponsorship of an award scheme;
- cause-related marketing, where the company contributes a donation to the charity in return for each product sold in order to encourage sales;

- support in kind, which includes: giving company products or surplus office equipment; making company facilities available, including meeting rooms, printing or design facilities; help with mailings;
- secondment of a member of staff to work with the charity, where a member of the company's staff helps on an agreed basis whilst remaining employed (and paid) by the company;
- offering 'internships' or work experience to a charity beneficiary or student at an educational institution;
- contributing a senior member of staff to the charity's management board;
- providing expertise and advice or training;
- encouraging employees to volunteer;
- organising a fundraising campaign amongst employees, including encouraging employees to give through payroll giving;
- advertising in charity brochures and publications.

Companies are increasingly looking for low-cost ways of giving support. The 2000 Finance Act has enabled companies to donate listed shares or securities and obtain tax relief in respect of this (see page 87). Offering free use of facilities, providing advice, donating product and equipment that is no longer required, encouraging staff to volunteer or collect or donate money will all cost much less than making a cash donation.

Companies will always receive more applications than they will have the budget to respond to. Community involvement budgets have not expanded in line with demands for support and many companies now focus their grant-making quite narrowly. Some larger companies will have set up small grants schemes in regions or towns where they have a major factory or business presence. Some have matching schemes, where they match money collected or donated by employees. Some will have developed special grants programmes and others will have a 'charity of the year' for their major donation and as a focus for encouraging staff involvement.

British Airways collects money from passengers

'Change for Good' is an in-flight initiative run by British Airways (BA) in partnership with UNICEF UK since 1994. The programme enables customers to donate their spare coins and notes during a flight using the collection envelopes provided. UNICEF then collects and changes this money, using it to help transform the lives of millions of children worldwide. To date, more than £22 million has been raised to support projects in over 50 countries. Other airlines have since followed the example of BA and run similar schemes.

British Airways also encourages staff in the UK to volunteer for Action for Street Children, an organisation that helps children around the world who are living or working on the streets as a result of being orphaned, abandoned, or having run away from home because of physical and/or sexual abuse. Giving up annual leave, the BA volunteers join the Action for Street Children team for trips of between three and seven days to support projects in Bulgaria, Brazil, Zambia and India.

There are many ways in which a company can help, unlike other funding sources which only provide money. Although you might not get very much in cash donations, there may be better – and equally valuable – ways companies can help you. Try to work out how best companies can support you, based on their level of giving, what they are interested in and the different forms of support they might give – and then approach them with an interesting proposition which they will find difficult to refuse. You might start by getting some modest item provided free and then try to deepen the relationship and escalate their level of support.

Major company programmes

Some of the largest companies now run large-scale programmes in partnership with a national charity or charities. The following are two examples:

Nestlé Make Space Campaign with 4 Children. The campaign aims to create a network of contemporary, dynamic and safe out-of-school clubs for 11–16 year olds. Developed in consultation with young people, Make Space clubs offer social opportunities and activities in a safe environment by providing 'chill-out' and 'quiet' zones, computer access and sports, arts and other activities. There are now more than 1,200 clubs with a Make Space 'Cabinet' of young people having been created to provide them with the opportunity to comment on what matters to them.

Citibank's Finanacially Speaking programme runs in partnership with SpeakersBank. This programme involves schools in East and South London (Citibank is headquartered at Canary Wharf). A competition is organised with each school, where students are asked to speak on some topic relating to money – this could be anything from the importance of saving to setting up an enterprise or buying Fairtrade. Winners are invited to the Citibank HQ for a final speak out. Citibank staff help out as volunteers.

The different types of companies that give

Multinational companies

Most multinational companies have global giving programmes, generally tied to areas where they have or are developing business interests. Some multinational companies, such as IBM and American Express, have an international structure for managing their giving, with budgets set for each country and a common policy for the sorts of activity they are interested in supporting. With others, community involvement policy remains a purely local matter for company management in the country concerned, although some have tried to transfer projects and ideas from one country to another.

Leading national companies

The giving of leading companies is well documented in the *Guide to UK Company Giving*. This gives information on the scale and scope of the company giving programmes of the top 500 corporate donors, with enough information to be able to identify those companies that might be interested in supporting you.

More than half the top companies are members of the PerCent Standard organised by Business in the Community (BitC), which set an aspirational target of 1% of pre-tax profit as a recommended level for community support (in cash and kind). 2006 was the last year of the PerCent Standard, as leading companies recognise the need to develop a more rigorous accreditation. BitC is developing a new standard to encourage companies to report more holistically on their community investment. Some of the largest companies publish brochures which describe their community involvement programme or specific schemes that they sponsor.

The leading national companies will often be supporting large national charities as well as having their own sponsorship schemes, making smaller donations to local charities, and sponsoring events in the area where they are headquartered or where they have a major business presence.

B&Q – community investment improves customer service

For more than ten years B&Q has been working towards helping disabled and older people shop with confidence. As inclusion and sustainability are important parts of the company's values, B&Q has established over 300 partnerships nationwide between its stores and local disability groups to develop training on disability awareness and improve its service to disabled people.

In seeking to achieve this, B&Q has:

- introduced the 'Daily Living Made Easier' product range
- encouraged and paid staff to learn British Sign Language
- provided induction hearing loops and wheelchairs in all stores
- improved accessibility of all B&Q stores.

The function of the partnerships is not charitable. The purpose is to create a better shopping environment for disabled customers. B&Q argues that if it gets it right for disabled people, then it can get it right for most people and, in the process, it increases sales to disabled people (a traditionally under-served group), increases overall employee satisfaction, retention and productivity rates, and enhances its brand.

In recognition of its work, B&Q was awarded the Enhanced Accessibility Award at the RADAR (Royal Association for Disability and Rehabilitation) People of the Year Awards in December 2006.

Larger local companies

In any city or region there will be large companies that are important to the local economy. They will often feel a responsibility to support voluntary action and community initiatives in those areas, and value the good publicity this provides. If yours is an important project, make it part of your fundraising strategy to develop a good relationship with the larger companies in your area.

There are also companies with a regional remit. The water, electricity and ITV's regional television operators all have a specific geographical area within which they operate, even if they are part of a multinational company. Their community support will be confined within these regional boundaries.

Smaller national companies

The larger companies, because of their size but also because their giving is well documented, are often overwhelmed with requests for support. But there are also companies that are less well known and with smaller charitable budgets which receive far fewer approaches. And there are newly floated companies whose giving will only really develop once they have become public. Such companies can provide opportunities for the enterprising fundraiser.

New economy companies

The end of the last century and the early years of this have seen the growth of a new economy based on the IT revolution (the internet, mobile phones etc.) and also on new ways of delivering utilities and other services to consumers. Many of these companies are too busy developing their business to put any real effort into philanthropy. But some – as well as their founders, who now rank amongst Britain's leading rich – are attracted by the concept of 'venture philanthropy', which involves a much more hands-on approach to giving. They are prepared to invest substantially in one or more key projects which have the potential to make a real difference and be replicated, providing cash and other support over a longer timeframe and becoming personally involved in the development of the project. Others, as their business and profit base are consolidated, may give in a more traditional way.

Examples of new company giving

- *Dyson Limited* manufactures domestic appliances, including the well-known Dyson Cyclone. Support is channelled through the Dyson Foundation which received £2.8 million from the company in 2005. A range of charitable causes is supported, although there is some preference for supporting educational projects in the field of design and technology by means of free resources, bursaries and hands-on workshops and lectures in local schools and universities.
- *Informa plc* is an international provider of specialist information to the academic and scientific, professional and commercial business communities. In 2005 the company donated £143,000 to charity. The Informa Community Committee is responsible for the company's community activity and has identified key areas which include: payroll and company giving; disaster relief funding; match funding; staff volunteering; community/charity partnerships; and provision of product discounts for minority and disadvantaged groups.
- *Innocent Drinks*, producers of natural fruit drinks and 'smoothies', has established a grantgiving charity (The Innocent Foundation) that works in partnership with community-based projects and NGOs. Although based in the UK, the majority of support is given to overseas projects, especially in those countries from which Innocent sources its ingredients. Each year, 10% of the company's profits are given to the Foundation, which has helped support work in Brazil, Colombia, Costa Rica, Ecuador, Guatemala, India and Indonesia.

Examples of venture philanthropy

- *McKinsey & Co.*, the management consultancy group, has backed the Ashoka Foundation, which supports 'social entrepreneurs', as its worldwide social partner, offering three-year bursaries. Substantial *pro bono* support is also provided, with staff encouraged to get involved as members.
- *SHINE*: Support and Help in Education, has been set up by a group of city people as a vehicle for their philanthropy. Focusing on literacy and numeracy projects, support is given to disadvantaged, disengaged and challenged children and young people (7–16 years) in Greater London and Manchester.
- *Body Shop International* promotes and supports campaigns on the environment and in support of indigenous peoples, linking together its own giving, its purchasing of raw ingredients, and the involvement of its staff and customers.
- *Impetus Trust* is a pioneer of venture philanthropy in the UK. Impetus offers donors the means to make the biggest difference with their money by enabling charities to achieve a positive change in their performance. By focusing entirely on an integrated investment package comprising long-term financing of charities' infrastructure, hands-on management support and capacity building

delivered through projects run by volunteer associates, Impetus helps to fill an important gap in funding.

Smaller local companies

Smaller, local companies (known in European jargon as small and medium-sized enterprises, or SMEs) are often overlooked. Almost everyone targets the large companies because good information is available. However, there is a wide range of local companies, from manufacturers on trading estates to accountants and solicitors in the high street. The majority of SMEs are involved in activities in their local communities. Many of these firms are privately owned, and the approach will often be through the managing director or senior partner.

The best sources of information on what companies exist in your area are:

- the local Chamber of Commerce, where most of the more prominent local companies will be members;
- the Kompass directory of companies, which is regionally organised and can now be searched online;
- the local council: the business department might produce a list of major business ratepayers. The economic development section may have a list of major employers;
- the local newspaper, which will carry stories from time to time that mention local companies, and may provide information on new companies planning to set up in the area;
- postcode directories, where you can identify large users;
- you – by walking the streets and keeping your eyes open, you can often identify local companies that it could just be worth approaching.

It is likely that most of the smaller companies you approach will not have a donations policy in place and may well make their giving decisions on the basis of the personal interests of their managing director or senior partners. Some may never have made a charitable donation before and may not know about the related tax advantages available to them, so be prepared to tell them about these opportunities.

Some of these companies may prefer to give in kind – for example, a prize for a raffle or advertising in a souvenir brochure for a fundraising event. It might be easier to approach these companies for this sort of support in the first instance, and later on, once they have given something, to persuade them to make a cash donation.

Who decides and who to write to

Larger companies will have a manager who is responsible for dealing with charitable appeals, although a donations committee (which includes senior management) may have the final say. The largest companies may also employ specialist staff (rather like a foundation) to assess the applications and make recommendations. Some large companies such as Lloyds TSB operate an independent foundation which sets policy and decides on applications. With medium-sized and smaller companies, it is nearly always the most senior executive who decides.

You should write in the first instance to the person who deals with charitable appeals. Make sure that you have the name and job title correct. If you have a top-level contact, or if one of your members or volunteers is an employee of the company, then use them.

Getting started

You should try to find out as much as you can about the company and about its possible interest in supporting your project, but remember that:

- companies generally have less well defined policies than trusts, although you can often determine a pattern to their giving;
- the chance of an application 'out of the blue' getting substantial support is low;
- companies are more conservative in their giving, and are less likely to support innovative projects (at least until they get established) or anything that is risky or controversial;
- company policies change more frequently than those of trusts, because of mergers, take-overs, or a fall or rise in profits. So ensure your research is up-to-date. Consulting a directory, or even having a copy of the company's annual report and accounts is not enough; they may have been taken over since then. Check the financial press on a regular basis.

Nonetheless research is important, not just into policies, but also into contacts. Here are some tips.

1 Find out what, if any, previous contact you have had with companies, any previous fundraising approaches you have made, and with what success.
2 Identify and match possible funders with various aspects of your work. In particular, try to find any local companies that are known for their generosity and might have an interest in supporting your cause.
3 Find out whether any of your board members, volunteers or supporters have any personal contact with the companies you plan to approach – and whether they know people who have credibility in the business world who can help you do the asking.

4 Enlist a senior business leader to assist you with your fundraising. This can be someone to serve as chair of a development or fundraising committee, or just to contact a few colleagues and sign a few letters.

5 Contact Business in the Community to find out about its membership or to help you identify local companies through its regional network.

Ethical issues

Receiving support from companies can be problematic if the business values or practice of the company conflict with what your organisation stands for. There are two approaches. Some organisations will accept money from anyone, on the basis that the money can be used to do good. Others define certain types of company that they will not accept support from. Tobacco, alcohol, gambling, armaments, extraction industries, polluters and companies operating in the developing world that underpay their workforce are all areas of business activity that can cause problems. An ethical stance is of particular importance where the work of the charity is directly connected with the issue or where the relationship is high profile. Health and cancer charities would find it hard to accept money from a tobacco company; peace and international relations organisations have similar problems with arms manufacturers; and so on.

Decide your ethical policy before approaching companies. It should be agreed by the management committee and minuted. You might want to define and agree a policy in consultation with staff, although sometimes this can be contentious and create divisions. In such cases it may be better to treat each decision on an ad hoc basis whilst moving towards some sort of consensus on policy.

Sometimes the issues are clear cut. It is relatively easy, for example, for a health charity to decide whether to accept money from a tobacco company, or a youth charity from a drinks company. The product relationship with the cause is clear, and all the charity has to do is agree a position on the issue.

There are two organisations that chart the ethical behaviour of companies, which can provide you with the information you need to formulate an ethical donations policy:

- EIRIS (Ethical Investment Research Services) researches companies on the FT All-Share Index. Its main aim is to advise on socially responsible investment. A charge is made for its services;
- Ethical Consumer Research Association produces *Corporate Critic*, which rates over 50,000 companies on their ethical performance at www. corporatecritic.org.

155

Ten ideas for getting support from companies

1 Put yourself in the position of the company. Why should it want to give its shareholders' funds to you? Why should it choose your charity, rather than any of the other organisations that make contact? Think about the benefits the company will get from supporting you and mention these in your appeal letter. If you are looking for sponsorship, then these benefits will be at the heart of your proposal.

2 Suggest something specific for the company to support, and in your letter say why it should be interested. It is often best to think of something quite small if you are approaching the company for the first time.

3 Use all the contacts you have in the company to help get your project supported. Do you know the chair, the managing director or any other senior member of staff? Or their spouse, who may be able to put in a good word for you? Or if you telephone, can you get into conversation with the chair's secretary or personal assistant so that he or she becomes interested and enthusiastic?

4 Think of all the ways in which the company could help. Cash might not be the best way for the company to give support. Might it be easier to offer staff time, perhaps giving you some expertise you lack? Or the use of a vehicle? Or access to company staff to circulate an appeal or to sell your Christmas cards to? It is likely that everyone else will be asking for cash. The company may find it easier to give in kind, but once it has done so and got to know you and your work, cash support may become easier to obtain next time.

5 Consider whether there is a senior executive of the company (the more senior the better) who might become a trustee of your charity – or serve on a fundraising or development committee. They can bring new ideas, good organisation and a wealth of business contacts to your organisation that will be worth many times the value of a donation. Such an invitation, even if refused, may be seen as flattering. If this level of involvement is too much, a request for advice may succeed.

6 Do you have any volunteers who also work for the company? They may be able to help you 'from the inside', and it will do you no harm if you mention their support for your organisation in your appeal letter, though you must remember to check that they are happy to be mentioned first!

7 Don't assume that every company will give. Make parallel approaches to a number of companies.

8 Consider who might be the best person to make the approach or sign the letter. It may not be you but could be another senior business executive who has already supported your organisation generously. Their endorsement of your work can provide a comfort factor for other companies.

9 Every time you buy anything from a company, ask for a discount. This will save you money, but it is also a way of getting them to support you.

10 Check if the company is registered for payroll giving and, if it is, ask if you can promote your cause to employees. You will find more on payroll giving in chapter 4, section 4.5.

8.2 Cash donations

This is the most obvious way that a company can be asked to support your organisation, but also the most expensive for them, so most cash donations are small (under £200). You are more likely to be successful if you offer a 'shopping list' of specific items, rather than a vague request for general support. Some companies match their employees' fundraising.

Tax and company giving

The 2000 Finance Act made giving tax-effectively straightforward for companies.

1 Donations: the company simply pays the full donation to the charity under Gift Aid and then deducts the total amount of its charitable donations from its pre-tax profit calculations at the end of the year. The level of benefit a company can receive in return is restricted on a sliding scale according to the amount of the donation, up to a maximum of £250 in benefits.

2 Business expenditure: any expenditure by a company which is wholly and exclusively for business purposes is also deductible against corporation tax liability. This will cover most sponsorship and advertising payments to charity.

3 Shares: companies are able to get tax relief for gifts of certain shares and securities to charity. See the HM Revenue & Customs website www.hmrc.gov.uk for more information.

8.3 Gifts in kind

Giving things rather than money is often easier for a company. The value of the gift to the charity will always be much more than the cost to the company. Companies can give:

- products for use by the charity
- products as prizes or as lots to be auctioned
- old stock and ends of lines for resale in charity shops
- professional and technical advice *pro bono* (without charge)
- facilities such as meeting rooms, conference facilities, training.

If a company donates articles that it makes or sells in the course of its trade, or an article that it has used in its trade (this can include computers and furniture), then this can be treated as a tax-deductible business expense. Donated items whose 'book value' (value as given in the accounts) is written off before the donation is made (unsaleable or damaged stock, ends of lines etc.) also attract full tax relief. See *The Fundraiser's Guide to the Law* for more detailed treatment of this.

There are organisations which act as 'clearing houses' for gifts in kind, such as Kind Direct (formerly Gifts in Kind UK).

Some practical tips on how to set about getting support in kind

1 Make a list of everything you need – a 'wish list'. This can include services as well as products (such as the design for a leaflet you plan to produce).

2 Go through the list and try to identify companies that might have what you require. Personal knowledge is fine but you might also want to use business directories.

3 Make contact. Writing a letter can act as an introduction but you will probably need to follow it up with a phone call or personal visit. State your request, saying that it is for a charity and indicating how well used it will be and how important it is to your organisation's future.

4 If the company refuses to donate it, it might be able to give you a hefty discount. This is worth getting and can be a fall-back position in your discussions.

5 Be positive and enthusiastic. It can be very difficult for the company to refuse if it knows what you want and how important it is for you. It will always cost the company far less to donate the item than it would cost you to purchase it.

6 Say thank you. Report back subsequently on the difference the donation has made. Send them your annual report. Try then to recruit the company as a cash donor.

8.4 Employee volunteering and secondments

A major resource that companies can offer is their staff time. This can be provided in a number of ways.

- *Employee volunteering*: many of the large companies encourage their staff to volunteer, usually out of office hours, on the basis that this enhances the skills of their employees and promotes good community relations. Some companies make matching donations to the projects their employees are involved with. *Cares* is a national campaign run by Business in the Community that aims to engage employees in their communities through volunteering.

- *Professional skills*: banks, law firms, accountants, advertising and PR companies can all encourage staff to give their professional skills free of charge or to become trustees. Even where this is not done, you can always ask.

See chapter 16 for more on volunteering.

Another type of support is a secondment, where the company loans you a member of staff full time for an extended period. There needs to be a good reason why the company would do this, as it is an expensive form of support. Schemes might include:

- challenges for middle and senior managers. These might be in the form of an assignment of, say, 100 hours to complete a specific task for the charity, which can help the employee develop new skills in a different setting;
- secondments linked to a major programme which the company is supporting, where the loan of the member of staff is part of the package;
- pre-retirement secondments as a alternative to early retirement or redundancy. These would normally be on a full-time basis for one or two years. Secondments can also be set up for people 'between jobs' in the company.

Many companies also encourage staff to volunteer after retirement; REACH (Retired Executives' Action Clearing House) and RSVP (Community Service Volunteers formerly the Retired and Senior Volunteering Programme) both act as placement agencies for retired volunteers.

Employee volunteering is not only valuable in itself, but is strategically important since you will be building a relationship with a member of staff who can then act as an intermediary in asking the company for other forms of support, including cash donations.

8.5 Getting companies to advertise

Companies will often take an advertisement in a publication – possibilities include:

- your annual report
- programmes produced specially for fundraising events
- conference folders; pads and pens
- leaflets aimed at your service users and others
- posters, including educational wall charts.

However, you do need to think through whether you actually want an advertisement or company logo to appear prominently in your materials.

Advertising can be broken down into two categories:

- *goodwill advertising,* where the primary purpose of the advertiser is to support a charity and to be seen supporting a good cause; this creates goodwill for the company rather than selling its products;
- *commercial advertising,* where the advertiser wishes to reach the audience that the charity's publication goes to, and the decision is made for purely commercial considerations.

What are you offering to advertisers

Before trying to sell the advertising, you need to recognise what you are offering. If it is goodwill advertising, then the prestige of the event, the nature of the audience, the location and any celebrities who will be present will be major incentives. Price is less of an issue than the work of the charity, although the advertiser will want to know the circulation and readership of the publication, any special characteristics of that readership and any particular connection between it and their product. If it is commercial advertising, these details become much more significant.

Pricing the advertising

The first consideration when pricing the advertising is the format of the publication. A lavish souvenir brochure is different from an annual report, and this in turn is very different from a single colour newsletter produced on your computer. There are two factors to consider when deciding the cost of the advertising.

- How much you want to raise? Divide this target by the number of pages of advertising to get a page rate.
- How much are advertisers prepared to pay? For commercial advertising this is especially important. Try to define the value of your audience to them.

Once you have decided a page rate, then you can then set prices for smaller spaces that are slightly higher than pro rata. For example, if the page rate is £250, then a half page might be priced at £150, a quarter page at £85, and eighth page at £50. You can ask for higher sums for special positions, such as the back cover, the inside front cover and facing the contents page. For a regular publication, you could offer a series discount for taking space in several issues.

Getting the advertising

In order to appear professional, produce a rate card which contains all the information that the advertiser needs to know, including:

- deadline for agreeing to take space
- deadline for receipt of artwork and address where it is to be sent
- publication size
- print run
- use of colour on cover and inside pages (four-colour, two-colour, black and white)
- page rates, including special positions, size of advertising space, and whether VAT is chargeable
- payment details.

The covering letter

On the last Friday of every month, come hail, rain or shine, our team of 150 volunteers pushes a copy of the 'Community News' into each and every one of the 5,000 letterboxes in Newtown. We know our readers eagerly await its arrival, because they write and tell us, telephone us, and stop us in the street to tell us so.

There are many reasons for its continuing popularity – lots of local interest stories, on-the-spot photographs, and our fearless reporting of local issues without political bias of any kind. Our regular features – the crossword, gossip, cookery and gardening columns, the over '60s angle and Young Mum's Forum have all helped us make 'Community News' Newtown's No.1 Good Read, and we aim to keep it that way.

Advertise your company's products and services with us and get your message into 5,000 letterboxes each month. An advertisement rate card is enclosed with full details. If you have any queries, please don't hesitate to call me.

[From *Sell Space to Make Money* (now out of print)]

A simple brochure or covering letter which sets out the reasons for advertising is useful, but posting copies out will generate little response. The way to sell advertising is on the telephone, where you make a call to follow up a letter you have sent. For larger advertisers, you might try to arrange a personal visit. You have to find the person who can make the decision, grab their attention, persuade them, and not go away until you have a commitment. Of course, the majority of people you approach will say 'no'; but your job is to persuade a significant proportion to say 'yes', and to get them to take a larger space than they might instinctively go for.

8.6 Business sponsorship

Sponsorship needs to be carefully defined. It is not a donation, and the fact that you are a charity is largely irrelevant. It is a business arrangement. The charity is looking to raise funds for its work and the company wants to improve its image, promote and sell its products or entertain its customers. The sponsor's contribution is usually money, although it could be a gift of goods (such as a car), or services (such as free transport), or professional expertise (such as promotion or marketing consultancy), or the use of buildings (such as an exhibition centre), or free promotion (such as media coverage in a newspaper).

Many companies will provide much more in sponsorship than they would as a donation, but only so long as the commercial benefits warrant it. Developing links with the major national and local corporate sponsors could be an investment in your future that is well worth making now. For more detailed coverage of this topic, see *Finding Company Sponsors for Good Causes.*

Who sponsors?

Most sponsors are commercial companies. There are four main options for sponsorship:

- businesses wanting to promote themselves, to create a better image or generate awareness in the local communities where they operate. This includes those companies with an 'image problem' – for example, mining and extraction companies associated with the destruction of the environment who want to project a cleaner image by being associated with a conservationist cause;
- businesses wanting to introduce or promote a product or service. This could include a new brand of toothpaste or beer, or a supermarket opening in the area. Public awareness is important if a product or service is to get accepted, so companies may be open to proposals that give a product or service more exposure;
- companies looking for entertainment opportunities to influence customers, suppliers, regulators, the media and other opinion formers. They may be interested in sponsoring a prestigious concert, a theatrical event, an art exhibition, a horse race or a sporting event, which would provide them with an appropriate entertainment opportunity and the opportunity to meet and mingle with celebrities;
- companies that are committed supporters of your organisation. You may be able to offer them something that they would like to sponsor, even if it is partly for philanthropic reasons.

Why companies like sponsorship

- It helps them get their message across.
- It can enhance or change their image.

- It can reach a target audience very precisely.
- It can be very cost-effective advertising or product promotion.
- Further marketing opportunities may develop from the sponsorship.
- It generates good publicity for the sponsor, often of a kind that money can't buy.
- It generates an awareness of the company within the local community in which the company operates and from where it draws its workforce.
- Sponsors can entertain important clients at the events they sponsor.

What can be sponsored?

There is an extremely wide range of things that can be sponsored, including:

- cultural and sporting events;
- mass participation fundraising events, such as a marathon or fun run;
- the publication of a report or a book, with an attendant launch;
- the production of fundraising materials, leaflets and posters, or the sponsorship of a complete fundraising campaign;
- conferences and seminars, especially to specialist audiences (such as doctors) where promotional material can be displayed;
- vehicles, where the acknowledgement can be painted on the side;
- equipment such as cars or computers produced by the company;
- competitions, awards and prizes;
- scholarships, bursaries, travel grants.

The bulk of corporate sponsorship money goes to sport, with motor racing, golf, tennis, athletics, football and cricket all receiving huge amounts. These offer extensive media coverage, good opportunities for corporate entertainment and an association with a popular activity. But as a charity you will not be competing for a share of the same budget.

Arts organisations will know that the arts is another big recipient of sponsorship – business support for the arts runs at around £150 million a year. Arts sponsorship is promoted by Arts & Business, which describes itself as acting 'as a crucible where businesses and arts organisations come together to create partnerships to benefit themselves and the community at large'. Social sponsorship is much smaller by comparison, but is a growing area. The 'market' is less crowded and there are all sorts of imaginative ways in which companies can sponsor events and activities run by charities.

Identifying possible sponsors

First you should decide what benefits your proposed activity can offer a sponsor. Is it access to a target audience? Access to public personalities? A prestigious event with entertainment opportunities? Once you have done this, you can begin to define companies that might be interested. They may be national companies looking for national publicity, or a major company located in your area or a purely local concern looking to develop its local presence. Remember that if you are looking for a substantial sum, only the larger companies will be interested.

Then draw up a list of potential sponsors. Do some research to find out what the company has sponsored before, what sort of sums it might possibly provide, and whether it might have any current interests or concerns which could be met through sponsorship. For example, a development company that has just completed a residential estate will be interested in marketing it, or a new shopping centre may need a promotional event to coincide with its opening. These are opportunities for sponsorship.

You need patience. Sponsorship can take a long time to negotiate, and it is best to plan well in advance. Start discussions at least a year before the proposed activity is to take place.

The sponsorship package

Before you make your approach, you need to prepare a written proposal, which will outline the project and highlight all the benefits to be gained by the company. It will also have a price for the sponsorship which will reflect as much the benefits to the company as your own need for money. In your proposal, you should describe:

- the nature of the project or activity, and how it is likely to work;
- the audiences that will be reached and the publicity that will be obtained. These should be quantified as far as possible (how many column inches of coverage and in which newspapers; how many and what sort of people will attend the event; how many posters will be displayed; how many hits the website will receive etc.). Remember that the company will be primarily interested in reaching those people who are its target audience and you have to demonstrate how you will do this;
- the geographical coverage – is it a national or a purely local activity?
- the image that will be projected through the event, and how this will fit in with what the sponsoring brand or company might be looking for;
- the specific advertising opportunities that will be available on poster hoardings, the sides of vans, in the event programme, on TV and in the press;
- some of the other benefits that the sponsorship might confer on the company – the effect it will have on staff, on business contacts, and on government and other authorities;

- the cost of the sponsorship – and the value of the sponsorship benefits. You can also try to assess how this compares with other ways of achieving the same promotional objective.

All this should be produced in a professional (though not necessarily expensive) way, together with photographs and press coverage from previous sponsored events, and brief background material on your organisation and its work.

Where the money will come from

Which budget head the money comes from is important, as this will determine who will make the decision and what sort of return is needed. The following are the main options.

- *Marketing*. The company may be undertaking all sorts of activity to market its products and brands – all within an annual budget. The marketing manager will be making choices about what promotional options to pursue based on the cost and expected return. If you are asking for sponsorship, then you have to demonstrate the return you can provide – and show that this is a cost-effective option.
- *Corporate image*. Very large companies have a central budget to promote their name, image and logo. Often this is handled alongside their charitable support, and sometimes even out of the same budget. The return to the company may be more intangible than with product or brand sponsorship, but this is all part of the corporate image building process (which includes corporate advertising and PR). A good example of how this can pay off is demonstrated by the following example: Shell was involved in an oil spill on the River Mersey in the 1980s. The judge fining the company said that the fine would have been far larger but for Shell's excellent record in sponsoring the arts and the environment.
- *Employee relations*. The human resources budget is often a company's biggest single budget; investing in better staff relations can be a cost effective way of enhancing staff loyalty, retaining and even recruiting staff.

Making the approach

Having identified a potential company and developed your sponsorship proposal, there is a variety of ways in which you can approach the company.

Approach the person who will make the decision directly. For product promotions, this will be the brand manager. For corporate PR, it may be the director of corporate affairs. Try to make an appointment to visit the company to give a presentation of your work and discuss the sponsorship opportunities. Only then will you be in a position to find out about the company's needs and how you can meet them.

- If you cannot arrange a meeting ring the marketing department to find out what sorts of sponsorship they consider and who to send the proposal to. Send a summary proposal to see if it sparks any interest and follow this up with a phone call a few days later to try and arrange a meeting.
- There may be an advertising agency or marketing consultant who will introduce sponsorship opportunities to sponsors. They will sometimes charge you a fee; more usually they will receive a commission from the sponsor. It depends who retains them, and in whose interests they are acting.

Contractual issues

Sponsorship involves your giving something in return for the money you are receiving, so you need to agree terms through a contract. This can be set out in a legal agreement (for larger sponsorships) or in the form of a letter. You need to be clear about the following.

- How long the arrangement will run. Is it for one year, thus requiring you to find a new sponsor next year? Or can you get a commitment for several years? What happens at the end of this period – does the sponsor have a first refusal on the following year's event? Most successful sponsorships last for several years, and the benefit builds up over the sponsorship period. But companies don't like being tied to sponsoring something indefinitely – their sponsorship programme would begin to look stale.
- The fee to be paid, and when the instalments are due.
- What benefits are to be delivered in return for the fee. These should be specified as clearly as possible, so that you know precisely what you are contracted to deliver.
- Whether VAT is chargeable. This will depend on whether your organisation is registered for VAT and the extent of the benefits offered to the sponsor. If VAT is chargeable, this should be discussed at the outset, and the fee agreed should be exclusive of VAT.
- Who will pay for what costs. Who pays for the additional publicity the sponsor requires is something that is often forgotten. There needs to be a clear agreement as to who is responsible for what, so you can ensure that everything is covered and there are no misunderstandings later on.
- Who is responsible for doing what. You will need to clarify who will do the public relations, who will handle the bookings, who will invite the guests, whose staff will receive the guests and so on.
- Any termination arrangements in the event of the activity having to be cancelled.

- Who is responsible for managing the sponsorship – a named person on both sides.
- Whether the sponsor is a 'commercial participator' under the terms of the Charities Act 1992 (see page 169), when the requirements of the Charities Act will apply.

If everything is written down and agreed, there will be fewer problems later – and it ensures that everything has been properly thought through at the outset.

8.7 Joint promotions and cause-related marketing

Many larger charities are involved in promotional activity to help market a commercial product – this is often known as cause-related marketing (CRM). This can bring in large amounts of money and expose the name of the charity to millions of people for little or no cost. The same idea can also be adapted for use by local charities through local promotions.

Commercial promotions can include on-pack and licensing promotional deals, affinity credit cards, competitions and awards, the use of phone lines, and self-liquidating offers. What they have in common is that they present an opportunity to raise money for your cause and to project your charity to new audiences, but they require that you work with the company and on its terms to achieve this.

This arrangement benefits both the charity and the commercial partner. It differs from sponsorship in that you are promoting the company's product or service (in return for a payment) as the primary purpose of the arrangement. But as with sponsorship, you will need to make a business case for it.

Profitable partnerships

A research report based on a survey of 2,000 randomly selected adults conducted by the British Market Research Bureau found the following:

- over 65% of the sample had participated in a CRM campaign. Three quarters of them either switched brand, tried out a product or increased their usage because of CRM; four out of five felt more positive about certain purchases, more loyal to a company or brand; and there were clear benefits to the charity, many stating such campaigns provided an easy way for them to give their support;
- some 90% had heard of at least one CRM campaign and nearly half could spontaneously name a specific company or brand involved in a campaign;

- two out of three people believed more businesses should become involved. However, a small percentage felt CRM was exploitative or that it was inappropriate for business to become involved in social issues in this way.

Getting started with promotions

Joint promotions are quite difficult to arrange. You must first talk about the possibility of your developing promotional links with companies with a marketing or advertising agency.

You need to decide whether you are the type of charity which can expect a commercial link of this sort. It has been generally accepted that national household-name charities and those addressing popular causes (such as helping children) are more likely to benefit from this area of fundraising than the less well known charities or those addressing difficult causes such as torture or slavery.

Calor promotes ChildLine

Calor is actively involved in fundraising for ChildLine, the UK's free, 24-hour helpline for children. Calor's Gift of the Gas campaign has successfully raised over £67,000 for the charity since 2005 through a 'cylinder retrieval' scheme, where Calor donates £5 for every unwanted Calor gas cylinder returned to a Calor Gas Direct outlet. Calor has pledged to continue the scheme until 31 December 2007, which will enable ChildLine to answer more children calling 0800 1111 in danger or distress. The company's target is to reach £100,000 by the end of 2007.

You can wait until companies or their promotional agencies contact you (they may not), or you can try to take the initiative yourself by contacting companies that might be interested. You can also contact promotion agencies (that are not retained by you) to make them aware of the opportunities you are offering which they could include when appropriate in their sales pitch to companies.

If you are approached by a promotional agency pitching for business, this does not mean that anything is certain. It may be working independently, hoping that a good idea that involves your charity can then be sold to a company. In nine out of ten situations, these ideas come to nothing, and you may find you have put in considerable effort without getting any payback.

Issues with sponsorships and joint promotions

Sponsorship involves a close working relationship with a company. Therefore you will need to be sure when you enter into any sponsorship agreement that this relationship will benefit your organisation and will not damage your charity's reputation. With commercial promotions the relationship is even closer. The charity is actively promoting the products of the company, so it is important that the product you are associated with is good value and good quality. With both arrangements it is important that you have no ethical problems in associating with that company. You should develop an ethical donations policy before you apply for any sponsorship or suggest a joint promotion – agreeing in advance which types of company you are happy to work with and which you are not. (See *Ethical issues* page 155.)

There is also the question of who will benefit most from the arrangement. How much you should expect to receive from a sponsorship or commercial promotion is also a difficult question. It may be worth a great deal to them to be linked with you. Any negotiation should start from what you think the association is worth to them. Your need for money should not dim the value of your commercial worth.

Finally, there are important legal issues arising from the 1992 Charities Act (and still applicable following the Charities Act 2006). The 1992 Act defines a 'commercial participator' as 'any person who carries on for gain a business which is not a fundraising business but who in the course of that business engages in any promotional venture in the course of which it is represented that contributions are to be given to or applied for the benefit of a charity'. In other words, high street shops often promote products on the understanding that part of the sale price will go to charity – for example charity Christmas cards published commercially state explicitly that for each pack sold a certain sum will go to charity. The Act also covers advertising and sales campaigns or other joint promotions by companies with charities. If the activity falls within the provisions of the Act, this then requires:

- a written agreement in a prescribed form between the charity and the commercial participator;
- the public to be informed how the charity will benefit from its involvement, which shows what part of the proceeds or profits are to be given to the charity. This is a matter for professional advice.

The Charity Commission also suggests that trustees should consider the following points before allowing the charity's name to be associated with a particular business or product:

- the relationship is appropriate and will not damage the particular charity or the good name of charity as a whole;

- the proposed fundraising venture is a more effective way of raising money than others that might be considered, and that the terms of the arrangement are generally advantageous to the charity;
- that the arrangement is set out in some detail and kept under review, such that the charity's name is not misused or improperly exploited, and that the charity has the right to prevent future use of its name if the arrangement proves unsatisfactory. It may be worth taking legal advice in drawing up the terms of the arrangement.

Resources and further information

See also general lists at the end of the book.

Organisations

Arts & Business
Nutmeg House
60 Gainsford Street
Butler's Wharf
London SE1 2NY
www.aandb.org.uk
Tel. 020 7378 8143

Business in the Community
135 Shepherdess Walk
London N1 7RR
Tel. 0870 600 2482
e-mail information@bitc.org.uk

Charity Commission
PO Box 1227
Liverpool L69 3UG
www.charity-commission.gov.uk
Tel: 0845 3000 218
Fax 0151 7031 555

Community Service Volunteers
(for the RSVP programme)
237 Pentonville Road
London N1 9NJ
www.csv-rsvp.org.uk
Tel. 020 7278 6601

Companies House
Crown Way
Cardiff CF14 3UZ
www.companies-house.gov.uk
Tel. 0870 3333 636

CRASH
The Barley Mow Business Centre
10 Barley Mow Passage
London W4 4PH
www.crash.org.uk
Tel. 020 8742 0717

EIRIS (Ethical Investment Research Services)
80–84 Bondway
London SW8 1SF
www.eiris.org
Tel. 020 7840 5700

Kind Direct (formerly Gifts in Kind UK)
9th Floor
11–15 Monument Street
London EC3R 8JU
www.inkinddirect.org
Tel. 020 7714 3930

PerCent Standard
c/o Business in the Community

ProHelp
c/o Business in the Community

REACH
89 Albert Embankment
London SE1 7TP
www.reach-online.org.uk
Tel. 020 7582 6543

Publications

The following publications are available from the Directory of Social Change. Prices were correct the time of writing, but may be subject to change.

Corporate Fundraising, 3rd edn, ed. Valerie Morton, CAF/IOF/DSC 2007, £22.95

Finding Company Sponsors for Good Causes, Chris Wells, DSC 2000, £12.95

The Fundraiser's Guide to the Law, Bates, Wells & Braithwaite, DSC 2000, £19.95

Guide to UK Company Giving, 6th edn, John Smyth & Denis Lillya, DSC 2007, £39.95

Other publications

Building relationships between the third sector and the private sector
This publication can be downloaded for free on the Business in the Community website.
www.bitc.org.uk/resources/publications/bitcare_toolkit.html

Kompass (series of directories)
Windsor Court
East Grinstead House
East Grinstead
West Sussex RH19 1XA
www.kompass.com
Tel. 01342 335866

Yellow Pages
www.yell.co.uk

9 GOVERNMENT FUNDING

In recent years there has been a significant increase in the amount of funding that the voluntary and community sector (VCS) receives from government. The Labour government has viewed the sector as an important 'partner' in delivering its policies, and has increased funding and other forms of support accordingly. Opposition parties have also been attracted by the sector's standing in developing their competing policy agendas. Although many initiatives have been controversial and some have even been opposed by the sector, the sector's increased importance to the government's agenda is undeniable.

Although the amount of statutory funding has increased substantially, only a relatively small proportion of it will be directly accessible to most organisations. However, if you are prepared to research the possibilities thoroughly and tailor your application to meet government objectives, this can be a worthwhile route to follow.

This chapter outlines recent developments, the different types of government funding, including from central government, regional and arm's-length bodies and local authorities, and suggests ways of accessing support.

Details of organisations and publications referred to in this chapter are on pages 210–212.

9.1 Background to government funding

In the past, income from government represented a much lower percentage of voluntary sector income than donations from trusts or from the general public. However, this is no longer the case. It is very difficult to determine exact figures, because of the lack of effective data collection by statutory funders and the fact that funding is allocated by so many diverse agencies and in many different ways. However, it appears that more than a third of the sector's income now comes from statutory sources – an annual figure in the region of £10 billion – which puts statutory funding at least on a par with funding from any other source.

The 2002 Cross-cutting Review

The main reason for this growth in statutory funding comes from the government's drive to involve the sector in the delivery of public services, which has corresponded with a shift towards funding being awarded as service delivery contracts or on a commissioned basis rather than in the form of grants. Over half of statutory funding for the voluntary sector is now distributed in the form of fees for the delivery of services.

Many of the important policy initiatives in this respect have come out of HM Treasury's 2002 *Cross-cutting Review of the Role of the Voluntary and Community Sector in Service Delivery*. This review made a number of recommendations, based on five key areas for reform:

- to involve the Voluntary and Community Sector (VCS) in the planning as well as the delivery of services;
- to forge long-term strategic partnerships with the sector;
- to build the capacity of the sector;
- that it is legitimate for service providers to factor in the relevant element of overhead costs into their cost estimates for services delivered under contract (full cost recovery);
- to implement the National Compact (see page 177) at all levels.

Several of the recommendations have resulted in large-scale strategic initiatives that have affected how the voluntary sector functions and how it relates to government.

ChangeUp

The ChangeUp programme is designed to improve the infrastructure and support available to frontline voluntary and community sector organisations. The initiative primarily supports second-tier and umbrella organisations that provide advice and services to other organisations.

ChangeUp initially created six national 'hubs' of expertise, composed of organisations working in partnership, to improve voluntary and community sector infrastructure in the following areas: performance improvement, workforce development, ICT, governance, recruiting and developing volunteers, and financing voluntary and community sector activity. Around 130 regional and local consortia were also set up throughout England along similar lines, to address the particular sector infrastructure needs in those areas. To achieve this, a total of £150 million was provided by government for the period 2004–08.

Outside of the main umbrella bodies and the larger national charities involved in the hub consortia, many organisations felt that this money was not used as effectively as it could have been. The Capacitybuilders agency was set up in June 2005 to manage and improve the ChangeUp programme at arm's length from government. Capacitybuilders launched a review of the role of the national hubs, concluding that there were significant deficiencies in the hub structure. As a result Capacitybuilders announced that there would be an open, competitive tendering process for the provision of 'national support services' to the voluntary sector later in 2007. This effectively spelled the end of the national hubs as originally designed.

Following a lengthy consultation with the voluntary sector, Capacitybuilders launched its Destination 2014 strategic plan in 2007, which described its aims and objectives for the years up to 2014. At the same time the agency launched a draft framework for the national support services – its outline plan for voluntary sector infrastructure after the hubs. The draft framework proposed that the 'support services' be organised around four themes: Finance, Performance, Workforce and Voice. Although the focus on Voice (campaigning and advocacy) was welcomed, there was consternation that volunteering and governance had been subsumed under the Workforce theme.

Capacitybuilders was allocated another £88.5 million in the Third Sector Review for the 2008–11 period (see page 177), roughly half of what was allocated for the previous four years. The biggest challenge for Capacitybuilders, however, will be to convince the sector at large that the new 'support services' will provide accessible support for a diverse range of organisations at the front line, and not simply swallow up future funding by replicating the deficiencies of the hubs.

Futurebuilders

The Futurebuilders initiative also came out of the 2002 cross-cutting review. The programme aims to increase the sector's delivery of public services by providing funding primarily in the form of loans. The idea is that low-interest loans enable the organisation to develop sufficiently to become 'investment ready', meaning that they are able to compete for service delivery contracts from statutory bodies.

At its inception the fund focused on five themes, deemed to be areas where public services could be improved by increased voluntary sector participation: community cohesion; crime; education and learning; health and social care; and support for children and young people. The initial amount to be invested was £150 million up to April 2007.

In May 2007 the Office of the Third Sector announced that it would be re-tendering for the delivery of Futurebuilders. The Third Sector Review (see below) confirmed that an additional £65 million would be allocated to the fund for the 2008–11 period. Importantly, the scheme will now be open to fund any area of public service delivery, and will seek to fund social enterprises as well as charities.

The 'Third Sector Review'

Since the 2002 review, the amount and the pace of change in the relationship between government and the voluntary sector has been such that the Treasury and the Cabinet Office felt it necessary to conduct another review in 2006, the so-called 'Third Sector Review', billed as the largest ever consultation with the voluntary and community sector. Consultation events were held throughout England, with over 2000 people from more than 1000 organisations taking part, and 253 written submissions were made.

The goal of this review was to determine the 'future role of the third sector in social and economic regeneration' and set out a '10-year vision' for the sector and its relationship with government. As such this review's scope was not limited to the sector's role in delivering public services, but planned to encompass the sector's wider role in society (and by default in the government's future agenda). The report highlighted the following areas that government will focus on in its relationship with the 'third' sector:

- enabling voice and campaigning – enabling individuals and groups' voices to be heard;
- strengthening communities – building active, strong and connected communities;
- transforming public services – creating an environment where third sector organisations can contribute fully to transforming public services;
- encouraging social enterprise – supporting social enterprises to start up and thrive;
- supporting the environment for a healthy third sector.

The review was expected to be a major milestone in the relationship between the sector and government, but the final version seemed more like a missed opportunity. It provided a summary of recent initiatives and a glimpse of the immediate future, but very little discussion of what is planned beyond 2008. A series of key commitments related to each theme were laid out, but concrete actions were relatively limited. In contrast to the 2002 review, which contained 43 recommendations, this review contained only 36 'actions', many of which had already occurred. More is not necessarily better, but given that this review had a broader focus and higher aspirations, it was somewhat disappointing.

Despite these deficiencies, the review's themes do describe the direction that much government policy towards the sector will take in future years. The involvement of the sector in delivering public services will continue to expand, particularly in certain areas such as health and social care. Social enterprise is also clearly a priority for the government, and resources will increasingly be made available to develop this area. The focus on enabling voice and campaigning and the importance of the Compact was largely welcomed by the sector.

The government also clearly perceives an important role for the sector at the local level and has provided some limited support to develop this. The review recognises a number of longstanding problems, such as the prevalence of short-term funding arrangements, even if the stated commitments and actions to address them are vague.

The review trumpeted that £515 million would be provided to the third sector during the period of the 2007 Comprehensive Spending Review (2008–11). This seems roughly accurate based on the main proposals in the report, which are outlined below:

- **£80 million small grants programme**, to be administered by local funding bodies for local projects/groups. This fund was announced in response to sector feedback about the significant decline in small grants funding. Initially it was described as supporting 'community capacity building projects', but the final review stated that it would 'provide core funding to grass roots community organisations supporting community action and voice'.
- **£50 million endowment fund for local funders** such as Community Foundations. This will provide capital grants to help generate income and lever in matched funding from other sources, which would then be allocated as grants for local projects/groups.
- **£30 million Community Assets Fund**, to facilitate the transfer of capital assets such as buildings to community ownership (primarily from local authorities), to be managed by the Big Lottery Fund. This fund will be developed in line with Making Assets Work – the Quirk Review of Community Management and Ownership of Public Assets.
- **£10 million investment in social enterprise** (announced in the 2006 Social Enterprise Action Plan), including £1.8 million annually during 2008–11 for RDAs to improve support for social enterprise.
- **An extra £6.5 million for the Safer Stronger Communities block of Local Area Agreements**, intended to support the capacity of local groups to participate in the design and delivery of LAAs (see section 9.4). However, this is not ring-fenced for sector involvement, although local authorities are 'encouraged' to do so.

- **£10 million for community anchor organisations** and community asset and enterprise development. There was almost no detail on this proposal in the review. The Department for Communities and Local Government will have ultimate responsibility and there will likely be a connection to the Community Assets Fund described above.
- **£117 million of investment in youth volunteering** through the national framework for youth volunteering, run by V. V is a registered charity which manages corporate donations that are matched funded by government, and then distributes grants for volunteering projects.
- **£88.5 million for Capacitybuilders and £65 million for Futurebuilders**, for the period 2008–11.

The amounts attached to these programmes are not insignificant but the overall impression is one of compromise between some good policy ideas and a tight fiscal environment for the foreseeable future. £80 million in small grants is welcome, but this amount pales in comparison with the amount of small grants funding that has been phased out in recent years. £50 million to endow local funders is a good idea but will probably only be able to provide endowments of less than £1 million for each funder. Given the proposed size of individual investments, £30 million for the Community Assets Fund won't even come close to providing one investment in every local authority area in England. Continued investment in Futurebuilders and Capacitybuilders is at roughly half the level as the last spending period.

The Compact

The importance that the government places on the voluntary sector has also been reflected in the National Compact drawn up between government and the voluntary sector in 1998. This, for the first time, attempted to define their roles and mutual responsibilities (*Compact on Relationships between the Government and the Voluntary Sector*, Home Office and NCVO, 1998). The Compact was later supplemented by a series of Codes of Practice which provided more detail on specific areas such as funding (*Funding: a Code of Good Practice*, Home Office and NCVO, 2000). Its importance was reinforced in the 2002 cross-cutting reviews, and more recently in the Third Sector Review (*The Future Role of the Third Sector in Social and Economic Regeneration: Final Report*, HM Treasury and Cabinet Office, 2007).

Despite repeated efforts to strengthen awareness of the Compact within the voluntary sector and government, the Compact's principles have not become fully embedded in the relationship. Therefore in 2005 the Home Office announced that a new post of Compact Commissioner would be created to champion the Compact and strengthen its full implementation at all levels of government. In autumn 2006 the Compact Commissioner was appointed and in April 2007 the Commission itself was launched.

The first Compact Commissioner, John Stoker, described the Commission's role as 'an independent body operating through influence'. It is not an ombudsman, because the Compact is not a legally binding agreement, but seeks to function as one by finding and promoting best practice and by providing guidance and advice for the voluntary sector and government. However, there is significant support in the voluntary sector for the Commission to be given statutory powers – to make it more of a real ombudsman – in order to crack down on pervasive bad practice by government funders. However, this approach does not appeal to ministers or the Commissioner himself, and is not likely to be considered any time soon.

The Third Sector Review announced that funding for the Commission would continue during 2008–11, and confirmed that the Compact and associated codes will be reviewed, with the aim of having revised documentation in place by 2008/09. Further details were not available at the time of writing, but according to the Commissioner, this review would seek to:

- reaffirm the principles of good partnership working;
- bring the detail of the Compact and codes of practice up to date;
- improve the delivery of the parties' commitments and provide a better framework to allow adherence to them to be assessed.

The 2002 cross-cutting review also recommended that the process of setting up local compacts be accelerated and expanded throughout England. Progress on local compacts has been slow – by 2007 nearly all areas had a local compact or were working on developing one, but in many areas this was not finalised and a significant number of areas still had no local compact at all. Further, there is a wide variation between areas in the awareness and effectiveness of local compacts. Organisations working at the local level should find out about their council's progress and get a copy of their local compact. The website www.thecompact.org.uk contains information about local compacts in every local authority area, as well as advice and examples of best practice.

Changes at the local level

Along with these high-level strategic changes in the relationship between the voluntary sector and government, the relationship at the local level has also changed drastically in the last decade, and it looks like more change is in the pipeline. In the 1990s many services were tendered out to the private and voluntary sector by both local authorities and local health trusts. Many voluntary organisations, particularly in health and social welfare fields, now have contracts or service-level agreements with clear targets and timetables to fulfil. Initiatives such as Futurebuilders are intended to drive forward this trend. At the same time most local authorities have seriously reduced their dedicated grant programmes for voluntary organisations. Local authorities have been criticised for getting services from voluntary agencies on the cheap, whilst the voluntary sector has been criticised for relinquishing its independence.

In addition, since 1997 an extensive range of area-based programmes has been generated by central government which engage regional bodies and local authorities in partnership arrangements with the voluntary and community sector. Indeed, by late 2002 these had become so numerous that they had to be reviewed by the Regional Coordination Unit, with a view towards streamlining and simplifying the various funding streams.

The development of Local Strategic Partnerships (LSPs) and associated Local Area Agreements (LAAs) throughout England is related to the proliferation of area-based programmes. These developments are part of a significant and possibly fundamental shift in the relationship between the voluntary sector and statutory bodies at the local level (see section 9.4).

In summary, in recent years the relationship between government and the voluntary sector has become both closer and more complex, with many different relationships and many potential opportunities for funding which bring their different demands and responsibilities.

9.2 Applying for government funding

If you are thinking of applying for government funding, whether from central, local or regional government, or from the many related statutory agencies, known as non-departmental public bodies (NDPBs, formerly known as quangos), there are a number of things you need to bear in mind:

- funding programmes can change frequently. Criteria and priorities may vary from year to year, or the fund may only be available for a year or two and then disappear or change into something quite different;
- the funders themselves can change frequently. There have been four serious reorganisations of central government departments since 2000, which have fundamentally altered the composition, function and title of nearly half of the departments of central government;
- announcements are commonly made at very short notice, and you typically have less than six weeks to put together an application;
- because of the way departmental budgets are set, few programmes offer funding for more than a year at a time, and even if funding is awarded for multiple years this is not always guaranteed;

- for most programmes the number of applicants is far greater than the funding can support. Typically only between 5 and 20% of applicants will be successful;
- because funds are public money, there are usually extensive monitoring and reporting requirements, which can be time-consuming and difficult to manage.

Despite these challenging characteristics, government funding can be a very important part of any organisation's fundraising strategy. The level of involvement will vary according to the type of work you do and the time you can devote to fundraising. Some organisations, such as those working in health and social care, may not have a choice – the nature of their work and the funding environment is such that they will need to establish close relationships with statutory bodies at many levels. It is best to consider government funding as part of a mix of funding sources, in order to reduce the risk of becoming dependent on one source and compromising the organisation's independence, which can be a risk with statutory funding in particular.

With government funding from any level, you should remember that it is not enough for you to show that your organisation is doing good and important work. You must be able to demonstrate that the work falls within the government department's own strategies and helps it to meet those aims and objectives. This key point is well stated by John Marshall, formerly head of grants and funding policy at the Active Community Unit of the Home Office (now part of the Office of the Third Sector), and now national coordinator for grants at Capacitybuilders:

> *Government grants are primarily designed to meet departmental policy objectives and programme outcomes. These should of course be reflected in the published criteria for grants. Applications are, therefore, expected to demonstrate clearly how they will help departments achieve their objectives. Too many applicants seem to assume that the core work of their organisation is reason enough to secure a government grant. I am afraid that no matter how effective or important the work of your organisation, you need to show how it meets the objectives of the funder.*

Identifying which departments or agencies are most relevant to your organisation and the work that you do is the first step in the process. Most central government departments are primarily concerned with national organisations and projects that have a national significance. Devolution has meant that, apart from departments which have a UK-wide remit, such as the Foreign and Commonwealth Office, the Ministry of Defence and the Department for International Development, voluntary organisations should approach the relevant departments within their own country – in Scotland,

Wales, and Northern Ireland most grantmaking is handled by the departments within the Scottish Executive, the National Assembly for Wales and the Northern Ireland Executive respectively. NDPBs have their own geographical areas of responsibility which mostly fall within the four countries, but this is not always the case.

Once you have identified which departments or agencies are most relevant, you need to develop an understanding of what their policy objectives are, as well as how your work might fit in. You will need to obtain their policy documents, read and try to understand them, and keep track of how their policy develops over time. Always be absolutely clear about what their mandate enables them to support. This will help you to avoid wasting time on inappropriate applications; and if you do make an application, to stress in it how you will be helping them to meet their objectives. Keep in mind that they are funding projects to help deliver on targets that they need to meet, so understanding what these are is crucial.

As with all fundraising, it is important to develop relationships with people. This can be difficult but can really make the difference between success and failure. In the short term, these contacts may be able to help you by explaining the application process, the programme's criteria, and what sorts of projects they are looking for (although they may not always be willing or able to do so). In the longer term, these people can be a better source to tap for information about policy developments and even potential future funding schemes. Try to identify key contacts and have a conversation, or even schedule a meeting, about what their priorities are, as well as your own. This may be more difficult for smaller, regionally or locally-based organisations to do on a national level, but it is still worth trying.

Developing a good relationship with the funder will serve you well over the long term, as organisations that successfully deliver projects and have established a reputation for themselves as trustworthy are likely to be the organisations that government funders are most interested in working with. Remember that your reputation is important – and successfully delivering projects is one way to establish that. Organisations which develop good working relationships with departments are also more likely to receive grants in aid or strategic funding for their general work.

Another important constraint of government funding at all levels is that it works to an annual timetable ruled by the financial year which runs from 1 April to 31 March. All grants (except contracts) have to be approved within an annual budget. Although the Treasury has repeatedly issued guidance stating that departments have the power to make multi-year funding awards where appropriate, awareness of this principle has been very slow to take root. Indeed, an investigation by the House of Commons Public Accounts Committee in 2005 found that 70% of grants administered by the Home Office were for a year or less.

Most departments have firm deadlines for submitting an application, usually in the spring or autumn before the financial year in which the grant will be made. This means that you have to plan your programmes and budgets well in advance. Always check the schedules attached to the programmes, and be forewarned that they may change due to unforeseen circumstances. Departments find it difficult to anticipate the number of applications they will receive, and this can lead to delays in the funding being awarded. Also, grants administered by central government departments must usually be approved by the relevant minister; in most cases this is routine but if the minister becomes involved in the selection process the schedule can be severely disrupted. Even if you have been successful, any significant delays in awarding the funding may mean you need to adjust your project plan, budget, and proposed outcomes accordingly. In extreme cases, you may even need to seek redress under the Compact.

Finally, always remember the little things – *read the directions,* and, as with applications to Lottery funders, trusts and foundations, be sure to provide all the information required. If you aren't certain about something, seek advice from grants officers in the department or agency before you send in a completed application form. If they can't (or won't) help you, try to get advice from a colleague or even contact another organisation that could help. It is usually too late to ask questions once you have sent in the application. In most cases you won't be able to retract, alter or add to the information once you have sent it.

9.3 Support from central government

The voluntary sector receives financial support from central government departments and agencies (NDPBs) in a number of ways. Ultimately all funding comes from the taxpayer, of course; the Treasury then allocates funding to departments according to tri-annual Comprehensive Spending Reviews and the Chancellor's annual budgets. Once departmental budgets are set, there are several routes the funding can follow to reach the voluntary sector. The main routes are described below and illustrated in the figure which follows:

1 funding directly administered by central government departments;
2 funding which is channelled through the Government Offices for the Regions or Regional Development Agencies;
3 funding which is administered by NDPBs or other executive agencies;
4 local partnerships of various types (including Local Strategic

Partnerships and Crime and Disorder Reduction Partnerships);

5 funding distributed by local authorities, increasingly on the basis of grants awarded to certain local authorities for projects in those areas;

6 funding channelled through the NHS or primary care trusts.

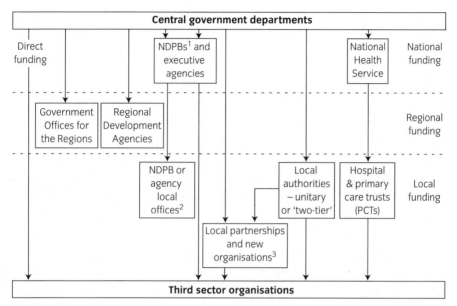

Source: National Audit Office

Notes
A variety of central and local government bodies provide TSOs with funding.
1 Non-departmental public bodies, e.g. the Legal Services Commission.
2 e.g. the 47 local offices of the Learning and Skills Council.
3 e.g. LSPs – Local Strategic Partnerships; CDRPs – Crime and Disorder Reduction Partnerships.

Reproduced from the National Audit Office report Working with the Third Sector, *29 June 2005*

Funding flows from government bodies to the third sector

Funding for the voluntary sector also takes the following forms:

1 funding programmes directed specifically at voluntary and community organisations;

2 grant-in-aid to individual voluntary organisations on an annual review basis – increasingly characterised as 'strategic funding';

3 funding programmes covering a wider constituency than the voluntary sector alone, often administered by NDPBs such as the Arts Councils and Natural England;

4 special departmental initiatives to tackle a problem and to research, test and pilot new approaches/methods;

5 special initiatives, often interdepartmental, and often in selected areas, to tackle a problem through local partnerships comprising the public,

private and voluntary sectors;

6 service contracts, which occur most extensively at local authority level and particularly involve voluntary organisations working in aspects of health, disability and social welfare;

7 loan schemes, usually low-interest and repayable over a longer period, which support increasing an organisation's capacity, or the development of social enterprise.

These types of support are not listed above according to their relative size. Although central government gives large amounts of money to voluntary organisations each year, most of it goes to organisations already being supported, and much of it will not be available in an open application process.

The administration of central government funding programmes varies, mainly because of departments' different requirements and practices and the different outcomes they are trying to achieve. This partly explains why it is almost impossible to determine with certainty how much funding is available in any given year. Based on the figures in the following table, a rough estimate is around £460 million per annum. This includes funding distributed directly by the department or through an executive agency such as an NDPB, and excludes funding from the National Lottery. It also includes several significant funds which are relevant to the voluntary sector but not exclusive to it. If these funds are excluded, the total amount of funding specifically for third sector groups would be closer to £300 million. The figure includes primarily grant programmes, but also some contract-based funding and loan funding. The common denominator is that these programmes distribute funds in a competitive process for which voluntary sector organisations and social enterprises are eligible.

The main ways that grant programmes operate are described below, with specific examples provided in the table which follows:

- programmes which fund multi-year projects, where the fund will not reopen to applications until that two- or three-year period ends;
- programmes which have rolling annual funding rounds, but have a fund value which includes awards for multi-year projects that were successful in previous rounds. This means that only a proportion of the funding will be available for new projects in any given financial year;
- annual grants programmes with a specified amount of funding for the stated financial year, for projects to take place within that year or the following year;
- programmes that have an annual budget and accept applications and award funding on a 'rolling' basis throughout the year. This usually means that applications are accepted until the funding runs out.

Main competitive funding programmes from central government relevant to third sector organisations

Department/ Scheme	Most recent funding period	Fund value for period shown	Funding process			
			Multi-year rounds + awards	Annual rounds + multi-year awards	Annual awards	Awards made on ongoing basis
Cabinet Office						
Adventure Capital Fund (Local Investment Fund & other partners) ±	2003 onwards	variable				☐
Community Assets Fund (Big Lottery Fund)	2008–11	£30m			unknown	
Office of the Third Sector Active Communities Strategic Funding § β	2006–07	£5.6m	☐			
Office of the Third Sector Social Enterprise Strategic Funding §	2007–10	£2.4m	☐			
Office of the Third Sector Volunteering and Charitable Giving Strategic Funding § β	2006–07	£6.1m	☐			
Office of the Third Sector Small Grants Programme †	2008–11	£80m			unknown	
Department for Communities and Local Government						
Connecting Communities Plus – Strategic and Project Grants	2006–09	£18m	☐			
Connecting Communities Plus – Community Grants	2006–09	3m				☐
Ethnic Minorities Innovation Fund ‡	2006–08	£3m	☐			
Faith Communities Capacity Building Fund	2007–08	£4.5m		☐		
Innovation and Good Practice Grants (Housing Corporation)	2007–09	£1.5m	☐			
Tenant Empowerment Programme (Housing Corporation)	2006–07	£3.64m				☐
Third Sector Strategic Partners Scheme §	from 2008	unknown	☐			

Department/ Scheme	Most recent funding period	Fund value for period shown	Funding process			
			Multi-year rounds + awards	Annual rounds + multi-year awards	Annual awards	Awards made on ongoing basis
Department for Culture, Media and Sport (non-lottery funding)						
Community Radio Fund (Ofcom)*	2007–08	£500,000			❑	
Designation Challenge Fund (Museums, Libraries, Archives) *	2006–08	£3.8m	❑			
Grants for War Memorials (English Heritage and Wolfson Foundation) *	2007–08	£100,000			❑	
Historic Buildings, Monuments and Designed Landscapes (English Heritage) * †	2007–08	£8m				❑
Listed Places of Worship Grant Scheme	2007–08	£15m				❑
National Capacity Building Programme for the Voluntary Sector (English Heritage)	2006–07	£1.4m		❑		
Memorials Grant Scheme	2007–08	variable				❑
PRISM Fund (Museum, Libraries, Archives) *	2006–07	£250,000			❑	
Regional Capacity Building Programme for the Voluntary Sector (English Heritage) †	2007–08	£630,000				❑
Repair Grants for Listed Places of Worship (English Heritage and Heritage Lottery Fund) *	2007–08	£24.5m		❑		
Department for Children, Schools and Families (formerly Department for Education and Skills)						
Children, Young People and Families Grant Programme	2008–09	£11m		❑		
Community Champions †	2005–08	£9m			❑	
Independent/State School Partnerships Scheme	2006–08	£3.4m		❑		
Local Network Fund for Children and Young People †	2006–08	£40m		❑		
National Voluntary Youth Organisation Grant Scheme ‡	2005–08	£21m	❑			
Parenting Fund	2006–08	£14m	❑			
Safeguarding Children, Supporting Families Grant Programme ‡	2005–08	£4.2m	❑			

Department/ Scheme	Most recent funding period	Fund value for period shown	Funding process			
			Multi-year rounds + awards	Annual rounds + multi-year awards	Annual awards	Awards made on ongoing basis
Strengthening Families Grants ‡	2005–08	£3.5m	□			
Department for Environment, Food and Rural Affairs						
Bio-energy Capital Grants Scheme Round 3 (AEA Energy and Environment) *	2007–10	£7.5m		□		
Countdown 2010 Bio-diversity Action Fund (Natural England)	2006–08	£4m	□			
Business Community Reuse Fund (Royal Society of Wildlife Trusts)	2007–08	£1.5m			□	
Environmental Action Fund ‡	2005–08	£7.14m	□			
English Woodland Grants Scheme (Forestry Commission) * †	2008–09	£17.7m				□
Rural Stress Action Plan (Rural Stress Information Network) ‡	2005–08	£1m		□		
Sustainable Development Fund (National Parks) †	2005–08	£1.6m				□
Department of Health						
Opportunities for Volunteering Scheme (Volunteering England and other partners)	2008–11	£6.7m		□		
Section 64 General Scheme of Grants	2008–11	£17.2m		□		
Social Enterprise Fund	2008–11	£73m		□		
Department for International Development						
Civil Society Challenge Fund *	2007–08	£14m		□		
Conflict and Humanitarian Fund *	2007–08	£14.5m		□		
Development Awareness Fund *	2008–09	£1.5m			□	
Governance and Transparency Fund *	2007–11	£100m	□			
Department for Business, Enterprise and Regulatory Reform (formerly Department of Trade and Industry)						
Business Incubation Development Fund *	2005–08	£5m	□			

Department/ Scheme	Most recent funding period	Fund value for period shown	Funding process			
			Multi-year rounds + awards	Annual rounds + multi-year awards	Annual awards	Awards made on ongoing basis
Equality Awareness Capacity Building Funding *	2005–07	£2.5m	❏			
Financial Inclusion Fund – Face to Face Debt Advice Project	2006–08	£45m	❏			
Low Carbon Buildings Programme (Carbon Trust) *	2006–09	£78.5m		❏		
Department for Transport						
Road Safety Challenge Fund	2006–07	£250,000			❏	
Department for Work and Pensions						
Financial Inclusion Fund – Growth Fund Contracts ±	2006–08	£36m				❏
Foreign and Commonwealth Office						
Global Opportunities Fund *	2007–08	£70m		❏		
HM Revenue & Customs						
Grant-in-Aid Funding Programme §	2007–08	£2m			❏	
Home Office						
Connected Fund	2007-08	£500,00			❏	
Independent Sexual Violence Advisors Fund	2006–07	£2m			❏	
SARCS Fund: Provision for Sexual Assault Provision Centres	2007–08	£1.1m			❏	
Victims Fund: Supporting Victims of Hate Crime	2007–08	£250,000			❏	
Victims Fund: Supporting Victims of Homicide	2007–08	£250,000			❏	
Ministry of Defence						
Veterans Challenge Fund	2007–08	£750,000				❏
Ministry of Justice (formerly parts of the Home Office and Department for Constitutional Affairs)						
National Offender Management Service Grants	2007–08	£500,000			❏	
Victims Fund: Provision for Victims of Sexual Offending	2007–08	£1.25m			❏	

Notes
1. Where a fund is administered by an external body (i.e. NDPB) this is indicated in brackets
2. The time period and fund value shows the most recent information available at the time of writing
3. Time periods shown refer to either one financial year (00/00) or multiple years (00–00)
4. Variable = the amount of funds awarded each year is not fixed
5. Unknown = the fund value and/or funding process had not been announced at the time of writing

Key
* = fund is not exclusively for the voluntary sector
‡ = fund will not continue beyond the time period shown
§ = fund is technically 'grant-in-aid' but is open to competitive bidding
β = total amount shown is for first year of 3–5 year awards
† = administered regionally or locally
± = not grant funding (i.e. contracts or loans)

Annual grants-in-aid to voluntary organisations

The distinction between grants and grants-in-aid is not always clear even within the Civil Service. Nor, for that matter, is the distinction between grants and contracts always clear – it can sometimes be difficult for civil servants to determine which model is most suitable to achieve the desired outcomes.

In a document published in May 2006, *Improving Financial Relationships with the Third Sector,* HM Treasury sought to clarify the distinction between these types of funding.

- *Grant* – 'a financial transfer used to fund an activity because that activity is in broad alignment with the funder's objectives'.
- *Grant-in-aid* – 'payment by a government department to finance all or part of the costs of the body in receipt ... where the government has decided, subject to parliamentary controls, that the recipient body should operate at arm's length'.
- *Procurement* (contracting) – 'the acquisition of goods and services in line with the government's policy of value for money, normally achieved through competition'.

Grants-in-aid are therefore distinguished from other types of funding in that they tend to be given on a continuing basis to bodies towards their operational or core costs. Although the organisations may have to re-apply on an annual basis, this is not usually in a competitive process. These organisations are closely linked to particular government policies and interests and many have owed their genesis as voluntary organisations to joint initiatives arising between government departments and/or their agencies and voluntary sector interests.

This form of funding can be mildly controversial – there is a sense in the voluntary sector that certain organisations have benefited from stable, unrestricted and longer-term funding in the form of grant-in-aid, perhaps to the detriment of others doing similar or more ground-breaking work. There is a perception that some organisations have been able to negotiate grant-in-aid as a result of their stature and influence rather than on merit.

There may be an element of truth in this, but the reality is more by accident than design. Most organisations receiving grant-in-aid have simply built up a good relationship with the funder and a track record of successful delivery. Their funding status has been achieved almost organically, as a result of many years of working in partnership with the statutory funder. Unfortunately, the nature of grant-in-aid means that unless you are already on the list, it can be hard to get yourself on it, and therefore the politics of the voluntary sector may come into play.

This may be behind the recent trend to repackage some long standing grants-in-aid as so-called 'strategic funding'. An example of this is the Active Community Unit's (ACU) strategic grant programme for 2005 (the ACU has since been incorporated into the Office of the Third Sector). Prior to the launch of this programme the ACU distributed around £6 million annually to about 30 organisations in the form of grant-in-aid, as unrestricted funding to support their work. In 2005 this funding scheme was repackaged into an open, competitive funding programme called the ACU Strategic Funding Programme. The programme had a much more prescriptive outlook about why organisations were being funded – specifically to promote the ACU's strategic objectives and provide a 'voice' back to government on the voluntary sector's behalf. A smaller number of organisations were eventually awarded the funding, for a period of up to five years with annual reviews.

Most departments fund some organisations in this way, but it can be difficult to find out which they are. For illustration purposes some further examples of grant-in-aid are provided below (this list is not exhaustive).

- Department for International Development (DfID) Partnership Programme Agreements are agreements between DfID and 'influential UK civil society organisations', which set out how to meet and deliver the Millennium Development goals, primarily the poverty reduction strategy. The agreements provide 'strategic' funding for between three and five years. Recently funded organisations include Action Aid, Islamic Relief and Oxfam.

- HM Revenue & Customs provides grant-in-aid to fund the core costs of voluntary sector organisations that promote the take-up of tax credits and child trust funds.
- The Office for Criminal Justice Reform (OCJR), part of the Ministry of Justice, provides grant-in-aid funding directly to Victim Support, a national charity with local branches throughout England, Wales and Northern Ireland, which helps victims of crime.
- The Home Office gives grant-in-aid to several organisations assisting refugees, asylum seekers and immigrants, including the Refugee Council, a charity which provides advice and support, and the Immigration Advisory Service, which provides free legal advice and representation services.

Joined-up thinking

The government has been talking about 'joining up' policy for the voluntary sector for many years. Many attempts have been made to this end but progress has been painstakingly slow, at least from the voluntary sector's point of view. Indeed, 'joined-up government' is a laudable principle that seems to fall down in practice for many policy areas, not just vis-à-vis the voluntary sector. Departments find it very difficult to operate outside their own institutional culture and priorities, and adequate coordination between national, regional and local levels on complex policy initiatives is extremely difficult to achieve. Further, the nature of politics means that many initiatives are abandoned before they have adequate time to deliver fundamental change. This can have a very demotivating effect on both civil servants and on those of us in the voluntary sector who work with government – neither may be convinced that the next big initiative will be around for very long.

In 2006 two significant changes occurred which have the potential to make real progress in joining up policy for the voluntary sector across government. In May 2006 the policy areas related to the voluntary sector and communities were transferred out of the Home Office, to allow it to focus on its core functions of policing, immigration and anti-terrorism. Of particular importance was the fact that the Active Communities Unit – the main entity responsible for the voluntary sector – was moved to the Cabinet Office. Together with the Social Enterprise Unit, formerly in the Department of Trade and Industry, a new 'Office of the Third Sector' was formed within the Cabinet Office, which is charged with coordinating policy across government for the voluntary sector. The sector was given its own Cabinet Office minister for the first time.

Alongside the establishment of the Office of the Third Sector was the launch of the Charity and Third Sector Finance Unit within the Treasury, also in the spring of 2006. The purpose of this office is to act as a policy and strategy development network in the Treasury, bringing together all aspects of tax policy, spending and financial services relating to the voluntary sector. It is expected that this new office will work closely with the Office of the Third Sector in future years.

Whilst the full impact of these developments remains to be seen, they are an indication of the voluntary sector's increasing importance to the government's agenda, and should lead to real progress in terms of 'joining things up'.

Partnerships and special initiatives

In recent years there has been a proliferation of initiatives generated by central government to tackle specific problems, frequently in areas of particular disadvantage. Through these central government has sought to stimulate new initiatives and cooperative work at the local level by the development of a variety of partnerships across all sectors, public, private and voluntary/community. These often involve huge amounts of money. They include:

- New Deal for Communities
- Sure Start
- Supporting People
- Connexions
- Children's Fund/Children's Trusts
- Crime and Disorder Reduction Partnerships

For many of these programmes, certain localities, or zones, have been selected in areas of particular need to receive additional funding for innovative approaches. These initiatives do not operate like competitive funding programmes. In general they run to the following pattern:

- each selected area is allocated a certain tranche of money by the lead central government department to reach particular objectives with clearly targeted outcomes;
- a partnership is formed of the public, private and voluntary sector organisations with a clear interest in the programme;
- a separate managing body is set up responsible for drawing up a strategy and budgeted programme of activities over the lifetime of the scheme;
- within this programme voluntary organisations may be funded for an agreed activity or service which forms part of a wider strategic plan.

Although the opportunity to join such a partnership may seem attractive, the many additional administrative tasks and incessant meetings can create a very heavy workload, so you need to be sure that your organisation has the capacity to cope and can allow for it when putting project budgets together.

Local voluntary and community groups within the location of a special initiative should be alert to the possibility that the partnership body may decide to provide a community fund in their area. See chapter 6, section 6.2, for more on community foundations.

The plethora of partnerships operating at local level is part of the reasoning behind the introduction of Local Strategic Partnerships across England. LSPs operate as the 'single co-ordinating partnership for an area ... linking the neighbourhood to the regions, co-ordinating across and between partnership activity'. They are intended to be the 'partnership of partnerships', playing a strategic role in coordinating activity and allocating funding locally. The 2006 Local Government White Paper and Local Government and Public Involvement in Health Bill contain many proposals intended to make these partnerships more effective (see section 9.4).

Regionalisation

Regionalisation is part of the government's modernisation and devolution programme. The idea is that regional government offers greater involvement and control to local people and organisations. Devolving funding streams away from central government to regional agencies 'closer to the ground' clearly fits with this approach. Much government funding for each of the nine English regions is initially channelled through a number of regional structures, the main ones being Regional Development Agencies (RDAs) and Government Offices for the Regions (GORs).

A cross-departmental unit, the Regional Co-ordination Unit, was set up in 2002 to give more coherence to the work of the GORs. It carried out a review of area-based programmes, with a view to finding ways to amalgamate some programmes in order to streamline and simplify the various funding streams. As described above, the rationalisation of many funding programmes is already well under way and is set to continue in future years.

The introduction of RDAs added an important new tier to government, but one which is not democratically accountable except in Greater London. RDAs have been given specific statutory responsibilities for economic development and regeneration, competitiveness, business support and investment, skills, employment and sustainable development. Whilst their thinking seems to be business-led, their decisions will increasingly affect the work of voluntary organisations that have formed into regional networks to be able to make an input into their thinking and their work. RDAs are also set to play a key role in supporting social enterprise.

Until 2002, RDAs were responsible for overseeing the Single Regeneration Budget (SRB). However, RDAs called for freedom from restricted budgets and power to decide their own spending priorities, according to regional needs as expressed in their strategic plans. As a result the SRB ceased to function after the transition year, 2001–02. Now RDAs are financed directly through a Single Programme Budget (the 'Single Pot'). This pooled budget consists of funding from six government departments, with the majority being supplied by Communities and Local Government (CLG).

The allocation of the Single Pot between each RDA is determined in large part by a formula, which is agreed between the Department for Business Enterprise and Regulatory Reform (formerly the Department of Trade and Industry) and the RDAs based on the economic situation in each region. Priorities are reflected in each RDA's three-year corporate plan (currently 2005–08), which sets out how the RDAs intend to use their money.

Government has stated that RDAs have flexibility to support voluntary and community sector organisations in the delivery of both social and economic outcomes, but many RDAs have strictly defined their role in regeneration and the promotion of business and enterprise and are not necessarily oriented towards involving the voluntary sector. However, the 2007 Third Sector Review and the 2006 Social Enterprise Action Plan provide a clear indication of the RDA's role in supporting social enterprise.

The decline of SRB has undoubtedly had an impact on funding available to the voluntary sector from RDAs. A report by the Local Community Sector Taskforce in 2006 stated that 'we are in no doubt that the wind down of SRB … has placed additional pressures on the sustainability of local community groups and projects'. It went on to estimate that up to £3 million per year was needed for each region to ensure that community sector activity was not threatened by the end of the SRB. It is difficult to say with certainty what long-term effects this will have on the voluntary sector's activities at the local/regional level.

The proposals in the 2006 Local Government and Public Involvement in Health Bill concerning Local Strategic Partnerships and Local Area Agreements may also impact the relationship between RDAs and the voluntary sector in the future. Along with other key statutory bodies, RDAs are 'named partners' on LSPs, and much of their funding may become subject to negotiation according to local priorities as part of LAAs (see section 9.4).

Funding to local groups

Whilst, as a general rule, central government departments support national work or initiatives with a national significance, and leave the funding of local and community activities to local government, in recent years they have initiated a number of time-limited programmes. Usually these involved devolving responsibility for overseeing the programme to the regional Government Offices or an external agency, and then administering the programmes through agencies 'closer to the ground', such as community foundations, rural community councils, councils for voluntary service and even grantmaking trusts. Initiatives of this type have included the following.

- Community Resource Fund (1999–2002) – managed by the Community Development Foundation and the Community Foundation Network, for the Active Communities Unit of the Home Office (now the Cabinet Office).
- Neighbourhood Support Fund (2001–06) – managed by the Community Development Foundation and two other bodies for projects in the 40 most deprived areas of England.
- Community Champions Fund (1999–2008) – delegated from the DfES (now DCSF) to the Government Offices for the Regions and then to local administrators.
- Local Network Fund (2001–08), administered for DfES (now DCSF) by a network of of 57 voluntary sector organisations with community development and grant making experience.
- Adult and Community Learning Fund (1998–2004) – administered for the DfES (now DCSF) by NIACE, the national organisation for adult learning.
- Neighbourhood Renewal Fund Community Chests and Community Learning Chests (2001–06) – delegated by ODPM (now CLG) through the Government Offices and administered by local organisations.

With the exception of the Community Champions Fund and the Local Network Fund, which will continue until April 2008, most of these programmes have now ended, and in some cases the funding attached to them has been or will be incorporated within the scope of Local Area Agreements. One of the largest small grants programmes, the Neighbourhood Renewal Community Chests, which provided £100 million during its operation, ended in April 2006. Funding that would have been provided under this programme in the form of small grants is now distributed according to the agreements in each LAA. This may or may not include a small grants component – it will depend on how the LAA is negotiated in each area.

These small grants programmes have been effective because the application processes have tended to be less complicated and the local administration has made the interaction between funder and applicant easier to manage. The programmes usually offer smaller amounts of money, which have a proportionally higher impact on these groups since many of them do not employ professional staff or have capital assets to maintain. If the increasing importance of LAAs does in fact lead to the phasing out of such small grants programmes, this will be a real cause for concern for the local voluntary sector.

The Local Community Sector Taskforce report in 2006 recommended that £35–50 million be set aside during the 2007 Comprehensive Spending Review for 'Community Micro Grants' to 'develop social capital and build community capacity', in order to maintain local sector activity. The Third Sector Review did announce an £80 million small grants programme, for 'grass roots community organisations supporting community action and voice'. This funding is welcome but it remains to be seen to what extent it will mitigate the impact of the transition to the LAA framework.

Although in general most centrally administered grants programmes are primarily for organisations and projects with a national reach, this is not always the case. Several recent grant schemes have been expressly for local projects or have contained a local or community 'stream' of funding, where a certain amount of the total funding has been set aside specifically for local groups or projects. Some examples follow.

- *Connecting Communities Plus Community Grants*. This CLG programme is administered by the Community Development Foundation (CDF), and supports the government's strategy to increase race equality and community cohesion. Larger 'strategic' and 'project' grants took up the majority of Connecting Communities Plus funding but £3 million was earmarked for local community groups and projects to apply for.
- *Parenting Fund*. Administered for DCFS (formerly DfES) by the National Family and Parenting Institute (NFPI), this fund supports organisations working with parents, families and children who face significant challenges. The first round (2004–06) supported national as well as local projects, but the second round (2006–08) was only available for projects in specified urban areas in England where need was deemed to be greatest.
- *Faith Communities Capacity Building Fund*. The Community Development Foundation is also responsible for running this fund on behalf of CLG. The aim of the fund is to promote inclusion and community cohesion through supporting faith and inter-faith organisations to strengthen their capacity and communications network. The fund contains a Small Grants Capacity Building stream for local community groups doing inter-faith work.
- *Connected Fund*. This Home Office programme provides small grants to support small, locally managed community groups and organisations tackling gun and knife crime and gang issues in their local areas.

Another recent development involves local authorities increasingly acting as applicants for grants from central government, typically from Communities and Local Government. This means that particular programmes will be available in some areas and not others – it will depend on whether the local authority put in an application and whether it was successful. It also means that local authorities may choose to deliver the objectives of the programme in very different ways, according to the proposals they set out in their bids. Occasionally local authorities may choose to provide funding directly to the local voluntary sector through such programmes, but usually this is through forming partnerships or commissioning work from specific groups.

Non-departmental public bodies (NDPBs)

The official definition of an NDPB is 'a body which has a role in the process of national government, but is not a government department or part of one, and which accordingly operates to a greater or lesser extent at arm's length from ministers'. Their boards, which are charged with the responsibility for their work, are composed of appointees. Increasingly board members are being selected through open competition. Much of the work of government is carried out by these semi-autonomous bodies.

It would be foolish to attempt too many generalisations about NDPBs; they are so many and so varied. However, they can be broken down into three main types by their legal status:

- executive bodies – the most powerful type of NDPB, and the most directly linked to departmental authority. They carry out a wide range of operational and regulatory functions and usually have their own budgets. NDPBs of this type are most likely to distribute funding to the voluntary sector;
- advisory bodies – these usually comprise groups of experts or representatives of organisations with particular knowledge or expertise. They are created to advise government on one particular issue, usually narrowly defined. They are unlikely to distribute funding to the voluntary sector but may be important in other ways, as they may influence policy development;
- tribunals – these have a judicial or quasi-judicial function, on any number of issues or topics.

The main point for the fundraiser to remember is that they also operate according to the annual financial round (1 April to 31 March). They receive their funding from the government department to which they are related and they are accountable to its minister, who may exert pressure on them as considered necessary.

Like central departments, they disburse funds according to their strategies. It is important to understand these and to obtain full details of their funding programmes along with their annual report. Be sure to check on their deadlines for grant applications, their grant conditions, the range within which grants are made and any requirements for match funding. You will face strong competition. NDPBs usually fund local authority and private sector initiatives as well as those from the voluntary sector, so it is important to appreciate and be able to demonstrate the particular strengths of your voluntary organisation in meeting the agency's objectives and grant criteria.

Many national NDPBs such as English Heritage and Natural England have regional offices which decide on grantmaking through close contact and understanding of their local constituency. It is important to build up a good working relationship with these offices. With all agencies it is best to discuss your proposals first with relevant grant officers.

Increasingly NDPBs that relate to the voluntary sector are being set up with voluntary sector management. The best example of this is Capacitybuilders, which manages the ChangeUp programme. Although it is officially an NDPB of the Cabinet Office, its board and some of its management team come from the voluntary sector.

The following table includes the main NDPBs that may be relevant to the voluntary and community sector – it is *not* a comprehensive list of all NDPBs.

Main non-departmental public bodies relevant to the third sector and the departments which fund them

	Executive	Advisory	Tribunal
Cabinet Office			
Capacitybuilders	❏		
Futurebuilders England		❏	
Department for Communities and Local Government			
Advisory Panel on Beacon Councils		❏	
Community Development Foundation	❏		
Commission for Equality and Human Rights	❏		
Community Forum		❏	
English Partnerships/Commission for New Towns	❏		
Housing Corporation	❏		
Natural England	❏		
Residential Property Tribunal Service			❏
Standards Board for England	❏		
Women's National Commission		❏	
Department for Children, Schools and Families (formerly Department for Education and Skills)			
Children and Family Court Advisory and Support Service (CAFCASS)	❏		
Independent Advisory Group on Teenage Pregnancies		❏	

	Executive	Advisory	Tribunal
11 Million (Office of the Children's Commissioner)	❑		
Quality Improvement Agency for Lifelong Learning	❑		

Department for Culture, Media and Sport

	Executive	Advisory	Tribunal
Advisory Committee on the Government Art Collection		❑	
Advisory Council on Libraries		❑	
Alcohol Education Research Council	❑		
Arts Council England	❑		
Big Lottery Fund	❑		
Churches Conservation Trust	❑		
English Heritage	❑		
Heritage Lottery Fund	❑		
National Endowment for Science, Technology and the Arts (NESTA)	❑		
National Lottery Commission	❑		
Olympic Lottery Distributor	❑		
Sport England	❑		
UK Film Council	❑		

Department for Environment Food and Rural Affairs

	Executive	Advisory	Tribunal
Advisory Committee on Business and the Environment		❑	
Advisory Committee on Consumer Products and the Environment		❑	
Commission for Rural communities		❑	
Darwin Advisory Committee (Darwin Initiative)		❑	
Environment Agency (EA)	❑		
Forestry Commission	❑		
National Forest Company	❑		
(Natural England	❑		
Science Advisory Council		❑	

Department for Innovation, Universities and Skills (formerly Department for Education and Skills)

	Executive	Advisory	Tribunal
Higher Education Funding Council for England (HEFCE)	❑		
Investors in People	❑		
Learning and Skills Council (LSC)	❑		

	Executive	Advisory	Tribunal
Office for Fair Access	❏		
Sector Skills Development Agency	❏		
Department for Transport			
Disabled Persons Transport Advisory Committee (DPTAC)		❏	
Department of Health			
Care Standard Tribunal			❏
Commission for Patient and Public Involvement in Health (CPPIH)	❏		
Expert Advisory Group on AIDS (EAGA)		❏	
Health Protection Agency (HPA)	❏		
Independent Advisory Group on Sexual Health (IAG)		❏	
Learning Disability Research Advisory Group		❏	
Mental Health Review Tribunal (MHRT)			❏
National Strategic Partnership Fund	❏		
Department for Work and Pensions			
Disability Employment Advisory Committee		❏	
Disability Living Allowance Advisory Board		❏	
Health and Safety Executive (HSE)	❏		
Independent Living Funds	❏		
National Employment Panel		❏	
Social Security Advisory Committee (SSAC)		❏	
Foreign and Commonwealth Office			
British Council	❏		
Westminster Foundation for Democracy	❏		
Home Office			
Office of the Immigration Services Commissioner	❏		
Advisory Board on Naturalisation and Integration		❏	
Ministry of Justice (formerly parts of the Home Office and the Department for Constitutional Affairs)			
Family Justice Council		❏	
Independent Monitoring Boards	has its own special NDPB status		
Youth Justice Board	❏		

The list includes UK-wide departments and central government departments in England. There are equivalents in most cases in the other three countries of the UK, for example the Scottish Arts Council, Historic Scotland, Scottish Homes, Scottish Law Commission, Scottish Natural Heritage, Scottish Museums Council; the Arts Council of Wales, Countryside Council for Wales, Council of Museums in Wales, Welsh Historic Monuments, Housing for Wales; the Arts Council of Northern Ireland, Northern Ireland Museums Council, Northern Ireland Community Relations Council; Northern Ireland Environment and Heritage Service, Northern Ireland Housing Executive. In addition there are agencies specific to that country, for example the Welsh Language Board and the Bòrd na Gàidhlig (Scottish Gaelic Language Board).

Getting information and using websites

If you don't know the relevant internet address, the following are good starting points and have links to other sites:

- *www.direct.gov.uk* – the government information service site provides an index of sites, including departments, councils, NHS Trusts and non-departmental public bodies;
- *www.gnn.gov.uk* – the government's official news service, containing all press releases from central and regional government as well as NDPBs;
- *www.civilservice.gov.uk* – the website of the UK Civil Service; provides information about public bodies including NDPBs.

The departmental websites often contain detailed criteria and often downloadable application forms. Although the quality and accessibility of information and the regularity of updates varies, they contain information on government policy, recent press releases, transcripts of speeches and consultation papers.

The *governmentfunding.org.uk* site, managed by Directory of Social Change, has been developed to assist fundraisers in navigating the maze of funding available from central government. The site contains the following features:

- searchable database of information on grants from central government for the voluntary sector, together with downloadable application forms and guidance;
- personalised user profile, with the option to save searches and grant information, and receive e-mail alerts on new and updated schemes which match criteria selected by the user;
- news page containing important news articles from the sector press, with searchable archive;
- comprehensive Help & Advice section which contains general funding help, including an A-Z index of key terms and links to other relevant sites;

- Bulletin Board online forum where users can post questions and comments;
- Directory of Users feature, which allows organisations to make their organisational contact details and aims available to others online.

9.4 Local government

Local government is an important source of funding for many voluntary groups. Local authorities distribute funds from their own budgets, in grant form but increasingly by contracting for service delivery, and also administer grants programmes on behalf of central government departments, notably Communities and Local Government. It is difficult to generalise because funding arrangements vary from one local authority to another and are subject to frequent changes.

It is important for fundraisers to be aware of the organisational structure of their local authority, and of the decision makers whose responsibilities are in line with their organisation's priorities.

Organisational structure

Local government reorganisation has led to a confusing variation in the types of local authority. Unitary authorities, which carry out the full range of local government responsibilities, co-exist in England alongside so-called 'two-tier' areas, where county and district councils share responsibilities. London borough councils carry out the full range of local authority duties, and in Scotland, Wales and Northern Ireland regional government also co-exists with smaller local authorities.

Historically, the leader of the largest party on a local authority has been designated leader of the council and has faced re-election annually, but in recent years many local authorities have reorganised their styles of operation, developing cabinets of executive councils, mayoral offices, and a role for other councillors as 'backbenchers', scrutinising and influencing policy. The Local Government White Paper and the Local Government and Public Involvement in Health Bill (2006) stipulates three choices for councils: a directly elected mayor, a directly elected executive of councillors, or a leader elected by their fellow councillors with a clear four-year mandate. At the time of writing these proposals had not become law.

Further changes to local government may arise as a result of the Lyons Inquiry final report, *Place-Shaping: a Shared Ambition for the Future of Local Government*, published in March 2007. Sir Michael Lyons was initially given the task of reviewing local government finance, but the terms of his inquiry were extended to cover the strategic role of local government more broadly. Lyons examined local government's role in what he called 'place-shaping', meaning 'using powers and influence creatively to promote the well-being of a community and its citizens'. The report presents 'options for future governments' that are likely to influence the future development of local government policy.

The pace of change at local authority level underlines the importance for local organisations of keeping abreast of changes in the system operating in their authority. The local authority itself should be your first point of call, but the Local Government Association is also a useful resource for information.

Local Strategic Partnerships and Local Area Agreements

The creation of a range of local area strategies by central government (see 'Partnerships and special initiatives' page 192) has inevitably brought many voluntary and community organisations into a closer working relationship with their local authority since these initiatives are governed by boards with voluntary sector representation.

The 2000 Local Government Act brought in Local Strategic Partnerships (LSPs), which have been established throughout England in the years since. LSPs are local partnerships between local authorities, local representatives of statutory bodies such as the NHS and police, the private sector and the voluntary sector. Around 360 LSPs have now been set up. The 2006 Local Government White Paper and subsequent local government bill contained many proposals to enhance their role, seeing them take the 'strategic lead' in local areas and becoming the mechanism through which 'sustainable communities' are achieved.

Under the proposals, local authorities would be charged with leading LSPs because of their democratic accountability. The LSP is intended to develop the Sustainable Community Strategy, which sets out the vision and priorities for the area's future. This is then spelled out in detail in the Local Area Agreement (LAA), which defines outcomes for the next three years, negotiated between central government (as represented by the regional Government Office) and the LSP, around these themes:

- children and young people
- safer and stronger communities
- healthier communities and older people
- economic development and environment.

LAAs are designed to rationalise the many area-based funding streams and their associated targets and budgets, to reduce bureaucracy and give local communities greater control over how resources are deployed to meet local priorities. Many area-based funding streams related to these key areas have already been merged under the rubric of LAAs, following on from the review of Area Based Initiatives and the Small Grants Action Plan in 2002. To date, each LSP has had the option of continuing to allocate funding according to the themes, or of pooling resources into one single pot, and it is likely that the 'pooling' solution will become prevalent in the future.

Fundamental questions remain about how LSPs and LAAs can work effectively in practice, especially as far as the voluntary sector is concerned. Between 2001 and 2006, £60 million of funding was provided through the Community Empowerment Fund (part of the Neighbourhood Renewal Programme) to set up and maintain Community Empowerment Networks in the 88 Neighbourhood Renewal Areas in England. These local structures facilitated VCS participation in LSPs in those areas. However, the vast majority of LSP areas have not had any funding specifically earmarked for VCS participation. Given the probability of a tighter fiscal environment in future years, it looks as though funding for the 88 will not be extended either. The 2007 Third Sector Review announced an extra £6.5 million for VCS participation in LSPs, but this is not ring fenced.

Even if they are able to participate effectively in LSPs, there is no guarantee that local voluntary groups will be able to access funding locally in the same way as LAAs become more widespread. The White Paper recognised the need to maintain small grants programmes for local organisations, but there is no guarantee that this will be the case, and much of the funding for delivering LAA targets may be in the form of contracts, or go to single organisations that are involved in the LSP and are commissioned to run larger projects to fulfil the LAA targets. The Third Sector Review announced several initiatives to support local groups, but largely avoided addressing the impact of LAAs on the numerous funding streams these groups have come to depend on.

Because of devolution, the situation outside England is somewhat different. In Wales, the nearest equivalent to LSPs are Community Strategy Partnerships, which were scheduled to evolve into Local Service Boards during 2007–08. These exist in all 22 Welsh local authority areas, and bring together the key local partners, including the voluntary sector. The equivalent to the English LAA in Wales is the Local Service Agreement – these are set to be agreed by individual areas with the Welsh Assembly Government in the years up to 2010. In Scotland there is no direct equivalent of LSPs/LAAs, although many aspects of the community planning system (introduced under the Local Government in Scotland Act 2003) have similar principles and themes. Community Planning Partnerships have been established in each of the 32 Scottish local authority areas as part of this system.

Local compacts

Local compacts have been or are being developed throughout most areas in England. Similar to the national compact, these set out the mutual responsibilities that the local authority and local statutory bodies have with the local voluntary sector. There seems to be a wide variation in the quality and effectiveness of local compacts – local organisations should try to find out how much progress their local authority has achieved so far, and whether the agreement seems to be functioning as it should. For more information, including case studies, an information bank, and a register of local compacts, see www.thecompact.org.uk.

Local contacts

For grants and other forms of advice and help, get in touch with the range of local authority officers who are responsible for information and support services relevant to your organisation. In many local authorities there are specialist grants officers with the specific remit of providing funding information to voluntary organisations, and these are obviously a first port of call. Find out if your local authority has such an officer and subscribe to any bulletins on funding or other useful services that are offered.

You may also need to develop working relationships with officers dealing with regeneration, employment and training and with links to European Structural Funds. The Government Offices for the Regions and the Regional Development Agencies have key roles in these areas, and any contacts you can develop will be helpful. However, officers in your local authority may also be able to provide you with advice and direct you as necessary to relevant officers in the regional bodies.

It is worth noting that although many decisions are made by councillors, briefing sessions by council officers can be hugely influential. Assuming that councillors are solely responsible for decision making can lead to missed opportunities – as at central government level, there will be many different people behind the decisions that are made.

The establishment of Local Strategic Partnerships across England and the increasing importance of Local Area Agreements means that making contacts and forging relationships with members of these partnerships is also crucial. In many areas, particularly in the 88 Neighbourhood Renewal Areas that received Community Empowerment Fund money, there may be established networks of voluntary organisations set up to represent the voluntary sector on the LSP. In many cases this will be led by an already established support body, such as the local council for voluntary service. If you want to be able to participate in the activities of LSPs and have an influence on the decisions they make, you will need to become actively involved in some way.

Whilst it is vital to contact the specialist grants officer (if there is one) or to find the officers responsible who service the committees relevant to your work, you should also find out the names of the councillors serving on committees, particularly the chair. You should also try to enlist the support of your local councillors in the ward where you are working, whether they are from the party in overall control of the council or in opposition.

Find out their interests

Before approaching councillors and council officers, it is sensible to find out how much your local council gives for your area of work and the particular projects it supports. This information is readily available in the minutes of council and committee meetings.

It is also interesting to find out what other councils are doing. If yours is one of the councils which is spending very little on voluntary organisations, it may be useful long-term ammunition to be able to underline this point to your council by making suitable comparisons – though this will probably not help you much in the short term where getting the council to increase its budget is unlikely.

Vital research

You should get to know the working procedures of your local council. Find out:

- what principal responsibilities each tier of local government in your area has, particularly with regard to your own area of activity;
- what each relevant council's stated policies are. If, for example, a council lays strong emphasis on providing educational facilities and services, you may be able to take advantage of this when applying for a grant for an educational component of your work;
- how and when decisions on grants are taken. You need to know both the procedure and the timetable;
- what organisations the council has funded in the past, and the amounts it has given in individual grants. This more than anything else will give you a picture of the council's general approach and preferences;
- which councillors and council officers will be involved in the decision to fund you, and which are likely to be sympathetic to your organisation.

Making your case

Once you have identified the councillors and council officers whose support you need, it is advisable to spend time interesting them in your organisation. Invite them to events, which will also be a good opportunity for them to meet your colleagues. If there are people with local influence on your board or who support you in some way, persuade them to talk to some of the key councillors and officials about the value of your work. Check these local VIPs' political persuasions first, and 'match' them with councillors with similar political views.

It is a good idea to prepare the ground in this way before you make any formal application for a grant, so that you have a fair idea of what will be acceptable and what will not. Make sure that all those responsible for contacting and lobbying councillors are properly briefed: first, on the local importance of the organisation (backed up by figures, analysis etc.); second, on how your work relates to the policies and priorities of the council; and third, on what the council can do to help. If councillors receive conflicting or muddled statements from a variety of sources, this can do considerable damage to your case.

You may find it difficult to prioritise spending time in interminable meetings or phone calls with representatives of statutory bodies, but keep in mind that in any community, even larger urban areas, a relatively small number of people will make the majority of decisions across all sectors. These people may wear many different hats so, for example, the chief executives of local businesses, PCTs, police and even councillors may also be trustees for charities in the area.

The somewhat trite adage that 'fundraising is friendraising' has a good deal of truth in it. This does not imply that by developing relationships with important people in the community you are trying to curry favour with them to do things which aren't above board – that certainly should not be your goal. The point is rather that you are trying to establish relationships to give you access – to be able to advance your cause, find out important information, and have a level of influence on decisions where it is appropriate. If you aren't a known quantity, whether on an official or unofficial basis, this will be much more difficult.

Particular considerations

Apart from information particular to your council, there are criteria which all councils are likely to use when considering your proposal. You should take these into account at an early stage.

- How well do the work and objectives of your organisation fit in with your council's stated policies and priorities?

- Are there any organisations in the area doing similar work? If there are, do these organisations receive local authority funding? Are there sound reasons why the authority should fund your organisation as well as, or instead of, those it is already funding?
- How successful are you? Is your work of a high calibre? And what outside evidence can you provide to support this? How many people do you serve? And how many of them come from the local authority area? Are there other ways in which you can demonstrate local community support, such as membership or local fundraising?
- How well organised are you in terms of financial and administrative con- trol? Are you reliable? Is your work endorsed by way of grants from other official bodies?
- How strongly do the local people feel about you? Would local opposition be strong if you were forced to disband from lack of funds?

Media coverage

While you are talking privately to council officers and councillors you should also be directing your efforts at your local media to reinforce your message. Items on local radio and in the local paper about the importance and quality of your work, reviews and interviews in which you outline future plans of benefit to the community should also have an effect on councillors' opinions.

Support in kind

Local councils may be able to offer you support in kind as well as cash grants: secondhand office equipment and furniture; premises for your use either free or at a low rent; help with transport maintenance; staff second- ments; access to the council bulk-purchasing scheme which may offer lower prices than elsewhere. But you will only be able to find out if such support is available if your contacts with councillors and council officials are good.

At the time of writing, the Department for Communities and Local Government and the Office of the Third Sector were examining ways to facilitate the trans- fer of properties owned by local authorities to local voluntary sector groups. The first stage in this process was the 'Quirk Review', *Making Assets Work*. This contained a number of recommendations, including the need for better guidance and advice, a risk assessment toolkit for local authorities, smarter funding arrangements for asset transfer, and a promotional campaign to raise awareness.

The Office of the Third Sector's £30 million Community Assets Fund was also confirmed in the Third Sector Review. This fund will be managed by the Big Lottery Fund, and will support partnerships between local authorities and community organisations wishing to transfer assets. At the time of writing, specific proposals regarding the fund were out for consultation, but it was scheduled to be operating by 2008.

Asset transfer has the potential to either be a real boon or a minefield for local voluntary sector groups wishing to get involved. As the Quirk Review rightly recognised, risk needs to be assessed and managed properly in this sort of arrangement, to safeguard both parties and the public interest.

Regular contact

Whatever support you are looking for, you should be talking regularly to councillors and council officials, especially those who are of particular importance to you. Keep them informed of your activities throughout the year, not just when grant application time looms again. Establishing relationships shouldn't be just about funding. If it is you will find them more difficult to maintain, and you won't be maximising the other potential benefits.

Acknowledgements and personal thanks

And, as always, you must say thank you for any assistance you receive from your local council. Also remember to credit the council in publicity material, in media interviews and in formal speeches. The council (as well as councillors, who will always have one eye on the next election) needs a good press as much as you do.

Rate relief

In addition to giving you a grant, your local authority can also give you relief on your business rates. If you are a registered charity you are entitled to 80% rate relief on any premises you occupy for charitable purposes. This relief is reimbursed to the local authority by central government. Your local authority can also at its own discretion give you relief on all or part of the remaining 20%. Rate relief is given only if you apply for it and only for the current and following rate years (1 April to 31 March). It cannot be granted retrospectively. You can still apply for rate relief, however, even if your charitable status has not yet been officially approved by the Charity Commission (the office of the Scottish Charity Regulator in Scotland and HM Revenue & Customs Northern Ireland).

Once you have been granted rate relief, you should continue to obtain it automatically, but check your annual rates bill to make sure this is happening. Because of pressure on financial resources, many councils are now less willing to give discretionary relief. But it is certainly worth applying for it. And continue to apply for it each year, if you are unsuccessful at the first attempt.

In his final report Sir Michael Lyons noted that rate relief for charities is worth £700 million annually, and recommended that 'government should undertake its own review of the reliefs and exemptions in the system in order to consider whether current reliefs and exemptions remain justified'. No such review had been announced at the time of writing, but if this does take place the outcome could have a dramatic and potentially negative effect on charity finances.

Getting information

The Local Government Association puts out some very useful factsheets about the structures and responsibilities of local authorities which are also available on the web. More importantly, the funding advice officer in your local council for voluntary service, rural community council or their equivalents should be able to inform you about the committee structures of the council in your area, and provide you with contacts and information on funding programmes, etc.

Resources and further information

See also general lists at the end of the book.

Organisations

England

Capacitybuilders
77 Paradise Circus
Birmingham B1 2DT
www.capacitybuilders.org.uk
Tel: 0121 237 5100
e-mail info@capacitybuilders.org.uk

Charity and Third Sector Finance Unit
HM Treasury
1 Horse Guards Road
London SW1A 2HQ
www.hm-treasury.gov.uk
Tel: 020 7270 4558
e-mail CTSFU@hm-treasury.x.gsi.gov.uk

Communities and Local Government
Eland House
Bressenden Place
London SW1E 5DU
www.communities.gov.uk
Tel: 020 7944 4400
e-mail contactus@communities.gov.uk

Compact Voice
c/o NCVO
Regents Wharf
8 All Saints Street
London N1 9RL
www.compactvoice.org.uk

Futurebuilders England
3rd Floor
3–5 Rathbone Place
London W1T 1HJ
www.futurebuilders-england.org.uk
Tel: 020 7927 6340
e-mail info@futurebuilders-england.org.uk

Local Government Association
Local Government House
Smith Square
London SW1P 3HZ
www.lga.gov.uk
Tel: 020 7664 3131
Fax: 020 7664 3030
e-mail info@lga.gov.uk

Office of the Third Sector
Cabinet Office
35 Great Smith Street
London SW1P 3BQ
www.cabinetoffice.gov.uk/third_sector
Tel: 020 7276 6400
e-mail ots.publicenquiries@cabinet
office.x.gsi.gov.uk

RDA
National Secretariat
Broadway House
Tothill Street
London SW1H 9NQ
www.englandsrdas.com
Tel: 020 7222 8180
020 7222 8182

Regional Co-ordination Unit
Government Offices for the English
Regions
Riverwalk House
157–161 Millbank
London SW1P 4RR
www.gos.gov.uk
Tel: 020 7217 3111
e-mail rcuenquiries@rcu.gsi.gov.uk

Scotland

Futurebuilders Scotland
Communities Scotland
Social Economy Unit
Thistle House
Haymarket Terrace
Edinburgh EH12 5HE
www.communitiesscotland.gov.uk
Tel: 0131 479 5379
e-mail fbs@communitiesscotland.gsi.
gov.uk

Voluntary Issues Unit
The Scottish Executive
Area 2G
Victoria Quay
Leith Docks
Edinburgh EH6 6QQ
0131 244 3649
e-mail viu@scotland.gsi.gov.uk

Wales

Voluntary Sector Branch
National Assembly for Wales
Crown Buildings
Cathays Park
Cardiff CF10 3NQ
0845 010 3300 (switchboard)
e-mail voluntarysectorbranch@wales.
gsi.gov.uk

Northern Ireland

Voluntary and Community Unit
Department for Social Development
Level 3, Lighthouse Building
1 Cromac Place
Gasworks Business Park
Belfast BT7 2JB
www.dsdni.gov.uk
Tel. 028 9082 9424
e-mail vcu@dsdni.gov.uk

Websites

www.direct.gov.uk
The government information service site provides an index of sites, including
departments, councils, NHS Trusts and non-departmental public bodies.

www.gnn.gov.uk
The government's official news service, containing all press releases from central
and regional government as well as NDPBs.

www.civilservice.gov.uk
The website of the UK Civil Service, provides information about public bodies including NDPBs.

www.thecompact.org.uk
The official site of the Compact.

www.governmentfunding.org.uk
Information on grant funding from central government for the voluntary and community sector.

Publications

Cross-cutting Review of the Role of the Voluntary and Community Sector in Service Delivery, HM Treasury, 2002

The Future Role of the Third Sector in Social and Economic Regeneration: Final Report, HM Treasury and Cabinet Office, 2007

The Local Government and Public Involvement in Health Bill, Parliament, 2006

Making Assets Work: the Quirk Review of Community Management and Ownership of Public Assets, Department for Communities and Local Government, 2007

Place-Shaping: a Shared Ambition for the Future of Local Government, Department for Communities and Local Government, 2007

Report from the Local Community Sector Taskforce, Communities and Local Government, 2007

Strong and Prosperous Communities, Communities and Local Government, 2006 (the Local Government White Paper)

The UK Voluntary Sector Almanac 2007: The State of the Sector, NCVO, 2007.

Working with the Third Sector, National Audit Office, 2005

Working with the Voluntary Sector, House of Commons Committee of Public Accounts, Thirty-Second Report of Session 2005–06

10 THE EUROPEAN UNION

The European Union (EU) provides a huge amount of money for social and economic development in Member States, a small part of which is available to voluntary organisations. In 2000 to 2006 the amount received by the UK through the European Social Fund alone was around £5 billion. These funds go to regional and local government, regional regeneration initiatives, Learning and Skills Councils, as well as to voluntary organisations.

Getting money from Europe can be a long, slow and painstaking process. There is increasing competition for the available funds, and the programmes, priorities and guidelines are constantly changing. Each year, the EU agrees its budget. The budget year runs from 1 January to 31 December. You need to keep up to date and to make contact as early as possible, ideally a full year in advance. The budget is adopted in December but it will have been under discussion for the whole of the preceding year and so it is never too early to begin your research. However, you will be unable to apply until the official invitation to tender has gone out. More information is available from the publications and organisations listed at the end of the chapter. Where matching funds are required, you need to make sure that these are committed before you apply.

This chapter gives you an overview of what is available and how to access it.

Details of organisations and publications referred to in this chapter are on pages 227–228.

10.1 A new era for EU funding

After two years of negotiations, the EU has agreed the budget and regulations for the next round of Structural Fund programmes for 2007–13 (the previous edition of this book detailed the 2000–06 round). Due to the addition of new Member States into the Union, there will be less funding for the richer Member States, such as the UK, with more emphasis on employment and skills issues. In addition, to improve the administration of European Structural Funds, a more strategic approach has been adopted through the introduction of

Community Strategy Guidelines on Cohesion and National Strategic Frameworks to determine the structural spending priorities for member states.

Project activity funded by the current 2000–06 programme will continue until 2008. There is likely to be some overlap between the two programmes during 2007 and 2008 whilst the new programme starts up.

For 2007–13, each Member State will publish a National Strategic Reference Framework setting out its priorities for support from the Structural Funds. The Department for Work and Pensions (DWP) is responsible for the new European Social Fund (ESF) programme for England.

The DWP published the draft Operational Programme document for consultation on 30 October 2006. This document set out the proposed spending priorities and delivery arrangements for the programme. A 12-week formal consultation process ending on 22 January 2007 was instigated, with stakeholders encouraged to contribute their views. The publication of the consultation results is expected during 2007.

The previous round of funding was split into three areas: structural funding, budget line funding and contract and research funding. A number of reforms have been introduced as detailed below:

Structural funds

The most important of these are the European Social Fund (ESF) and the European Regional Development Fund (ERDF). They are controlled by Member State governments. The European Social Fund is of particular interest to voluntary organisations and therefore is discussed in some detail in section 10.2.

Budget line funding

There are more budget lines which offer opportunities for voluntary organisations to apply for funding, although eligibility is not necessarily limited to the voluntary sector. These budgets are controlled by officials in Brussels operating within one of the Directorates General (DGs) of the European Commission. A full list of budget lines for 2007–13 is given in section 10.3. To an extent, decisions on funding can be influenced by MEPs in Strasbourg, who can lobby on your behalf. Almost all applications have to have a significant transnational dimension and UK-only projects are not normally funded.

Contract and research funding

This is for specific work which the European Commission wishes to commission, on behalf either of itself or of another government. It is usually put out to tender and can support research across a range of issues in the areas of health, environment, socio-economic affairs, energy, transport and medicine. There are also opportunities to host European Commission conferences and events.

10.2 The Structural Funds, including the European Social Fund

There are several structural streams, with funding for the voluntary and community sector available from the European Regional Development Fund (ERDF) and the European Social Fund (ESF). The funds help to deliver the European Union's Cohesion Policy, which aims to narrow the gaps in development and economic performance among the regions and the EU Member States.

It has been agreed that the EU Structural and Cohesion Fund budget for 2007–13 will be €308 billion. This is smaller that the €336.1 billion budget proposed by the Commission, but still represents an increase of 21% compared with 2000–06. It represents over a third of the overall EU budget for 2007–13 of €864.3 billion.

The European Commission will allocate the Structural and Cohesion Fund budget to Member States according to criteria set out in the regulations. It is estimated that the UK will receive approximately €9.4 billion, significantly less than the €15.85 billion available in 2000–06. This is, as mentioned in the introduction, as a result of the EU enlargement and the UK's good economic and jobs performance relative to other Member States.

The new programmes had an effective start date of 1 January 2007, although the delay in agreeing the 2007–13 EU Financial Perspective means that the Structural Funds programmes will not be agreed and operational until later in 2007.

European Regional Development Fund ←

The European Regional Development Fund (ERDF) aims to reduce social and economic disparities between regions of the Union and therefore is only available in certain areas of the UK. It is essentially concerned with business growth and economic regeneration.

ERDF spending has four main priorities:

- promoting innovation and knowledge transfer, including research and development and building links between higher education institutions and businesses;
- stimulating enterprise and supporting successful business, including support for small and medium-sized enterprises and social enterprises;
- ensuring sustainable development, production and consumption, including encouraging take-up of renewable energy and building a better environment;

215

- building sustainable communities, including support for social enterprise, increase the attractiveness of deprived areas and improving access to employment and public services.

European Social Fund

The European Social Fund (ESF), the other main Structural Fund, aims to reinforce the link between itself and the guidelines and recommendations of the European Employment Strategy. The employment guidelines are currently grouped under the three main headings:

- attracting and retaining more people in employment;
- improving the adaptability of workers and enterprises;
- increasing investment in human capital.

These aims are supplemented by recommendations to each Member State. In recent years, the recommendations to the UK have focused on improving the employment prospects of disadvantaged groups, and tackling the skills deficit and gender gaps.

ESF intends to address the employment guidelines and recommendations by supporting policies set out on Member States' Lisbon National Reform Programmes. The UK programme sets out the government's strategy of increasing employment opportunity for all, in particular by helping disadvantaged groups move from inactivity to work.

The regulation sets the criteria for determining which Member States and regions are eligible for funding under the following three objectives.

Convergence Objective

The old Objective 1 has been replaced by the Convergence Objective which supports the economic convergence of the poorest Member States and regions. The following qualify for funding.

- Member States whose Gross National Income per head is less than 90% of the EU average are eligible for funding from the Cohesion Fund.
- Regions whose Gross Domestic Product (GDP) per head is less than 75% of the EU average are eligible for full Convergence funding from the ESF and ERDF.
- Regions whose GDP per head is above 75% of the EU average but less than 75% of the 15 'old' Member States are eligible for 'phasing-out' Convergence funding from the ESF and ERDF. This is also known as 'statistical effect' funding, since it provides transitional support for regions that would have qualified for full Convergence funding if the EU had not been enlarged to 25 Member States in May 2004.

Within the UK, Cornwall and the Isles of Scilly, and West Wales and the Valleys will qualify for 'phasing-out' Convergence funding. It is estimated that the UK will receive approximately €2.6 billion in Convergence funding.

Regional Competitiveness and Employment Objective

Objectives 2 and 3 have been combined under the Regional Competitiveness and Employment Objective and support projects to increase competitiveness, employment and skills in those regions that are not eligible for the Convergence Objective. Both the ESF and ERDF will operate within the Competitiveness Objective.

All of the UK, outside Cornwall and the Isles of Scilly, West Wales and the Valleys and the Highlands and Islands, will be eligible to receive funding under the Competitiveness Objective. It is estimated that the UK will receive approximately €6.2 billion in Competitiveness funding.

With the Competitiveness Objective, South Yorkshire and Merseyside will qualify for ring-fenced 'phasing-in' funding. This is to provide transitional support for regions that received Objective 1 funding in 2000–06, but no longer qualify because their economies have grown.

Co-operation Objective

The Co-operation Objective replaces the current Interreg Community Initiative and will finance cross-border and transnational co-operation projects. It will be funded by EDRF only. It is estimated the UK will receive approximately €0.6 billion.

What ESF provides

- Getting unemployed people back to work
- Careers advice, counselling and other measures to prepare unemployed people for work or study
- Vocational training
- Work placement
- Start-up aid for unemployed people
- Wage subsidies for employing unemployed people
- Capacity building for local and interest communities
- Training in firms threatened by change
- Any type of training that contributes to local economic development

---

The management of ESF now rests with the Government Regional Offices in England, the Welsh European Funding Office in Wales, and the Scottish

Objective 3 Partnership and the Strathclyde European Partnership (Objective 2 only) in Scotland. Applications for funding have to be made to these bodies. The application form, guidance notes and other relevant documentation are all available online at www.esfnews.org.uk.

Each English region, Scotland and Wales all operate their own application processes, and you are advised to check with your relevant body for application deadlines and to obtain copies of any relevant regional guidance and information.

The Global Grants programme

This programme began in 2001 and provides small grants of up to £10,000 to non-governmental organisations that would otherwise be unable to access ESF funding. Intermediary Bodies (IBs), local public, private or voluntary sector agencies appointed by the nine regional Government Offices in England administer the Global Grants. IBs award 100%-funded grants of up to £10,000 to small community based organisations that would not normally access ESF. Global Grants aim to help socially excluded groups move closer to the labour market.

After 2007, there will be another similar programme to the Global Grants programme, although the DWP has not yet decided on a name for the new programme. The upper limit of £10,000 may change.

10.3 Budget line funds

Funds are also accessible to voluntary organisations through budget lines. They provide funding for projects in areas such as education, training, the environment, consumer protection and information. They are distributed directly from the European Commission. Generally they require applicants to form transnational partnerships with organisations from at least two other Member States.

The following is a provisional list of the budget lines for the period 2007–13. It gives an indication of the many and varied fields of activity where the EU has an interest in providing funding. The list will vary from year to year and up-to-date information is available on the Europa website www.europa.eu.

At the time of writing €1 = 67p.

Budget line EU programmes proposed in reference to the financial programming period 2007–2013

Financial Framework Heading and Programme	Legal basis period	Global amount (current prices in EUR million)
Competitiveness for growth and employment		
Codecision programmes		
7th Research Framework Programme	(2007–2013)	54 582.1
Trans-European Networks – TEN Transport	(2007–2013)	8 013.0
Trans-European Networks – TEN Energy	(2007–2013)	155.0
Galileo	(2007–2013)	1 005.0
Marco Polo II	(2007–2013)	450.0
Lifelong Learning	(2007–2013)	6 970.0
Erasmus Mundus	(2004–2008)	230.0
Erasmus Mundus 2	(2009–2013)	501.9(a)
Competitiveness and Innovation Framework Programme	(2007–2013)	3 621.3
PROGRESS – Programme for Employment and Social Solidarity	(2007–2013)	743.3
European Year on Equal Opportunities for All in 2007	(2006–2007)	15.0
Custom 2003–2007	(2003–2007)	157.2
Custom 2008–2013	(2008–2013)	323.8(b)
Computerisation of the excise system (EMCS)	(2002–2008)	35.0
Fiscalis 2003–2007	(2003–2007)	67.3
Fiscalis 2008–2013	(2008–2013)	156.9(c)
Interchange of Data between Administrations, Businesses and Citizens – IDAbc	(2005–2009)	148.7
Interchange of Data between Administrations, Businesses and Citizens – IDAbc (continuation)	from 2010 onwards	126.0(d)
Safer Internet Plus	(2005–2008)	45.0
Safer Internet Plus (continuation)	(2009–2013)	70.0(e)
eContent Plus	(2005–2008)	149.0
Other expenditure (incl. nuclear decommissioning: 1 487)	(2007–2013)	5 492.7

Notes

(a) Total amount 2007–2013: 656.4

(b) Total amount 2007–2013: 358.8

(c) Total amount 2007–2013: 172.3

(d) Total amount 2007–2013: 215.6

(e) Total amount 2007–2013: 95.0

Financial Framework Heading and Programme	Legal basis period	Global amount (current prices in EUR million)
Cohesion for growth and employment		
Structural Funds	(2007–2013)	277 703.0
Cohesion Fund	(2007–2013)	69 707.0
Preservation and management of natural resources		
Council's decisions		
Market expenditure and direct aids (after transfer to Rural Development)	(2007–2013)	318 988.0
Rural Development	(2007–2013)	88 488.5
Common Fisheries Policy and Law of the Sea	(2007–2013)	2 411.6
European Fisheries Fund	(2007–2013)	4 339.7
Codecision programmes		
Life+	(2007–2013)	2 097.9
Other expenditure	(2007–2013)	274.2
Freedom, security and justice		
Council's decisions		
Integration of third-country citizens	(2007–2013)	825.0
Fundamental rights	(2007–2013)	96.5
Criminal justice	(2007–2013)	199.0
Terrorism	(2007–2013)	139.4
Crime	(2007–2013)	605.6
Codecision programmes		
European Refugee Fund	(2005–2007)	176.4
European Refugee Fund	(2008–2013)	628.0(f)
European Return Fund	(2008–2013)	676.0
External Borders Fund	(2007–2013)	1 820.0
Daphne	(2007–2013)	116.9
Civil justice	(2007–2013)	109.3
Drugs prevention & information	(2007–2013)	21.4
Other expenditure	(2007–2013)	1 834.1

Note

(f) Total amount 2007–2013: 699.3

Financial Framework Heading and Programme	Legal basis period	Global amount (current prices in EUR million)
Citizenship		
Codecision programmes		
Public health	(2007–2013)	365.6
Consumer Protection	(2007–2013)	156.8
Culture 2007	(2007–2013)	400.0
Youth	(2007–2013)	885.0
Media 2007	(2007–2013)	756.2
Citizen	(2007–2013)	215.0
Rapid response and preparedness instrument for major emergencies	(2007–2013)	133.8
Other expenditure	(2007–2013)	1 593.9
The EU as a global player		
Council's decisions		
Instrument for Pre-Accession – IPA	(2007–2013)	11 565.0
Macroeconomic Assistance	(2007–2013)	753.0
Common and Foreign Security Policy – CFSP	(2007–2013)	1 980.0
EC Guarantees for lending operations	(2007–2013)	1 400.0
Emergency Aid Reserve - EAR (g)	(2007–2013)	1 744.0
Codecision programmes		
European Neighbourhood and Partnership Instrument – ENPI	(2007–2013)	11 967.0
Development Cooperation and Economic Cooperation Instrument – DCECI	(2007–2013)	17 055.0
Instrument for Stability – IFS	(2007–2013)	2 879.0
Humanitarian Aid	(2007–2013)	5 614.0
Other expenditure	(2007–2013)	1 179.3

Note

(g) The commitment appropriations under the EAR are not included in the ceilings agreed in the Financial Framework 2007–2013. They will be entered over and above these ceilings.

Source: Europa Reference: MEMO/06/213 Date: 24/05/2006

Accessing the budget lines

Budget lines are handled in Brussels by the various Directorates General (DGs) of the European Commission (see box on pages 223–224), or through their Technical Assistance Offices. In order to get access to these funds, there are a number of fairly straightforward but lengthy processes.

1 Read the Vade-mecum on grant management. Since 1999, all DGs are required to meet the minimum standard set by the Vade-mecum on Grant Management, which was produced to deal with earlier problems of fragmentation and lack of transparency. The document's purpose is to provide an easy to follow reference guide for all those involved in grants, whether drawing up, proposing or evaluating programmes or processing individual applications (see website address at the end of the chapter).

2 Find out as much information as you can about the many programmes and budget lines that connect with your work. Be prepared to look behind the official label at examples of work that has actually been funded under a particular heading. There are considerable opportunities other than ESF, and it is often those organisations that find out about these first and make their approaches before others do that are successful. Useful starting points are suggested at the end of the chapter. The internet is perhaps the single most useful research tool when you are dealing with Europe. There is an enormous amount of information published on the main Europa website, and your biggest difficulty will be in navigating through it all. You can find your way to the websites of the relevant DGs, where background information and lists of current and previous grants are often available. But you can also ask people in other organisations where they have made approaches, and try to learn from their experience.

3 Once you have identified a suitable budget line or lines, make an initial contact with the relevant DG or Technical Assistance Office. The system appears to work in a rather more open manner than British government departments. Telephone systems are good and everyone speaks English. Fax and e-mail can also be useful at the preparatory stage. Establish whether what you have in mind fits in with the conditions of that particular programme. This can be done by asking for any written conditions or criteria. In addition, ask for the application deadlines and for information on how soon after the deadline a decision might be made. The 'call for proposals' will be published in the Official Journal of the EU, but by that time there may only be a couple of months left in which to submit an application. It is therefore useful to find out what calls for proposals are in the pipeline so that you can have a draft ready in advance.

4 At this stage, you may decide either to send in a firm application or to submit a brief outline of what you are proposing. Firm proposals are most suitable where you are approaching a large funding programme with tight requirements. Where this is not the case, it may be better to submit an outline in order to be able to discuss what you are planning with the relevant officials. It may be useful to meet officials in Brussels or the UK. This can be arranged simply and at relatively low cost. It will give you a chance to explain your ideas, and find out their priorities and any special requirements. Officials are accustomed to being seen in their offices and happy to discuss ideas – indeed many welcome it.

5 You will inevitably then be required to send in a formal application – and this is where the system can break down. The time it takes for a decision may well exceed one year (by which time your need may have altered). This is something that officials are only too well aware of and they will generally let you know the latest lead times.

6 Lobby. There may be value in lobbying MEPs – if you can find one interested in your project. They do not have any control over the budget, but officials are often influenced by their interest. It is however a risky undertaking, since it may be viewed by officials as interference.

Tips on making applications to Europe

- Don't expect clarity. Procedures vary from one office to another and even published guidelines change from time to time. Careful research is well worth the time and effort involved. You should refer to the relevant websites to ensure that your application meets with any changes and thus amend your application accordingly before finalising it.
- Talk about ideas, not money. Officials are there to develop their programme areas, not yours. You should be prepared to understand the wider picture, discuss your ideas and adapt them to meet their interests as well as yours for those budget lines and programmes where there are no clearly set out guidelines.
- Don't be in a hurry. Expect to be talking to officials early in one year in the hope of getting money in the next year. Sometimes it can take far longer than this. Response times in some departments are very protracted. In other words, plan ahead.
- Think partnership. This is becoming increasingly important for projects. It takes more time, but adds strength to your application.
- Consider using an expert to help you make your initial approach: there are now a good number of people based in Brussels and elsewhere who specialise in this sort of work. There are also a number of liaison groups that can advise you, such as the Euro Citizen Action Service (ECAS).
- Note and observe any deadlines.

- Be clear where your co-funding will come from.
- Make your proposal succinct and absolutely clear. A well-thought-through and clearly articulated proposal is much more likely to convince the reader.
- Provide all the accessory information requested.
- Don't underestimate the red tape. Ensure that you begin nothing before you have a signed contract, and make sure everything is fully documented.
- Save a copy of your application.
- Do not be intimated by the euro jargon. If you do not understand something – ask!

Directorates-General and services of the European Commission

In the European Union, the staff of the main institutions (Commission, Council and Parliament) are organised into a number of distinct departments, known as Directorates-General (DGs), each of which is responsible for specific tasks or policy areas. In searching for European funding it is critical to decipher under which DG your project fits (it may be more than one).

The Directorates-General are divided into four groups: Policy DGs, External Relations DGs, General Service DGs and Internal Service DGs. Internally, many of the DGs are referred to by their abbreviations (provided in the parentheses below).

Policy DGs
Agriculture and Rural Development (Agri)
Competition (Comp)
Economic and Financial Affairs (Ecofin)
Education and Culture
Employment, Social Affairs and Equal Opportunities (Empl)
Enterprise and Industry
Environment (Env)
Fisheries and Maritime Affairs (Fish)
Health and Consumer Protection (Sanco)
Information Society and Media (Infso)
Internal Market and Services (Markt)
Joint Research Centre (JRC)
Justice, Freedom and Security
Regional Policy (Regio)
Research (RTD)
Taxation and Customs Union (Tax)
Transport and Energy (Tren)

External Relations

Development (Dev)

Enlargement

EuropeAid Co-operation Office (Aidco)

External Relations (Relex)

Humanitarian Aid (Echo)

Trade

General Services DGs

Communication

European Anti-fraud Office (OLAF)

Eurostat

Publications Office

Secretariat General

Internal Services DGs

Budget

Bureau of European Policy Advisors (BEPA)

Informatics

Infrastructures and Logistics

   Brussels (OIB)

   Luxembourg (OIL)

Internal Audit Service (IAS)

Interpretation

Legal Service

Personnel and Administration

Translation (DGT)

After your application is approved

Once you have agreement from the appropriate DG to support your project, you will be asked to sign a contract with the Commission with a number of conditions. Possibly the most onerous of these are the reporting requirements, which are especially complicated as they need to be done both in sterling and in euro. You should always get professional advice about the problems of fluctuating exchange rates, which can leave you with either less or more money to spend than you had planned for. Make sure also that you only charge for expenses that were included in your original project budget. If changes to this become necessary, get agreement from the Commission first; you do not want to be put in the position of having to refund money. Finally, it may appear obvious, but it is extremely important that you submit your report and evaluation on time and in the required format, particularly if you expect to be applying for EU funding again.

If your application is not approved

As with other sources of funding, the DGs receive more applications than they can accept, so failure need not mean that your project was completely unsuitable. You can ask for feedback, for information about successful applications, and for the percentage of successful applicants. You may be able to revise your proposal and try again under a different heading or indeed under the same heading the following year.

10.4 Issues around European funding

1 **Contract funding:** European funding is contract funding, not grant funding. If your project application is approved, you must do what you said in the application. If you use the money for activity not detailed in the application form you may be deemed to be in breach of contract and thus have to pay back any European monies claimed.

2 **Co-financing:** European funds rarely pay 100% of the costs of running a given project. The money given to top up the European money is known as match funding or co-financing. Until recently, it has been the responsibility of organisations to secure match funding from another source in order to obtain European funding. However, the majority of ESF funding in England is now distributed in a system known as Co-financing. Under Co-financing GORs distribute ESF funding via a variety of intermediary bodies, such as Learning and Skills Council, Jobcentre Plus, Connexions Partnerships, Business Link, Regional Development Agencies and some local authorities. These organisations are responsible for finding the match funding, which they then combine with their ESF allocations to create a single funding stream.

3 **A European dimension:** Many of the budget line funds are conditional on you working in partnership with like-minded organisations in other Member States. In most cases you will be expected to name these transnational partners in your application. The implication of this is that you should build relationships with like-minded organisations across Europe even before you consider submitting a proposal. Go to conferences, use e-mail, and develop contacts by joining any relevant European networks and liaison groups. If you do not have a transnational partner, you can also ask officials of the relevant DG to help you find one.

4 **Delays in decision making and payments:** Applications can take a long time to process. For budget line funds this can be as long as a year. For ESF funds a delay of three months is not unusual. You are strongly advised not to start your project until formal approval has been received.

Different European funding streams have different payment systems. The relevant guidance notes should give you details. However, be aware that the reality does not always follow the theory. Payments may be delayed for a number of reasons, the most common being that the claimant organisation has not provided all the required information.

Resources and further information

See also general lists at the end of the book.

Organisations

Department for Communities & Local Government – for ERDF
Eland House
Bressenden Place
London SW1E 5DU
Tel. 020 7944 4400
Fax 020 7944 4104

European Briefing Unit
University of Bradford
Bradford BD7 1DP
Tel. 01274 235821
Fax 01274 235820
e-mail ebu@bradford.ac.uk
Provides training courses on applying for European funding.

European Citizen Action Service (ECAS)
83 Rue du Prince Royal
B-1050 Brussels
Belgium
www.ecas.org
Tel. + 32 2 548 04 90
Fax + 32 2 548 04 99
e-mail admin@ecas.org

European Commission
Tel. (main switchboard)
+32 2 299 1111
Websites
main site: http://europa.eu.int
for Vade-mecum:
http://ec.europa.eu/enterprise/standards
_policy/vademecum/index.htm.
Official Journal:
http://eur-lex.europa.eu

Information Diffusion Europe Associations a.s.b.l. (ID's)
Rue Saint-Georges 99
B-1050 Brussels
Belgium
Tel. +32 2 735 13 01
Fax +32 2 735 53 09
e-mail id.s@skynet.be

Publications

The following publication is available from the Directory of Social Change. The price was correct at the time of writing, but may be subject to change.

A Guide to European Union Funding for NGOs, 13th edition, ECAS 2007, vol. 1: £27; vol. 2: £24; Set: £40

References

'Structural Funds Regulations 2007–2013'. Regional Policy Inforegio. http://ec.europa.eu/regional_policy/sources/docoffic/official/regulation/newreg1 0713_en.htm

'Community Strategic Guidelines on Cohesion 2007–2013'. http://ec.europa.eu/regional_policy/sources/docoffic/2007/osc/index_en.htm

'Financial Programming and Budget'. http://ec.europa.eu/budget/documents/annual_budgets_reports_accounts_en.htm

'Q&A on the legislative package of EU programmes for the financial programming period 2007–2013'. Europa Rapid – Press Release. http://europa.eu/rapid/pressReleasesAction.do?reference=MEMO/06/213&format=H

'The Cohesion Fund – A boost for European solidarity'. *Inforegio*, panorama No.14, September 2004.

'Vade-Mecum on Grant Management'. European Commission.

'The ESF 2007–2013' .European Social Fund. http://ec.europa.eu/employment_social/esf2000/2007–2013_en.html

European Social Fund. ESF Website News, News magazine. http://www.esf.gov.uk

'The Cohesion Fund at a Glance'. Regional Policy – Inforegio. http://ec.europa.eu/regional_policy/funds/procf/cf_en.htm

'Directorate-General'. http://en.wikipedia.org/w/index.php?title=Directorate-General&printable=yes

11 INCOME GENERATION AND CONTRACTS

Earned income is an extremely important source of income for charities. According to NCVO's *UK Voluntary Sector Almanac* out of a total income for the sector of £127.7 billion in 2004–05 (excluding housing associations, private schools and some professional associations), £13.4 billion came from earned income. There are all sorts of ways in which charities can earn income. They can charge for their services. They can enter into contracts with health, education and care providers. They can sell consultancy, information and publications. Developing earned income can be a key element of a fundraising strategy for many organisations.

The growing importance of income generation has led to the concept of 'social enterprise', which is now being encouraged by a number of national networks and grants funds. There are two reasons for this: the wish by service providers and also by charities to see more health, welfare and educational provision being undertaken by the voluntary sector; and the idea that income generation can lead to a more sustainable future for an organisation by reducing the dependency on fundraising success. Social enterprises include:

- commerical enterprises which have been established to achieve a social objective, such as to encourage recycling or address global warming;

- commercial enterprises which have been set up to provide training or create jobs in areas of high unemployment or for people who are hard to employ;

- business activities involving the sale of goods or services by non-profit organisations.

Running a successful social enterprise requires different skills from running an organisation funded by grants and donations. Sales and contracts have to be won, costs have to be recovered from income, selling replaces fundraising as a key function, and success also depends on entrepreneurial ability as well as good management.

Details of organisations and publications referred to in this chapter are on pages 241–242.

11.1 Why income generation?

For a long time charities have drawn the bulk of their income from grants and through public fundraising. Earning income by charging for services has traditionally been seen as more appropriate for a private sector organisation, and this kind of entrepreneurial approach used to be seen as inappropriate for charities. Since the 1990s, however, there has been a major shift in attitudes. The contracting out of services by government has meant that many charities have become adept at tendering for business and entering into service-level agreements; alongside this, increasing numbers of charities have developed income streams from other sorts of trading activities, including charging for services and selling donated goods through charity shops. This income generation brings a number of advantages.

- You are helping to create a more robust organisation. The more you earn the less you will have to raise and the more viable and sustainable your organisation will become. A wider range of income streams makes you less dependant on any one source. Your own earned income can be more or less assured if you run your services well. If you generate a profit, this can provide funds for expansion and development.
- You can make a better case to funders by showing the breadth of your income and your ability to turn work funded by short-term grants into longer-term income-generating activities. Income generation can also take a lot of pressure off your fundraising – which is especially important when competition for grants is fierce.
- You can only sell services if they are needed, if they are of sufficiently high quality, and if someone is prepared to pay. This can add an important dimension to your quality standards and strengthen the link between the service you provide and the user on the receiving end.
- Income generation reduces dependency on outside support and major grant sources, gives you much greater independence from funders and freedom to speak out on behalf of your organisation – and, more importantly, its users.

11.2 Income generation options

Income generation means undertaking a commercial enterprise, usually with the aim of recovering costs or making a profit. This could include:

- charging the users of a service for providing that service;
- providing a service under contract for a body such as a local authority;
- selling items made by beneficiaries of the organisation;
- selling items to members, visitors and supporters;

- earning money through selling publications, running conferences, providing training, undertaking research or selling consultancy within the organisation's area of expertise;
- entering into a commercial activity completely unrelated to the work of the organisation simply to make money. The profit from your commercial activity is then used to support the main work of the organisation.
- commission from selling insurance-related products

Put like that it sounds a simple and logical thing to do – and, in the right hands and under the right management, it can be. But many find that generating income successfully is much more difficult than it seems. Some even make heavy losses. You need to ensure that you have the capacity to develop and manage a successful enterprise before you decide to get started.

There is a danger of getting diverted from pursuing your real objectives. Where the enterprise helps you deliver your mission, you will have no problem. But where it is done only as a means of earning money to support the real work of the organisation, then when the enterprise becomes too demanding of your time and resources, and where the income generated is relatively modest or even non-existent, it can divert you from your real work. If this is the case, then stop.

In this section we will look at the different ways of generating income, and the risks and opportunities that are involved.

Advantages of income generation

- It can provide an additional independent source of income for your work.
- It forces a more commercial approach to the management of your organisation, such that the cost and value of each product is known.
- It creates a more lively entrepreneurial approach.
- There is positive feedback – the more successful you are, the greater the income you will generate in return.
- It fits within current culture and attitudes.
- It can increase recognition of your organisation with potential supporters.

Arguments against income generation

- Asking donors for money is easier.
- With income generation, it's only the surplus (after meeting all costs) that is available to support your other charitable work.
- It makes the organisation too commercial, distorts priorities and distracts from the real agenda.
- Too often it loses rather than makes money.

> - Many organisations do not have the skills, the necessary commercial expertise, the management capacity or the organisational structure to undertake income generation activity successfully.

Charging for services

There is no problem under charity law with a charity charging for its mainstream services which it is providing in pursuit of its charitable objects (this is called 'primary purpose trading'). You can ask beneficiaries to contribute towards the cost of the services that they are receiving (even where these were previously provided free of charge). Much depends on the nature of your clientele. The audience at theatres and opera houses, for example, expects to pay for attending a performance (as well as for a programme, a drink at the bar and an ice cream).

The main argument against charging is that it might exclude those unable to pay (thereby creating a charity only or mainly for the rich). However, charging can bring a number of benefits.

- It forces the organisation to calculate the real cost of providing the service. Oscar Wilde once said that 'a cynic is somebody who knows the price of everything and the value of nothing'. Conversely, many charities know the value of everything, but the cost of nothing.
- Once you know the cost you can decide a subsidy policy. You don't have to provide the service either for free or at full cost. You might want to price it somewhere in between, and make up the shortfall through grants and other fundraising. You could decide to introduce a differential pricing policy (special rates for local residents, concessions for unwaged people, the over-60s and young people, for example). You could charge someone else – for example a local authority – who would pay the fees on behalf of people it is responsible for.
- You will need to invest in promoting the service to potential 'customers', so you will need to agree a marketing budget. This encourages you to tell the world about what you are doing, which could even help your other fundraising.
- It creates a different and possibly more equal relationship between the service provider and the service user.
- There is a demonstrable commitment from the service user to using the service, and an indication that what is being provided is what is needed and wanted.
- If the service is provided at above cost, it can generate funds which can be used to pay for other work.

Trustees should consider carefully the implications of charging fees for services, and the level at which fees should be set.

Contracts for services

The contract culture has brought massive changes into the voluntary sector. Voluntary organisations are now key providers of mainstream services in the health and social care fields. The government body becomes the 'purchaser', providing the funds and setting the guidelines for how the service is to be run and who is to benefit. The charity is the 'provider', running the service and hoping to recover costs and even make a surplus.

Take, for example, residential care for older people which used to be provided by the local authority but which is now contracted out to a range of commercial and not-for-profit providers. The purchaser selects a provider (either by negotiation or through a tendering process). The contract is not awarded on price alone, but also on quality and the provider's ability to run the service. The contract (sometimes called a service agreement) is then issued which defines the service to be provided and the payments to be received.

The contract culture opens up a range of income streams, but requires certain skills: you need to be aware of potential pitfalls.

- The arrangement is quite different from a funding relationship. The payment is not a grant; it is for a service and may have penalties for non-performance, which increases the level of risk. The price is fixed at the outset and the terms are set by the provider (which is the other way round from a funding application, where the applicant sets out what they want to do and seeks funding for it).
- The fact that you are a charity is often irrelevant. The purchaser is buying the best available service at the best price. You won't get anywhere by saying 'give it to us because the charity benefits'.
- Costing the bid is vital. A charity should submit a bid that ensures full cost recovery or is priced to make a surplus. Some have submitted bids at below cost, hoping to raise the balance through fundraising – don't! It is not a proper use of charity funds to subsidise public sector services, and underfunding can soon lead to financial crisis.
- The contract work may be a diversion from the real mission of the charity, and be undertaken solely because the money is there.

There are examples of charities being bullied by purchasers. One charity was asked to provide a complete statement of costs incurred in running a highly successful contract. A renewed contract was then offered at cost price. Desperate to get the work, the charity agreed to it. This should not be allowed to happen. Organisations cannot survive on this basis. Commercial providers would not tolerate this sort of behaviour.

Quality of service

Whatever the service you are providing, you should ensure that your users are receiving the best quality service possible in relation to the cost. Often there is a trade-off between *quality* and *quantity*. You might want to extend the service to as many users as possible; or you might want to focus on fewer people and ensure that you have a greater impact. Regarding quality you need to be aware of the following terms:

- *inputs*: the resources you apply to addressing a problem;
- *outputs*: the activities you undertake and the number of people benefiting;
- *outcomes*: the effect of those activities on the beneficiaries – for example, how someone becomes more effective as a result of some training, and what they then do with their increased skills and abilities;
- *impact*: the long-term change that you are able to create.

It is important at the outset to develop ways of measuring outcomes and impact, which you can either do yourself or by using an outside evaluator. If you can demonstrate high-quality service, user satisfaction, successful outcomes and long-term impact as well as your ability to deliver value for money, this will become important in helping you market your organisation and sell its services.

Full cost recovery

Most voluntary organisations struggle to find funding to pay for their overhead costs, and according to acevo, the Association of Chief Executives of Voluntary Organsiations, this can 'lead to underinvestment in management and leadership, internal and external infrastructure, strategic development and governance'. This situation is made worse by funders that prefer to fund the direct costs of projects rather than pay for overheads or provide core funding. An organisation has to find a way of paying for its overhead costs – its office, its management, its governance, its promotion and PR, its fundraising and so on. Failure to pay for these costs will make the organisation unsustainable. The solution is full cost recovery (FCR).

If you budget for FCR, you ensure that the pricing of your contracts and the fees you charge for services (and the grants you are seeking to subsidise the costs), reflect the full costs of delivering the service, including a reasonable allocation of overhead costs. The UK government first endorsed the principle of FCR in its 2002 review, 'The role of the volutary sector in service delivery'.

The review stated that *'Funders should recognise that it is legitimate for providers to include the relevant element of overheads in their cost estimates for providing a given service under service agreement or contract.'* The review suggested a deadline for statutory funders to implement FCR by April 2006. This is now current practice; and it is a practice that you should try to adopt generally for all your fundraising and for the budgets you produce to support your proposals.

Exploiting skills and expertise

Many voluntary organisations have developed specialist skills and expertise which they can sell. This could be part of the dissemination process, encouraging better working practice and enabling similar projects to be developed. Or it could be done simply to generate income. Home Start Consultancy, for example, is a resource centre for local Home Start projects, providing them with training and support – for which they charge a fee. Child Poverty Action Group provides training on welfare matters and publishes the *National Welfare Benefits Handbook*. Both these organisations are exploiting their expertise whilst directly pursuing their mission.

Think about whether you could:

- organise training courses
- organise conferences
- sell publications or information sheets
- hire out your facilities
- offer consultancy.

You also need to think about these questions:

- Is there a market for what is being offered? If so, will it pay an economic price? As with other forms of income generation, it is vital to know the costs involved.
- Does your organisation have the marketing skills and the administrative capacity to make it a success? Could you link up with another organisation, maybe a specialist training organisation or publisher?
- Do you have a marketing plan and a budget? Too many organisations produce a publication, and only then start to think about what to do with it. This can prove to be an expensive mistake, leaving you with lots of unsold copies and only a small income.
- Is what you are planning a one off project or can it be repeated? If it is repeatable, you will be able to spread your start-up costs over a longer period.

Example

A women's training charity was already funded to run courses for unemployed women who wanted to return to paid work. It negotiated a contract with a big local employer to run a version of its 'Moving into Management' course for selected employees. The employer paid the charity the market rate for the training, rather than the subsidised charity rate, because it recognised that it was buying a high-quality service. The employees acquired new and very relevant skills. The charity found a new source of income (and generated a surplus) from selling its existing skills to a new market.

Selling products made by beneficiaries

Do you have or could you develop any of the following?

- Products made in sheltered workshops by people with disabilities or impairments.
- Products made in the developing world.
- Training programmes for the long-term unemployed, homeless or people with special needs.
- Produce from a city farm or community garden.

This may be the main purpose of your organisation, or simply a spin-off benefit. You must ensure that what is being sold is of marketable quality, and that there is a market which you can reach – whether through a retail outlet, by mail order to supporters or by wholesaling the merchandise to a retailer.

Selling gift items to supporters

Some larger charities raise money through catalogue trading, where new goods are offered to supporters and to the general public by mail order or through local agents. Even successful, well-resourced national charities with a strong track record in this kind of trading may still earn as little as a 10% profit on sales after the cost of the merchandise and all selling and management costs are taken into account. The following are important.

- The merchandise must be of a high standard and live up to promises made in the catalogue. The goods should also reflect your values – in the materials (using recycled paper, for example), through the design or through how and where they are produced. The catalogue should include a coherent range of products rather than a collection of unrelated items, and the range must appeal to your target market. The goods must be available in sufficient quantity to meet likely demand, or your supporters will lose confidence in you. And you must make sure that you price the items so that there is a reasonable profit margin.

- Promotion. You can sell your merchandise successfully through a charity shop, but you may be subject to VAT and have to pay business rates unless the shop is selling mainly donated goods or items produced by the beneficiaries of your charity. If you sell through a catalogue, this will need vigorous promotion, usually by direct mail, and you will then start to build up a list of regular purchasers. Some sales will be made through word of mouth and personal contact; most will come from sending the catalogue to previous purchasers, to your supporters and to selected mailing lists.
- Control and administration. Catalogue trading involves buying, warehousing and order processing. The operation will need to be well managed. You will need to price the merchandise so as to pay all the costs and generate a surplus, and keep costs to a minimum. There may also be cash flow problems, as you will be buying in stock well in advance of getting sales income.

On a more modest level, many smaller charities produce and sell some of the following in an attempt to raise money:

- Christmas cards and gifts to their supporters;
- souvenir items to visitors (at heritage sites, museums and arts centres);
- publicity material, such as tee-shirts and lapel badges.

Done well, these can generate useful income and carry a logo, a slogan or a message, thereby publicising the cause. You need to be clear at the outset whether you are producing and selling the items to raise money or to generate publicity. Sometimes a charity gets into this sort of trading because it believes its supporters want it to, or it sees other charities doing it and feel that it ought to. 'It might end up selling quite small quantities of Christmas cards, for example, and be making a loss, therefore it could be concluded that the staff's time would be better spent asking supporters directly for money'.

Promotional items that can be sold to raise money with the charity's name, logo and message

- Greetings cards
- Calendars
- Diaries
- Address books
- Pens and pencils
- Tee-shirts
- Wallets
- Mugs
- Posters
- Mouse mats

This form of trading does not directly further the work of the charity, and its success should be judged by the amount of money generated in return for the amount of effort, capital, risk and management time put in. It is also an activity where a separate trading company may need to be set up (see below).

Charity shops turning donated gifts into cash

Charity shops selling donated items such as secondhand clothes are seen on many high streets. Most charity shops are simply retail outlets, selling merchandise to generate a profit for the charity. Some aim to be information points, promoting the cause and the work of the charity and recruiting new supporters. Whatever the purpose, running a shop requires a considerable management effort, as it is becoming increasingly difficult to attract customers and make money now that charities are in competition with each other as well as with commercial discount outlets for clothing and other goods. The following are some of the key factors for running a successful shop.

- *Location*. Finding the right location is essential. The shop must be sited in a place that can attract passing trade. It must be near enough for the voluntary helpers who will staff it. And you have to balance these needs with the rent you have to pay.
- *Staffing*. Most charity shops depend extensively on volunteers for their staffing. The usual pattern is to employ one professional manager for a shop of any size, who will coordinate a team of 20–40 volunteers. Some shops have a separate volunteer committee which runs the shop. Training, recruitment, supervision and management are vital to success.
- *The merchandise*. Charity shops tend to sell three types of merchandise: goods donated to the charity by well-wishers in order to raise money (such as secondhand clothing, household items, books and jewellery); goods produced by the beneficiaries of the charity (for example in sheltered workshops and rural development projects); and promotional items produced by the charity (such as greetings cards and tee-shirts). Quality is important, particularly when the shop is selling donated goods which need to be cleaned, repaired, sorted and priced before they are sold.

For further information, contact the Association of Charity Shops, a forum for those charities (large and small) which are running charity shops.

Letting space in a building

Some charities have premises which they can use to generate an income, whether by hiring out office space, conference or seminar rooms, or by running a commercial service on the premises (such as a print shop or community café). You need to ensure that you have the management capacity to do this and that you can make it financially worthwhile, and you need to assess the risks involved. For further information, Community Matters produce a book on *Managing your Community Building*.

Commission from selling insurance-related products

Just as some supermarket chains offer financial services, some charities have a range of insurance products aimed at their particular client group. For example, older people's charities (travel insurance), animal charities (pet insurance), etc. These are underwritten and supported by major insurance companies such as AXA and Norwich Union.

11.3 Problems and issues

The need for an entrepreneurial approach

Reliance on grants can discourage an entrepreneurial approach. Voluntary organisations usually budget, raise the money and then spend it. The idea of a revenue budget with income generation targets can be an alien concept. The idea of using marketing and selling techniques to generate income, and of strategic investment (spending money now to produce a return later on) will need a change in attitude, new skills and new approaches.

Kinds of people and skills needed

You may need to recruit people with different attitudes, and possibly to adopt a different reward system and salary structure, with incentives and benefits. This may mean moving outside your traditional networks and recruiting from the private or social business sectors.

Losing the vision

Voluntary organisations are driven by a shared vision of a better society. The work that they do, for the most part, reinforces that vision. When the main purpose becomes making money, a new set of attitudes starts creeping in, and many organisations become concerned that they will lose their internal cohesion. The same can happen when the fundraising department of a large charity becomes distanced from the operations of the charity.

Some organisations prefer to keep their income generation work separate and trade through a completely separate trading company or non-profit agency, even where there is no legal requirement to do this (see below).

Charity law

When your income generation activity is conducted in pursuit of your charitable objects (which is often called primary purpose trading), or if it involves the sale of products made by your beneficiaries or the sale of donated goods, there are no problems. But if you are generating income outside these three categories, you may encounter charity law problems and tax problems. But this will only be significant where:

- the trading activity is substantial and involves the use of the charity's assets (it is not a proper function of a charity to get substantially involved in a non-charitable trading activity or to apply its assets for this purpose);
- a profit is being made, which would be taxable if generated directly by the charity. Very often after allocating all relevant overheads, a charity will find that it is not making any real profit from the trading activity;
- the charity's resources are being put at risk. If the scale of your trading is large, this will inevitably involve risk – the risk of making a loss. There are cases, including some large well-known national charities, where large losses on trading have had to be made good, and it is not proper to use charitable funds for this purpose.

In such circumstances, you may need to organise your trading through a separate company which is owned by the charity and operates for its benefit. This is tax-effective, as the profits of the trading company can be Gift-Aided to the parent charity. This is an extremely technical area and you will need good professional advice on how to structure your trading. Consult a professional, or see the *Voluntary Sector Legal Handbook* for more information.

Sources of capital

There will also be a need for money to invest in the enterprise. There are various options.

- *Borrowing*: You can only borrow money if your constitution allows you to. There are a number of socially responsible banking services that specialise in lending out money to good-cause organisations at below commercial levels of interest and without the onerous guarantees or security that commercial lenders may require. A wide range of social investment funds are now available to invest in social enterprises. The pioneer in this field is the Triodos Bank. The Charities Aid Foundation has also developed its Venturesome fund. Futurebuilders has been set up by the government to invest in charities seeking to deliver public services. The Local Investment Fund has set up eight regional community loan funds. And there are lots of other sources, many belonging to the UK Social Investment Forum, which is a network for ethical, social, community and green investment institutions. A wealthy trustee or an outside benefactor may also be prepared to advance you the money you need.
- *Savings*: You may be able to use some of your free reserves to invest in income generation, or allocate some of your annual surplus to an income

generation fund. You must make sure that you use your charitable money only for charitable purposes. Investing in income generation is acceptable if this is a primary purpose activity. If it is a commercial rather than a charitable activity, then the money will need to be provided as an investment. This will require an assessment of risk and returns, and independent professional advice on whether this is a reasonable way to invest the charity's funds.

- *Grants*: Few funders are interested in financing commercial activity, even where the money generated will be used to support the charity. The Esmée Fairbairn Foundation is an exception amongst the large foundations, and has one of its programmes focusing on making grants and loans to support social enterprise. In fundraising for a social enterprise, you will need to convince the funder not only of your ability to run a successful business, but also that it represents a really good and secure investment in your future sustainability and in achieving your objectives.

Resources and further information

See also general lists at the end of the book.

Organisations

Association of Charity Shops
Central House
14 Upper Woburn Place
London WC1H 0AE
www.charityshops.org.uk
Tel. 020 7255 4470

Business in the Community
135 Shepherdess Walk
London N1 7RQ
www.bitc.org.uk
Tel. 0870 600 2482

Charities Advisory Trust
Radius Works
Back Lane
London NW3 1HL
www.charitiesadvisorytrust.org.uk
Tel. 020 7794 9835

Community Matters
12–20 Baron Street
London N1 9LL
www.communitymatters.org.uk
Tel. 020 7837 7887

Futurebuilders England
3rd Floor
3–5 Rathbone Place
London W1T 1HJ
www.futurebuilders-england.org.uk
Tel: 020 7927 6340
Fax: 020 7927 6341

Local Investment Fund
www.lif.org.uk

Triodos Bank
Brunel House
11 The Promenade
Bristol BS8 3NN
www.triodos.co.uk
Tel: 0117 973 9339

UK Social Investment Forum
www.uksif.org

Venturesome
www.caf.org.uk/default.aspx?page=6903

Publications

The following publications are available from the Directory of Social Change. Prices were correct at the time of writing, but may be subject to change.

Charitable Status, 6th edn, Julian Blake, DSC, £12.95

The Fundraiser's Guide to the Law, Bates, Wells & Braithwaite and Centre for Voluntary Sector Development, DSC 2000, £19.95

The Voluntary Sector Legal Handbook, 3rd edn, Sandy Adirondack & James Sinclair Taylor, DSC 2008, £50 (voluntary organisations), £80 (others) (available early 2008; check www.dsc.org.uk for details)

PART
three

TECHNIQUES

▶▶▶▶▶▶▶▶▶▶

12 EVENTS AND FUNDRAISING FROM THE GENERAL PUBLIC

Some of the most traditional forms of fundraising remain the most effective, both in terms of amounts generated and the ability to give again and again. This chapter looks at events and other methods of fundraising – public collections, raffles and lotteries – which can involve the general public in your work and, potentially, turn them into long-term givers to your organisation.

Details of organisations and publications referred to in this chapter are on pages 267–268.

12.1 Fundraising events

A successful and repeatable fundraising event can be extremely valuable for you. It brings all kinds of direct and indirect benefits. However, for every successful event that attracts new supporters, another could fall flat, get rained off or have the sponsor pull out at the last moment. You must always evaluate the fundraising potential against the risk of losing money. A well-run event can make money, take your message out to a wider public, involve existing supporters and bring in new supporters. But many absorb a great deal of energy for very small returns. This section is concerned mainly with ticketed events, while mass participation sponsored events are dealt with in section 12.2. For more detailed information, see the 'How to' guide *Organising Special Events* (details on page 267).

Objectives of an event

If you decide to hold a fundraising event you must be very clear what you want it to achieve. Is it mainly to raise money or to interest new people in your organisation? Set a clear primary objective for the event. This will help define it and create measurable targets for what you want to get out of it.

Events can be of any size and complexity. The main idea is to offer an enjoyable experience in return for the participants' money. Both elements are important. It is not just about generating as much money as possible; if people enjoy themselves, they will be happy to participate on another occasion.

In 2006 the Medical Foundation for the Care of Victims of Torture organised an evening featuring well-known authors, including Zadie Smith and Andrew Motion, reading extracts from their favourite books, the twist being that none of the pieces chosen could be from their own work. The evening was counted a success, raising funds through entry and raffle tickets, and awareness of the cause. This is an example of a particular type of event that will attract a particular type of person and generate funds and publicity.

Whatever your event, there are five principal groups of people likely to be involved: sponsors, the media, the performers, the audience and the charity. Get them working in harmony and you are well on your way to success.

Sponsors

Your sponsors will support the event in order to meet their own business objectives (for example it gives access to their target audience – such as motorists for car dealerships – or key opinion formers, celebrities, etc.). In order to attract sponsors, you will need to show them how your event can help them achieve their objectives. If you make the most of the next ingredient (the media), then your sponsors will regard the event even more enthusiastically.

The media

The media is in business to report events such as yours, especially if there is a celebrity involved or if the event is genuinely newsworthy. Well-known names and celebrities attract the media more than anything. You may be able to get some coverage by talking about the good work you do or the fun of the event. If the event is considered significant enough, a newspaper, radio or television station may become a 'media sponsor', offering you free advertising and press coverage to promote the event in advance, thereby extending your audience reach, in addition to providing a good picture feature of the event itself.

The performers

The performers are central to the event itself: the band booked to play at a ball; the auctioneer undertaking the sale; or the football teams and celebrity players taking part in a charity match. They also have something to gain from participating. It could be a fee (although try to get a reduced fee or a free performance), or positive publicity and an association with a worthy cause – which is good for their image.

The audience

About 10% of the public attend charity events. Some go simply because they want to participate in the event; many consider it a way of supporting a charity. People do not go to a charity auction feeling the same way as if they were going to a commercial auction. They are much more likely to bid generously. People going to a charity concert expect to hear something about the organisation involved or to be asked to contribute to a collection. Their enjoyment of the occasion will in part be determined by the quality of the performance (get that wrong and you risk your reputation), and in part by the degree to which the charity benefits.

The charity

The final ingredient is you and your organisation. Your involvement gives the event a focus – the main reason for its happening is to raise money to support your work. The audience may come because they are your supporters, or because they are interested in your cause. The performers will not come to just any event, because they may have many other commitments. An event for your organisation should be something that strikes a sympathetic chord with them. The sponsors will decide to back the event because of your reputation and the audience that you can deliver for them. Your contacts with celebrities, such as a member of the royal family, and other well-known people can be a further incentive.

Deciding what to organise

One starting point for deciding the sort of event that would be best for you is to examine your market. What will have the most appeal for your supporters or the group you want to target? Who is likely to attend the event? What are their interests? Will they bring their friends? Are they old or young? Active and energetic? How much do they know or care about your cause? How much disposable income do they have? What are you and your helpers interested in – and what contacts do you have (access to performers, for example)?

Alternatively, think about the major types of event and see whether any seem appropriate. A short list might include:

- sporting events
- musical and cultural events
- balls, dinners, auctions and other entertainment events
- exhibitions, festivals and fairs.

Most events are run on a one-off basis – although you may want to repeat one if it is successful, thereby creating a regular source of income for your charity and building on the experiences from previous years. The first time you hold an event, it will take longer to organise – so try to develop events that can be repeated. Some events take place over a period – for example, a knockout football competition or a film festival. More complicated (and more risky) events should be left for when you have more experience.

Depending on your plans, you may need some sort of licence (to run the event, to collect money in a public place, or to run a bar). Check the legal requirements with the local authority and any other relevant regulatory organisation, before you start any detailed planning. There may also be tax implications.

Event management

It is important to allow enough time to organise your event, as it often involves more effort than you think. There are three main ways to do this, each with their own drawbacks and advantages.

1   *Doing it yourself* (or getting another member of staff to do it) will help you learn how it should be done and provide you with the experience to do it better next time. However, if you haven't run an event before you may jeopardise the chances of success by your inexperience. You would certainly need to take advice from more experienced people.

    The single biggest problem in doing it yourself is the time investment. How much money could you be raising if you were not organising this event? All events require attention to detail, checking and double checking at every stage. If you are in the middle of a busy fundraising programme, then being responsible for something that requires so much of your time may not be sensible.

2   *Engage a professional.* Sometimes an event will be run through a sporting or theatrical body which does this on a regular basis. You could engage them to do the whole thing (and try to persuade them to do it free as a charitable contribution). If not, there are professional event organisers in the musical, sporting and entertainment fields who will do all the day-to-day organisation for you – for a fee. If you hire a commercial event organiser on the basis that a proportion of the ticket price or the proceeds goes to them, they will be a 'professional fundraiser' under the terms of the Charities Acts (1992 and 2006), and certain requirements will need to be met to comply with the Acts. See the box on page 295, and also *The Fundraiser's Guide to the Law* for more information.

3   *Establish a committee of volunteers.* The key appointment will be the chair, which could be you. This need not be someone who has run an event before, but they do need to have strong leadership qualities and

the good management sense to link the commercial needs of the event to the requirements of the charity. You will probably then need to select a multi-disciplinary team that embodies all the skills necessary to make the thing work: from people with the sporting or musical background to deal with the programme, to the accountant who will tell you whether VAT is chargeable on the ticket sales and what the legal requirements are. Give yourself plenty of time to find the right people.

Fundraising events and tax

When income to a charity is given freely there is no tax payable on it. However, many events involve the sale of tickets to the public. This is considered trading rather than fundraising and may be liable to tax. This is a complicated area involving both VAT and income tax. There is a tax concession for those organising occasional events, which allows the income from such events to be treated as a donation and be free of tax. For further information on tax and VAT exemptions, see the HM Revenue & Customs website guidance notes on trading by charities (www.hmrc.gov.uk/charities) or contact them directly for advice on your particular situation.

There are several important aspects of successfully managing the event.

- *An accurate budget*. You have to control costs if you are to run the event profitably. Your budget will show how many people you will need to attract and what price to charge for tickets. You will need to make an early assessment of all the likely costs and the potential sources of income and include something for contingencies. On the income side it is worth making a high and low estimate to illustrate what may happen in different circumstances. This will highlight the risk involved.
- *Time*. You can organise an event in a short time, but the longer you leave yourself the better. The best is an annual cycle, with the planning of the following year's event starting just after the completion of the current one. Booking a venue or obtaining the services of the performers may take a lot longer and may dictate how far ahead you need to plan.
- *Legally binding contracts*. You will need to set up arrangements with performers, the venue and any sub-contractors, expressed through some formal written agreement. This sets out precisely what has been agreed and is signed by both parties to confirm the agreement and to avoid disagreement later on. It is especially important to agree how any money is to be split (both expenditure and income); who has the rights to any recording of the event; who is responsible for what costs; and what the obligations are in the event of cancellation. Look at cancellation clauses and the costs involved to do this. Where considerable sums are involved, the agreement should be drawn up by a lawyer.

- *Good administration and record keeping.* For your first event, you will have to start from scratch; but the next time will be much easier, since you will be building on experience. Keep records of everything – for example, whether insurance is needed, where to go for it and how much to pay. Immediately after the event, have a review – document what went really well, what went wrong or could be improved, what suggestions there are for doing better or raising more money next time.

Reducing the risk

Apart from accurate budgeting and cost control the best way of reducing risk is good planning, organisation and marketing. However, things have a habit of not going to plan, so you need to think about your exposure to risk and how to reduce it. There are several ways of doing this.

- *Financial sponsorship.* Get all the costs of the event covered by a sponsor, so that any money raised goes to your cause, a message that is likely to encourage ticket sales.
- *Commitments and guarantees.* One way of running a charity ball is to have a committee of say 20 people, each of whom agrees to get 12 people to come to the ball. They take responsibility for selling the 12 tickets, or for paying for them themselves if they are unable to find others to contribute. This means that you have a guaranteed attendance of 240 people – enough to fill the venue or make sure that the event is a success.
- *Cost cutting.* You can try to get as much as possible lent, donated or sponsored for the occasion, so that you do not have to pay for it. Venue costs, performer costs, and the cost of prizes can all be substantial, and if they are too high can jeopardise the success of the event. Not having to pay or paying much less is a simple way both to get more out of the event and to reduce risk.
- *Insurance.* It may be possible to insure against public liability, theft or damage (in case something goes wrong), and even against the possibility of bad weather for an outdoor event.

Promotion

Effective promotion can turn an event from a modest success into a really profitable one. Decide who will want to come to the event – your target market – and how best to reach them.

Local radio can be a powerful promotional tool for local events. Many radio stations send mobile recording studios; others may send a reporter to cover the event live. This sort of link creates a promotional momentum. The station will want to give frequent plugs during the run-up to the event, mentioning the date and how to get tickets. Another possibility is to offer free tickets as prizes to be given away by the radio station.

You can also advertise. Think about posters and handbills displayed or distributed locally, advertising in the press and being included in listings magazines.

One way of encouraging publicity is to feature celebrities who may be attending the event or performing at it. For sporting and musical events, the performers will be one of the main attractions. Alternatively, you can invite a celebrity to act as compere, to open the event, present awards or announce raffle winners. Having famous names adds credibility, and encourages people to come along and stay until the end.

You also need a strategy for getting people to come if ticket sales are slow, but not so disappointing as to have to cancel. Once you are sure the event is going to run, it is important that it is well attended. At that stage it is more important to see that people are there than that all the tickets are sold. This means that you should be prepared to give tickets away to groups who might be interested in coming – through schools and student unions for young people's events, through hospitals and other institutions, or via a media promotion.

Sponsorship

Events offer a sponsor a range of facilities and benefits. Sponsors need to know a good deal about the event and its expected audience before they will make a commitment – how many people are expected, who they might be and how they will be exposed to any advertising messages.

You should have a clear idea of how much money you need from a sponsor and what you can give in return. You might be offering special hospitality facilities, opportunities to meet famous people, to place the sponsor's message in a prominent place, or the chance to publicise the sponsorship through the advertising or public relations undertaken for the event. See chapter 8 for more on company sponsorship.

One of the key items that can carry a main sponsor's message, and those of other advertisers, is the brochure (this is known as 'goodwill' advertising, as the advertisers are seen to be supporting a good cause). Almost every event needs a brochure or programme containing details about it, which can also generate income. Each copy can either be given away free (to create maximum circulation) or be sold on the day to generate further income.

Also, if the event requires prizes, these can be asked for and provided as a form of sponsorship from either a local or national company depending on the size and potential of your event.

Developing extra income

For many events, such as a dinner-dance or a ball, the ticket price will cover the cost of putting on the event and not much more. If you want to generate money for your work, you will need to devise ways of getting those attending to give or spend while at the event, such as:

- holding an auction, raffle or prize draw;
- giving out donation forms for each person to fill in, making an appeal during the evening, or collecting money from those present. To make sure that people respond generously, you should say what the money is for and perhaps suggest a level of donation. You could also offer a prize (donated, of course) for the table that contributes the most.

Spin-off for future fundraising

A great advantage of a successful event is that you can build up an audience for future occasions. By collecting the names and addresses of those who have attended, you can invite them to participate next time.

Try to capture the interest of the people who attend so that they learn about your cause and understand the importance of your work. You can also add the participants' names to your database, although if you are planning to send them other fundraising appeals not directly connected to the event, you should make sure that they are happy for you to do this. See Appendix 4 for information on the requirements of the Data Protection Act.

Organising a particular type of event can help you reach out to a new audience. For example, if you are interested in people involved in education you might think about an exhibition of children's paintings; or if you want to appeal to people who have an interest in the arts you might organise a benefit screening of a film or performance of a play.

However, you need to be careful. People attend or take part in charity events for many different reasons. It may well be that a substantial number of those attending are not interested in your charity but were attracted by the event itself. Therefore, sending them expensive appeal literature over a long period may simply be a waste of money. It is much better to ask them what they want to receive from you – if anything – and give them that. The response rates to this kind of strategy are usually as high (if not higher) than the blanket approach, but at a lower cost to you.

Shelter's 'Walk for Home: Manchester'

In the autumn of 2006 Shelter organised its first 'Walk for Home' event in Manchester. Over 150 Mancunians took part, led by XFM DJs, Paul Tonkinson and Adam Cole, walking a route that encompassed some of the significant sights of the City – including Old Trafford where the walk started and Urbis, the city's Centre for Urban Culture. The walk both raised money for Shelter's projects in the city and publicised the issues of homelessness in Manchester.

12.2 Walks, runs and challenge events

Another traditional but highly successful fundraising method is an event where participants are sponsored by their family and friends depending on what they achieve. Almost anything can be sponsored, for example:

- giving up smoking (number of days without a cigarette up to a specified limit);
- slimming (amount of weight lost during a set time);
- marathon runs (kilometres run plus a bonus for completing the course);
- penalty shoot-outs (goals scored if you are the penalty taker, or goals saved if the goalkeeper);
- even cycling in the Himalayas!

In deciding what sort of event to organise, find something that will be sufficiently popular to attract lots of participants as well as being straightforward to run. You also want something that you can repeat, building on your experience and success to achieve greater returns the next time you run it.

A sponsored event can be used to get across an important message about your cause. For example, an environmental charity might organise a sponsored clean-up of litter from an area of countryside; or a health charity might organise a fun run. However, remember that people often feel they are supporting their friends' participation in an event rather than making a donation to your charity.

If the event does not attract enough participants, or they cannot generate enough sponsorship money, you may not hit your target. So think carefully about what will attract your target audience, and whether you can reach them. If it is young families, think of something that will involve the whole family at the weekend – such as a fun run or a sponsored swim.

You will have four main audiences for your event:

- those who have participated and enjoyed the experience before – so it is important to keep a record of who has participated in previous years and in what events;
- your supporters. Mail your members and donors – they may be interested in doing something to help raise money;
- those who are interested in the particular activity you have chosen (cycling, walking, marathon running, etc), but who may not know about your work – although their participation gives you the opportunity to interest them in it;
- those involved in your organisation: your management committee; your staff (their involvement in a sponsored event can improve morale and teamwork); and your beneficiaries.

The National Deaf Children's Society (NDCS) and Charity Challenge Events

The National Deaf Children's Society (NDCS) and Challenge Events NDCS have been running charity challenges for over 10 years. Their first event, an Arabian Nights Bike Ride to Jordan in 1996, proved a huge success with 150 people taking part and £300,000 raised for the charity. Since then the NDCS has organised charity challenge events all over the world and has raised £7 million from these alone. Over the years the charity has expanded its programme and now offers not only international treks but also UK events, corporate events, and UK and international marathons. All events are deaf friendly, linking in with the mission of the charity, and many deaf participants as well as parents of deaf children have taken part in challenges, ranging from Trek the Inca Trail to the Flora London Marathon. National advertising and mailing campaigns are employed to recruit participants, and have proven successful in both attracting a new and varied audience, as well as bringing back past participants keen for more challenges. NDCS has also set up a stand alone website – www.ndcschallenges.org.uk – specifically for Challenge Events NDCS.

Organising a mass participation event

Break up your plan for the organisation of your event into three parts.

Before the event

At this stage, you will need to:

- decide the event and agree the route or venue;
- get necessary permissions and insurance;
- plan the promotion and recruitment of the participants. Since the ultimate success of the event depends on the amount raised, it is important to get your target number of participants. You can then encourage them to raise more money by: setting a minimum sponsorship requirement which they guarantee to pay; giving them a target, both in terms of the number of sponsors they should aim to get and how much to ask for; having an entrance fee for participating in the event;
- prepare carefully the sponsorship forms and explanatory materials about the work of your organisation. The form must describe exactly what is being done, but should also say why the money is needed. It should list the names and addresses of sponsors; a phone number to contact the sponsor if they fail to produce the money they have promised; and the amount pledged. You want to encourage sponsors to be generous. They need to know how many miles (or whatever) they are likely to be paying for. Most sponsors do not know what level of sponsorship is expected, and are guided by what others have written before, so encourage participants to approach their more generous supporters first. Alternatively you might indicate some preferred amounts. Some people may prefer to give a fixed sum. The form should also allow for this and for the opportunity to Gift Aid sponsorship;
- provide advice and support to participants to help them collect pledges;
- organise volunteers and stewards to help on the day;
- confirm the route;
- prepare a certificate of completion for participants to take away after the event.

You will be surprised by the range of sums that people are able to raise. This depends as much on the effort put in by the participants (which you can of course encourage) as on their financial circumstances.

On the day

You need to make sure that everything runs smoothly, that there are sufficient helpers, and that they are properly briefed. You also need to ensure that participants are welcomed (especially any celebrities who are participating); that newspaper and radio reporters are met on their arrival and briefed about anything unusual (including anyone participating in fancy dress, any stunts, anything unusual about what the money will be used for); that there is information at the start of the event to advise performers and the public what the route is, where the refreshment and toilet facilities are, and for events that involve physical exertion, where medical help can be obtained. You will need to have sufficient helpers to staff the various check-in procedures, to mark the route and to certify completion.

After the event

Key activities at this stage are:

- collecting the money. This is primarily the responsibility of the participants. Keep a register of all those who took part and stress the importance of collecting the money by a deadline date. Follow up by phone, letter or e-mail. You can also provide an incentive by offering a prize for the largest amount actually raised by an individual or a team;
- thanking those who helped;
- recording the names and contact details of those who took part.

Finally you should review the whole event from planning through execution. This is important as it will enable you to identify what you did well, but also your weak points and problems, so that you can improve on everything the next time you do it.

Sponsored event checklist

1 Make sure you plan and set objectives well ahead
2 Choose the right activity for your target audience and cause
3 Set a date and find a suitable venue
4 Get any permissions you need, for example to use a public place
5 Produce sponsorship forms
6 Involve other organisations, as they can be a good source of participants
7 Organise local publicity and get media sponsorship
8 Get local business sponsorship to cover costs and pay for any prizes being offered
9 Prepare for the day: ensure you have all the stewards, equipment and information that you need for the event
10 Thank all the participants

---

11   Chase up all uncollected pledges

12   Make Gift Aid claims

13   Log all details on your database

14   Evaluate the results against your objectives

12.3 Collections

Collections can still be an effective way of raising money. They require a good deal of planning, a well-briefed and enthusiastic team of volunteers and equipment, for example collection boxes. The main benefits of a collection, aside from the money raised, are that it reminds your local volunteers about your cause, and gives your organisation a noticeable presence for the period of the collection. This type of fundraising can be done in various ways and the two we cover in most detail are:

- house-to-house collections, where you knock on doors and ask for support, or leave an envelope and information about your work, and call back the next day;
- street collections and collections in public places. Typically here a collector will have a collecting box, and may give some token in return for the donation (such as a sticker).

But you might also consider:

- collecting boxes placed on shop counters, in pubs and in restaurants for people to leave their small change;
- static collecting devices placed outside shops;
- collecting boxes in supporters' homes, where they can leave their small change or ask their friends to contribute.

Please be aware that, at the time of writing, the 2006 Charities Act has just become law and that there are provisions in the Act which will affect the licensing of public collections. These may require you to obtain a 'certificate of fitness' from the Charity Commission and/or a permit from the local authority in whose area your collection is due to take place. You should contact the Charity Commission and your local authority to make sure you are in compliance with any new legislation.

Organising a house-to-house collection

A successful house-to house collection requires:

- carefully recruited volunteers
- well-chosen streets in which to collect
- good advance planning

- delivery of collecting materials in good time
- reliable collection of envelopes
- careful recording of donations.

House-to-house collections have worked well in the past for both national and local charities, and are a good way of asking everyone in a specified area to give their support. The collectors need to be well briefed. They are the link between your organisation and the public, and may be asked all sorts of questions about the work of the organisation and how it spends its money, which they will need to answer accurately and enthusiastically.

The first step is to obtain any permits you may need from your local council (or any other relevant licensing authority). You will need to specify the date or timescale of the collection, the localities in which you intend to collect and the manner in which the collection will be carried out. A licence may be refused on several grounds, including that:

- it will cause inconvenience to the public;
- it is on the same day or the day immediately before or after another collection;
- the expense is too high, or too little will be generated for the cause;
- the promoter has not acted properly in past collections.

The detailed requirements for conducting a collection are set out in the regulations attached to the 1992 Charities Act, however, as mentioned above, you will need to check on any new requirements concerning collections contained in the 2006 Charities Act. The regulations cover such things as who can collect money and how the collection has to be run. You only need a licence for a collection in a public place (a place to which members of the public have access) or when you are collecting in more than one location. A collection restricted to a private house, school, office, public house or hospital does not require a licence – although, once more please note that the Charities Act 2006 has extended the definition of a 'public place'. However, even if you are not collecting cash (if you are going from house to house asking for jumble or paper, for example), you still need a licence to collect in a public place.

If you are organising a national collection (throughout the whole or a substantial part of England and Wales) then you can obtain an order from the Charity Commission authorising the collection. For details of the rules on collections in Scotland and Northern Ireland, consult the Scottish Council for Voluntary Organisations and the Northern Ireland Council for Voluntary Action.

Before applying for a permit, you should plan how you will run the collection. Local knowledge should help you decide which sorts of houses are likely to be responsive. For larger collections you may want to collect throughout the area.

An important factor is the group of volunteers that you have. Typically you may want one volunteer to take responsibility for one street, probably the street they live in or one nearby. Volunteers can be recruited on a networking basis or by telephone or e-mail. Ideally you will want to approach people for this activity who have identified themselves as having an interest in your organisation – they might have made a donation or got involved in some other activity. There may be too many to approach face to face or, if you are carrying out a national campaign, may be spread over too large an area, so the most practical way to ask them to get involved is over the phone – see chapter 14, section 14.3, for more information on using the telephone.

Once you have recruited your volunteers it is important to provide training and induction. For example, a general briefing about the charity and its work; the purpose of the appeal; when they should collect; how they introduce themselves; what to say; what difficult questions to expect; and so on. You can arrange a training session, brief people individually, or prepare a pack containing all necessary information.

The collectors' main function is to deliver an envelope on which there is a message, possibly with an accompanying brochure or letter from the charity. A couple of days later, the collector should return to collect the envelopes. Undoubtedly they will encounter a wide range of responses, ranging from hostility, through apathy, to enthusiasm. There will always be some people who are genuinely interested in what you are doing, which is a good opportunity to supply more information and even recruit a new member or volunteer.

The returned envelopes should be handed into a central point, and opened under the supervision of two people, with the amounts from each address logged. Try to keep track of how much money comes from each area, for future reference. If you can, have your collectors make a note of those giving money who show a particular interest in the organisation, as you might want to approach them to do something else for you. However, you may find that this is difficult with larger collections in more than one area.

There is always the possibility of fraud by someone carrying out an unauthorised collection in your name. If you receive any reports of unauthorised collecting, investigate them as fast as you can, as any bad publicity could damage your organisation and the voluntary sector as a whole. Under the 1992 Charities Act you have the power to prevent unauthorised collections by seeking an injunction from the courts.

Checklist for organising a small-scale local collection

1   Make sure your chosen date does not clash with holiday periods or other collections.
2   Seek any authorisation you need: from the police or local authority.
3   Identify your target areas and locations for collecting and what time to carry out the collection.
4   Recruit your volunteers.
5   Prepare any materials you need, such as collecting boxes or envelopes, leaflets about your work, details of any membership scheme, and stickers.
6   Brief your volunteers about the work of the charity, and provide some basic training in effective asking.
7   Organise how the money will be received and accounted for. Bank all proceeds immediately upon receipt.
8   Thank volunteers, telling them how much they raised and how important this will be to your work.
9   Follow up on those donors who have been noted as being particularly interested in your organisation.
10 Debrief your volunteers. Find out what went well, and what not so well. Suggest ways of doing better next time. Keep a record of which locations or neighbourhoods did best.

Organising a street collection

Running a street collection is in some ways more difficult than a house-to-house collection as volunteers tend to be less enthusiastic. The collecting has to be concentrated into one day and you, the organiser, have to provide enough collectors to cover the whole of the collecting area.

As with a house-to-house collection, you will need the relevant permits and should apply to your local council for them, as well as any other relevant authority. Do this well in advance, as others may have already laid claim to particular collection dates and sites. If you have a regular annual day for this activity or a regular collection week, you will still need to apply each year.

There are two main requirements for a successful collection.

1   You need plenty of volunteers to carry out the collection. Draw up a rota for each collection point, using people for not more than an hour or two.
2   Choose locations to give collectors access to the maximum numbers of people. A busy shopping street or centre are often good choices. The ideal site is one where you are visible to passers by as they walk up a street. This gives the potential donor time to think about giving. If you

are stationed immediately outside a busy entrance to a shop, people have to make a split-second decision to give. If you make it difficult, this gives them a reason not to give. Please do also note that, as mentioned above, the 2006 Charities Act has expanded the definition of a 'public place' where permits may be required. So do make sure that you cover all your locations in terms of checking what permits you will need.

You also need to cultivate a positive attitude in your collectors. Although they are not allowed to solicit on the streets, they should not shrink back from passers by. A collector who is prepared to look people in the eye and station themselves in the middle of the thoroughfare – being careful not to cause an obstruction – will do much better.

You will need a sealed collection device that is easy to carry, convenient for the public to put money into, and easy to get the money out of again after the collection. The main choice is whether to go for a more expensive plastic collecting box that can be reused, or whether to use a cheaper disposable box. This will depend on your future plans. A number of commercial suppliers now provide a range of collecting receptacles that can be personalised with your charity's name and logo.

It is a good idea to have your collectors wear a sash or vest with your charity's name on it. Then people can see at a distance what cause is being collected for. It is not good enough to hope that passers by can see the label on your tin. You may wish to offer sticky lapel badges indicating that someone has given. This can help spread the idea in a busy town centre as well as alerting other collectors that these people have donated already. It is also useful to carry some general leaflets about your organisation for donors who are interested in knowing more about what you do.

Checklist for a street collection

- A good date and location for the collection
- Any permits you may require to carry out the collection
- Lots of enthusiastic volunteers
- The right equipment: stickers or flags to offer people, and collecting boxes suitably labelled to advertise your organisation
- Printed information about your appeal to brief the volunteers, and to hand out to interested passers by
- Local publicity
- A proper system for receiving and banking all the cash that has been collected

---

12.4 Raffles and lotteries

Raffles and lotteries are a commonplace method of fundraising and can be used successfully by both large and small organisations. According to the Gambling Commission more than £75 million raised by large society lotteries benefited charities in 2005. All lotteries are regulated, but the regulatory authority depends on the status of the activity. However, the main authority to be aware of for charitable purposes is the Gambling Commission.

Some definitions

Lotteries come in many forms, and have different names.

- *Lottery*: formal name for a game of chance by sale of tickets. This could be a private lottery, a small lottery, a society lottery, a local authority lottery or the National Lottery.
- *Raffle*: colloquial name for a lottery, usually with non-cash prizes.
- *100 club*: a group of 100 people participating in a lottery on a monthly basis. Tickets are purchased by monthly subscription and the draw is each month.
- *Tombola*: a small-scale game of chance at an entertainment event, usually involving the purchase of tickets to win bottles and other donated goods. Each ticket usually wins a prize.
- *Sweepstake*: a lottery where the winner is decided by drawing lots; for a sweepstake on a horse race, for example, the winner is the participant who has drawn the name of the horse that wins the race.
- *Skill game*: where the outcome is decided by some measure of skill (including a tie break to choose the winner from all those submitting correct answers). Sometimes the element of skill required is very small, and the format is used to get around lottery regulations.
- *Competition*: the same as a skill game. Skill games and competitions can also be free entry, where they are used extensively in sales promotions. Because a measure of skill is involved, these are not technically lotteries, which are games of chance.
- *Free entry draw*: this is a skill game or prize draw used in sales promotion, where there is no charge for entering.

For the purpose of regulation, lotteries are divided into four categories (apart from the National Lottery, which is separately regulated by the National Lottery Commission): small lotteries, private lotteries, society lotteries and local authority lotteries.

Each type of lottery has a different set of regulations which are covered in full in the Gambling Commission's publication *Lotteries and the Law*, which can be downloaded from its website – www.gamblingcommission.gov.uk. See Basic lottery rules, below, for general descriptions of each type of lottery.

Basic lottery rules

- *Small lotteries*
  One-off events with prizes up to the value of £250 (non-money prizes can be of any value); no registration required.
- *Private lotteries*
  Not-for-profit lotteries, which may be run within any residential environment, workplace or club; no registration required.
- *Society lotteries*
  Those lotteries with proceeds in a single lottery of over £20,000 or with cumulative annual proceeds of more than £250,000; requires registration with local authority or the Gambling Commission, depending on the level of ticket sales; tickets must not be sold for more than £2.
- *Local authority lotteries*
  Promoted by a local authority; required to register with the Gambling Commission.

Prizes

Some people buy tickets to support your charity; others may be attracted by the prizes. As a lottery gets bigger, the lure of prizes becomes more important. You can offer either cash or non-cash prizes.

Getting goods or services donated as lottery prizes can be a good way of getting support from companies. For a small or a private lottery, prizes can be collected from local companies and shops, and need not be more than £5–£20 in value. Having a wide range of prizes that you can display at the event will help sell the tickets. It is not usually necessary to offer cash prizes.

For larger raffles you need to focus on a smaller number of better prizes. The main prizes are what will encourage people to buy tickets. An unusual and imaginative prize is more attractive than a money prize, and sometimes will not cost a lot to organise. For example, a museum supporters' group might arrange a personal tour with the director followed by a dinner. Allow plenty of time to find good prizes that are consistent with your organisation's aims. Prepare an outline of your plans or, for major raffles, a special brochure highlighting the advantages of being associated with the raffle. You should contact potential prize donors well before the event, and companies will want crediting for their support, possibly on the tickets themselves, at the prize giving, and in any press coverage.

Promotion

Everything hinges on selling tickets. If the prizes are right and the price not too high (£2 per ticket is the current maximum that you can charge), tickets are best sold on a personal basis. For small raffles where the tickets are sold at an event, this is not difficult but needs careful planning. Identify a group of key volunteers for the evening and ask them to go round and visit everybody present. You can also contact supporters prior to the event, and ask them to ask their friends and at their place of work.

For a society lottery, where you aim to sell tickets to a wider public, more will need to be done. You can send tickets to your supporter base. Although some may be annoyed by this, enough usually accept the tickets and sell them on or buy them themselves. Local groups or volunteer fundraisers are often excellent at selling raffle tickets, especially when they actively sell in their workplace or neighbourhood. Ring them up to see if they will do it, and to offer them encouragement.

The draw

In a small raffle, the draw for the prizes is the moment of drama. Build the timing of the draw into your plans for the event. It should be announced at regular intervals leading up to the draw as an aid to selling tickets. Ideally, the draw should be the finale, thus encouraging people to stay to the end of the event. Getting a celebrity to present the prizes can add to the excitement. This is a good opportunity for a photograph. Invite a photographer, or arrange for a member of staff to take pictures of prizes, prize winners and celebrities.

For a larger raffle the situation is different. Few members of the public will want to attend the draw, although the date and place should be clearly publicised on the tickets. There is an opportunity to use the draw to invite donors and sponsors to meet senior staff and trustees, and to try to enlist their support for the next year.

To gamble or not to gamble

Organisations with a strong religious tradition (and some others) may find this area of fundraising problematic. Even with the prevalence of the National Lottery, they may not wish to be involved in any form of gambling. It is not important what you personally think about selling lottery tickets, or whether there is any evidence that links buying lottery tickets with addictive gambling. What is important is that you are clear about your organisation's attitude. If there are good reasons to believe that gambling might be a contentious issue, you should make sure your organisation has an agreed policy on it.

12.5 Working with patrons and celebrities

Association with a well-known personality can lift your organisation from obscurity into the limelight. Celebrities can help in many ways. For example, their presence at an event will be a potential draw. They can inspire members and donors, and can turn your fundraising event into a roaring success.

Probably most important, though, is their potential for attracting media coverage. If a well-known broadcaster is prepared to lead a press conference announcing a new campaign, the press is going to be much more interested than when an unknown charity executive says the same thing. Similarly, photo editors are more likely to publish a photo of a well-known and photogenic actor opening a new facility, than when a local councillor is doing the same thing. So it may be worthwhile cultivating any contact or connections you have to people who will attract positive media attention.

A local charity can of course get good local coverage by using people who are well-known in their own area. You may not be lucky enough to have a famous musician or footballer living in your village, but it is still worth cultivating contacts such as councillors, business people or local TV and radio presenters, who may be pleased to get involved.

Celebrities give their time for the same reasons that anyone else wants to support the charity – they think it is worthwhile and that their contribution can make a difference. However, it is not just having celebrities associated with your organisation, but the way you use your celebrities that will have an impact.

Using celebrities effectively

Try to find a relevant celebrity. People who have had direct experience of an issue or problem will be a much more powerful advocate for the organisation and the cause. For example, the actress Susan Hampshire is dyslexic and has supported the British Dyslexia Association for many years. Celebrities should also be matched to your target donor audience.

Well-known people can be used in a wide variety of ways – from becoming a patron or joining your board of trustees to appearing in photo calls, launching publications, giving out prizes or participating in fundraising events.

When asking a celebrity to help, you need to think carefully and discuss with them the best way for them to get involved. They want their association with you to be a success, but may not have unlimited time to give.

You also have responsibilities to them. Celebrities have their reputations to consider, so they are unlikely to want to be associated with bad publicity or with controversy. They may be used to a level of personal support and attention that is difficult for small organisations to sustain – everything from having detailed briefings as to what they are expected to do, to having speeches written for them, being collected by taxi or car and driven back after the event, and being accompanied and looked after whilst they are there.

Managing celebrities

It is often said that celebrities are the most difficult of people to work with. Some well-known people demand to be treated as celebrities in all aspects of their lives; others can be deeply appreciative of the opportunity to be involved at all. It is important to build your relationship with such people carefully – as indeed you should do with anyone who contributes to your organisation in any significant way.

Because celebrities can bring you great benefits, you should treat them professionally and politely, and try to make sure that their contribution is meaningful for you and satisfying for them. Control access to your celebrities tightly. You should make sure they are not being asked to do too many things too frequently, or even being asked to do things that they have specifically declined to do.

Appearance fees are always an issue. Most performers do not expect or want to take fees from charity events, and certainly should not be encouraged to do so. You should be prepared to pay reasonable expenses – and only consider paying the most nominal amounts as a fee, and then only in exceptional circumstances and possibly as a donation to a charity of their choice.

If you are recruiting a celebrity for an event, they will need to have a very clear idea of what is going to happen and precisely what is expected of them. Will they be making a speech? Who will write it for them? Will a car be provided? When must they arrive? When can they discreetly slip away? Who will greet them and look after them whilst they are with you? Will there be a presentation of flowers or a public thank you? Do they have to shake hands, speak to and be photographed with your main sponsor? Who will brief them on what to say? Who will be responsible for formally thanking them afterwards on behalf of the organisation? And so on. They will also want to be told how much their presence has helped; how many extra people have come this year; how much extra money was raised; and how many reporters covered the story.

Sometimes you have to deal with them via an agent or personal assistant. Working with an agent can be both a help and a hindrance. They could be more concerned with fees and payments, and may not want their client to do something for nothing. On the other hand, being associated with you can bring the celebrity a lot of good publicity, so there is also benefit to their client. Try to get a direct line to your celebrity as soon as you can. But the agent can be helpful in identifying long-range opportunities and availability; they can also help you get an idea of what the celebrity is looking for from the arrangement, as well as their likes and dislikes.

Resources and further information

See also general lists at the end of the book.

Organisations

Charity Commission
www.charity-commission.gov.uk

Gambling Commission
www.gamblingcommission.gov.uk

HM Revenue & Customs
(for VAT matters)
www.hmrc.gov.uk

Northern Ireland Council for Voluntary Action
61 Duncairn Gardens
Belfast BT15 2GB
www.nicva.org
Tel. 028 9087 7777

Scottish Council for Voluntary Organisations
Mansfield Traquair Centre
15 Mansfield Place
Edinburgh EH3 6BB
www.scvo.org.uk
Tel. 0131 556 3882

Publications

The following publications are available from the Directory of Social Change. Prices were correct at the time of writing, but may be subject to change.

The Fundraiser's Guide to the Law, Bates, Wells & Braithwaite and Centre for Voluntary Sector Development, DSC 2000, £19.95

Organising Special Events, John F Gray & Stephen Elsden, DSC/CAF 2000, £14.95

Tried and Tested Ideas for Local Fundraising Events, Sarah Passingham, DSC/CAF 2003, £16.95

The Voluntary Sector Legal Handbook, 3rd edn, Sandy Adirondack & James Sinclair Taylor, DSC 2008, £59 (voluntary organisations), £89 (others) (available early 2008; check www.dsc.org.uk for details)

Other publications

Institute of Fundraising Code of Practice on Charity Challenge Events

Institute of Fundraising Code of Practice on House to House Collections

Institute of Fundraising Code of Practice on the Management of Static Collection Points

Institute of Fundraising Code of Practice on Outdoor Fundraising in the UK

Institute of Fundraising Code of Practice on Raffles and Lotteries

Institute of Fundraising Code of Practice on Scottish Charity Law in Relation to Fundraising and Public Charitable Collections

Institute of Fundraising Code of Practice on the Telephone Recruitment of Collectors

13 Capital and Big Gift Campaigns

In addition to your regular fundraising activity, your organisation may need to raise money to launch a major new service or embark on a large-scale building programme. This chapter gives a brief introduction to when and why you might undertake a capital campaign, and how capital and big gift campaigns tend to be structured.

Details of organisations and publications referred to in this chapter are on page 276.

13.1 The case for a capital or big gift campaign

As responsibility for care and welfare has shifted away from the state, either because of increasing expectations and rising costs or as a consequence of the contract culture, charities are finding themselves needing more and more capital funding. Schools and hospitals need money to develop their facilities and for equipment; organisations caring for older people need to meet the needs of a growing older population. The National Lottery continues to fund (or part fund) national, regional and local arts, heritage and sports projects where there is a requirement for matched funding (see chapter 7). All this suggests that capital fundraising will continue to grow. This increase in the demand for funds could result in a decline in response rates and a resistance to giving. It also means that those seeking funds in a highly competitive climate will have to look for ways of improving their effectiveness.

Charities have always been able to attract big gifts, and in recent years attention has turned to using big gift fundraising as one of the principal components of a capital campaign. The techniques tend to be used in the context of a large one-off appeal for a particular project, such as the £134 million raised for the conversion of Bankside power station into Tate Modern.

There is another way of using the device of the capital campaign, which is common to universities in America, that is to launch a campaign as a focus for an organisation as a whole as well as its fundraising. For example the NSPCC's Full Stop Campaign to end cruelty to children reflects the mission of the charity and gave opportunities for fundraising.

Campaign phases

A campaign to raise a significant sum must be properly planned and is likely to go through a number of clearly defined phases:

- the planning stage
- the case document, which sets out and justifies the purpose of the fundraising
- the business plan or feasibility study, which sets out the plan and timescale for the fundraising
- the research
- the recruitment of an appeal committee
- the private giving phase, in which major gifts are sought
- the launch
- the public giving phase
- the consolidation.

Going through all these stages not only ensures that the appeal is properly planned and organised. It also allows a reasonable timescale for the appeal, links it with your expenditure plans and alerts you to any cash flow shortfalls. It may take over two years from start to finish; a very large target may well take longer. You need to consider the question of investment and risk. When plans have been approved and the staff have been taken on, trustees can get nervous about the chances of the original outlay being recouped. This demands an understanding of the appeal process and faith in the people charged with its success.

Issues to consider

One issue is the degree to which a capital campaign will interfere with your ongoing fundraising and affect future fundraising prospects. This will vary with each organisation, and depends on the campaign strategy and the relative sizes of your capital and revenue fundraising budgets. For a £50 million a year charity raising £5 million of capital, there is likely to be some overlap. And if your existing supporters have made a substantial donation, you may not be able to ask for another one so soon afterwards. However, for a small charity raising a relatively large sum, the momentum, excitement and interest that are generated by the campaign will probably add to the regular income received rather than detract from it.

Difficult cash flow decisions may need to be taken. There will be considerable costs involved in the early months, especially if a professional fundraising consultant is retained. No campaign is cost-free; a budget for administration and publicity material will need to be included. A properly planned and resourced campaign will stand a much better chance of success. However, there may come a point at which you question whether the campaign will succeed. If you take the view that it will not, then you should pull out. This is not an easy decision to take but it is better to withdraw at an early stage than to be seen to fail publicly.

13.2 Planning a campaign

Planning a capital campaign involves the following stages.

1 *Planning the project for which the funds are being raised.* You need to be able to justify the need for the project as vital to the work and future of the organisation; otherwise, people won't give. You will need to prepare a business plan for the project, to assure yourself that you can raise the money and that you will have enough to keep going once it has been completed. Major campaigns are by definition very public, so potential failure is also public. It would be highly embarrassing if the project folded after completion for lack of the funds to run it. You will need detailed costings and drawings.

2 *Doing a feasibility study.* Many organisations take on a consultant to get advice on how to conduct the campaign. One of their first steps will be to conduct a feasibility study to identify whether the campaign is likely to be successful. This is important, as it will also highlight any inconsistencies or ill-conceived ideas.

3 *Planning the structure of the campaign.* At this stage it is advisable to recruit a campaign committee to lead and oversee the fundraising. The key appointment is the chair. The committee's function is to raise big gifts, so people should be appointed for their asking capacity and their networks, as well as their interest in your organisation. You may also want to establish sub-committees to oversee the running of other elements of the campaign such as events, publicity and media coverage, and to harness volunteer help. These committees will need to be supported by either paid or volunteer workers who are well briefed, efficient and available.

4 *Reviewing likely funding sources.* A vital planning tool is a table setting out the number and size of donations needed. This lists the gifts that you plan to acquire, helps you identify possible donors and sources, and gives guidance on the level of support to ask for. Always start from your existing donor base and contacts. Who do you already know with the ability to make a big gift? Then move on to other strategic sources of

funding. Is there a well-known trust whose support would act as a lever in approaching other funders?

5 *Documentation and research to back up the above.* For major gifts, you should undertake some preliminary work on likely sources. You should certainly explore possible government and trust grants.

6 *Preparation of the case statement.* This is a vital document, which will be the strategic plan for the appeal. It will include sections covering the following:

- a background to the charity and its history
- a description and justification of the project
- the costs of the project
- a costed breakdown of the individual components of the project
- the gifts needed to achieve this target
- the plan for raising the money (including any fundraising events)
- the sources of money expected.

This report needs to be professionally presented.

7 *Identifying the people or organisations who will provide the lead gifts for the campaign* and approaching them to see if they will help. This is usually done by drawing up lists of leading business people and other influential people gleaned from a wide range of sources, including personal knowledge and contacts. They will meet infrequently, but are there to help solicit the largest gifts through their contacts and credibility. Once again, the appointment of the chair is critical as they will be the public figure leading the campaign. These first large gifts will set the tone for the appeal and boost your confidence.

8 *Ensuring the support of your trustees.* One key issue is the degree to which your trustees are committed to the campaign. It will be extremely difficult to approach people for support if the trustees appear to be unenthusiastic.

Leadership

The leadership of the campaign is extremely important. There are two key principles to bear in mind.

- People often respond better when asked by their peers, that is those who are at or above their own level in business or society.
- Response will be better if the person asking has already given and given generously. One question they are very likely to be asked by those they are approaching for donations is if they have given themselves.

The qualifications to look for in the chair and in campaign committee members are that they have the resources to give major gifts on the scale you need (either personally or through the company or foundation they are associated with); that they have good networks which will provide important potential givers; and that they are able and willing to ask others to support the appeal both in person and by letter.

The first stage is to identify people to help you plan the campaign. Since initially you are asking for advice rather than money, it will be easier for them to agree – but they will probably expect to be asked for a donation later on. A group of two or three senior people with an interest in your work can form the planning group. Their role is either to act as the formal leadership of the appeal or to select that leadership. They should be well respected in the community and, if possible, not have been associated with a similar appeal in the recent past – if they have, their asking capacity may have been diminished. As already mentioned for other groups, they also need to have a good network of contacts to draw on.

You need to understand why such important people might want to work for your cause. There are many reasons. Some people will do it because they genuinely believe in and support the cause; others find an approach from a senior person in the community difficult to resist; others find the link with other business people attractive for their own purposes; some are motivated by the notion that they might get recognition; and some just like the challenge of achieving something worthwhile. They will appreciate efficient administration and being provided with the back-up they need. This will ensure that their time is effectively used (and not spent in lots of committee meetings).

Many people will not know how to ask effectively, so you may need to provide some training in the principles of effective asking and an induction to the work of your organisation.

13.3 Managing the campaign

The private phase

With all the building blocks in place, you should be ready to begin the task of asking for money. At this stage, everything is still done privately, without fanfares of publicity. It is accepted practice to plan to have a proportion of the target in place before you go public.

The first step is to get the financial commitment of your campaign committee. It is important that your early gifts are of a sufficient size to give a lead to those that follow. Through the process of developing and refining the appeal document, most committee members should already be aware of the scale of donations that are needed. They will have been engaged in discussions about what is expected of other prospective donors, and will be familiar with what might be expected of them.

Once they have made their own commitment, they should move on to the task of approaching others. You will already have drawn up lists of prospective donors. They can add new names from their own contacts and decide how best to approach them.

The task of asking for big gifts is best done by the committee members themselves, with you, the fundraiser, providing smooth administration. Once you have identified who should approach a potential donor, a wide variety of methods can be used, from an informal sounding out at a dinner party, to a personal letter, to an invitation to see the project – whatever the person asking feels most comfortable with.

People usually take time to decide on big donations, and this is especially true for large public sector grants. Do not expect a decision within the course of a single meeting. You might need a series of meetings – starting perhaps with a reception, followed by informal chats – that culminate in the prospective donor being asked to help and offered a range of possible ways of doing so. In addition to money, they can be asked to give support in kind and the names of others who might be approached.

The objective of the private stage of the appeal will be to have a proportion of your pledges in place to provide a basis on which to roll out your fundraising programme for the completion of the appeal. You might decide that 25% or even 50% of your target will be what you require; you should take into account your particular situation and set this figure accordingly. This will give a real boost and legitimacy to the appeal when it is launched publicly, and it is wise to launch your appeal to the public only when you are confident of its success.

Table of gifts needed for appeal

It is always sensible to break down the total appeal target into the numbers of gifts of different sizes that you will need to raise. This table is an example showing how this might be done.

No. of gifts	Amount p.a. £	4 year value £	Total over 4 years £	
2	25,000	100,000	200,000	
8	10,000	40,000	320,000	
20	5,000	20,000	400,000	
40	2,000	8,000	320,000	
70			**1,240,000**	**Total**

The public phase

The public phase should start with an official launch. This can be done in a number of ways depending on how the campaign is structured. It should certainly include a press conference and might also involve an event to which you can invite prospective donors.

In the public phase of the appeal, much of the money will be raised from larger numbers of people making smaller donations. This phase will have several objectives: to take the appeal to a wider audience; to assist the task of the big gift fundraising; and to give those who were unable to donate at a high level the opportunity to give at a more modest one.

A media communications campaign is important to raise the profile of your appeal. Some big appeals recruit committees or involve media professionals on a voluntary basis to advise on this. You should certainly have someone working on your media communication strategy, as this will affect your other fundraising activities.

Events are an important component of your campaign, as they attract media coverage, and reach out to a wider audience. You may want to set up a volunteer committee to take responsibility for events, as they take a good deal of time to organise. (See chapter 12 for more on event management.)

Direct mail can also be used, targeted at people your personal approaches have not yet reached. It is important, though, that this be left towards the end, so that nobody gives a small donation in response to a letter where they might otherwise have given a bigger donation if asked personally. A mailed appeal at this stage is also more likely to produce results if people can see that the target is close to being reached.

For very large national campaigns, you may need to have a regional committee structure to harness opportunities at a regional level. The regional chairs should be appointed as part of the campaign structure, and they then recruit people in their area. In this public phase their role will mainly be helping to stimulate and co-ordinate events to raise support and get publicity for the campaign in their area.

The consolidation phase

Consolidating what has been achieved in the first stages of the campaign will ensure that you make the most of the efforts and the contacts you have made for your continuing fundraising. This phase includes a number of key steps:

- bringing in all the money that has been pledged. During the campaign you will have received promises of support that may not yet have materialised. This is the point to follow these up;

- closing the campaign. When the target has been realised there should be an announcement (to get publicity for the success of the venture) and a celebration involving some sort of reception or event. Key volunteers, prominent supporters and sponsors, staff and others who were centrally involved in the appeal can all be invited;
- thanking those involved;
- setting up a development committee for the future. You may have generated your income on a somewhat ad hoc basis up to this point; the creation of the right structure for the charity and its future fundraising can help ensure that the momentum is not lost. This may involve setting up a permanent development committee to carry on the fundraising, or a high-level advisory committee. During the course of the campaign, you will have gained the confidence and enthusiasm of a number of key contacts. Those who have been particularly effective should now be encouraged to take more permanent places within the structures that you have created so that they can continue to help you;
- further fundraising. With these people and structures in place, you are in a position to approach people who did not give to the campaign, and to begin to go back to those who did give for further support.

Resources and further information

See also general lists at the end of the book.

Organisations

The Institute of Fundraising has a Directory of Consultants with a search facility on its website – www.institute-of-fundraising.org.uk (under 'Information about Fundraising') – that can be used to source someone to help you with a capital or big gift campaign.

Publications

The following publications are available from the Directory of Social Change. The price was correct at the time of writing, but may be subject to change.

Capital Campaigns, Trudy Hayden, DSC/IOF/CAF 2006, £22.95

Find the Funds, Christopher Carnie, DSC/CAF 2000, £16.95

14 DIRECT MARKETING

Marketing is not just for commercial companies, nor is it only about selling. Fundraising demands a range of marketing skills. In a sense, this whole book is about marketing – marketing a cause to someone who can contribute money and/or time to supporting it. This chapter looks at the link between marketing theory and fundraising and covers some fundraising methods and media that are being used by charities today.

Details of organisations and publications referred to in this chapter are on pages 313–314.

14.1 Marketing – a brief introduction

Marketing is often described in terms of the four Ps – product, price, place and promotion. For this chapter, one more P has been added – planning.

Planning and market analysis

Marketing planning starts with a clear understanding of an organisation and its work, the market in which it is operating, its competitor organisations (in the non-profit, the public and the private sectors), and the attitudes of potential supporters.

Useful tools for this include:

- doing a SWOT analysis for your organisation, in which you concentrate on the internal strengths and weaknesses, and the external opportunities and threats (see chapter 3 for more on this);
- market share analysis, which measures what proportion of a given sector of donated income you are currently receiving – for example, how much support is given by local companies, and how much of this your organisation is receiving;
- market research, which identifies the attitudes of your potential or actual supporters to giving to the cause in general, and to your particular charity.

All this will give you a better idea about the people and groups you should be targeting.

Product

The service your organisation provides is, in marketing terms, the product. It consists of the following ingredients:

- the actual 'tangible' product or need which your charity exists to meet;
- what the donor gets from association with you;
- any extra benefits: for example, an invitation to meet a person who has been helped, or attendance at a special event each year.

You are competing for a share of your supporters' disposable income. You have to tempt them to buy your product rather than someone else's, so you need to make your product as interesting as you can.

Each product you create will have a life cycle. According to marketing theory, you will need to re-promote your product from time to time to keep it up to date, attractive and in people's minds.

Charities also have a range of fundraising products which they market to their donors. These might include a major donor programme, membership subscriptions for broader support, a regular giving scheme to increase committed support, and a schools fundraising scheme for younger people. These can all happily co-exist, so long as they are not in competition with one another.

Price

Donors do not automatically know how much to give. You need to steer them towards what is likely to be achievable and affordable to them, while also meeting your own requirements.

The most obvious way of doing this is to ask for a precise amount, for example, 'We are asking each person to give £25.' However, this can raise the question, 'Why £25?' The response to that is to give an idea of what the money can achieve – '£25 can help us dig a well in Africa.' The donation may not actually be spent on that, so be careful that the wording does not create a binding obligation to spend the money in a certain way. You may commit a breach of trust if you say you are definitely going to dig a well and then use the money for another project instead.

There are three useful approaches in this type of situation:

- a shopping list of tangible items, illustrating a range of things at different prices that the donor's money might be spent on;
- a range of levels of support from which the donor can choose;
- a range of possible frequencies (annual, quarterly, monthly). You will find that smaller amounts given more frequently are likely to yield larger

annual donations. This is because people respond to the headlined figure more than to the actual cost.

The price you ask determines both the type of supporter you get and the amount of benefit you generate for your organisation. This will be the donation minus the cost of fundraising and administration. A monthly £5 donation might cost as much to service as a £25 one-off donation, and could be immediately swallowed up by administration costs. There can be a tendency to ask for too little. People are more generous than you think, so you need to make sure you ask at the right level. For example, with potential major donors you will do yourself a disservice asking for only £50 – not because it is expensive to administer, but because they might have given a great deal more.

Place

Place in marketing terms refers to the means by which people give. It will usually be closely linked to promotion. For example, a personal request to help provides an opportunity to write a cheque and hand it over. A request made in a speech or on the radio should include a means by which people can contact you and make a donation (for example, a mailing or website address, or a telephone number). Think carefully about how people are expected to get their money to you, whether it is with a donation form, a collection bucket at the door at an event, a credit card hot-line or a secure website.

The place will determine not just what you can ask for, but also how people view your organisation. For example, if you decide to raise money from an annual ball, you will only interact with a certain group of people in a particular atmosphere. You could also appeal to a wider audience by running a series of special coffee mornings (like Macmillan Cancer Support's 'World's Biggest Coffee Morning'). The two approaches might ultimately achieve the same result in terms of money raised. However, they would have done this by using completely different techniques, from quite different sources, using different resources and helpers, and in the process creating a completely different perception of your organisation by the participants.

Promotion

How do you present yourself to the public? Promotion is not only the medium, but also the message. The message is conveyed by a whole range of things within your control. Your name – or at least the title of your appeal – sends an important message, particularly if you have made this name well-known. People recognise World Wide Fund for Nature (WWF) or Save the Children, and these names evoke images of what the charity is doing.

How you present yourself creates an impression of credibility, urgency, dynamism, and so on. Most important is how you express your needs in your written and visual material. Is it a rational or emotional appeal? Is it supported by human content? Good designers and copywriters can create the image you require for your organisation, if they are well briefed. See chapter 15, section 15.3 for more on this.

The medium of your promotion is another important ingredient. Are you going to rely on personal recommendation to get your message across? Or are you going to use TV, radio, newspaper advertising, direct mail, posters, house-to-house visits, company promotions, booklets, events, one-to-one approaches (by telephone or face to face), your website?

These five Ps are interdependent; if one factor is changed then it will affect all the others. The rest of this chapter looks in more detail at the key marketing techniques that you can use for fundraising.

14.2 Direct mail

The post still provides one of the most flexible and powerful tools in fundraising. A postal appeal or direct mail programme can provide both regular and immediate income. The key is to build up and maintain an active and enthusiastic base of supporters. This takes time, effort and money to get started. Postal appeals will not provide immediate income for organisations which do not yet have an active supporter base. This will need to be developed, in order to provide an audience for your appeals.

The three main elements of a mailing programme

- *The audience*. There can be an enormous variation in the response rates you achieve, particularly between cold audiences (your potential new supporters) and your existing donors (who are more likely to respond).
- *The message*. What you tell them and what you ask for are extremely important. You need to devise a powerful message that will move people to give. The creative approach, that is the way you present the story you are telling them, and the 'offer', what you are asking them to do, are the two most important components of the message.
- *The timing*. Some times of the year may be better than others. For example the period leading up to Christmas is a good time for charity appeals, as it is a time when people feel predisposed to give. If there is a good reason for the appeal, for example as a response to a natural disaster, then the immediacy of the need and demonstrating that you are responding efficiently and effectively means that you should get your appeal out as quickly as you can.

Good direct mail entails sending a clear personalised message of the length you want, to whom you want, when you want. It will need:

- a selection of people to send the appeal to;
- a mailing pack – often a leaflet with a covering letter, some mechanism for replying (also known as a response device) and an envelope for the donation to be returned in;
- an efficient administrative system for dealing with the response.

There are three broad categories of direct mail, which fall into two types of promotion:

Acquisition (or recruitment) of supporters

- 'cold' mailings to people with whom you have had no previous contact;
- 'reciprocal' mailings, where you mail sections of your supporter base with another organisation's appeal and they do the same.

Supporter development

- 'warm' mailings to your existing members and supporters.

Response rates on warm mailings are the highest, but can vary dramatically depending on what you are asking for – legacies, committed gifts, one-off donations – and the creative treatment you decide to use – for example, is it an emotive, hard-hitting story? Reciprocal mailings to other people's supporters also work relatively well – these people are known charity supporters and already respond to direct mail. Response rates on cold lists also vary enormously, from virtually nothing to as much as 3%, depending on the cause and the list you are mailing to. Then once people have given, they become part of your warm list and your next challenge will be to motivate them to give again.

The power of the medium comes not only from the ability to target your message precisely, but also because you can get the same message out to large numbers of people, which provides an economy of scale. The idea is to make the medium as personal as possible, as if you are writing to a friend or colleague. However, as your supporter base gets bigger, the opportunities for making your mailings personal will diminish. This depersonalisation will inevitably have an impact on your returns; one way of addressing this is to break down your base into smaller groups and send them slightly different messages. This is called segmentation. You will certainly want to say something different to your existing donors from what you say to those who have not yet given. You may then want to subdivide further – for example, separating higher value donors and those who support you with a monthly direct debit, from people who make lower value one-off donations.

Ways to personalise mailings

A personalised communication works far better than a general 'Dear Supporter' letter. If you are writing to thousands of people, you may have to make it more general in appeal but there are still ways to make it appear more personal.

1 Mailmerge your letter or have it laser printed so the donor is addressed by name, for example 'Dear Mr Radcliffe'. Alternatively, if you are writing to a small select group you could handwrite the donor's name in the salutation at the start of the letter and your sign off ('Yours sincerely') as well as your signature.

2 Personalisation is not just a matter of name and address. It also includes any detail about them or their giving which you can incorporate into the body of the letter – such as the amount of the last gift and the purpose for which it was given.

3 Use an ordinary stamp rather than having the letter franked. If it is an urgent appeal test use a first-class stamp, which can further increase the returns.

4 Have a handwritten postscript at the end of the letter which reinforces the message. This can be printed.

5 Ensure that the response device has the donor's name on it – this will also help you administer and acknowledge the gift when it comes back to you.

6 Use a reply envelope with your name or that of the appeal letter's signatory on it (as well as the organisation and reply address), so that the reply letter is addressed to someone and not to an anonymous organisation.

Components of a mailing

The components of a mailing vary widely. A well-used model consists of five parts:

- an outer envelope, with a window to show a name and address on the reply device or at the top of the letter. The envelope can be overprinted with a message to encourage recipients to open it;
- the letter as the main communication, which should be written to interest and involve the prospective donor as much as possible;
- a coupon or reply device to summarise what the appeal is about, give examples of expected donation levels, and carry any codes and donor identity so that you can keep track of responses;
- a reply envelope to return the reply device and donation. Use Freepost if you can. Making it easy for the donor to reply will increase the response considerably, but include a note that the use of a stamp will save the charity money;
- a leaflet: this can help to provide more detail and illustrations of the need that are highlighted in the letter. A leaflet is not always necessary but can be helpful in building a clearer picture for the donor.

This type of pack allows you to include as much information as you feel you need. However, be careful of over-wordy appeals, as they may go unread. Use pictures to tell the story, case studies and quotes to illustrate that you can make a difference, and graphic devices to break up the text. Think carefully about the envelope and external appearance. This is essential to increase the chances of people opening it rather than putting it straight in the bin. The best-planned and most attractive appeal letter will be completely wasted if no one reads it.

Getting the message right

Like any other printed communication, getting the message right is at least half the battle (the other half is getting it to the right people at the right time). For a mailing, however, there are a number of other things to be aware of.

- *The proposition*. Each mailing should have a central proposition. It might, for example, be '£21.60 can help a child in distress' or 'urgent action is needed to save the rainforests of Brazil'. This central idea should be the visual and verbal theme throughout the mailing pack.
- *The request*. You must be absolutely clear what you want. A good letter will repeat the request for help several times. Then there can be no mistaking what you want the reader to do.
- *The length of the message*. There is no rule about this. The important thing is to say what you want to say, and say it effectively. Focus on quality of writing rather than length.

Warm mailings

Sending appeals to your own donors is one of the most profitable ways of raising money. Not everyone can expect to raise £1 million by mailing 80,000 people, although it has been done. The principle is to get the audience, the message and the timing right.

The relatively high response that you can get from warm mailings (to previous donors) is the main reason for building a supporter database. When you include the longer-term support from regular givers and membership subscriptions, you might be able to raise as much as £10 for each £1 of fundraising costs. You will be communicating with one of your most committed audiences. Get the approach and message right and you will raise money; get it wrong, and you can lose support from those you rely on.

There are varying views about how often you should write to your donors. Some people feel that twice a year is too much, while other organisations keep in touch at least once a month (when all the different communications from them are included). Trustees often take a very conservative view of this, which can effectively block the sensible development of your direct mail income. Testing is sometimes the only way for you to prove the point that more frequent mailings can be productive. If you find it cost-effective to mail more frequently, then do so; if not, then don't. Alternatively, ask your donors how often they would like to receive information from you. If your supporter base is large enough, divide it into different segments depending on how often each group wants to hear from you. However frequently you plan to contact people, you need to develop a mailing strategy and have a good idea of your programme for the year.

A sample annual mailing plan

A – appeal, R – Annual Report, I – Information Mailing/Survey, U – Upgrade mailing

	April	June	Aug	Oct	Dec
Committed Givers	U	A	I	A	A
Major Donors	U	R	I	A	A
Active Donors	U	A	I	A	A
Lapsed Donors	A	I	A		
Enquirers/Prospects	A	I	A		

An example of a possible mailing plan, taking into account the need to appeal regularly to good but uncommitted supporters, report back to major donors with an annual report, give core donors an opportunity to upgrade the value or type of their support, and approach lapsed or prospective donors less frequently. Each of the different segments in the plan will require a different package, even if appeals are going out at the same time.

You could develop a newsletter or magazine to keep your regular donors or members informed about and involved in your work. This will be useful in creating a context within which you continue to solicit their support. However, most organisations will be using direct mail to seek money directly. It is beneficial to vary what you are sending them in order to make a high-frequency mailing programme less repetitive. For example:

- invite them to become regular givers. This can be extremely effective and very appealing to donors if you start by asking for a small sum each month. But the response rates will be smaller than for a single donation;
- ask them to organise an event or participate in a local collection. This can help get new initiatives going locally. The majority of Oxfam shops started with an appeal for volunteers in the locality;
- suggest that they leave you a legacy. This will not produce cash now, although you can offer an extra option of making a donation as well or instead.

Cold mailings

It is all very well to dream about the returns you could get if only you had an active supporter base of 10,000 people – you have to acquire them first. One of the main ways of doing this is through cold mailings ('cold' because, to your knowledge, the person receiving your letter has not demonstrated any warmth to your cause before).

You will need to compile names and addresses from available sources or rent lists from a list broker. The main differences between warm and cold mailings lie in the cost and the message. Because the people you are contacting are not your existing supporters, you can expect a poorer response from them. Thus to get the same amount of money you may need to mail to 10 times as many cold names at 10 times the cost. Then there is also the cost of renting the list. This often forces fundraisers to look for a cheap way of reaching the large numbers necessary to get a response of any size.

Most of the recipients of a cold mailing will not know much about you, so you will need to give a basic description of your work and some reassurance about its value and importance. This may be through endorsements from well-known people, or giving answers to frequently asked questions (like the amount spent on administration), or by highlighting your achievements and successes.

Not all of the people on any purchased list will necessarily be unknown to you. Some may be existing supporters and you should check for and exclude them before mailing. You could find yourself in an awkward situation if what is perceived as an inappropriate message is sent to one of your major donors.

Other ways to identify good lists in advance are to find out whether the list is already mail responsive, whether there is a high percentage of people on your own list of donors who are also on this list, and whether they seem to be the same sort of people as your typical donor.

Before you purchase or rent a new list, you should check whether the list has been used recently, how old it is, whether it has been updated recently (you do not want to be sending letters to out-of-date addresses or to people who have died). Also check whether the list has been regularly checked against the Mailing Preference Service list, in order to remove all those people who have asked not to receive unsolicited mail.

Evaluating mailing lists

Eleven questions to ask before you buy a mailing list:

1 Are the people your supporters or someone else's? If they are your supporters, could you get them to endorse your appeal?
2 Are they mail order responsive? If this is a list of mail order buyers or postal
   donors they will be more used to responding in the post.
3 Is this a compiled list or a list of someone's customers/supporters? Compiled
   lists do not respond well.
4 Are the people on the list similar to your own donors: by age, gender and
   attitude?
5 How up-to-date is the list and when was it last updated? Don't buy names of
   people who are no longer there.
6 Is there a name and home address for each person?
7 Are these people buyers/donors or just enquirers?
8 Have these people bought or given recently? Can you take only the recent ones?
9 Is there any information on frequency of activity? The more frequent the better.
10 When was this list last mailed? The more recently the better.
11 What was the amount of money on average that was given/paid? Are these
   people likely to be able to give what you need?

Getting the right mailing lists is essential when you are trying to find new supporters.
The difference between getting a good mailing list and a poor one may be as much
as five times.

[*Commonsense Direct Marketing*, Drayton Bird]

Cold mailings rarely pay for themselves, but if you are not continually adding
to your supporter base it will gradually decline as existing supporters die,
move or lose interest. You have to balance the cost of acquisition against the
likely support you will continue to receive from those who do respond. If half
the donors continue to support you, your original acquisition cost is easier to
justify. Some may even go on to leave you a legacy.

When starting from scratch, a direct mail programme will need a certain
amount of initial investment. Depending on the sort of response rates you
get, you may find that the programme does not begin to generate any surplus
for three to four years. However, at that point the income should gradually
build up, given good management of the programme, and should provide
long-term for your organisation.

Local charities may have a significant edge here. It may be easier to find suitable local lists, the local connection can generate additional interest in the
work, and cheaper methods of distribution than mail become possible.

If you are doing a large-scale mailing, test it on a small quantity of the names first to see whether enough people are likely to want to support your appeal to justify mailing the entire list.

Cold mailing issues

1   *Buying other people's lists*. Many members of the public regard selling mailing lists as an invasion of their privacy and do not like to receive unsolicited mail. These people will contact you from time to time and complain in the most vocal way. Be prepared with your response.

2   *It can appear a waste of money.* If only 3% of people respond, then 97% will be throwing it away – which is why it is sometimes referred to as 'junk mail'. It is those who reply, not those who do not, who make direct mail an effective fundraising method, but you have to watch the response rates and mail-out costs to ensure that you are being cost-effective. Even if you are, those that are not responding may think you are wasting both your money and the world's resources. Therefore, for example, using recycled paper can give the right signals, despite its greater cost.

3   *It is expensive*. You must ensure that you have the capacity to invest in this form of fundraising, which requires a large expenditure commitment, a significant degree of risk and a payback period of several years. If you can't do it properly, then don't do it at all.

Reciprocal mailings

One answer to the low response rates of cold mailings is to undertake reciprocal mailings. The idea is that your best potential donors are those people who have recently given to you (warm mailings); but the next best are those who are giving to similar organisations. These people are likely to be socially concerned and are known to respond to direct mail appeals. They may also be happy to support two similar causes, so if you mail your supporters with an appeal from a similar charity and they mail your supporters with their appeal, you will both gain. And that's how it usually turns out in practice. Typically, response rates can range from 2.5% to 10%.

Try to arrange to mail a similar organisation to your own, even if they are a near competitor. When undertaking this type of activity you will want to devise a simple policy to safeguard your interests and those of your donors. Note that it is good practice to give your supporters the opportunity to opt out of being included in reciprocal mailings.

Looking after your own supporter database

The most valuable resource you have is your own database of donors, members and supporters. Guard it carefully and manage it properly. Keep it up to date by adding all new donor contacts as soon as possible. Change donor details as soon as you are advised of them – for example, a change of address or a death. Check for duplicates regularly as sending the same mailing twice to a donor can cause aggravation and wastes money. Do not delete people who have 'opted out' of receiving direct marketing materials from you. Hold them on your database with a code that shows they should not be mailed. If you then get their name from another source, you will not risk annoying them by appearing to disregard their instruction.

Keep track of people who are not giving. Just because someone has not responded for a year or two does not mean that they won't respond in the future – but they are less likely to do so. Do not delete them from your list but put them in a separate coded segment in one of your mailings, and examine the results. You would expect the response and average donation to be lower than your most profitable segments, but is it so low that it is no longer worth mailing these names? Or should they be mailed just once a year? Maybe you could try ringing some of your list to see why they have not been giving before you remove them. Or you could try a different tack with them, for example, asking them for a legacy or trying to reactivate their giving with a more hard-hitting appeal.

A mailing strategy – simple donor pyramid

Legacies
Major Donors
Committed Givers
Multi Donors
New Donors

This is a broad approach followed by many organisations. The idea is that your direct marketing programme will move individual supporters up through this pyramid. Getting the first gift may be done on a continuous basis with cold mailing, advertising or other mass appeals. Once on board, you will aim to upgrade supporters to the next level of the pyramid. Of course it is not necessarily true that only people who made major donations to you will leave a legacy – any level of donor may do this as well as people who have never supported you.

Before setting up a supporter database and using the information you have collected, it is essential to make sure you comply with the Data Protection Act (see Appendix 4).

Managing your data

As much as possible your mailings should be planned a year to 18 months ahead. Segment your data records into different groups depending on when they became a supporter, how much and how they gave, and other relevant characteristics. The larger your supporter database, the more you can segment it. Plan different messages for each segment. For example, what are you going to say to your regular supporters? Are they to be taken for granted and not written to or thanked and otherwise left alone ... or treated just like any other supporter ... or made to feel special?

Ensure that your mailings are producing the expected results and that the costs are kept within budget. Monitor costs. Get competitive quotes for all items of expenditure and make sure your suppliers keep within this. Plan and monitor expected income (maybe based on results from the last comparable mailing). Useful measures are:

- the response rate (the percentage of people mailed who respond);
- the average donation (how much each person gives on average);
- the combination of these two factors, which is the yield (the money received per 100 people mailed).

It is usually better to focus on both response rates and average donations – as you can do different things to improve each. Improving the response rate is part science and part judgement. The science is in the appropriate testing of your mailings. You can test almost any aspect of what you mail by sending a slightly different message to a small sample set of the group that you are mailing, and then comparing the results. Test your letter, your message, how you personalise it, and test one group against another. Whatever you do, test just one thing at a time, and ensure the group is large enough to give a statistically valid result. Testing is the way you learn from experience and improve your performance over time.

'The Good Mailing Guide'

1 Use emotion in your writing
2 Include stories about individuals
3 Ask for money, directly
4 Use simple language, avoid jargon
5 Make all written material visually attractive

6   Portray your beneficiaries as 'doers' rather than as 'victims', not as helpless, but needing your help

7   Catch the reader's attention immediately, perhaps with a snappy headline

8   Use someone specific as the signatory – this could be someone well known, your director or chair, or a frontline worker

9   Get the timing right

10   Make the reader give

11   Appeal to the reader's conscience

12   Read what you are sending before sending it – would you give in response to your own appeal letter?

This is a list of success factors developed by Oxfam after studying 10 years of appeals to supporters.

Getting help

Direct mail is a highly specialist fundraising method. You will need to be skilled at:

- writing effective copy
- producing a cost-effective mailing package
- knowing how much to ask for
- planning a mailing programme
- selecting the best lists to rent
- testing (and coding) the response
- knowing what response rates to expect
- evaluating your performance.

You may not have all (or indeed any) of these skills but you can use:

- *professional consultants*, who specialise in this medium. Since you are paying for their expertise, it is as well to know precisely what you need, brief them well, and have a contract that sets out precisely what they are expected to do and for how much;
- *direct marketing agencies*. For the hard-pressed, a direct marketing agency will carry out all the necessary functions for a fee. This has the advantage of getting the work off your desk, but it can be expensive;
- *freelance help*. Designers and copywriters are available freelance, and can be used in conjunction with yourself or with other sources of help and advice;
- *fulfilment agencies or mailing houses*. The mailing can involve a great deal of work, sorting out which letters go to which people and putting everything into the right envelope within a reasonable time. Mailing houses will perform these functions at a much greater speed than you are

likely to be able to manage, unless your mailing is quite small. Another advantage of using a mailing house is that it can help you claim a postal discount for bulk mailings;

- *other charities with direct mail programmes*, who might be prepared to share their knowledge and experience with you.

As with other areas of fundraising the key to direct mail is to start small, experiment and build up. You need constantly to analyse response rates and test new ideas before rolling out your mailings to larger groups of donors.

Door drops

Door drops are another method of acquiring new donors. They require a mailing pack similar to the sort that you might prepare for a cold mailing and can be delivered by the Royal Mail, by agencies that specialise in delivering unaddressed mail or by volunteers.

The advantages of this type of cold donor recruitment are that it is cheaper to deliver than mail and can be distributed to large areas of the country quite cost effectively. The disadvantages are that it is not personalised, gets lower response rates and so needs to go to larger volumes to achieve equivalent returns to cold mailing, and has a higher rate of anonymous donations.

14.3 Using the telephone for fundraising

The telephone has been a key fundraising medium since the early 1990s. Both incoming and outgoing calls are important for the fundraiser. Incoming calls include enquiries and telephone pledges in response to an appeal. Outward bound telemarketing, which requires some skill, can be used for a whole range of promotional and fundraising activities.

Also, as a result of the high numbers of people now owning mobile phones, more charities are incorporating donations via SMS or using text messaging as part of their fundraising programme.

Donation lines

Special response lines for people to call in and make a donation are commonplace. Donors appreciate being able to make credit (or debit) card donations by telephone in response to an appeal.

You can use a separate number for the response line, which should be answered by someone briefed to receive these calls. Answer machines are not ideal; donors want to speak to a real person. However, if you do need to use an answer machine make sure that the message is clear, that donors are told exactly what information to leave and that the answer tapes are long enough to record a number of calls.

If the calls come through a switchboard or receptionist it is important that there is an effective procedure for answering calls, and that the person taking the call knows what to do. If you spend a good deal of time out of the office, you will want information about people phoning in passed to you quickly.

Premium telephone lines

There are special lines offered by British Telecom through its Valuecall Service. One arrangement shares the revenue between the telephone company and you, the subscriber. The caller pays a premium rate per minute at peak times, and slightly less at other times. The line can be used in conjunction with radio, TV or a mailed appeal, or to receive donations or give out information.

Other special numbers available give the caller access to you at local rates irrespective of where they call from, and you are charged for this. Or they can allow callers to telephone you at your expense.

Answering services

For some campaigns, you will want to have someone actually answering the phone, but you may not have the facilities or staff to do this. One option is to use volunteers. You will need to identify and brief the volunteers, and for large appeals you may want to get additional telephone lines installed. Another option is to use a telephone agency, which will have the necessary equipment and trained operators. Not only will they answer the phone, but for an additional charge they will deal with any follow-up mailings and provide a detailed analysis of the response. This service can be quite expensive, so be sure to get a quote first.

Recruitment and renewals

The telephone can also be used to recruit people to do house-to-house collections, to recruit and keep in touch with people participating in a fundraising event, and so on. It is also an excellent way to get people to renew their membership or increase the value of their committed regular gift.

You may consider using the telephone simply to find out if your supporters have any questions to ask you. Too many telephone calls (and also too many fundraising letters) are concerned with what the charity wants to tell its supporters rather than listening to the supporters' ideas, questions and concerns. Why not simply ring people up to find out if they are happy with what they receive from you and whether there is anything else they would like to know? You may find out some very interesting things about who your supporters are and be able to begin to identify some trends in their behaviour. However, if you are going to do this you must be prepared to listen to their ideas, and if they ask you not to ring them again, don't.

Another good use of the telephone is raising money for an emergency. If there is a famine and people are dying, or a spell of bitter weather is giving older people hypothermia, then this is a good reason to call your supporters.

What can be achieved using the telephone

In 2005 Cancer Research UK carried out a telephone campaign talking to women who had taken part in its annual Race for Life. This event involves women of all ages and all levels of fitness who sign up to walk, jog or run five kilometres to raise money to help fund Cancer Research UK activity. With the Race for Life conversion campaign Cancer Research UK wanted to offer women a different way to support the charity. It was felt that a telephone call would be the most relevant medium to approach them to rekindle their support. The phone could be used to talk to them about the impact of their giving and motivate them to give again, and also to engage them in a conversation about the work of the charity and its plans for the future.

The approach focused on the supporter's race experience; each call was tailored to the individual, referring to the race they had taken part in and the year in which they had participated. This was enhanced by the use of questions devised to engage the supporter in a 'real' conversation about their experience.

The campaign was a great success, recruiting almost 6,500 new committed givers who will contribute £1.3 million to Cancer Research UK's work over a five-year period. Of the people called, 12.4% set up a regular gift (against a target of 7.2%), 93% of which was by paperless direct debit.

The telephone is an expensive way of contacting people, so it needs to be used effectively. It is unlikely to be a cost-effective way of soliciting one-off low value donations (unless they are taken by debit or credit card). However, it comes into its own when you want to develop your donors by moving them from being occasional givers or just people with an interest in your organisation to committed monthly donors (as in the case study from Cancer Research UK detailed in the box above), and it can be particularly helpful for negotiating the amount of the donation. Response rates can be as high as 50% or more when calling past donors, which is well in excess of normal mailing response rates. However, you will still need to send them a letter and form to set up their regular gift, unless you can offer paperless direct debits. So you will probably expect around 60% of pledged donations to be converted into actual support.

Getting your message across on the telephone

Successful outbound telephoning needs a good script containing:

- information about the caller and the organisation represented;
- confirmation as to whether it is a good time to talk. For example, if the person being called is about to have a meal they may not wish to stop and talk, so carrying on with the call may cause annoyance. You might also mention how long the call is likely to take;
- reference to previous support or past contact. When calling people who have supported you before, it is important to refer to their past help and thank them;
- a short introduction about the current progress of the organisation and its plans will help set the scene for a request for further help;
- a call to action. As with any other form of communication, you should not assume that supporters will necessarily know why you want their support unless you state it explicitly. The call to action must be very direct and clear, and should state precisely what you want them to do;
- a follow-up reminder. You can say that any pledge made over the phone will be followed by a letter or form to sign. This follow-up should be done as soon as possible to achieve maximum response.

If you plan to use the telephone, then you need to include a space on response devices and in your promotional literature for supporters to give you their phone numbers (it is useful to have both home and mobile phone numbers). There is also then the implication that if they give you this information, they do not mind being called. If you do not have records which contain telephone numbers, you may need to look these up. For larger campaigns, there are organisations that can source this information for you; they will also check for anyone who has registered with the Telephone Preference Service not to receive telemarketing calls.

You will need to recruit and train your callers; this is definitely not something just anybody can do. Successful callers will have an easy outgoing confidence that is communicated over the phone. Though many people are used to the phone, put them in a situation where they have to ask a supporter to give, and they become reluctant and tongue-tied.

Using an agency

You may want to outsource your telephone solicitation by sub-contracting the work to an agency. This can be very helpful for a major telephone campaign. But the use of an agency to solicit funds means that it has to comply with the requirements of the 1992 and 2006 Charities Acts.

Telemarketing and the requirements of the 1992 and 2006 Charities Acts

If you employ an agency to make calls on your behalf, then it is a 'professional fundraiser' under the terms of the 1992 and 2006 Charities Acts. There are a number of requirements:

- a written agreement between the charity and the professional fundraiser in a prescribed form;
- a written statement to be given to potential donors that details what the money is to be spent on and what proportion of their donation will be used to pay the costs of the fundraiser. With the new Act, which became law in 2006, this statement will have to include the amount the 'professional fundraiser' will be paid for fundraising for the appeal; or if the specific amount isn't known, a reasonably accurate estimate of what they will receive should be given;
- a cooling-off period. When a professional fundraiser uses the telephone to solicit money or to sell goods to raise money for your charity, and people respond with payments, then the professional fundraiser must, within seven days of receipt of the payment, write to people who have given or paid more than £50 giving them the right to cancel. The donor then has seven days to cancel the gift. This only applies to telephone solicitation by a professional fundraiser or commercial paticipator, and not to funds solicited by the charity's own staff or by volunteers, who are not covered by these provisions.

The agency will need to make a statement about the fact that it is being paid to fundraise for you and now to say exactly how much it is being paid. This may antagonise donors if it is not handled carefully. You will need to be prepared to get involved with the preparation of scripts and be ready to modify them if necessary during the campaign. You will also need to keep in touch with the campaign, visiting the agency to listen to live calls to check that your charity's reputation is being maintained. For a major campaign, carry out tests with an agency. This will incur start-up costs, but will lift much of the burden of the work at this stage from you. If the test looks like being successful, you can then explore the logistics of doing the campaign in-house.

Whichever way you set about it, you need to make sure of two things: first that your supporters are happy to be telephoned and, crucially, that they have not registered with the Telephone Preference Service; and second that telemarketing is a cost-effective method of fundraising for you.

Short message service (SMS) or text messaging

One relatively recent addition to phone fundraising has been SMS or text messaging. Numbers of text messages sent in the UK are growing at an extraordinary rate, with just one month's total topping 3.7 billion messages. The Mobile Data Association predicted 40 billion messages would be sent in 2006.

People are conducting an extraordinary amount of business on their mobile phones, and charities have been quick to use this medium. The main use of SMS is to solicit an immediate one-off donation, particular for a disaster appeal, such as for the 2004 Tsunami in Asia, when over £1 million was raised by text messaging alone. However, there are other potential uses including ordering brochures about the charity and its fundraising appeal, and the launching of mobile internet sites which can send simple forms – such as a Gift Aid declaration – to the phone user to be filled out.

14.4 Personal solicitation

Meeting and speaking to potential donors face to face is an extremely powerful fundraising technique. There are several forms of personal solicitation currently used by charities:

- recruiting committed supporters in the street or from door to door in their homes
- talks at public events
- visits to people's homes
- making presentations at private meetings.

All these give opportunities for persuasion, questions to be asked and answered, and for reassurance on matters of concern. The degree of personal interaction between the charity and the donor is what sets this apart from other fundraising techniques.

Door-to-door cold solicitation

This type of face to face fundraising can be daunting, as there is usually no known history of support or expressed interest in the charity as a reason for the visit. Though this sounds a thoroughly unpromising way of winning supporters, it can work very well when the fundraisers are specially trained. The technique is unlike house-to-house collecting, in that you will usually be asking for a regular or high-value gift, and so part of the process may need to take place inside the home rather than on the doorstep. However, as for house-to-house collections, there are licensing requirements.

Though some organisations (such as the Karuna Trust) have been doing this type of fundraising for many years, since the late 1990s it has grown very rapidly.

Basically there are two well-established methods. The first is 'one-step' door-to-door fundraising. The fundraiser will visit a household and make an immediate proposition to give. Because the money is being asked for 'there and then' (to be paid by direct debit), a licence, under the House to House Collections Act 1939 is required, just as for cash collections (but see below for changes to the law).

The second method is a 'two-step' or 'multi-visit' process. Individual fundraisers are usually assigned an area that is relatively well-known to them, perhaps close to their own homes; and they will visit streets which they have identified as good prospects for fundraising. They will then call at individual houses, very specifically **not** asking for support at that time but initially leaving information about the charity and making an appointment to return another time once the householder has had an opportunity to consider whether they wish to give their support. Both the Home Office and the Charity Commission have confirmed that *under current legislation* this method does not require a local authority licence provided there is absolutely no proposition put to the householder during the initial interaction (but again see below for changes to the law).

Both types of fundraising have in the past sometimes been used on behalf of a group of voluntary organisations which are being promoted to the donor all at the same time (the 'basket approach'). This is largely falling into disuse in favour of a 'solus' (individual charity) approach.

With either method, the fundraisers need to put in a lot of footwork and be prepared for many rejections. However, it can be a very effective method of recruiting committed givers. It is also particularly suitable for getting support for local community projects where donors can see the need and the benefits on their own doorstep.

If this technique is of interest to you, you will either need to train and run your own team (which can take a lot of time and effort) or employ an agency to do it for you. It is highly advisable to contact the PFRA (Public Fundraising Regulatory Association); this is the charity-run voluntary organisation which promotes best practice in street and doorstep fundraising. It can provide you with details of experienced and accredited agencies, or advice on how to do it yourself.

Street solicitation

This type of face to face fundraising, sometimes known as clipboard fundraising or 'chugging' (originally a negative term coined by journalists by eliding the phrase 'charity mugging', there is now a movement to reclaim the term and give it positive connotations as an elision of 'charity hugging') was brought to the UK by Greenpeace from Germany in the late 1990s. Since then it has mushroomed.

The principle is that small groups of trained fundraisers set up on a busy street or in a shopping centre to recruit committed support (usually with a monthly direct debit). Under current legislation it is far from clear whether a licence is required, and different councils take vastly different positions on the need to 'regulate' this activity. What is agreed is that cash should not be collected, and tables or displays which cause an 'obstruction' should not be placed in the street. The PFRA has voluntary agreements in place with a large number of councils which obviate the need for a licence – check directly with the Association about how you can access those schemes. Collectors should always wear branded tabards or jackets so that they are clearly recognisable as working on behalf of a particular organisation.

Currently these teams are mostly run by fundraising agencies and the cost is based on the number of new supporters recruited, not the value of the individual gift. This type of recruitment is expensive but can be very cost effective if people agree to make regular monthly gifts. Once again, if you are considering using this fundraising method, contact the PFRA for advice and information.

Legal changes for door-to-door and street solicitation

Under the Charities Act 2006, which started to come into effect during 2007, there will be significant changes to the licensing regime for all the forms of face to face fundraising. It will no longer be necessary to obtain a licence for door-to-door collecting, but you will be required to inform the relevant local authority of your *intention* to collect. With street solicitation, you will definitely need a licence, but councils will be obliged to be much more flexible in issuing them than is often the case at the moment. The exact way in which the new law will work is, at the time of writing, not completely clear. So seek expert advice from the PFRA or from your local council before proceeding.

Presentations at events

You might get the chance to make a presentation at meetings, conferences or other events. This is an opportunity to speak directly to people about the work of your organisation and its needs. With an experienced speaker, this can also be a good opportunity to ask for money. If you are speaking at someone else's event, you may need their approval if you plan to ask for immediate donations or to distribute fundraising literature.

Your presentation needs to be carefully thought out. Why should that group of people be particularly interested in your work? The answer could be that they may not be interested, but have been attracted by the activity you have organised. You need to engage their interest if you want to get their support.

Next, you need to decide how you want your audience to respond. You could give out information with donation forms included, carry out a collection at the exits, or write to participants afterwards.

Other people's events offer you new audiences, but you can also organise your own events for existing and potential supporters. These could be visits, study tours or open days to see your organisation at work, small discussions with an expert speaker so that they can discuss the problems you are addressing in greater depth, or receptions, perhaps at the home of a well-respected donor and possibly with a guest speaker and some sort of presentation afterwards.

Such events can be excellent for fundraising. They will make your existing donors feel important and give them a better understanding of the issues. This may lead them to give more substantial support or to volunteer.

Warm visits

Warm visits involve face to face meetings with people who have already supported you or with whom you already have contact. There are two reasons for doing this:

- to talk about your work rather than specifically to ask for money, so as to find out more about their interests and develop a closer relationship with them. This is an investment in the relationship which you hope might lead to more committed giving or a legacy;
- as part of a major appeal, when you need to get support and are making a personal presentation on the work of the organisation to a potential new supporter.

How to prepare for visiting a donor

- Have precise information on the individual's past support so that you can thank them and tell them what you have been able to do with their money. Try to locate a particular interest or concern of theirs and show how you are working in that field. In other words, listen first and suggest second.
- Be well briefed about the work of the organisation, so that you can talk about current efforts and future plans in an informed and interesting way. Take photographs or leaflets with you to show the donor.

- Have some idea of the support you need, and the ways in which they might be able to help you, so that if the opportunity arises you can introduce the idea of further support.
- Know about tax-effective giving – this can be one excuse for being there in the first place – and tell them how their money can be used even more efficiently, by donating it tax effectively.

You will need to fix an appropriate time and place for the meeting. The charity's offices are often the best place because this gives people a better perspective about the work of the organisation. Alternatively, some people will feel more comfortable in their own homes. You can go along as well, but the best person to do the actual asking is the person who introduced the potential donor to you, and they need to be properly briefed.

Don't be in too much of a hurry to make the ask; this needs to be correctly timed and may even come at a subsequent meeting, after the person's interest has been stimulated and they have had time to consider whether to support you. Try to listen to what the potential supporter is saying, and respond accordingly. Fundraising is not about telling someone what you think they should know; it is about engaging their interest and understanding their needs.

Resources to develop for face to face solicitation

If you would like to use personal solicitation as a fundraising tool for committed and major gifts or legacies, here are some suggestions for what you will need.

- People who are really good speakers and presenters. You might decide to develop a panel of people who are interested in what your organisation is doing and good at speaking at meetings.
- Existing donors who are prepared to speak to potential new donors. There is nothing like having people say, 'This organisation is great, and I've given to it' for motivating others to give.
- Volunteers with skills that are similar to those required for warm visits.
- Good hand-out material that can be used to illustrate the points you are making. For presentations you may want to use PowerPoint, an overhead projector or a flipchart, or even a short film on video or DVD to help get your message across.

All visits should be prepared with care. Rehearse the presentation thoroughly. If at all possible practise on a colleague or friend who can give you constructive criticism – and advise you if the presentation is too long or too short. You should try to predict what questions will come up. Go prepared with photos, brochures, budgets and plans so that you can use these as prompts. Finally, remember to leave some information with the potential donor, or you could send this as a follow-up to your meeting. Most people will not make up their minds immediately, and will be guided, reminded or helped to respond by what you have left with them or sent afterwards.

Throughout the meeting, you should give people the opportunity to ask questions. If you are not getting much feel for how the meeting is going, ask some questions yourself. Do they feel it is an important issue? Do they think the project will achieve what it is setting out to do?

At some point you will need to make the request for money. There are different ways to do this. One is to say that you want them to consider helping in one of several ways. A more direct approach might be to explain the urgency of the need, and then simply ask for money. Always try to ask for a specific amount based on what you believe the supporter may be able and willing to give. Don't be overcautious when making your ask – when you are making a personal one-to-one presentation like this, the potential donor is expecting to be asked and will respond according to what they can afford. If anything, slightly *over*-estimate – this is a classic example of 'don't ask, don't get'!

14.5 Advertising for support

Advertising in a newspaper or magazine can be used to promote your cause or to raise money, but it is expensive. You can raise money directly through making an appeal, or indirectly by recruiting members or volunteers or generating enquirers for further information (whom you might approach for support later on). Advertising is extremely successful in raising money for an emergency or disaster, or when a particular issue has hit the headlines. At times like this, your advertisement will reach people when they know that something needs to be done – and you are offering them a way of helping.

There are various ways for you to advertise:

- in the press – taking space in national or local newspapers, through display advertising or small ads (also known as 'off the page' advertising);
- in magazines and journals (general interest or specialist);
- loose inserts in a newspaper or magazine;
- posters (both billboard advertising and smaller posters displayed on notice boards);
- on TV and radio.

Nine questions to ask before you advertise

I find it useful to start work on appeal advertising by thinking of myself as person to person fundraiser, about to set off, ringing the doorbells of potential donors. Like a salesman (for that's what I am), I ask myself these questions:

- Which are the best doorbells to ring?
- How have I identified them?
- What kind of people live behind these doors?
- What's the best time to 'call', remembering the clamour for their attention?
- What's their lifestyle; their attitudes; discretionary income; knowledge of and sympathy for my organisation's work?
- How do I best get a hearing?
- How do I get them to open the door and invite me in?
- What shall I ask them to do and how can I most successfully get them to do it?
- How do I retain their continued interest and practical support?

Not until I have answered these questions am I ready to see how my charity's need can be translated into the 'calls' I'm going to make in printed advertisements. I'm not writing to a mass audience. I'm writing to individuals; to the reader, my press ad (like my mailing), must come as a personal message, telling her or him of a need, so that it evokes a personal reaction and response. But the initial impact needs to be swift, or it will never retain attention.

[Taken from *The Printed Fundraiser*, by Harold Sumption (1916–1998)]

Newspaper advertising

The main problem with press advertising is the high cost, even for a limited amount of space. So messages have to be succinct and eye-catching. However, you can select your audience through the known readership of the paper or magazine; you can also predict whether your issue is likely to be given editorial coverage and, if so, whether this will be done sympathetically.

A guide to what you should be able to raise through press advertising is a 3:1 revenue to cost ratio. However, most organisations will not achieve anything like this, and many find that the returns are substantially lower than the costs. It may be that what you can achieve with advertising could also be achieved more cheaply with an effective and well-targeted communications campaign.

Opportunistic advertising

The most exciting aspect of advertising is its flexibility. You can place an advertisement almost immediately, so if a disaster or some other high-profile event happens one day, you could be appealing for help the next morning.

What might be classed as a disaster? This is not necessarily a serious emergency, but what your public is being told is serious by newspapers and other news media. A famine overseas is an obvious example, or the domestic disasters that occur from time to time, such as a major oil spill. Then there are the regular 'disasters' that are perceived or stage managed, such as the plight of homeless people in the winter highlighted by appeals run by Crisis or Shelter around Christmas, when the weather is getting cold and public sympathy is high. Timing is everything, and one estimate is that 30% of your response is likely to come just from getting this right.

Acquisition advertising

This is all about finding new supporters who can be profitably appealed to at a later date. For example, you might find it a good idea to take newspaper space to publicise a particular issue affecting your beneficiaries and invite donations to support your work in this area. You might not make much surplus over the costs of the advertising, yet you might acquire the support of many new donors who subsequently go on to give more substantial sums on a regular basis. Decide before you start how much you can spend to recruit a new supporter. Some organisations are happy if they can find new supporters for £50 each, although in the end it depends on how much you expect to raise from each supporter in the longer term.

Awareness advertising

If no one knows much about you or if you want to launch a new campaign, you may need to build public awareness first, rather than immediately try to raise money or recruit supporters. Awareness advertising is expensive and its impact is difficult to measure, and it often demands the use of very large spaces with the advertising continuing over a long period.

Although this approach is often used by large companies, it may not be the best way of using limited charitable funds. It may be that the effective use of PR will buy a good deal more awareness than any amount of advertising. However, one advantage of paying for the space is you can control both the timing and the content of the message.

Loose inserts

One of the main problems with buying space in newspapers is the size constraint. To buy an 18cm space across four columns in a national newspaper may cost as much as £4,000. So the space you will be able to afford is very limited. Loose inserts could be a better option. Depending on the publication, anything from a small leaflet to a Christmas gift catalogue can be inserted or bound into a publication.

There are four important differences between an insert and an advertisement.

- There is much more space available to you and you can even include an envelope with the insert, although the publisher may impose restrictions on the weight, size or shape of the insert, and the print cost will vary with the size of the insert. This makes inserts an ideal medium to describe your work and set out the different ways of supporting your organisation. Inserts can work extremely well for membership recruit-ment, campaigns for committed giving such as child and community sponsorship schemes, and those appeals that need space if they are to be promoted effectively.
- The cost per recipient is much higher, but inserts can be very cost-effective because of the combination of the space available to you, cost and value for money factors, and the ability to include a response mechanism as part of the printed insert.
- Inserts take time to arrange and print and so, unlike adverts, cannot so easily be produced to take advantage of topical events.
- They can be easily detached from the publication, without damaging it; on the other hand, they can also fall out and get lost, or thrown away.

Inserts also provide excellent opportunities for testing the message or format of an appeal.

Evaluating the results

You should always try to evaluate the effectiveness of any advertising you pay for by using a coded coupon, special reply address or phone number in the advertisement or insert. The coding should be done for the campaign as a whole, and for each separate promotion within it. This is the only way you can find out which medium works best for you. Results can then be measured in terms of:

- income raised per £ of media cost
- cost per new donor recruited.

In the case of awareness advertising, you can do research before and after to measure any increased awareness generated by the campaign – this is expensive, so is only really viable for major campaigns by large charities.

Posters

Posters fit least well into the fundraising area, largely because they don't eas-ily allow for an immediate response. But they are nonetheless an important promotional medium. They can range in size from the huge 96-sheet hoardings visible on main roads right down to the smaller posters and handbills used in windows and on notice boards.

Commercial posters

Posters are an extremely potent communications medium. Their impact depends on the size of the image and the extent of the coverage, but it requires a great deal of both to get your message across, and this is expensive. Charities can use the medium in small bursts to highlight a special week or the launch of a campaign, either nationally or in a chosen area. You could copy what political parties do at election time; they rent a site for a day to promote a poster which will generate controversy and media coverage.

However, opportunities for any direct response can be limited, although you can give a phone or text number as a contact. Posters are probably most useful as an awareness medium to support other fundraising activity.

Mini-posters and handbills

In a different league from commercial posters are small posters or handbills which you can use to publicise almost anything locally. These are attractive for fundraising, since they can be printed cheaply and displayed free. One commonly used idea is to print a poster as a part of one of your leaflets, so the leaflet folds out to become a poster.

Depending on what you are promoting, these mini-posters can be targeted at whomever you want. They can be put up in supporters' windows, in shops, on library notice boards, in community centres, in schools, or anywhere you feel you can reach your target audience. Volunteers can distribute thousands of posters and leaflets and create a highly visible campaign at little cost.

Advertising on TV

Television advertising is very expensive, so it is important to identify realistic objectives for any advertisement. If you simply wish to promote a message you should note the codes produced by CAP (Committee of Advertising Practice), which regulates the content of all TV commercials on channels and stations licensed by Ofcom. Alternatively you may want to advertise activities going on in the regions or around the country. The Children's Society and Christian Aid have both supported their national fundraising weeks by using TV advertising. This can give your volunteers moral support and make the public aware in advance of a special week or a house-to-house collection. Direct response advertising on TV (DRTV) is much more widely used. This differs from the classic commercial in that it invites donors to make a donation by phone with a credit card or to become a committed donor with a monthly gift by direct debit. Both Oxfam and the National Canine Defence League were trailblazers in this area of regular giving via DRTV; since many other organisations have followed their lead.

Air time can be bought in a range of ways. Individual spots can be purchased, but are extremely expensive at peak times. The evidence suggests that off-peak times such as afternoons and late at night are better for charity advertising. In this case, packages of spots might be purchased at a discount.

The choice of media depends on your objective: if it is to get a message across to a national audience then an independent network, Channel 4, breakfast TV, or a satellite or cable channel can be used. If you are a local charity or want to test your commercial in one region, then use the appropriate regional TV station.

Getting the message right can be difficult. If it has little impact, you risk wasting the chance to bring your charity to the attention of millions. But if you attempt to make it too strong and emotive, you risk having the advertisement turned down by the broadcasters or the regulators. It is advisable to check with the appropriate authority on what is acceptable before committing to too much expense.

TV commercials are expensive to produce. To cut down on costs, you can try asking the professionals to donate their services free, use existing film or slide-based material, use a personality (preferably in a studio), find a partner to share the cost, or get the advertisement sponsored.

If you are considering this type of advertising you may want to contact the Media Trust, an organisation established to help charities communicate more effectively. It has a Media Matching service to put charities in contact with communications professionals willing to donate their time and expertise.

Advertising on radio

Advertising on radio has the advantage that it is much cheaper than television, and can be tailored to a local audience. Radio time is bought in exactly the same way as TV time. National packages are available, but radio can be especially useful for supporting local or regional events. It would be quite normal for an advertising agency to place adverts with a dozen or so radio stations to cover one part of the country. For example, a concert, shops or a charity week can be promoted on local radio stations in the catchment area of the potential audience.

The creative possibilities with radio are considerable, but you will need help from professionals. Ask your local radio station whether it can help prepare your commercial. Radio lends itself well to competitions, to celebrity voices and to repetition. You can expect well-known voices to give their time free, if properly approached. The cost of production may range from hundreds of pounds to a few thousand. If you have to distribute tapes widely, this will be an additional cost.

Advertising issues

1 Seeing it through other people's eyes. In fundraising, it is necessary to illustrate the cause in some way. Images of the beneficiary and their needs are among the most powerful means of generating a response. But what effect might this have on the beneficiaries themselves or on public attitudes towards the cause? Organisations dealing with the problems of disability use much less harrowing pictures, especially when they are controlled by the people with disabilities. Many opt for positive and optimistic images.

2 Free or fee? A number of campaigns have been developed using free space whenever it becomes available. The disadvantage is that you have no control over the intensity or timing of your campaign.

Once you have decided to use advertising, there are two key decisions to take: how to design and produce your advertising and how to place it. You can do both, but you will never be able to purchase media as cheaply as a media buyer or an advertising agency. Developing a creative approach and producing the advertisement have traditionally been the function of advertising agencies. So unless you are conducting a small-scale local campaign, you are quite likely to need the input of an agency; you should budget for this.

Television and radio appeals

As well as paying for advertising there are opportunities for getting some sort of free coverage. One is the BBC's Lifeline appeal, which has been running for many years. The appeal is broadcast monthly in a slot on a Sunday. If you are successful in being selected to broadcast an appeal, the publicity and financial support generated can be considerable, although the sums raised vary widely.

There are other ways of using TV to get your message across than a direct appeal, and these can, if well coordinated, enhance your other fundraising work. The opportunities now include the Community Channel which was launched on Sky Digital in September 2005 by the Media Trust. Initially it only broadcast for three hours each day and its content was mainly concentrated on charity advertisements. Since then it has developed into a 24-hour, seven day a week service highlighting local and international issues as well as the charitable and voluntary sectors.

Editorial appeals

Each year, especially at Christmas, some TV magazine and news programmes feature a charity appeal. Blue Peter is a well-known example, supporting charities that appeal to children. In their case money is rarely sought – stamps, clothes, even mobile phones and other convertible items being the usual object of the appeal. Local and regional news programmes have similar appeals.

To get your charity featured, you must make yourselves known to the producers of the programmes, and in the first instance to their researchers. This should be done at least six months in advance, and preferably well before then. If you can create a link between the audience and the appeal, you are more likely to be successful.

Telethons

Telethons were a feature of the 1980s and 1990s and look set to continue to raise relatively large sums. They are to an extent a counterbalance to the pulling power of the large charities, as most of the proceeds are distributed to smaller and local charities.

- BBC Children in Need began appearing as a TV and radio appeal in 1980. It now raises over £30 million each year for children's charities.
- Comic Relief has been run every other year since 1985. It raised more than £63 million in 2007 for projects in Africa and in the UK. Sport Relief is run in the intervening years, and raised £18 million in 2006.

There are opportunities for charities to be featured as part of the telethon, but the main chance is to apply for a grant after the event from Children in Need and Comic Relief (see chapter 6 on grantmaking trusts).

Radio appeals

Radio must surely rate as the most under-exploited fundraising medium, as it holds many opportunities for the imaginative and energetic fundraiser. Possibilities include:

- *the Radio 4 Appeal* (previously known as The Week's Good Cause) which has been running since 1926. The amount of money you raise may not be huge, for example total income for appeals broadcast during the summer of 2006 varied between £668 and £37,000. However the value of having your appeal featured may raise your profile in other ways: one organisation received a legacy for £225,000 as a direct result of its appeal in this slot;
- *paid advertising* (discussed earlier in this section);
- *editorial coverage*. Nationally there are opportunities in programmes such as You and Yours. Locally, news and chat show programmes provide the best opportunities;

- *phone-ins*. It is always possible to phone in to a chat programme, or to get your supporters to do so, to express a point of view, promote an activity or make a request for support.

14.6 Fundraising on the internet

Since the late 1990s the internet has developed rapidly as a medium for communication and income generation. There are few fundraisers who are not aware of it, and new ways to use the web are developing all the time.

The growth of online shopping, online banking and personal electronic communications, whether e-mail, instant messaging or texting, has ensured that online fundraising is widely accepted by donors as simply another method of fundraising used by charities.

Donors and potential donors *are* online

According to the Office of National Statistics:

- 13.9 million households (57%) in Great Britain (14.3 million including Northern Ireland) could access the internet from home between January and April 2006, a rise of 26% since 2002 (August 2006);
- 69% of households with internet access had a broadband connection (August 2006);
- in 2002 about 10% of men aged 80 and over and just over 5% of women aged 80 and over said they used the internet;
- UK households spent £18.1 billion online on goods and services in 2004, a rise of 67% on 2003;
- 55% of adults who used the internet in July 2005 bought or ordered goods, tickets or services.

Different uses of the internet

For fundraisers, the internet provides many opportunities. Indeed it can support almost all elements of fundraising, from donor research and donor recruitment to event management, trading, donor development, tax-effective giving, donation processing and donor communication.

- It is an ideal medium to explain the details of your work to those who are interested. The number of charity websites has grown at an incredible rate in the last few years, and most take advantage of the ease of updating information to publish news about their latest campaigns on their website. The medium lends itself not only to providing this sort of information, but also to linking it with all other aspects of your organisation's work, such as recruiting new members, or encouraging people to attend events.

- For those organising events, the internet provides allsorts of opportunities. Auctions, ticket sales, telethons and sponsored events have been developed by many charities. Indeed, sponsored events work particularly well. Services such as *Bmycharity* and *Justgiving* enable supporters such as marathon runners to create their own fundraising page, e-mail their friends and families requesting sponsorship, and then watch as donations from around the world are received securely online, often with the tax-effective Gift Aid element added.
- *Justgiving* reported in 2005 that this method of fundraising does reach and recruit new supporters: 41% of donors on its site said they had not heard of the charity before, i.e. it was the personal request from their friend or relative that convinced them to give. In addition, the online element itself was attractive to many: 31% of donors said they would not have given if they had had to give cash or by cheque.

Online auction site eBay has now established *eBay for Charity* in the UK, enabling people selling items online to donate a proportion to their favourite charity. Charities themselves have for some years been using eBay to sell valuable donated items such as rare books to a global audience.

Online events show that charities can build valuable personal links with supporters and their networks of friends, colleagues and family. Some charities are using these relationships to offer information tailored to individual supporters' needs and preferences. For example, they can choose how often to receive e-mail newsletters, download a donation document to help them complete their annual tax return, and opt to receive alerts about particular activities run by the charity.

For organisations looking for more direct financial support there are a number of methods that can be used.

- *Simple appeals*. Many organisations now put appeals or opportunities to donate on their website as well as through more traditional channels, such as mail. Indeed, some charities have perfected the art of getting people to generate funds online without costing them a penny. For example, NSPCC, WaterAid and Whizz-Kidz have teamed up with corporate supporters to offer click-to-give sites: visitors click once a day and when a certain total is reached, the corporate supporter makes a donation.
- *Printed appeals*. Many internet users will be able to print the contents of screens that they view online. Thus a donation form, membership form or committed giving form can then be filled in with the relevant information and printed out to become a fully completed donation form. The

drawback of this is that it still has to be posted – and so still has many of the problems of direct mail, requiring an envelope, a stamp and a trip to the post box.

- *E-mail appeals*. As the number of your supporters with access to the internet grows you can collect their e-mail addresses and send fundraising appeals to them, provided you have their permission and adhere to data protection legislation (see Appendix 4).

- *Information provision*. The internet can be a very cost-effective way to supply information to your donors. Many charities strive to reach a wider audience and reduce their print bills by offering an e-mail newsletter to their donors.

- *Debit and credit card giving*. This remains the main focus of many organisations fundraising online, whether they are seeking one-off or regular gifts. Emergency appeals, which continue to benefit considerably from the opportunities of online fundraising, demonstrate how popular this method of giving can be. For example, between 6.16pm on 30 December and 6.16pm on 31 December 2004, the Disasters Emergency Committee website received 166,936 donations, raising £10,676,836 for the Tsunami Earthquake Appeal. This is the most money ever donated online in 24 hours, according to Guinness World Records.

- *Online shopping*. Charities that trade through catalogues are now putting these online to sell directly. The recent popularity of alternative or beneficiary gift catalogues such as the Good Gifts Catalogue and Oxfam Unwrapped has largely been driven by online sales. For example Oxfam offers alternative gifts such as the Alpaca Package where for £20 you can help 'farmers buy and look after these fluffy fellas, and make a living from their wool, with shears, shelter, food and fences.'

Using e-mail to keep in touch with supporters

Benjamin Franklin House at 36 Craven Street in London is unique being the only house lived in by the famous American that is still standing. It has two independent charities linked to it: the Friends of Benjamin Franklin House which is a UK registered charity and the Benjamin Franklin House Foundation, a US 501(c) (3) organisation. Though the house stands in the UK and therefore has a supporter base here, understandably it has a significant number of people in the USA who are interested in it.

As part of a capital campaign to raise funds to restore the house where Franklin lodged while in London between 1757 and 1775, the charity sent regular, accessible e-mail bulletins to donors and supporters all over the world. Using this simple medium these people could be kept updated visually with the progress of the restoration and informed when significant donations or funding came in. In this case e-mail provided a very immediate way of communicating to a disparate group without the need for mailmerging data, printing letters and sticking stamps on envelopes.

Since the house opened on 17 January, 2006, Franklin's 300th birthday, e-mail has remained a key, cost-effective medium for the communication of information and fundraising messages by the organisation.

Print - Close Window

From: "Benjamin Franklin House" <benjaminfranklinhouse@msn.com>
To: benjaminfranklinhouse@msn.com
Subject: Benjamin Franklin House - Last 'Countdown' Message
Date: Tue, 24 Jan 2006 22:27:08 -0000

Left: Benjamin Franklin's 300th birthday cake at the opening Gala
Centre: The Lord Mayor of Westminster experimenting with the musical glasses in the Student Science Centre
Right: Foreign Secretary Jack Straw and Ambassador to the Court of St. James's, Robert Tuttle cutting the ribbon to formally open Benjamin Franklin House

Dear Friends,

One week ago I wrote to say UK Foreign Secretary Jack Straw and US Ambassador to the Court of St. James's Robert Tuttle unveiled a precious heritage asset, the only surviving home of Benjamin Franklin as a dynamic museum and education facility.

The 1730s building served as the first de facto American Embassy, seat of Franklin's mission over nearly 16 years to keep Britain and America one under the Crown. Though unsuccessful, he planted durable seeds of a 'special relationship' that is a source of strength for both nations. It was a fitting tribute to Anglo-American Franklin, father of the US State Department, that two senior representatives of both governments came together on the steps of this practical, work-a-day Georgian residence which will speak of the past to future generations.

* **A Grand Celebration**

Polly Hewson, lead character in our museum-as-theatre Historical Experience, daughter of Benjamin Franklin's landlady (and Franklin's second 'daughter') wrote after his departure from Craven Street: "They all of them talk of you, and are now full of the thought of celebrating your birthday."

And so we were. On 17 January 2006, guests from across the UK, the US and beyond – over 350 of them – gathered at London's Banqueting Hall for a celebratory dinner and a most special 300th birthday party. Highlights included a Franklin Trumpet Voluntary arranged by well-known composer George Fenton, performed by the London Brass; delicious early American cuisine from William Norris; Franklin armonica master, Alisdair Malloy, who performed a piece written by Mozart for Franklin's amazing instrument; and Gala sponsor John Studzinski of HSBC who gave a superb introduction to Ambassador's Tuttle's erudite remarks. There was even a grand tiered birthday cake.

* **Successful First Days**

In the days since, some 150 members of the public have ventured to the House. In the largest extant Franklin artefact they have discovered the rescued original interiors have not a level angle among them. They have become immersed in our primary offering, the Historical Experience, and so must you too. It is unique and engaging using the 18th century spaces where so much took place as stage, blending live interpretation, leading edge sound, lighting, and visual projection to tell the rich story of Franklin in London in his own words. Tickets can be booked from our website www.BenjaminFranklinHouse.org.

Indeed, no dead hand of history here but also a Student Science Centre that will inspire young people through the science of Franklin's London years, when he explored everything from canal depths to daylight savings time, with the Gulf Stream thrown in for good measure. They will also learn about the Craven Street bones, remnants of an anatomy school run by Polly's husband. Outreach will bring American and British children together through the annual Benjamin Franklin Science Fair, giving them a chance to free their imagination and a common platform for discussing their shared history. Tuesdays we are only open to schools and our first groups are booked through March.

So too a living Scholarship Centre as a focal point in Europe for study of the myriad subjects with which Benjamin

The future of the internet for charities

While many charities are consolidating their initial experiences of online fundraising by developing more effective shopping sites, personalising donor information and ensuring their sites meet accessibility requirements, others are already experimenting with the latest opportunities. These include distributing information in RSS format ('really simple syndication'), featuring 'blogs' or more informal updates from staff and clients, publishing podcasts (audio files) of news or comment which can be listened to on a PC or a portable digital music player, and encouraging 'user generated content'. The latter can involve site visitors contributing comments, news, photos or even videos, and can make for a much more engaging website that both serves a wide range of stakeholders and reflects their needs and involvement with the charity. Recent examples include NSPCC's use of GoogleMaps to create a map of supporters involved in its Full Stop campaign and the Alzheimer's Society's campaign to solicit memories from supporters.

Yet other charities are embracing the opportunities of third-party sites such as YouTube, MySpace and Flickr to reach and interact with a large audience. Indeed, some US nonprofits have even begun holding virtual fundraising events and appeals in the virtual world of Second Life. Fortunately the income generated is very real.

Resources and further information

See also general lists at the end of the book.

Organisations

BBC Appeals Office
MC4 D1 Media Centre
Media Village
201 Wood Lane
London W12 7TQ
www.bbc.co.uk/info/policies/charities
e-mail charityappeals@bbc.co.uk

CSV Training and Enterprise
Tel. 020 7713 6840
www.csv.org.uk
e-mail information@csv.org.uk

Fundraising UK Ltd
(website for charity fundraisers)
www.fundraising.co.uk

Information Commissioner – for information on data protection
Wycliffe House
Water Lane
Wilmslow
Cheshire SK9 5AF
www.ico.gov.uk
Tel. 01625 545745/08456 30 60 60

**Mailing Preference Service (MPS) &
Telephone Preference Service (TPS)**
DMA House
70 Margaret Street
London W1W 8SS
www.mpsonline.org.uk
Tel. 020 7291 3310 (MPS)
e-mail mps@dma.org.uk
www.tpsonline.org.uk
Tel. 020 7291 3320 (TPS)
e-mail tps@dma.org.uk

Media Trust
3–7 Euston Centre
Regent's Place
London NW1 3JG
www.mediatrust.org
Tel. 020 7874 7600
e-mail information@mediatrust.org

**Public Fundraising Regulatory
Authority (PFRA)**
Unit 11, Europoint
5–11 Lavington Street
London SE1 0NZ
www.pfra.org.uk
Tel. 020 7401 8452
e-mail info@pfra.org.uk

Publications

The following publications are available from the Directory of Social Change.
Prices were correct at the time of writing, but may be subject to change.

Asking Properly, George Smith, White Lion Press 1997, £20

Building a Fundraising Database Using your PC, 2nd edn, Peter Flory, DSC/CAF
2001, £12.95

Data Protection, 2nd edition, Paul Ticher, DSC 2002, £18.95 (new edition
available early 2008; see www.dsc.org.uk for details)

Friends for Life, Ken Burnett, White Lion Press 1997, £15

Other publications

Commonsense Direct Marketing, Drayton Bird, Kogan Page 2000, £23.95

Institute of Fundraising Code of Practice on Face to Face Fundraising

Institute of Fundraising Code of Practice on Fundraising Through Electronic
Media

Institute of Fundraising Code of Practice on Reciprocal Charity Mailings

15 GETTING YOUR MESSAGE ACROSS

This chapter deals with how to put together materials (funding applications, appeal letters, annual reports and leaflets) that can be used to communicate a fundraising message. This is followed by a section on how your communications programme and contact with the media can be used to support fundraising work.

Details of organisations and publications referred to in this chapter are on page 337.

15.1 Applying to potential funders

The ability to write an effective letter or application is one of the most important fundraising skills to develop. The difference between a good and a bad application can be the difference between success and failure. Your application needs to communicate the needs of your organisation to potential supporters and will usually be the basis for the funder deciding whether to make a grant. More detailed advice can be found in the book *Writing Better Fundraising Applications*.

Planning your application

How you put together your proposal depends on who you are applying to; what their priorities and interests are; their procedure for selecting and assessing grant applications; what you need to say about your organisation; what you propose to do with the funds; and when you will be submitting the application. There are several factors to consider at this stage.

- *Application forms*. Does the donor require applications to be submitted in a standard format, or is there an application form? Increasingly, you may be offered the opportunity to apply by e-mail, or download the application form from a website (particularly for Lottery applications) and submit it electronically.
- *Application dates*. Most donors work to a grants cycle. For central and local government this is an annual cycle, while for many foundations grants are decided at quarterly meetings, and they may have a long list of

applications to consider. You can't just send off an application and assume you will get the money when you need it. You have to fit your fundraising into their grantmaking timetable, and this means planning ahead.

- *How many donors you plan to approach*. Even if you are sending the same proposal to a large number of donors, you should still try to personalise each one. This might include a reference in your covering letter to any previous contact, how the project particularly fits within the donor's guidelines and current interests and (if relevant) whether and how the donor will benefit from the association (this is particularly important to companies – see chapter 8).

- *The funder's potential for giving*. Large funders, including major trusts and government funding programmes, will expect quite a lot of detail. They are not just looking for good ideas, but for evidence of need and ability to deliver. Those who will make less significant donations, which includes smaller trusts and most companies, simply will not have the time to read a long application. They will want something clear and to the point – so a page or two is likely to be enough. You should try to include all the important points in your letter. If they need more information, they will ask for it.

- *The likelihood of success*. Fundraising is time consuming so it's best to concentrate on a few applications which you think stand a greater chance of success rather than scattering your efforts widely.

Targeting your proposal

Who you send your proposal to will depend on a number of issues.

- *Urgency*. If you need the money urgently, your best chance may be to approach those who have already supported you. You have already convinced them that your organisation is worthwhile, and they may be willing to support you again. However, first check any conditions they have on how long you need to wait before applying again.

- *Scale of need*. If you require a large sum, you can either apply for a few large grants from donors interested in your sort of work (or who have already supported you), or you can mount a wider appeal to a larger number of donors.

- *How many donors to approach*. Funders may want to know how many other people have been asked and who has already agreed to give. Again, careful targeting of a few is more effective than a more general mailing. You can use an early, generous donation to set an example to other donors. If you hope to obtain government support, it is usually best to secure this first, so you can tell other funders about it.

- *Type of project*. New projects and initiatives are more likely to be of interest than simply contributing to the operating costs of an organisation or providing a basic service. Try to construct the proposal to make your work appear new and exciting, showing that you are addressing matters of current concern in a fresh and innovative way. This is often simply a matter of presentation.

- *A personalised approach.* Try to personalise the approach as much as you can, referring to previous contact and support and making your application relevant to the potential funder's interests and concerns.

Content

Decide what you are going to ask for funds for – strategic development, capital costs, a specific piece of expenditure or a particular project. Read or re-read chapter 2, section 2.3 on making your case, before you go any further. Once you have established what you want the funds for, there are other points you need to consider:

- the aims and objectives of the project;
- the problem or need that is to be met;
- the urgency of the need, and whether there are consequences if nothing is done;
- the working methods to be used to meet your aims;
- why the method you have selected is the best or the most appropriate or the most cost-effective;
- the expected outcomes and achievements of the project;
- what it is about your organisation that makes it the most appropriate to run the scheme;
- if the work is innovative, what you will do to disseminate the experience gained from the project so that others can benefit;
- how you plan to monitor and evaluate the project;
- a clear budget for the work, which justifies all the expenditure;
- when the funding stops, what will happen in the future: will the project become self-sustaining? Will you find alternative funding, or finish?
- the other grants that can be (or have been) mobilised to add to the sum being requested from that particular donor;
- when the money is needed;
- any collaboration with other organisations and agencies;
- who else is supporting or funding your work;
- how you will bring in additional skills and resources, use volunteers and work with local community groups;
- your plans beyond the project, and how you will build on and develop your work during this next phase (which should at least be considered, even if you have no firm plans at this stage).

Broad checklist for a proposal

1. Do you have a strategy for the immediate project?
2. Have you planned ahead for when the funding ends?
3. Have you picked the right project for that funder and tailored your application to address their particular interests and priorities?
4. Have you done enough to establish your credibility and included a clear statement of your charity's functions and objectives?
5. Have you prepared a realistic budget and included a set of your most recent accounts?
6. Have you been specific about what you need?
7. Have you set an initial target for what you need to raise to start the project?
8. Is your proposal clear, concise and factual?
9. Have you included pictures illustrating the project or the problem you want to address?
10. Is it addressed to the right person?

How much to ask for

Do some research to find out how much each funder tends to give. This may be less than you need. In this case you will need to approach a number of potential donors, asking each to contribute part of the total. There are different ways of doing this. You can write to several sources, and ask each to contribute a share of the total (an appropriate proportion depending on their size). You can break down the project into separate components; each element might then become the subject of an application to a particular donor, and in each application you can highlight the particular importance of what you are asking for – as well as the value of the project as a whole.

Then you must decide on your strategy. Should you approach all your prospective donors at the same time? Or go to one first, hoping to gain their support before approaching the others? If you have a funder with whom you have worked closely in the past and who is prepared to make a commitment to support the project, their support might encourage others. However, if you have to wait to get commitment from one funder before approaching others, this can delay the funding process.

Whatever you decide, it is important to have a plan and make clear to everyone how you propose to raise the money you need.

Structure

When writing up your proposal, you should consider the following aspects.

- *Length*. The application length will vary depending on the funder being approached. For a major project (such as a new building) you will need to produce a detailed proposal. But you should also prepare an executive summary or a two-page covering letter that sets out the key points. For less complicated projects, keep the length to a minimum. This will make it much easier for the donor, who is probably receiving a steady stream of proposals. You can attach more detailed information if you feel that it will be of interest, or if you are requested to do so.

- *The key points*. At the heart of your proposal, you will describe the needs you are trying to address, the aims of your project, and how you will achieve them. Include as much detail as is necessary for anybody who is not knowledgeable about your area of work. Also show how you expect to measure the success of the project. Make sure you address the critical questions of accountability, equal opportunities and user involvement.

- *Credibility*. If the funder has had no previous contact with your organisation, they will want to be reassured that they can entrust their money to you. This can be done in a number of ways: providing CVs of key people; listing the names of well-connected committee members or patrons; mentioning the support you have previously received from other major donors or government bodies; providing evidence of other projects you have successfully developed; copies of good media coverage; independent evaluation of previous work; positive feedback from users, experts or others.

- *Recognition of the importance of the problem*. If the problem is not widely recognised, refer to authoritative reports or obtain endorsements from prominent people.

- *The budget*. Your budget will always be carefully scrutinised by potential funders. It needs to be clear, complete and accurate. Donors will want to know your major areas of expenditure and income. You should identify capital or other one-off costs, salaries, overheads and any other major operational costs. Similarly, income estimates will show the money you expect to generate from the project itself or through other fundraising, both during the lifetime of the requested grant and beyond. You should always attach your organisation's audited accounts for the latest year for which they are available.

Getting the budget right

Do not undercost your proposal. If you do, you will not raise the money you need to run your project effectively. So you should ensure that:

- every item that you expect to have to pay for is included;
- each item has a realistic cost;
- inflation is accounted for. Different funders will have different systems for dealing with this, but you don't want to find that the price of something has shot up just when you need to purchase it;
- administrative overheads associated with the project are put in where possible. The organisation as a whole functions to make the project happen and the cost of running the organisation also has to be covered;
- publicity costs are included.

- *Language and jargon.* Many proposals are badly written and boring to read. The application is a selling document – selling the idea of supporting your project to a potential donor. Avoid long sentences, long paragraphs, meaningless words, jargon (which means something to you but nothing to the reader) and waffle. Use short words, short sentences, short paragraphs, bullet points, bold text to highlight key features, headings and subheads to indicate the different parts of the application. Get someone else to read what you have written before you send it off – ideally this will be someone who knows little about your work, as they will then be in the same position as most of the people you will be sending your application to. They can challenge your assumptions and ask for explanations where things seem unclear.
- *Facts and figures.* Back up any claims about the extent of the need and the effectiveness of your methods with facts and figures. Everything may be 'desperate', 'urgent', 'important', 'unique'; but you need to prove this. Include just a few selected facts and figures in your proposal – you can also provide a wealth of detail in a background paper attached as an appendix to the application.
- *The human story.* Include short case studies and examples of how people have been helped and what they have gone on to achieve as a result of your help. This demonstrates that you are effective in helping people – which is what most donors are interested in supporting. Also, if you can, include pictures or photographs to illustrate the story you are telling.
- *Presentation.* Presentation can make a difference. Different standards and expectations apply to different donors. For example, a sponsorship proposal directed at the marketing director of a major company may need to look different from an application to a national foundation. Government

agencies and international donors have their own standards and preferred formats. Tailor your style of communication to your audience.

Making the application

To be successful you need to know as much as possible about the donor you are approaching. For example:

- what constraints are imposed by the donor (there is no point applying for something that they cannot or will not support);
- the typical size of the grants they award. Some funders make grants at two or three levels: large grants to major initiatives; medium-sized grants to national organisations or to projects they are especially interested in; and much smaller grants for local initiatives;
- the funder's interests and what they have supported in the past;
- who to write to (their name and job title), who makes the decisions and who they are advised by (so you can plan any lobbying);
- whether the funder expects any recognition or benefit for their support;
- their decision-making cycle and the best time to submit an application.

Research all the donors you plan to approach and keep this information on record. Suggest a meeting, or other ways to bring your work to the attention of the donor, such as inviting them to visit your project. Contact key advisers or trustees of the donor organisation (where you have good contacts) to tell them about your proposal. Above all remember that sending a completely inappropriate application is a waste of everyone's time – so read any guidelines carefully before applying. Also if you have the donor's telephone number or e-mail address, contact them to check whether you are applying at the right time, and if they still have funds available.

Following up a successful application

Your work does not stop once a funder has offered you a grant or sponsored your project. You need to check that all the conditions of the grant are noted. You will also need to fulfil any particular requirements of the funder and keep in touch. This might take the form of:

- *benefits*. Providing the benefits you have offered – for example with company sponsorship giving clear recognition of their support;
- *regular reports and feedback*. Whether this is a condition of the funding or not, you should keep your funder informed about how your project is progressing. This should include financial information, a narrative report and any technical details. This is important if you wish to apply to the funder again. Above all never forget that you are accountable for how the funder's money is spent and they will want to know exactly how it is being used –

some funders will only release the next tranche of funding when they receive satisfactory interim reports;

- *invitations to events and receptions*. This includes events organised specifically for the project they have supported, such as an opening ceremony for a building or a reception for an exhibition. Or you may want to organise a small reception especially for your funders, so that you can develop your relationship with them and get them more involved with other areas of your work.

Don't forget to thank your funders and acknowledge their support in appropriate ways, for example in your annual report.

15.2 Writing an appeal letter to supporters

The bulk of your supporter base will still hear from you most often by mail. Letter-writing is not just a question of raising money. All letters to your supporters are important whether the recipient responds or not. They create an awareness and can help build a relationship. This is important, particularly when a large proportion of the recipients will not respond.

If you get the communication right, this fundraising technique can be one of your best sources of continuing income – see chapter 14 for more information on direct mail.

Grabbing attention

'This Valentine's Day 500 people will die of a broken heart?'

[The British Heart Foundation communicating a powerful statistic about the numbers of people dying from heart disease on a day when many people are thinking about their loved ones.]

'Sponsorship can change your life too.'

'It's not often in life you feel as if you can really make a difference. Especially when it comes to the problems facing the developing world. With ActionAid, if you sponsored a child like Azeb you would be helping a whole community. Sponsorship that helps provide access to safe, clean water, healthcare, and education. ActionAid believe that only when these rights, which we take for granted, have been secured can children and their families begin to focus on developing a self sufficient future.'

[An extract from an advertisement by ActionAid, appealing personally to potential donors and clearly communicating how people in the developing world can be helped through support of ActionAid's sponsorship programme.]

There are several elements of an appeal letter to consider: the salutation, the entry, the appeal itself, the call to action, the signatory and the postscript.

The salutation

The salutation (Dear ...) should be made as personal as possible. When writing a small number of personal letters, you might top and tail them by hand. For larger volumes of correspondence, it is probably better to mailmerge all the elements you wish to personalise. Then for the biggest mailings you will need to have the personal information laser printed. Make sure you check people's titles; this is very important to some.

The entry

You need to grab the reader's attention immediately. If you don't, they may not get beyond the first paragraph. A letter from a respected celebrity or an impactful statement may make people read on; an intensely emotional opening to the letter can also work well.

The appeal message

Having gained the reader's attention, you must hold it. One way of doing this is to write in a simple straightforward way, clearly laid out with short words and sentences and a variety of paragraph sizes. Key ideas should be underlined, indented or otherwise highlighted. In terms of content, you need to:

- state the problem
- show how you can help resolve it
- demonstrate your credibility by showing what you have achieved in the past and others who have helped you
- indicate how much you expect the donor to give and what this will achieve
- make the call to action clearly.

You should also pay attention to the length of your letter. If it's too long your audience may lose interest before getting to the key message.

The call to action

The call to action is crucial, and where many otherwise well-written appeal letters fail. People can be reluctant to ask precisely and directly for what they want, yet that is exactly what is required. Start flagging up the call to action early on in the letter. Repeat it throughout the letter and make it absolutely plain near the end. It should consist of:

- what you want people to do
- how much you want them to give
- the payment mechanism (cheque, credit card, direct debit)

- when – how soon you need it (usually immediately, to create a sense of urgency)
- who to send it to (a personal name for replies will always be better than an anonymous department).

The call to action

For Ever, For Everyone

It's so amazing...

...people sometimes forget we're a charity

Could you imagine Britain without St Michael's Mount or the Lake District? Or Fountains Abbey, Hidcote Manor Garden or the White Cliffs of Dover? Or the hundreds of amazing landscapes, gardens, collections and historic buildings throughout our country?

All these amazing treasures simply have to be kept safe and open for everyone. And that is what the National Trust has pledged to do. Forever. Many places in our care are so familiar, so much part of our lives, it's easy to forget just how much it costs to maintain so much of our nation's heritage.

While we make savings wherever we can, costs keep rising, year after year. It all puts a terrific strain on our resources. Please donate £20 – or whatever you can – so we can keep our nation's most amazing places open for ever, for everyone.

One of our most exciting campaigns ever

A gift from you will help to make sure everyone is always free to walk through the breathtaking landscapes of the Lake District, or take idyllic family holidays on clean safe beaches in Cornwall. Or marvel at collections like the historic toys, games and dolls in the Museum of Childhood at Sudbury. We need your help so that future generations can enjoy the unique experiences now open to us all.

Please donate today if you possibly can. This will help us go on protecting the properties and places we all value – for you and generations to come.

[National Trust]

This appeal by the National Trust illustrates a direct call to action. What the charity wants the donor to do is clearly spelt out. The text is simple and direct. The example shows how you can write good copy to appeal to your donors – showing the benefits that will be obtained by responding and illustrating the cause in an attractive way.

The signatory

Picking the right person to sign the letter can make a huge difference to its impact. You may decide it should be your director, one of your trustees or, if you are a medical charity, for example, it may be some kind of expert such as a research scientist.

The postscript

Save an important idea for the PS. This is one of the most read parts of the letter so use it for your final argument to clinch the donor's support or reinforce the message. This can be produced in a printed typeface or a reproduction of the same handwriting used for the signature.

15.3 Using printed materials for fundraising

Getting the most out of your annual report

Every organisation produces some kind of annual report and this can be an extremely useful tool to support of your fundraising programme. It is an opportunity to promote your strengths, highlight the importance of the need, demonstrate your effectiveness, celebrate your achievements – and also raise money both directly and indirectly.

Eight reasons for producing a good annual report

1　A good annual report explains your organisation to the outside world. It tells the story of your aims, achievements, commitment and style of working.
2　A good annual report reports back to donors and others. A bad one can destroy a donor's confidence.
3　A good annual report is your sales brochure ...
4　A good annual report encourages staff and volunteers, giving them pride in their employer and their work.
5　A good annual report motivates and attracts ... whereas a bad one will put people off.
6　A good annual report gives a clear picture of sound stewardship, showing good use of your supporters' money.
7　A good annual report can directly solicit involvement and raise money.
8　A good annual report reinforces public trust and gives credibility to the organisation and the voluntary sector as a whole. A bad one can destroy credibility for all voluntary organisations.

[How to produce inspiring annual reports, Ken Burnett and Karin Weatherup]

Here are a few important points to take account of when preparing your organisation's report:

- *do* use illustrations and photographs liberally. They can often convey more than the printed word;

- *do* list major donors – after checking that they do not wish to remain anonymous and how their names should appear. This recognition will encourage them to think about giving a repeat donation, and encourage prospective donors to give;
- *don't* put your lists of supporters and committee members at the beginning. You are also writing the annual report to create interest in your organisation, and long lists of names can be off-putting;
- *don't* forget to include some sort of response mechanism: a form to fill in to send a donation or ask for more information, a phone number to call or website to visit. There is no point in provoking a reaction if your reader then has no obvious and easy means of contacting you.

Many standard fundraising techniques will also apply to your annual report. Be positive and communicate a sense of enthusiasm and achievement. You have more space than an appeal letter so you can use a range of techniques to get your message across. For example, why not try to include the following?

- *Drama*. Voluntary organisations revolve around dramatic issues – the fight against disease, giving children a chance in life, protecting the environment from destruction or whatever. Tell some good stories about what you have done.
- *Human interest*. Include case studies, interviews, profiles, testimonials or quotes to make your organisation more real.
- *Support*. Show how much people value your work, either through messages they have sent or endorsements they have given.
- *Boxes alongside the text*. Annual reports can look like a really daunting read. Try to break up the text with boxes, displaying facts, quotes, snippets of information or key points about your work.

You will have your own ideas as well, but above all remember that annual reports should be attractive and easy to read, even if some of the content may be challenging or even shocking.

Producing effective printed materials

Your annual report will be only one of a range of printed materials that you can use to promote your organisation and your cause. Creating effective fundraising and publicity leaflets and other literature is one of the fundraiser's most important tasks. Good fundraising ideas can be destroyed by poorly prepared or badly presented material. Good writing skills are vital, as well as a basic understanding of design and the production processes.

The process of creating printed material usually follows a similar path. The stages include:

- conceptualisation or visualisation, which may include producing a dummy or sample copy;
- setting aside a budget;
- copywriting and gathering together photographs and other visual material;
- design;
- print and production;
- distribution.

You may decide to take on some of these elements yourself, but it is likely that others will be done by outside suppliers and each stage might be produced by someone different. The more people that are involved the more things there are that can go wrong. There is also a greater risk of losing or watering down the original concept.

You need to decide who does what. Many people, even in a small organisation, feel they can write effectively. However, you need specific writing skills to present a good, clear, logical case and to express your ideas forcefully. This may require outside help. If you decide to use promotional consultants and designers, they may have the skills you need, but you have to brief them properly and be confident that they can produce what you need within your budget.

Some general principles of effective communication

You must be clear about what you are trying to achieve. Write down the objectives of each piece of communication, and include this in the brief to the writer and designer (if you are not doing it all yourself). Who is your target audience: volunteers and supporters, funders, professionals and others interested in the cause, other stakeholders (name them) or the general public? What are you aiming to do: increase awareness, communicate information (if so, what?) or raise money?

Decide on your primary audience and your objectives and concentrate on these. Other things will follow (such as raising awareness). But make sure the primary purpose is clear and the main message comes across.

Then identify who you expect to read the material and think about what tone is needed to appeal to them. If they are readers of a magazine or on a particular mailing list, you should know something about them and their interests. You also need to see if they have had any previous contact with you or knowledge about your work. You expect your past donors be fairly knowledgeable, and you will write differently to them than to those who know little or nothing about you. Try to develop a picture of who your existing donors are: their age, sex, interests, preferences and degree of commitment to the organisation. Once you have this picture in mind, you will be able to tailor your message to reach them more effectively.

Keep to your budget. You may have limited space (in an advertisement, for example) to get your message across. Print and postage bills on a mailing can be high. If you want to include photographs are these already available or will they need to be taken?

Ten suggestions for writers

1 Get to know your audience

2 Use simple, direct and everyday language

3 State your proposition boldly and clearly

4 Feature real, identifiable cases and people

5 Communicate the need

6 State clearly what the reader's support will enable you to achieve

7 Remember that cleverness rarely pays

8 Avoid seeming too professional

9 Remove any unnecessary detail

10 Give a clear course of action.

[Ken Burnett, author, lecturer and fundraising consultant]

Set a clear deadline for when you need the finished product, especially if it is going to be mailed or presented at an AGM. Things take longer than you think, so give yourself room for slippage and make sure that everyone involved sticks as close to their deadlines as possible.

Concept

You need to create a theme or style for your material and approach and you need headlines or slogans. These ideas can be generated through brainstorming the project. Gather a number of interested people together in a room, identify the object of the exercise and the rules of the brain-storming process, then get everyone to contribute as many ideas as possible, however unusual. A refinement process follows to select one of the suggestions or develop the approach out of several ideas. Out of this will come the general strategy which will in turn generate the actual copy.

At this stage, you will need a designer to produce some initial mock-ups. If you don't like the rough design, ask for a new approach before too much time has been spent. Backtracking later on will cost money and you may miss your deadlines. The visualisation need be no more than the front cover for a leaflet and a sample page – enough to give you an idea of how it will feel and look.

An insert produced by Christian Aid clearly and attractively illustrating the message of how the loan of a goat can make a significant difference to the life of a family in Mozambique. The goat project is just one example of how Christian Aid works and shows how a supporter's monthly donations could be spent.

Copywriting

Not everybody can write well. A good copywriter makes ideas come alive. However, small organisations cannot always afford to hire copywriters, so fundraisers often write their own materials. When hiring an outside consultant, always look at their portfolio to see what they have done for similar organisations. Brief them clearly about what you are trying to say and why, and who your target audience is. Some will have an instinctive understanding of your work while others may not.

Good copy needs a clear structure. The acronym AIDA is useful here. This describes the process of communication and persuasion:

- *Attention*: attract the reader's attention
- *Interest*: if you don't identify a reason for the reader to be personally interested, you will lose them
- *Desire*: to support your cause
- *Action*: the practical steps they will take to deliver this support.

Headlines, pictures and strong ideas all create a visual impact to attract the reader's immediate attention. Grab their interest by showing why you exist and the needs you are serving. Don't imagine that your supporters will continue to support you without a continuing reminder of the importance of what you are doing, or the human cost of ignoring the problem. You can generate desire by showing that things can be changed if they give their support. Action demands that you tell them what you want them to do and what sort of gift they are expected to make.

Keep everything simple and understandable. Avoid jargon. Organisations tend to develop shorthand ways of describing their work. This is useful when talking to colleagues, but can be meaningless to outsiders. Find someone outside your organisation to read your first draft. Ask them what they have and have not understood. You may have to agree the copy with other people in your organisation. Most people's reaction to checking someone else's text is to look for typographic errors and false statements, and then add their own thoughts, leaving accurate but heavily qualified text that loses all its punch and impact. Accept their comments, but remember that effective text cannot be written by a committee. Other people may have skills in providing the service or in running the organisation; yours are in fundraising and communication.

The KISS principle

An important principle is that of simplicity. KISS is the acronym often used to remind us of this:

Keep
It
Simple
Stupid!

Design

Design gives the printed piece its character. Good designers can lift the central idea from a piece of text and make it infinitely more compelling. The elements of this include the copy, the headlines and sub-heads, the photographs and illustrations used, as well as the design style. Other areas for consideration are the use of space, number of colours (the usual options are one, two or four-colour printing), the quality of the paper and whether to use recycled or wood-free paper, the use of text reversed out so that it appears in white, and blocks of the page overlaid with a tint of a second colour. When deciding all these, you should bear in mind that if the finished product seems too 'glossy', this can create an impression that you are spending too much on these materials – which can discourage people from giving. Conversely, if the finished product looks shoddy, then this can reflect on your competence.

You may already have a house design style, including the use of logos. If you do – and consistency is important – ensure that the designer is clearly briefed about this.

Remember also that your readers may not all have perfect eyesight. The RNIB can supply guidelines for making printed materials more legible to people with a visual impairment. Much of it is relatively straightforward, and relates to the size and style of the type and the use of coloured backgrounds. Make sure you brief the designer on how far their ideas should be constrained by considerations of this kind.

Illustrations can take many forms and help bring a design to life. Photographs are the easiest to use – but not if they do not make a point or are of poor quality. Photos should always be captioned, as captions are among the most read parts of any publication (and remember to credit the photographer). The best photos are those that show people doing things, rather than pieces of equipment, buildings or committee members posing for the camera. Illustrations, diagrams, plans and visualisations are a good alternative, especially for things that cannot yet be photographed (such as a building you are planning to put up).

A good designer will integrate all these elements for you. If you are using an outside designer, get a firm quote for the design cost before agreeing to proceed. Beware of how much the cost of corrections can add to your final bill. One way of saving money over a period is to design newsletters, handbills and leaflets that are produced regularly in a similar format in-house to a pre-designed format created for you by a professional designer.

Printing

The final stage is getting the finished material into print. If you are using outside printers get three quotes in order to obtain the best price possible – it is surprising how much prices vary, even on the most tightly defined jobs. You should even ask printers you deal with regularly to quote for new jobs. This does not demonstrate mistrust, but is good business practice.

Getting quotes

When asking for a quote, you need to be clear about the following points.

For dealing with designers:

- establish the date you will supply text and instructions to the designer and the date you expect to receive the completed job;
- sample visuals needed;
- format, size and price guidelines for the job;
- copywriting (who will do it, and when the final copy is needed);

- how copy will be supplied, for example, by e-mail attachment;
- photographs (what is required and by when, who will commission the photos, if new images are required, and when they are needed);
- illustrations (what is required, by when and who will commission them);
- who is responsible for proof-reading the text and checking design proofs.

For dealing with printers:

- date that the completed artwork will be sent to the printer, and the date required for receipt of the completed job;
- paper size and number of pages – printers use standard size sheets of paper, so the least wastage, the more economic the format of your job;
- print quantity – the more you print the cheaper each piece becomes. Short runs are particularly expensive but so is producing extra copies you do not need;
- paper quality – it usually pays to print on stock paper used by the printer which is bought in bulk; and colour of the paper – tinted paper is more expensive than white;
- number of print colours (one, two or four). One colour can look dull. Four colour, which uses a mix of four inks to create the effect of the full range of colours, is expensive, and the use of special inks (such as silver or gold) can also involve substantial additional cost. Two-colour offers plenty of scope for creative design and is reasonably cheap – bear in mind that you don't have to use black as one of the colours;
- photographs and halftone illustrations (this can add to the cost, but will increase the effectiveness of the communication). Will these be supplied as existing scans or will the printer have to scan them?
- what kind of proofs you want to see and how long you will have to approve them;
- folding – complicated folds will usually be more expensive than simple folding; scoring or perforation can also add to the cost;
- packing and delivery (the price usually includes delivery to one address).

15.4 Communications and dealing with the media

Effective communication of your message to the media is an essential ingredient of successful fundraising for two main reasons. First, it draws the public's attention to the cause or need. Without this attention and understanding, the task of the fundraiser can be much more difficult. If your meeting with the head of a local company coincides with positive articles in the press about your organisation's work, you will immediately be taken more seriously.

Initial steps for developing relationships with the media

- Keep a list of sympathetic media people to send promotional material to.
- Make contact with journalists, including those on local papers and radio, keeping them in touch with what your organisation is doing.
- Publicise your organisation's achievements both in its work and in fundraising (such as the receipt of a substantial grant or donation, or support from a government body or from a well known company) by sending out a press release. Follow this up with a phone call to encourage interest.
- Use beneficiaries to talk about the work of your organisation, either through interviews or through quotes in press releases.
- Issue a press release when the annual report comes out or when research is published on the cause. Try to get a feature written about it to coincide with publication, or make it newsworthy so that journalists will want to cover it.
- Stage a special event to generate media interest, especially one that illustrates the need or demonstrates the support that your cause is attracting: for example, delivering a petition signed by supporters to the Houses of Parliament when an issue of concern to your organisation is to be debated.

Good communication can also help position your organisation in relation to others in the same field. 'Why do we need so many charities, all apparently researching the same diseases? Shouldn't they all combine?' can often be a natural response from the public. Getting good media coverage can establish the special importance of your work and its particular ethos and contribution. If this is recognised by the public it can help eliminate an important barrier to their generosity.

News releases and press conferences

When you have something new to report, a news release to a selected list of newspapers, radio stations and TV channels is one of the most effective ways of publicising it. This can be in response to a recent development in your work, a major donation received, a new publication produced or research completed, a celebrity supporter joining your ranks, or some form of event designed specifically to highlight your work or generate publicity.

An effective news release answers the questions who, what, when, where and why. To be effective at a local level, it should have a clear local angle. Write it in the form of a short article, so that editors can use it verbatim, if they wish. Some might be really interested in the story and want more background information, which you can include separately. Picture editors appreciate photos.

If the event is of real interest, you might consider holding a press conference where you invite journalists to come and hear a story directly, but expect to be closely questioned on the project and your organisation. The timing of a press conference is critical. Its proximity to other important news stories can make or break yours, though you may have relatively little control over this. For example if there is a major political development or financial scandal, there will be little space in the newspapers for other news breaking at the same time. You also need to know the schedules and deadlines that journalists are working to.

Location is important. An interesting venue can add to the feel of the story – for example launching a campaign to save a piece of eroding coastline on a beach. However, the venue should also be easily accessible to journalists. You might want to hold a press conference at an event which is guaranteed to get good coverage itself – such as a national conference.

One way of giving a press conference added interest is to announce that it will be attended by some well-known people, renowned either for their entertainment value or for their serious interest. An actor or celebrity will often use pithy words for journalists or be well rehearsed in the photo call for photographers. Similarly, reporters will know that senior figures at press conferences can usually be drawn on the issues.

If you are using a celebrity, having a conference chaired by a senior person from your organisation will help control the questions and steer them away from the celebrity who might not always know the answer. To get your message across with no deviation or hesitation, it is a good idea to have some sort of rehearsal beforehand. If you can't manage this, you will need to give the spokesperson a full briefing. See chapter 12, section 12.5, for more on working with patrons and celebrities.

For those who cannot get to the conference, put together a briefing pack. Some of the fullest coverage from a press conference comes from journalists who have not even attended. But you might never have got this coverage without having organised the conference in the first place.

Photo calls and events

The media are always attracted to the unusual, the famous and the picturesque. A photograph to illustrate your cause or an element of it in an unusual setting may be just what you need to get media coverage. For example, a few years ago the organisation Volunteer Reading Help publicised their relationship with Southern Water with a photo call featuring the Olympic swimmer Duncan Goodhew, who is also dyslexic, reading to a seven-year-old girl underwater in a swimming pool! This put the work of the organisation in an unusual setting which tied in with both their sponsor and the celebrity.

The challenge with these sorts of activities is not just to organise them successfully, but also to select an activity that is relevant to your work so that any publicity can be linked to it. Needless to say, don't encourage dangerous stunts. If anything goes wrong, your organisation will receive the blame, whether it was your fault or not.

Damage limitation

If a negative story about your organisation that is untrue is featured in the media, it is important to act quickly and in a constructive way. The first people to contact are your key donors. They need to be reassured and given the facts. Next you should reply to the offending article as swiftly as possible. Though the damage may already have been done, it can be mitigated by an article or letter in reply. Then you should issue a statement to other newspapers/magazines/television stations and to your own staff and trustees setting out the facts of the matter.

You may get advance warning of media interest. If so, establish the facts; identify a spokesperson to put a rational and consistent case to the media; or consider inviting the senior management of the newspaper or the television station to withdraw the offending article.

If the bad coverage has a substantial element of truth, you are in a less defensible position and need a different approach. Accept responsibility for the situation, identify the immediate action already taken to remedy it and invite the newspaper to do a follow-up article in a more positive vein, which can help rehabilitate your organisation.

In all these situations there are a number of useful guidelines:

- ensure that the staff of your organisation do not speak to the media unless they are specifically authorised to. There is nothing so damaging as the leaked report or an inept interview from a well-meaning staff member;
- make sure that you establish the facts at an early stage and that these are accurate. Then make them well known;
- make sure that your internal communication systems are working well, that you can get any new twists of the story across to colleagues speedily, and that trustees and supporters are kept informed;
- if you don't already have one, draft an emergency plan in which you anticipate possible disasters and allocate responsibilities accordingly.

Media relations and campaigning

For campaigning organisations, communication with the media is a major tool in helping them to achieve their aims. It has important implications for fundraising. Sometimes campaigning and fundraising are seen as separate activities that require different people and skills. However, if the campaign is an intrinsic part of the organisation's reason for existing, when it gets good coverage, good fundraising results may follow.

Not all not-for-profit organisations are set up with campaigning as a major part of their work, but many need to campaign on particular issues from time to time or seek to set themselves up as the experts in a particular area. This creates an interesting opportunity, since the media will often turn to the organisation when they need informed comment on an issue.

Try to get your organisation regularly mentioned in the media by:

- issuing news releases;
- setting up events which will attract publicity. Better still, use these same skills to set up interesting fundraising events that the media will want to cover;
- holding press conferences;
- writing to the letters page of newspapers and magazines.

Timing is all important in media work, not only because of their deadlines, but also your need for coverage to enhance your fundraising. Media exposure should happen just before you launch a major fundraising initiative and be targeted towards the people you are approaching for support – in whatever form you can obtain it.

Integrating fundraising and your media communication programme

Your media relations should be integrated with your fundraising so the former maximises your fundraising potential, and vice versa. Ideally if someone has a specific communications role, they should be asked to produce plans to show how they can best support the fundraising needs, at the same time as meeting the communications objectives of the organisation.

In small organisations, overseeing media communication is unlikely to be a separate function, and will probably be carried out by a senior member of staff. However, everyone should be encouraged to recognise the importance of good communication in generating extra funds for the organisation.

One option is to appoint an agency to take care of this for you. Some work mainly with the non-profit sector, or you could use a commercial agency interested in your cause and willing to take you on as a client at a reduced fee. As mentioned in the previous chapter, the Media Trust has a service linking voluntary organisations with media companies and individuals who will undertake *pro bono* work or charge lower fees for this type of client. Any agency you use needs to be briefed well if it is to present your work appropriately. You can monitor the results through the use of a press cutting agency. This will show you whether you are being sufficiently effective.

Resources and further information

See also general lists at the end of the book.

Organisations

Media Trust
3–7 Euston Centre
Regent's Place
London NW1 3JG
www.mediatrust.org
Tel. 020 7874 7600
e-mail information@mediatrust.org

RNIB
www.rnib.org.uk
For 'clear print' and 'See it Right' guidelines.

Publications

The following publications are available from the Directory of Social Change. Prices were correct at the time of writing, but may be subject to change.

Charity Marketing, Ian Bruce, ICSA 2005, £22.95

The DIY Guide to Powerful Publicity, Moi Ali, DSC 2006, £18.95

The DIY Guide to Public Relations, 2nd edn, Moi Ali, DSC 1999, £16.95

How to Produce Inspiring Annual Reports, Ken Burnett and Karin Weatherup, DSC 2000, £14.95

Writing Better Fundraising Applications, 3rd edn, Michael Norton and Mike Eastwood, DSC 2002, £18.95

Writing for Change, fahamu 2000, CD ROM £20

16 FUNDRAISING WITH VOLUNTEERS

Volunteers can be an extremely useful resource. In 1998 the National Survey for Volunteering estimated the value of formal volunteering (which is defined as any voluntary activity undertaken through or for an organisation or a group) as being worth £40 billion a year. More recent research done by the Institute for Volunteering Research, an initiative of Volunteering England, surveyed eight European not-for-profits (including the National Trust) and put the return on investment for volunteers as varying between 1:3 and 13:5. This chapter looks at ways volunteers can contribute to fundraising.

Details of organisations and publications referred to in this chapter are on pages 346–347.

16.1 Working with trustees and management committee members

Some organisations are run entirely by volunteers, and do not employ paid staff. Some – like the Samaritans – use volunteers to carry out the service delivery, but use paid staff for administration, coordination and fundraising. Citizens Advice, on the other hand, use both volunteers and paid staff for advice giving. Many others use volunteers on an ad hoc basis, or to bring in extra expertise. But whatever the structure of your organisation, you will have at least one important set of volunteers: your trustees or management committee members.

Your management committee is a key element of your fundraising structure. The ideal is to have a balanced, well-briefed, motivated and forward-thinking team of people who can provide energy and direction. One of the main roles of the management committee is to ensure that you have sufficient resources to carry out your current work and your development plans. This means having a strategic view of the organisation's fundraising potential, and ensuring there is sufficient expertise and administrative support within the organisation to raise the money that is needed. So for the fundraiser, it is vital to get people onto the management committee, or fundraising sub-committee if there is one, who will ask the right questions, think long term, advise on crucial issues, suggest useful contacts and bring clear thinking to the fundraising.

But what if your management committee does not or cannot do this? Depending on the size of your organisation and the amount of contact you have with the committee, there are several steps you or your director or other staff members can take.

- Identify the potential contribution that an effective management committee can make to the running of the organisation and to the fundraising.
- Discuss this potential with individual members who recognise the problem and want to help sort it out.
- Undertake an 'audit' of the skills, experience and expertise that you would like amongst your committee members.
- Identify and approach appropriate new people who may be willing to bring these skills and expertise onto your committee.
- You can then draw up a plan for reforming the committee, replacing those who have lost interest and setting a new agenda for the committee, and allocating roles and responsibilities to individual members.

Getting the most from your management committee

Collecting a group of skilled and experienced people is only the first stage. You need to get the most out of this group and ensure their continuing interest and involvement. Voluntary organisations often assume that committee members and trustees instinctively know what is expected of them or hope they will create a fulfilling role for themselves. But it is much better to spell things out from the start so that everybody is clear about the expectations. Here are a few ideas.

- Give each new person a proper induction. Show them the work of the organisation and introduce them to some of the beneficiaries, so that they understand the impact of the organisation. Introduce them to members of staff so they understand who does what, and give them leaflets about the work of the organisation.
- Discuss with each person exactly what they might contribute. It is better to ask for specific contributions and commitments rather than for help as required, and for something significant for a limited period.

- Agree matters like regular attendance at meetings, remuneration of expenses and training or attendance at conferences.
- Review their contribution (as a group if everything is going well, or individually if it isn't) on an annual basis.
- Find ways of keeping them motivated by continuing to impress on them the importance of the organisation's work, showing them its successes and achievements, involving them in discussing matters of current interest or concern, and continuing to expose them to your frontline work.

16.2 Recruiting and using volunteers

Volunteers are frequently used to raise money for an organisation – to run charity shops, to organise local fundraising activities, and to act as fundraising support groups. There is a range of fundraising tasks which could not be carried out without them – either because the organisation would not have sufficient time or the capacity to do certain types of fundraising in the first place, or because, if volunteers were not being used, the money could not be raised cost effectively. Volunteers can also assist fundraisers by providing administrative support and back-up.

Volunteers can be used in your fundraising in all sorts of ways, and volunteer management means more than just finding the people to do the work. In order to get the best out of your volunteers, they need to be chosen well, placed with imagination, given satisfying work to do which matches their skills and interests, and managed with skill. They are not simply there to be deployed as cheap labour in the worst jobs. Rather, they can add hugely to the resources available to you, enabling you to do more with less and to do it better.

If you use volunteers, you can also take advantage of this fact to support your fundraising case.

- You can show the numbers of volunteers and the amount of volunteer time you are mobilising. This shows that other people share an enthusiasm for what you are doing, as well as your own good sense in mobilising people's time for your cause.
- You can illustrate the value of volunteering to your organisation by estimating the value of the time put in or the work done by the volunteers – for instance, you can multiply the number of volunteer hours by the average wage and place a monetary value on volunteer contributions – some funders will use this as co-funding.
- In your annual report you can show the value of volunteering and how this enhances the service you are providing and makes it more cost-effective.

Types of work that volunteers can do

Membership of committees

Some fundraising can be done or overseen by committees. These might consist of volunteers, many of whom will also get involved in other aspects of the organisation's work. Different organisations use different committees (some use none at all). There are a number of models for fundraising committees.

- A fundraising strategy committee will usually report to the management committee. It monitors and develops the fundraising across the organisation, but is purely supervisory. This group will not actually raise money.
- A fundraising advisory committee is a looser grouping. It consists of a wide range of people, chosen for their occupation or experience. It can be a useful source of ideas and a means of getting new ideas taken up by the organisation.
- An event committee can be crucial when fundraising events are being organised. It is likely to be an ad hoc group specifically created to organise a ball, film premiere or other activity (see chapter 12, section 12.1, for more on events).
- A campaign committee is most effective where individuals are recruited specifically to help raise large sums for a major appeal. Members are chosen because of their ability to give substantial donations themselves and for their willingness to ask others to give (the rich, significant philanthropists, leaders of industry and commerce and those in charge of government programmes). Meetings are rare, and the role of the chair in leading the group and ensuring that the money is raised is crucial (see chapter 13 for more on capital and big gift campaigns).
- Local committees are groups of local representatives of your organisation. They should be activists and be prepared to get involved in any activity that is needed, including fundraising, public speaking and media work.

The role of any committee must be clearly thought through. Starting with the right brief is the key to recruiting the right people.

Administration

There are many ways in which volunteers can help you administratively:

- addressing and stuffing envelopes for a newsletter or an appeal;
- dealing with the response to appeals – banking the proceeds, sending thank-you letters, and data-entering the names of those who responded;
- assisting with membership renewals;
- answering the telephone;
- editing newsletters;

- doing research;
- organising public meetings;
- acting as a speaker to attend community groups and/or accept cheques.

Volunteer jobs should match the skills of the volunteers you are using. Also they will need supervision and support if you are to get the most out of using volunteers.

Fundraising

Volunteers can raise money (and other support) in various ways:

- house-to-house and street collections;
- organising a fundraising event, such as a sponsored walk, where depending on the size and scope of the event, a team of volunteers can be entirely responsible for running the event;
- getting gifts in kind or brochure advertising;
- selling raffle tickets or Christmas cards;
- staffing charity shops.

Much of this fundraising work can be done largely unsupervised. Many people get a real satisfaction out of this sort of work, doing something useful in their spare time and working with a group of like-minded people. Inevitably, they will be representing the charity and people will ask them about what the organisation is doing. It is important that they understand the work of your organisation and share its values: in a sense they are acting as your ambassadors. Some sort of induction is helpful, so that they can be briefed about the organisation and meet some of the staff and beneficiaries.

Who volunteers?

Many different types of people volunteer for all sorts of reasons. You may find that they can be people with the least time on their hands.

- People who have a particular connection with a cause may be willing to volunteer out of a sense of commitment.
- Recently retired people may have time to give, and be willing to do something useful and challenging. There are a number of schemes that promote senior volunteering and which act as a link between the volunteer and organisations needing them. The best known are REACH (formerly the Retired Executives Action Clearing House, which is an independent charity) and RSVP (Retired and Senior Volunteer Programme, run by Community Service Volunteers).
- Employees. Employees in the Community Network, which is part of Volunteering England, promotes and supports employee volunteering. Many companies encourage their staff to volunteer. A few offer time off during the

working week, but most expect the volunteering to be done in the evenings or at weekends. Some have a grants scheme, which entitles employees to receive a small grant for the organisation they are volunteering with.

- Professional skills volunteering. Lawyers, accountants, surveyors and others are encouraged to volunteer by their professional associations, using their special skills for the benefit of a community or charitable organisation. Many lawyers work with law centres and citizens' advice bureaux, for example.

- Unemployed young people including recent school-leavers and graduates yet to get their first job might want to volunteer for work experience. New Deal for the long-term unemployed has a Voluntary Sector Option where young people can work with a voluntary organisation in their community as a route back to employment. Some of the leading charities receive requests to volunteer from recent graduates seeking a career in the voluntary sector.

- People between jobs. The expectation of lifetime employment in the same job or sector no longer exists for most people, and temporary unemployment or part-time work are features of modern life. People between jobs need to maintain their confidence and keep up their skills; people with part-time work may have time to spare; women with children growing up may find they have time available and want to start thinking about a second career. All these groups are potential volunteers, who see volunteering as an opportunity to widen or enhance their own experience.

- Young people at school and college or in youth organisations. Student Volunteering England, Youth Action Network and schemes such as Changemakers encourage young people to become involved and develop social enterprise skills as an important part of their informal education. Also the Rank Foundation runs a 'Gap' scheme which enables 17 to 24-year-olds who are experiencing a gap in their education or work experience from unemployment 'circumstantially or through lack of opportunity', to work with charitable projects that the foundation is already supporting.

- Some people who are interested in your cause will just arrive on your doorstep or ring up asking to volunteer.

If you need help with a project that sounds interesting, then just ask. If you ask enthusiastically, you may find that people are prepared to help out. Remember that if you do not ask people will not know that you need help.

Volunteer recruitment and selection

The recruitment and selection of your volunteers is an important task. As with a paid member of staff, there should be a proper job description, and the volunteers should be selected according to their ability to do that job. You need to decide your policy on remuneration – whether you are going to offer to reimburse out-of-pocket expenses or even give some sort of honorarium or allowance. There are two important points to consider.

- *Equal opportunities*. If you don't offer expenses, or if you put pressure on volunteers not to claim expenses, then this could have equal opportunities implications. You may also want actively to encourage the participation of certain groups of people as volunteers, such as young people, unemployed people, people from minority ethnic communities, disabled people or older people, and you might develop ideas for actively recruiting from such groups.
- *Unemployment benefit*. If you recruit unemployed people for voluntary work, you will need to adhere to Department for Work and Pensions' requirements; otherwise the volunteer may lose benefit. When the Jobseeker's Allowance was introduced the requirements were relaxed in an attempt to encourage volunteering by unemployed people. Check the details of these opportunities at your local JobCentre or relevant volunteer organisation.

Recruiting people locally

Where you need a number of volunteers in one place – perhaps to help in the office or with a fundraising event – a range of recruitment opportunities exists. People occasionally turn up at your office or telephone you for information. If they seem interested, then you could ask them directly if they would like to become a volunteer.

Your publicity leaflets – or an article in your newsletter which asks for support – may offer the option of giving support in time as well as with donations.

Public meetings and other speaking engagements, including your organisation's annual general meeting, are opportunities to make your need for volunteers known. Those attending might offer, or know someone who might be interested.

Your local volunteer centre will keep a list of people looking for volunteering work. The TimeBank Campaign also recruits volunteers and there are now also websites providing this service such as www.do-it.org.uk.

You might try to get a feature article on your organisation, its work and its need for volunteers in the local newspaper, or you could consider taking paid advertising space just as you would for a paid job. Many local radio and television stations run social action programmes with the help of Community Service Volunteers, which assist organisations to recruit volunteers. As with a newspaper, you can also try to get coverage for a volunteer recruitment campaign or a feature about your work, or ring a phone-in programme and make your request on air.

Recruiting people with specific skills

To recruit people with more specialist skills you need a rather more directed approach.

- To find an accountant you might seek the help of a local accountancy firm; or for a lawyer, contact a local law firm.
- Professional bodies and associations are good hunting grounds for recently retired people with spare time who want to help. You could offer to give a talk, or suggest an article or a free advertisement in their newsletter.
- If you know exactly what you want, then by asking someone in that field if they know anyone who could do the job, you may eventually find someone who is prepared to take it on.

Unsuitable as well as suitable people will volunteer. So the next step is selecting from the people who have expressed an interest – which you may want to do through an interview and taking up references, just as for a paid job. Don't lower your standards simply because someone offers to help you. You need to take particular care where people are expected to represent your organisation in public or where they will be handling money. Where volunteers are in contact with children and young people or vulnerable adults, other checks will be required (contact the relevant volunteering umbrella organisation for your part of the country for details).

You will need to agree terms and conditions with your newly recruited volunteers, and set these out in some form of 'contract' or letter of agreement:

- the nature of the job to be done;
- the hours expected;
- the supervision and support offered, and any training that will be given;
- grievance procedures;
- what expenses are to be paid;
- any notice to be given on termination of the arrangement (by either side).

All these need to be discussed and agreed.

Management of volunteers

Like any members of staff, volunteers need managing.

- As mentioned above, any volunteer should have a clear job description.
- You should set them specific and achievable objectives.

- There should be an induction process, so that they see and understand the work of the organisation, meet members of staff (who will also need to appreciate the role and contribution of the volunteer) and be helped to get started.
- You should train them in what they have to do, so that they can do the job effectively, and continue to provide on-the-job training as necessary.
- You should ensure that they have enough information to do their job, and that they are briefed about recent changes and developments in the work of the organisation.
- You should supervise their work, give them feedback on how well they are doing, and congratulate them when they have made a positive contribution. Because they are not being paid, they need other forms of reward – recognition and appreciation are extremely important.

Resources and further information

See also general lists at the end of the book.

Organisations

Changemakers
Unit 502
New Loom House
101 Back Church Lane
London E1 1LU
www.changemakers.org.uk
Tel. 020 7702 1511

DoIt
www.do-it.org.uk

NCVO
Trustee and Governance Information
e-mail trustee.enquiries@ncvo-vol.org.uk

Rank Foundation
Youth Projects – England & Wales
28 Bridgegate
Hebden Bridge
West Yorkshire HX7 8EX
www.rankfoundation.com
Tel. 01422 845172
Fax 01422 844329

REACH
89 Albert Embankment
London SE1 7JP
www.volwork.org.uk
Tel. 020 7582 6543
e-mail volwork@btinternet.com

RSVP
c/o Community Service Volunteers
37 Pentonville Road
London N1 9NJ
www.csv.org.uk
Tel. 020 7278 6601
e-mail information@csv.org.uk

TimeBank Campaign
www.timebank.org.uk

Volunteer Centre Network Scotland
www.volunteerscotland.org.uk

Volunteering England
London Office
Regent's Wharf
8 All Saints Street
London N1 9RL
Birmingham Office
New Oxford House
16 Waterloo Street
Birmingham B2 5UG
www.volunteering.org.uk
Tel. 0845 305 6979 (for both London
and Birmingham offices)
e-mail volunteering@volunteering
england.org

Wales Council for Voluntary Action
www.wcva.org.uk
Helpdesk 0800 2888 329
e-mail help@wcva.org.uk

Youth Action Network
Crest House
7 Highfield Road
Edgbaston
Birmingham B15 3ED
www.youthactionnetwork.org.uk
Tel. 0121 455 9732
e-mail info@youthactionnetwork.org.uk

Publications

The following publications are available from the Directory of Social Change.
Prices were correct at the time of writing, but may be subject to change.

Keeping Volunteers, Steve McCurley & Rick Lynch, DSC 2007. £14.95

Recruiting Volunteers, Fraser Dyer & Ursula Jost, DSC 2002, £14.95

The Charity Trustee's Handbook, Mike Eastwood, DSC 2001, £9.95

Essential Volunteer Management, 2nd edn, Steve McCurley & Rick Lynch, DSC
1998, £19.95

The Good Practice Guide for everyone who works with volunteers, Volunteering
England 2002, £12.50

The Good Trustee Guide, 4th edn, Kevin Nunan, NCVO 2003, £25

A Management Companion, Tim Cook & Guy Braithwaite, DSC 2000, £16.95

APPENDIX 1

Institute of Fundraising Codes of Fundraising Practice and Code of Conduct

The Institute of Fundraising's Codes of Fundraising Practice set out the best practice standards for fundraisers operating within the UK. Each Code covers a separate fundraising technique or issue, as well as an overarching Code of Conduct setting out the framework of ethical behaviour for fundraisers. The Codes not only provide information on relevant areas of the law but also outline recommended practice based upon the highest standards of fundraising.

All 4,000 individual and 250 organisational members of the Institute have already committed to meet the best practice guidance outlined within the Codes. The Codes are the best practice criteria upon which the forthcoming self-regulatory scheme for fundraising is built.

The Codes are drawn up by working parties composed of representatives of the various interested constituents in a particular field, and undergo an extensive consultation process through the charities affiliated with the Institute of Fundraising, regulators and government. As new areas of interest are identified, so new Codes are drafted, under the supervision of the Institute of Fundraising Standards Committee.

Codes of Fundraising Practice

Acceptance or Refusal of Donations

Accountability and Transparency in Fundraising

Best Practice for Fundraising Contracts

Best Practice for Major Donor Fundraising

Charities Working with Business

Charity Challenge Events

Committed Giving in the Workplace

Data Protection

Event Fundraising

Face to Face Fundraising (on the street and house-to-house)

Fundraising from Grant Making Trusts

Fundraising in Schools

Fundraising through Electronic Media

Handling of Cash Donations

House-to-House Collections

Legacy Fundraising

Management of Static Collection Points

Outdoor Fundraising in the UK

Payment of Fundraisers on a Commission Basis

Raffles and Lotteries

Reciprocal Charity Mailing

Scottish Charity Law in Relation to Fundraising and Public Charitable Collections in Scotland

Telephone Fundraising

Telephone Recruitment of Collectors

Use of Chain Letters as a Fundraising Technique

Volunteer Fundraising

Guidance

Guidance for 'In Aid Of' Volunteer Fundraisers

Model Contracts and Standard Forms of Agreement

Forthcoming Codes

Best Practice for Fundraising Consultants

Direct Mail

Legacy Fundraising (Revision)

Copies of the Codes of Practice and Code of Conduct can be downloaded from the Institute of Fundraising's website:

www.institute-of-fundraising.org.uk

For further information please contact the Policy Team at:

Institute of Fundraising
Park Place
12 Lawn Lane
London SW8 1UD

Tel: 020 7840 1046
Fax: 020 7840 1001

Email: codes@institute-of-fundraising.org.uk

Appendix 2

The Fundraising Standards Board

The Fundraising Standards Board (FRSB) was set up in 2006 and launched to the public in 2007 to implement and oversee a transparent self-regulatory scheme for fundraising in the UK. The FRSB exists to provide a robust and accessible complaints procedure for members of the public, to ensure accountability in fundraising and to increase public confidence in charitable giving.

Charities and other fundraising organisations that join the scheme will use the scheme's 'tick' logo to demonstrate their commitment. This is underpinned by the complaints procedure for members of the public should they have a problem.

Self-regulation offers a vital opportunity to increase public confidence and trust in charitable organisations and to raise awareness of the high standards of fundraising to which they work.

FRSB membership: what does it mean?

By becoming FRSB members, charities and other fundraising organisations will be demonstrating that they are committed to best practice and accountability in fundraising.

Any organisation, however big or small, that engages in fundraising from the general public should sign up to the FRSB scheme. By signing up to the scheme, organisations will be committing to:

- Adhere to the Institute of Fundraising's Codes of Fundraising Practice and the FRSB's new Fundraising Promise (see below)
- Use the FRSB scheme 'tick' logo on their fundraising communications
- Promote the Fundraising Promise through their work and communications
- Ensure a robust procedure is in place for dealing with fundraising complaints from the public
- Select a complaints coordinator who will act as the primary point of contact with the FRSB
- Abide by the FRSB adjudications

What are the standards in fundraising?

Fundraising Standards Board scheme members must adhere to the Institute of Fundraising's Codes of Fundraising Practice (see Appendix 1 or www.institute-of-fundraising.org.uk) and the Fundraising Standards Board's new Fundraising Promise (see www.frsb.org.uk).

The Fundraising Standards Board's Fundraising Promise is a commitment made to the public by charitable fundraisers. It has been compiled in consultation with fundraisers and is based on six key pledges that centre on honesty, accountability and transparency. It is a commitment to the highest standards of practice, and to ensure that all fundraising activities are open, legal and fair.

The FRSB provides a complaints procedure for members of the public and responsive mechanisms for remedy and redress in situations where individuals are unhappy about fundraising conduct. The FRSB will investigate all complaints received about organisations that are members of the scheme and that are concerned with a breach of the Institute of Fundraising's Codes of Fundraising Practice, or a breach of the FRSB's Fundraising Promise, provided that the complainant has first directed the complaint to the charity concerned.

Who should join?

Any organisation that engages in fundraising from the general public should join. That includes registered charities, voluntary and not-for-profit organizations who receive financial donations, membership subscriptions, gifts in kind or services and facilities from members of the public, founders, members, patrons, supporters or businesses. This could be through collections, appeals, legacies, events, payroll giving, sponsorship, online giving or through fundraising efforts of others.

Charities and voluntary organisations pay an annual fee based on a sliding scale according to the levels of voluntary income. Fees start at £30 for the smallest organisations, rising to £1,800 for the largest.

For further information contact:

Fundraising Standards Board
Hampton House
20 Albert Embankment
London SE1 7TJ
Tel: 0845 402 5442
www.frsb.org.uk

APPENDIX 3

Institute of Fundraising response to the Charities Act 2006

The Charities Bill finally received Royal Assent to become an Act on 8 November 2006, marking the most significant change to charity law in over 400 years. This represents the outcome of a prolonged process of consultation between government and the voluntary sector. There is a broad level of consensus within the sector in support of the main provisions of the Act, with the proviso that the effectiveness of this Act will lie in the drafting of regulations and guidance.

The Act addresses three areas in particular that will impact directly on fundraising. These are:
• public charitable collections
• fundraising statements
• self-regulation for fundraising organisations.

Details are contained in Part 3, Chapters 1 and 2 of the Act and can be viewed at http://www.opsi.gov.uk/acts/acts2006/ukpga_20060050_en.pdf

Public charitable collections

The review of the law relating to public charitable collections revises the hotch-potch of regulation, some dating back to 1916, much of which is either unfit for purpose or fails to address modern fundraising practices. Part III of the Charities Act 1992 was never implemented as it was seen to be unworkable, and current regulation is diverse, confusing and inconsistently applied and observed.

The Act reflects a high input from the sector. It should ensure that all types of fundraising activity seen as charitable by the public, taking place in all areas seen as public places, are notified to one authority. The new Act expands the definition of a 'public place' where permits are required to include any highway and any place where members of the public have access to that which 'is not within a building, or if within a building, is a public area within any station, airport or shopping precinct or any other similar public area.' This is a change from the current law, which presently excludes supermarket or station forecourts.

The Act sets out a new scheme for the regulation and licensing of public charitable collections, be they on the street, door-to-door or in another area of public access. In short, the new system will mean that:

- all charities that wish to collect (apart from the very smallest collections) will first have to obtain a public collections certificate from the Charity Commission.

Charities will then have to:

- apply for a permit from the local authority if they wish to collect on the street;
- notify the local authority if they wish to collect door to door;
- obtain permission from the landowner if they wish to collect on private land.

The Institute of Fundraising believes that this is a fair scheme because:

All forms of collections are covered:

- street collections, or door-to-door;
- cash, direct debits or goods.

It is proportionate:

- the very smallest charities will only be required to notify the relevant local authority if they are undertaking a public collection;
- other charities will be required to obtain a public collections certificate first, to show that they are fit and proper to collect. Those charities that wish to conduct door-to-door collections will then have to notify the local authority. Charities that wish to conduct street collections will have to apply for a permit from their local authority.

It is equitable:

- local authorities will only be able to refuse to issue a permit against clearly defined criteria set out in secondary legislation.

Fundraising statements

Professional or commercial fundraisers raising money for charitable purposes or charitable organisations will be required to make appropriate statements about their role and how much of the money raised will benefit the charity or cause concerned. The Institute believes that this will promote public confidence in such ventures and in charity fundraising more generally. Detail as to how fundraising statements will operate will become more apparent in the draft regulations that will follow, and there will be an opportunity for the sector to debate the mechanics of this measure, at that time.

Self-regulation of fundraising

The Charities Act supports the development of a self-regulatory structure for fundraising organisations. It does, however, reserve powers for the Secretary of State to regulate in this area should the sector not prove successful in regulating its own activities.

The Fundraising Standards Board has been established to implement and operate a transparent and open self-regulatory scheme for the fundraising sector. For more information please visit www.frsboard.org.uk.

For further information, please contact:

Megan Pacey
Director of Policy and Campaigns
Institute of Fundraising
Tel. 020 7840 1009
e-mail meganp@institute-of-fundraising.org.uk

APPENDIX 4

Fundraising and the 1998 Data Protection Act

Many people are concerned about the uses to which information about them may be put, and in particular about 'junk mail' and 'junk phone calls'. Annoying people is never a good way to raise money from them, so it is important to take these concerns seriously. It is also a legal requirement. As well as being the law, the 1998 Data Protection Act provides a sound framework for good practice in the way you handle personal data. This framework is set out in the eight Data Protection Principles (see box).

The Data Protection Principles

1. Personal data shall be processed fairly and lawfully and, in particular, shall not be processed unless –
   (a) at least one of the conditions in Schedule 2 is met, and
   (b) in the case of sensitive personal data, at least one of the conditions in Schedule 3 is also met.
2. Personal data shall be obtained only for one or more specified and lawful purposes, and shall not be further processed in any manner incompatible with that purpose or those purposes.
3. Personal data shall be adequate, relevant and not excessive in relation to the purpose or purposes for which they are processed.
4. Personal data shall be accurate and, where necessary, kept up to date.
5. Personal data processed for any purpose or purposes shall not be kept for longer than is necessary for that purpose or those purposes.
6. Personal data shall be processed in accordance with the rights of data subjects under this Act.
7. Appropriate technical and organisational measures shall be taken against unauthorised or unlawful processing of personal data and against accidental loss or destruction of, or damage to, personal data.
8. Personal data shall not be transferred to a country or territory outside the European Economic Area unless that country or territory ensures an adequate level of protection for the rights and freedoms of data subjects in relation to the processing of personal data.

This appendix looks at the main implications of the Data Protection Act for fundraising, but it is only a summary and is not necessarily a full statement of the law.

It is the 'Data Controller' that is responsible for complying with the Act. Where you are working for an organisation, the Data Controller will almost always be the organisation, not an individual staff member or volunteer. In the discussion below (unless the context indicates otherwise) 'you' generally means 'your organisation', or you as a representative of the Data Controller.

You must assume that any database used for fundraising is covered by the Data Protection Act. This applies wherever the people on the database come from – your own members, a list of people who have made enquiries, a list taken from a reference book, or a bought-in list. It even applies in most cases if you are taking the names from paper files, rather than computer ones. Once you start to compile the list, even before you use it for fundraising, Data Protection will apply.

The key points are:

- Did the people on the list know you might use it for fundraising? If not, your use of the information is unlikely to be 'fair'.
- Were people on the list given the chance to opt out of their data being used for fundraising? If not, again your use might well be 'unfair'.
- If people have ever told you not to use their details for fundraising, are you sure that you have 'suppressed' their names from the list before you use it?
- If you are using someone else for part of the work – such as an agency that will do telemarketing on your behalf, or a mailing house – do you have a suitable written contract in place with the other agency?
- If you are phoning people to ask for support, have you checked that their number is not on the Telephone Preference Service register? It is an offence to call a number on the register for any sort of marketing, unless they have given you permission to market to them by phone.
- If you use a website, or if you share information with organisations overseas, are you complying with the special rules about transferring data abroad?

Fair processing

Any use you make of people's data must be fair (First Principle). The Act says that it is unfair if you collect information from someone without them knowing, or at least being easily able to know, who you are and what you will use the information for. These facts may be completely obvious; in that case you don't specifically have to make a Data Protection statement. However, things that are obvious to you may not be so clear to the Data Subject. So it is usually best to leave no room for doubt by saying clearly what you will use the information for. You do not have to use any specific language: 'We will keep your details on file so that we can contact you in future about our activities' is friendlier than 'We will hold your data under the Data Protection Act for direct marketing purposes'.

It is particularly important for you to consider data that will be shared:

- *within an organisation*, for example transferring it from the membership department to the fundraising department;
- *between organisations*, including passing it on from a charity to its associated trading company or sharing your list with another voluntary organisation.

In both cases you need to make sure that all relevant purposes are identified. In the second case you also need to indicate the type (or even the identity) of any organisation the data will be passed on to.

If you obtain the data from someone other than the Data Subject, you must make sure the Data Subject knows what is going on as soon as possible. This means that in your first contact with them (whether by phone or in a letter) you should make it clear who you are and all the uses that you will make of the information you now hold.

You may also want the organisation from which you get the data to guarantee that it has told the Data Subject about the actual or potential disclosure to you. (It may well be its responsibility if it didn't, but it's you that will get the irate phone calls and letters.)

Once you have obtained data, you must only use it in ways that are 'compatible' with the purpose(s) specified when you obtained it (Second Principle). Although some may wish to argue that fundraising is 'compatible' with membership, for example, you will avoid any future misunderstanding by having it clearly as a purpose in its own right.

You must also meet at least one of the 'conditions' for fair processing (in Schedule 2 of the Act). For fundraising or marketing you will generally be best able to meet either:

- the first condition – consent from the Data Subject; or
- the sixth condition – that it is in your legitimate interest and doesn't infringe the rights, freedoms or interests of the Data Subject.

If you decide to seek consent, note that you need a response from the Data Subject. A letter saying 'we will do this unless we hear back from you' meets the requirement to provide information, discussed above, but you cannot assume consent from those who do not reply.

The right to opt out of direct marketing

Data Subjects have an absolute right to opt out of direct marketing, which includes fundraising and probably includes approaches seeking support of any kind. The basic right is that they can 'require' you in writing not to use their details for direct marketing. However, you cannot leave it entirely up to the Data Subject to take the initiative, because of your responsibility to be 'fair' when obtaining information.

If you are obtaining the information directly from the Data Subject, in order to be fair you should give them the opportunity to opt out there and then, preferably through an opt-out tick box. With information that you have obtained from someone else, make sure the Data Subject knows clearly how to exercise their opt-out right.

Approaching someone who has given money in the past to ask for another donation counts as direct marketing, but following up a previous transaction does not – for example going back to someone who sends a donation without giving Gift Aid authorisation.

The opt-out only applies where the material is unsolicited. If you advertise something in your newsletter and someone phones up to ask for more information, you can, of course, send details even if they are marked on your database for 'no direct marketing'.

You must ensure that if you pass information to other organisations for marketing purposes, you exclude from your list anyone who has opted out. If you obtain a list from elsewhere you need guarantees that they have excluded those who have opted out.

Restrictions on telemarketing (phone, fax, e-mail and text message)

A separate piece of legislation, the Privacy and Electronic Communications (EC Directive) Regulations 2003, gives additional rights in respect of marketing carried out by electronic means. The Regulations cover, among other things, the Telephone Preference Service (TPS), the Fax Preference Service (FPS) and marketing by e-mail or text message.

You must not make a direct marketing call to any number that is on the TPS register. 'Marketing', in this context, includes any request for funds or support — donations, purchases, participation in fundraising events or activities, and so on. It doesn't matter whether the number is from your own database, from someone else's list or from the phone book. The only time you can make marketing calls to a number on the register is if you already have specific permission for this from the person you are calling. This applies to both private and business lines.

The Regulations also forbid sending unsolicited faxes to individuals and offer a Fax Preference Service (FPS) to businesses.

The TPS and FPS registers are run by the Direct Marketing Association. See www.tps-online.org.uk.

The restrictions on e-mail and text message marketing in the Regulations are less precise. E-mails to a business address, even if directed to an individual, are not restricted (but may not be welcome). E-mails to a private address may only be made with permission, unless the person is an existing customer and the promotion relates to a similar product or service to the one they have already bought or enquired about.

All e-mails must, as a result of various pieces of legislation, contain all the details that would normally be found on your headed paper — such as company number, charity number and real-world address, and must also provide a simple opt-out mechanism from receiving future marketing e-mails.

The provisions for text message marketing are essentially the same as for e-mails.

Using a Data Processor

If you employ another organisation to process personal data on your behalf they are likely to be a 'Data Processor'. Examples might include:

- sending names and addresses on disk to a mailing house;
- passing your donor database to a fundraising agency which will carry out a telephone appeal;
- using an external service to handle incoming donations in response to an appeal;
- using an agency to run an event for you, including issuing invitations and processing bookings.

In these circumstances, all the Data Protection responsibility remains with the Data Controller. In order to underline this, the Act says that there must be a written contract establishing this relationship. In addition, the Data Controller must be satisfied that the Data Processor has satisfactory security, so that the data can only be used for the agreed purpose(s) and in the agreed way.

If the Data Processor cannot show that their standard contract meets the Data Protection requirements you should take legal advice.

Transferring information abroad

The Act imposes, under the Eighth Data Protection Principle, additional restrictions on transferring data to countries that do not have equivalent Data Protection provision to the UK. Certain countries are automatically deemed to be acceptable; these include:

- those in the European Union;
- others in the European Economic Area (Norway, Iceland and Liechtenstein);
- those assessed as adequate by the European Union (at the time of writing Switzerland, Guernsey, the Isle of Man, Argentina and Canada).

For countries not covered above, you may be able to meet one of the conditions that overrides the Eighth Principle. These include:

- the consent of the Data Subject;
- transfers that are necessary in connection with a contract involving the DataSubject.

Failing that, you would probably need to secure adequate Data Protection through a contract with the recipient organisation.

The use of the internet is, by definition, worldwide. Placing personal details on a website is therefore likely to require consent. (Collecting personal data via a website, however, is no different in principle from collecting it on paper. You must provide all the relevant information and opt-outs, and must obviously maintain security, but it doesn't matter where in the world the person is when they provide their data.)

Additional points

Other provisions of the Act you may have to consider include:

- Is your data of good quality? The Act requires that it is accurate and up to date, as well as adequate, relevant, and not excessive.
- When you have finished using the data, do you have a policy for what happens to it? Under the Act you must not keep it longer than necessary.
- Are you confident that your data is not used in unauthorised ways and that it is kept secure? Again, this is a requirement of the Act. You should take particular care, for example, with financial information, including credit card details, to ensure that they do not get into the wrong hands and that your staff are reliable. You should also be aware of the risks when personal details are in transit — perhaps to a mailing house or other external agency, or on a laptop computer that is out of your office — and should have protocols for your staff giving information out over

the phone, in particular, in order to avoid them being tricked into revealing details of an individual to someone who could cause them harm.

- Have you checked whether your use of the data needs to be notified to the Information Commissioner?

Specific issues

One activity which might fall foul of the Data Protection Act is compiling speculative databanks on potential wealthy prospects. The whole point is usually to build up a profile in secret before deciding what is the most appropriate way of approaching them. On the face of it this appears to be a clear breach of the First Principle, especially if the material collected is not already in the public domain. However, it is generally felt to be acceptable, provided the information is not held in secret for any longer than strictly necessary. If this is a major part of your work, you may wish to take further advice.

Another common sticking point is the fear of putting people off getting in contact if you tell them up front that their details will be used for fundraising or marketing. Best practice is clearly to give the opt-out as soon as possible, but it may be legitimate to capture details for one purpose (a request for information, for example) and then to inform the Data Subject about future marketing before any use of the data is made for this purpose.

[*This appendix was provided by Paul Ticher, author of* Data Protection for Voluntary Organisations, 2nd edition, DSC, 2002.]

Useful Organisations

Directory of Social Change (DSC)
24 Stephenson Way
London NW1 2DP
www.dsc.org.uk

Publications
Tel. 08450 77 77 07
Fax 020 7391 4804
e-mail publications@dsc.org.uk

Courses and conferences
Tel. 08450 77 77 07
Fax 020 7391 4808
e-mail training@dsc.org.uk

Liverpool office
Federation House
Hope Street
Liverpool L1 9BW
Tel. 0151 708 0136
Fax 0151 708 0139
e-mail north@dsc.org.uk

Publishes a full range of titles for charities and voluntary organisations, including a large number of directories and handbooks for fundraisers. For a complete booklist, contact the Publications department, or go to the DSC website. Bookshop and library open Monday–Friday near Euston Station.

Comprehensive training programme covering all aspects of voluntary sector activity, including fundraising. For a copy of the latest Training Guide, contact the Courses and conferences departments or visit our website.

Organises Charityfair, the largest annual event for the UK voluntary sector, with a three-day programme of events and training. For full details, contact the London Courses and conferences department or go to the DSC website.

Charities Aid Foundation (CAF)
King's Hill
West Malling
Kent ME19 4TA
www.cafonline.org (gives access to all other CAF websites)
Tel. 01732 520000
Provides charitable and financial services to help donors make the most of their giving and non-profit organisations make the most of their resources, both in the UK and overseas. All CAF publications except those covering international research and some UK research are now available only via DSC (see above).

Charity Commission
Harmsworth House
13–15 Bouverie Street
London EC4Y 8DP

Woodfield House
Tangier
Taunton
Somerset TA1 4BL

12 Princess Dock
Princes Parade
Liverpool L3 1DE
www.charity-commission.gov.uk
Tel. 08453 00 02 18

Institute of Fundraising
Park Place
12 Lawn Lane
London SW8 1UD
www.institute-of-fundraising.org.uk
Tel. 020 7840 1000
Represents and supports the
professional interests of fundraisers at
all levels. Membership open to all
those working in a fundraising role.
Publishes good practice guidelines (see
Appendix 1) and runs a training
programme and annual conference.

**National Council for Voluntary
Organisations (NCVO)**
Regent's Wharf
8 All Saints Street
London N1 9RL
www.ncvo-vol.org.uk
Tel. 020 7713 6161
Fax 020 7713 6300
e-mail ncvo@ncvo-vol.org.uk
HelpDesk 0800 2 798 798
e-mail helpdesk@ncvo-vol.org.uk
The umbrella body for the voluntary
sector in England. Provides
information and advice to members
via the HelpDesk. Programme of
publications and events.

Other useful organisations

Use the page references in this list to find the page where full details of the
organisation are given.

Index